The Heavenly Muse: A Preface to Milton

A.S.P. WOODHOUSE 1963

Courtesy of University College Archives, University of Toronto

The Heavenly Muse

A Preface to ilton

A.S.P. WOODHOUSE edited by HUGH MacCALLUM

UNIVERSITY OF TORONTO PRESS

UNIVERSITY OF TORONTO

DEPARTMENT OF ENGLISH STUDIES AND TEXTS

Number 21

©University of Toronto Press 1972
  Toronto and Buffalo
  Printed in Canada
  ISBN 0-8020-5247-9
  Microfiche ISBN 0-8020-0274-9
  LC 79-185724

Contents

Editor's preface

This book grew out of many years of teaching and scholarship. While the literary interests of Professor A.S.P. Woodhouse were varied and wide-ranging, his most enduring commitment lay with Milton. His manuscripts reveal that he made several attempts to complete the present study – the first serious effort in 1943, the second a little over a decade later, the last in 1964 when, shortly before his death, he retired from the chairmanship of the Department of English of University College, Toronto, and resolved to devote himself to the completion of his work on Milton.

The problem for the editor, then, has lain in an excess of riches. The simplest answer would have been to reprint Woodhouse's published articles in their original form. Yet this answer entailed the neglect of a considerable body of unpublished material, including such fine and suggestive passages of criticism as the extended commentary on *Paradise Lost* in Chapter 8, and much of the discussion of the prose in Chapters 4 to 6. I decided, therefore, that an interweaving of published and unpublished criticism would provide a reasonable approximation of the book intended by the author. As a result, there are four kinds of source for the material gathered in this volume: published articles; manuscript revisions of published articles; unpublished chapters in manuscript; public lectures. Frequently it has been necessary to choose among three or four versions of the same essay, each having its peculiar virtues, and on occasion it has seemed advisable to weave together passages from two or more versions in order to retain the distinctive insights of each. In making this selection I have of course been guided by the aim of presenting the considered views of the author in their most lucid form, but I have also attempted to make clear the comprehensive and integrated character of his approach to Milton. Woodhouse held that in order to understand Milton the critic must grasp his thought and his experience, as well as his art. The unusual powers of synthesis which enabled Woodhouse to move toward this goal are revealed by the arrangement of material in this volume, and it is in the hope of rounding out the design that several important fragments (such as the section on Milton's treatment of the Son) have been included.

The result of this process of selection and arrangement, then, is not a new book. The core consists of criticism already published in article form, and this has been supplemented by material written for the most part many years ago. Much would no doubt have been altered had the author lived to complete his work. The most striking limitation of the present version is its neglect of the scholarship and criticism centred on Milton in the last two decades. Woodhouse intended to acknowledge his debts more fully and to take cognizance of new approaches and methods. He did not survive to do so, and the editor feels that such extensive revision is beyond his authority and competence. The reader is thus asked to bring to this book the same reservations and the same generosity that he would bring to a reprinting of articles that had been originally published during a lifetime of scholarship.

The lack of contact with recent criticism is not as serious a defect as it would have been in a lesser writer. The strength and independence of Woodhouse's thought, and the authority derived from his unusual mastery of the period, give to his work an enduring value. Many of his insights are formulated with such lucidity and force that they provide a lasting challenge to subsequent criticism. His view of Milton's humanism, with its stress on the tension between classical and Christian, leads to a recognition of important patterns in the poetry: thus his analysis of the interplay of secular and religious elements in *Comus* and his critique of *Samson Agonistes* as a Christian tragedy are seminal studies in Milton's awareness of convention and tradition. The same power of judgment is revealed in Woodhouse's interpretation of Miltonic doctrines. His essay on the creation is a fine example of judiciousness in recognizing, but not exaggerating, the poet's originality as a thinker. His study of such crucial themes as Christian liberty, the law of nature, divorce, church and state, and the Son of God, is conducted within the context of a general knowledge of Puritanism that has seldom been equalled. More caution, perhaps, is necessary in approaching his remarks on the dating and order of Milton's poems, and on the manner in which they reflect his development. In this field recent scholarship has provided new evidence and new interpretations (see my note on page 346). In spite of such progress, however, much remains problematical, and Woodhouse's firm sense of the canon of Milton's works continues to be useful and suggestive. Nor can his remarks on the dating of such pieces as *Ad Patrem* and *Samson Agonistes* be ignored.

In the end, however, this preface to Milton is justified by the way in which it returns us with new awareness to the poetry. In the last decade we have seen much fine criticism of the poetry, and particularly of *Paradise Lost* – one thinks of the readings of Milton's epic provided by Dennis Burden, J.B. Broadbent, Stanley E. Fish, W.G. Madsen, C. Ricks, J.M. Steadman, J.H. Summers, and many others. Woodhouse's commentary on *Paradise Lost*, written almost twenty years ago, inevitably reveals at moments its origin in an earlier epoch of criticism; yet it remains a firm, vital, and comprehensive treatment of Milton's great poem. Here, and in the studies of *Samson Agonistes* and *Paradise Regained*, fresh insight is united to a restorative sense of proportion and balanced judgment.

As anyone who sat in his classes soon realized, Woodhouse's power as a teacher was founded on his capacity for exposition. It was a point on which he himself took some justifiable pride. I remember, however, his comment on a colleague whom he greatly admired: 'That man is a teacher – I am an explainer.' The generous humility was as characteristic as his usual robust confidence, and yet the remark was at best only a partial truth. One might say, perhaps, that he was first an explainer, then a teacher. He fixed the object with an unwavering gaze, brought to bear on its interpretation a wealth of ordered knowledge, and produced an analysis which made one aware that beginning, middle, and end are more than rhetorical postures, and that subordination in sentence structure may be an important tool of thought. But there was nothing impersonal about this performance. Woodhouse had the power to awaken what he called 'the historical imagination,' and to create a lively and penetrating awareness of the history of the mind. And one further element commanded attention and allegiance: pervasive in all he said, reinforced by wit and by sanity of judgment, was his own passionate humanism. We can be grateful that so many of the qualities which made A.S.P. Woodhouse a great teacher have survived in his writing.

Readers familiar with the author's published work may find a more detailed account of sources useful. Chapter 1 ('Prospect: the study of Milton') was written in 1963–4 as an introduction to the planned volume. The first half of Chapter 2 belongs to the same period, and is a revision of material published in 'Notes on Milton's Early Development' (*University of Toronto Quarterly*, 13 [1942–3]: 66–101), while the second half reproduces the remainder of that article. The discussion of *Comus* in Chapter 3 is drawn largely from a lecture delivered at the University of London in 1956 which combined 'The Argument of Milton's *Comus*' (*University of Toronto Quarterly*, 11 [1941–2]: 46–71) with '*Comus* Once More' (*University of Toronto Quarterly*, 19 [1949–50]: 218–23), but it is supplemented by manuscript material on the genre of Milton's masque; the subsequent discussion of *Lycidas* and *Epitaphium Damonis* first appeared as 'Milton's Pastoral Monodies' (in *Studies in Honour of Gilbert Norwood*, ed. Mary E. White

[Toronto, 1952], pp. 261–78). Chapter 4 ('The reformer') was delivered as a public lecture in the mid-fifties; Chapter 5 ('The theologian, 1') is taken from a manuscript draft composed about 1956; and Chapter 6 ('The theologian, 2') draws upon the same manuscript but in addition reproduces the essay 'Notes on Milton's Views on the Creation: the Initial Phases' (*Philological Quarterly*, 28 [1949]: 211–36. Chapter 7 ('*Paradise Lost*, 1: theme and pattern') is an alternative version of the published essay 'Pattern in *Paradise Lost*' (*University of Toronto Quarterly*, 22 [1952–3]: 109–27), while Chapter 8 ('*Paradise Lost*: the elaboration of the pattern') is an unpublished chapter probably written about 1950. The final chapters are both revisions completed in 1963–4: Chapter 9 integrates material from '*Samson Agonistes* and Milton's Experience' (*Transactions of the Royal Society of Canada*, 3rd ser., 43 [1949]: Section II, 157–75) and 'Tragic Effect in *Samson Agonistes*' (*University of Toronto Quarterly*, 28 [1958–9]: 205–22); Chapter 10 provides a substantial revision of 'Theme and Pattern in *Paradise Regained*' (*University of Toronto Quarterly*, 25 [1955–6]: 167–82).[1] I am most grateful to the Royal Society of Canada, the University of Iowa, and the University of Toronto Press, for permission to use material from previously published essays. This work has been published with the aid of grants from the Humanities Research Council, using funds provided by the Canada Council, and from the Publications Fund of University of Toronto Press.

I wish to express my thanks to those who have given me help and advice during the preparation of this volume, and particularly to Professors Arthur Barker, J.M. MacGillivray, and Ernest Sirluck. I am also indebted to Miss Jean Jamieson, of the University of Toronto Press, for counsel and encouragement.

HUGH MacCALLUM

Author's preface

This book is the result of study and teaching spread over many years. It would have seemed more novel if it had been written earlier, but what it has lost in novelty it has, I trust, gained in maturity. Some of its ideas and interpretations were indeed set down in a number of published lectures and articles, and on these I have had time to reflect, I hope to advantage. I have, of course, profited over the years by work published by many scholars and critics. Of my predecessors and elder contemporaries I would mention with particular gratitude James Holly Hanford, William Haller, and E.M.W. Tillyard, all of whom I am proud to call my mentors and friends – and with all of whom I on occasion disagree! On almost all I have printed, including this book, I have had the inestimable benefit of the criticism and advice of my old friend Douglas Bush, surely the wisest as well as the most learned of critics; but all the faults that remain are of course my own. I have also had the benefit through the years of a number of brilliant students who have contributed to my knowledge and have forced me to define and defend my positions; of these I must not omit to mention Arthur Barker, Max Patrick, Ernest Sirluck, and Malcolm Ross, but other names in a long succession of honours and graduate seminars at Toronto would be too numerous to record. One other debt, this time from undergraduate days, I will take this opportunity to acknowledge: no one but myself can estimate how much I owe to the example of my earliest teacher, the late W.J. Alexander, under whom I studied various authors, but not Milton.

It is pleasant to record my gratitude to the Guggenheim Foundation for a fellowship given many years ago and for patience in waiting for the result, and to the various libraries in which I have worked – the British Museum, Dr Williams', the Union Theological, the Huntington, and my own university's library.

And there is yet one more debt, the greatest of all, but it I will keep for the dedication.

A.S.P.W.   1963–4

Ad matrem

The Heavenly Muse: A Preface to Milton

1
Prospect: the study of Milton

n the present state of literary criticism it seems desirable
that anyone who has the hardihood to write a book on a major English poet
should make quite clear the nature of his effort and its aim.

I

This *Preface to Milton* is, then, an essay in historical criticism. The means
used are those of historical study. The end in view is the elucidation of
Milton's individual poems and, more generally, of his mind and art. It has
no quarrel with modern criticism and is fully aware of the importance of
aesthetic analysis; but it prefers to undertake its analysis in the light of all
the relevant and ascertained facts, including the facts of Milton's experience
and thought as seen against the background of his age, the history of the
poetic traditions which he inherited, and the bearing of one poem (or prose
work) upon another.

   Inevitably such a book adopts certain principles and pursues certain
methods of investigation. These are not arbitrary, but are the outcome of
the studies from which the book took its rise. They are in the nature of
hypotheses to be verified in the only manner possible, that is, by applying
them to the elucidation of the poet's works and letting them stand or fall by
their general coherence or lack of it, and their ability or inability to illuminate the individual works. It is arrogant of any critic, whatever his school,
to imagine that he has said the last word on a subject, and naive of a reader
to expect him to do so. Sufficient if his work suggests a new and, within its

limits, a sensible and fruitful way of looking at the work. And this possibility, shared by historical criticism with other and more ambitious schools, is the first principle of the present effort. For it is a mistake to regard historical method as a mere corrective: a laborious endeavour to set right the facile mistakes of the unhistorical. It has, or at least may have, its own power of suggestion, of setting the facts in a fresh light, and of attempting a new point of departure for an examination of the poem.

It may do so in many ways, and among others by its power to invoke assumptions and expectations common to the poet and his original audience, but obscured or obliterated by time, so that they have to be painfully reassembled and cleared. This is a hard saying to the ordinary reader and to those critics who, by a sort of self-denying ordinance, reduce themselves to his level and approach the poem with a mind empty of the poet's prepossessions and, inevitably, full of their own. Two illustrations of the importance of recovering assumptions and expectations common to the poet and his original audience, the one aesthetic, the other intellectual, may be very briefly set down, for much will be heard of them below.

Nothing is more essential for the correct appraisal of a poem than that intuitive sense of the demands, the potentialities, and the limits of a particular genre enjoyed by a poet and his contemporaries; and nothing, clearly, is more perishable. No one who has witnessed the bafflement and boredom of unwilling beginners upon *The Faerie Queene* can doubt the truth of this observation, and no one who has read the complaints of critics about *Comus*. In Milton the problem is crucial because of his addiction to traditional forms and his bold and brilliant adaptation of them to his particular purpose. He relies upon an intuitive sense of the genre because he is obliged to take certain liberties with the traditional form. Thus in *Comus* half the difficulty disappears if one recognizes that this is not only a masque-like entertainment, but also an example of Spenserian allegory, and can recover a sense of the demands, potentialities, and limits of both forms: false expectations are swept away, and one is in a position to read the poem with intelligence and sympathy, alert to features of its pattern which may easily escape the ordinary reader. What is true of *Comus* is not less true of *Paradise Lost*, a classical epic on a Christian theme, with all that that implies of adjustment and adaptation, or of *Samson Agonistes*; and everyone knows how even a great critic and a learned, like Johnson, could be led hopelessly astray on *Lycidas* by a prejudiced and impercipient view of the pastoral monody.

There are intellectual assumptions and expectations, as well as aesthetic, which are certainly no less perishable; and they are specially important in poetry so doctrinal as much of Milton's. An example which, despite its obviousness, has often been ignored is found in a frame of reference common to Milton and Spenser, as to their contemporaries and predecessors, part indeed of the Christian inheritance, but one which strikes strangely upon the modern ear. This is the assignment of all experience, and indeed all existence, to one of two levels, commonly known as the *order of nature* and the *order of grace*.[1] To the natural order belonged not only the natural world, inanimate and animate, but man considered simply as a denizen of that world. Its law was the law of nature, which was apprehended in experience by reason, and which in its higher reaches included natural ethics, and even natural religion as distinct from revealed. Thus to the order of nature belonged all the ethical wisdom of antiquity. To the order of grace, on the other hand, belonged man in his supernatural aspect with all that pertained to revealed religion and to his salvation under both the law and the gospel. Its law was the revealed will of God, which was apprehended by faith; and it involved a special kind of experience called religious experience. Both orders were, of course, under the power and providence of God, and they had a common subject in man and societies of men; but, though related, they were not to be confused. This conception of the two orders was a frame of reference, not a body of doctrine, and on the precise relation subsisting between the order of nature and the order of grace there was room for a wide diversity of inference and emphasis. But one cannot appreciate the doctrine until one recognizes the frame of reference, which is sometimes formulated but more often simply assumed. The frame of reference is, as we shall see, as important for an understanding of Milton's ethics in general, and for his views on toleration, as it is for a true reading of *Comus* – that is, for a reading which lets us into Milton's meaning and directs us to a productive analysis of the poem's pattern; but indeed the frame of reference is in different degrees involved in most of his prose and in all his most serious verse.

That it is the office of the historical critic to recover such forgotten assumptions and expectations, aesthetic or intellectual, as we have illustrated by reference to *Comus*, is a second principle of interpretation adopted in this volume. A third, already implied in what has been said, is the legitimacy of hypothesis. The historical critic must never consciously run counter to the known facts, but he is not limited in his conclusions to them. To refuse, for example, to date a poem because there is no unambiguous external evidence of its year of composition is not caution but pusillanimity, and an invitation to perverse ingenuity in others. Among the early poems of Milton there are a considerable number whose dates can only be inferred, but they can be inferred with some degree of accuracy for there are enough poems whose dates are certain to permit the critic to detect the character and direction, the pattern as it were, of the poet's development, and his business is to fit the undated poems into this pattern. This illustration, from a matter apparently simple (until one attempts it) though in its way crucial, will suffice. The historical critic can and must make a free use of hypothesis, but with a sensitive regard to all the facts, and must then submit his hypotheses to experimental verification as defined above.

The historical critic, in the fourth place, must learn to know his author so intimately that he can detect what facts are relevant to this elucidation of his mind and art. Critics of other schools may seek to come directly at the nature of poetry and its relation to other activities. The historical critic, if he reaches this question at all, will do so by asking what is the nature of *Milton's* poetry and what its relation to *his* other activities. Granted that poetry is *sui generis,* a distinctive mode of experience and utterance, and not to be confused with other activities, it does not follow that it stands out of all relation to them, or that the relation in which it stands cannot in a given instance be determined.

Nothing has more bedevilled Miltonic criticism than the notion of two Miltons, operating in independence of each other, and sometimes at feud. It is a comfortable doctrine for Shelley (who likes Milton's poetry and his politics, but not his theology) or for Hilaire Belloc (who likes his poetry, but neither his theology nor his politics); but as a hypothesis it turns out to be utterly unverified and indeed nonsensical. There are in Milton tensions enough, as we shall see, but there are not two Miltons, only one; and the hypothesis, or rather the fiction of a poetical Dr Jekyll and a theological (or theological and political) Mr Hyde obscures a principal fact about the poet, namely, that he is so truly and naturally a poet as to think most deeply and cogently only in his poetry, or when, in his own phrase, he feeds (*Paradise Lost* 3.37–8)

> on thoughts, that voluntarie move
> Harmonious numbers.

Only in his poetry is full justice done to all sides of Milton's temper and doctrine. Only there are impulses and beliefs ordered and harmonized in so far as it was given to Milton to order and harmonize them; and the instrument on which this was achieved was the poem, with its power (as Milton recognized) 'to allay the perturbations of the mind and set the affections in right tune') (*Reason of Church Government,* Col. 3 [i]: 238). We are not left without strong indications from the poet himself of the relation of experience, thought, and art in his poetry. A fifth principle is, then, that anyone who would understand Milton must pay close attention to these indications, must explore as fully as he is able the interplay of experience, thought, and art in every poem analysed, and must try to determine its effect upon the poet himself.

There is a reason why this is peculiarly important in the case of Milton, and (though not easy) less difficult than with many other poets. But the attempt entails the invoking of other principles and the foundation of additional hypotheses, which must be explained at rather greater length.

II

Coleridge drew a luminous distinction between the imagination of Shakespeare and of Milton. Shakespeare, he said 'darts himself forth and passes into all the forms of human character and passion, the one Proteus of the fire and flood.' Milton, on the contrary, 'attracts all forms and things to himself, into the unity of his own ideal.' 'In the *Paradise Lost*, indeed in every one of the poems, it is Milton himself whom you see: his Satan, his Adam, his Raphael, almost his Eve, are all John Milton; and it is a sense of this intense egotism that gives me the greatest pleasure in reading Milton's works. The egotism of such a man is a revelation of spirit.'[2] It was some such perception also that led Macaulay to describe Milton's genius as essentially subjective or, as he called it, lyric.[3]

Critics have not been slow to read Milton's experiences in or into his poetry. Masson traced them, often with a rather heavy hand, in *Samson Agonistes* and other poems; and Hanford reversed his own earlier opinion in order to avail himself of similar clues to the personality of John Milton, Englishman.[4] Tillyard by seeking Milton at the centre of *Lycidas* has surprised the real subject of the poem,[5] but has not applied the same tactic to other pieces; and Saurat has made the valuable suggestion that Satan represents those elements in Milton's own temper and outlook which the poet recognized only to condemn.[6] But none of these critics has arrived at any general formula for the relation of experience, thought, and art in the poetry of Milton, which is essential for an understanding of the poet; and none of them – not even Tillyard in his analysis of *Lycidas* – has paid sufficient attention to Milton's art, which is essential for an understanding of the poems, and for an answer to the question how they complete his experience and supplement his thought. For the poems are not a mere record of past experience, but the realization of a new experience.

Insufficient attention to Milton's art and a tendency to view the poems as a mere record have had the natural effect of provoking a reaction against this kind of interpretation: a reaction which chimes in with the insistence of modern criticism that 'the play's the thing' and all other considerations irrelevant. But the contention of Coleridge and Macaulay regarding the quality and direction of Milton's imagination remains unassailable; and to it criticism must return. To recognize the relation of one of Milton's poems to his extra-aesthetic experience need not distract our attention from the poem or bereave us of any of the instruments of analysis put at our disposal by modern criticism. On the contrary, it brings into evidence one of the essential conditions under which the poem was conceived and composed, a condition antecedent to any which a purely aesthetic analysis will reveal. It may serve in some cases to discover the poem's dynamic: not the *how* of Milton's effects, which is the business of analysis, but the *why*. At the very least, it places the critic at the poet's point of departure, thence to follow his pattern, and perhaps to detect in it elements which might otherwise escape his attention.

Our concern, we have said, is with the poems of Milton, not with the nature of poetry in general. But it seems evident that poetry may, and perhaps must, embody two distinct kinds of emotion and effect a fusion between them. One may be called *experiential emotion* because it springs from the poet's experience of life, and appeals to the reader's experience of life, and this experiential emotion is in some degree interested. The other kind of emotion is purely aesthetic: it springs from the poem itself without reference to anything beyond it, and specifically from the poem's aesthetic pattern or significant form, and it includes, no doubt, for the poet his excited delight in the exercise of his craft, and for the reader the delight of perceiving the poet's skill. This we may call, for the sake of distinction, *aesthetic emotion*, and may recognize that it is, as compared with experiential emotion, disinterested.

The amount of experiential content and its significance vary greatly from poem to poem, and hence the weight of experiential emotion which different poems carry. In some it is very great. In others it is so small, or so insignificant, as to be almost negligible, and to reduce the poem to something like an exercise in aesthetic patterning. But where the experiential content is considerable, and where, in the poem, an aesthetic pattern is successfully imposed upon it, there is a fusion of disinterested aesthetic emotion with interested experiential emotion which transforms the latter. And this, essentially, is the new experience which the poem not merely records, but realizes. For the poet, to express the poetic experience is the same thing as to possess it. For the reader, to apprehend it in its fullest extent is to possess it in the degree possible to him.

The accuracy of this description may be in part confirmed by reference to the experience of the spectator or reader of tragedy. Aristotle was not wrong when he called the emotions aroused pity and fear. But these emotions are in themselves of the experiential, not of the aesthetic, order, and interested, not disinterested: we do not learn their nature in the theatre, but in life. In a tragedy, however, they are experienced under different conditions, and with pleasure; and the end is that release of emotional tension which Aristotle called *katharsis*. And one of the conditions of this whole experience, and an essential condition, is the presence of aesthetic pattern and the transformation of experiential emotion by the addition, the infusion, of aesthetic emotion. Thus the experience of the spectator or reader of tragedy casts, as it seems to me, an oblique light upon the experience of Milton in many of his poems. And when we come to *Samson Agonistes* the light will be no longer oblique, but direct.

Not all of Milton's poems start from an extra-aesthetic experience of much weight or contain an important element of experiential emotion. Some of his earlier efforts are principally exercises in aesthetic patterning. And this group, if it contains none of his greatest poems, yet contains a few of unsurpassed perfection: the *Epitaph on the Marchioness of Winchester*, *L'Allegro*, and *Arcades*. The fact is significant. For Milton is a master of pattern, and his concern for it by no means diminishes when extra-aesthetic experience and its attendant emotion are strongly present. Of Milton's patterns in general two characteristics may be observed: first, that they are essentially *structural* patterns, supplying a principle for the evolution of the whole poem and a firm basis for whatever is done by means of imagery and symbol, as might be easily illustrated from *L'Allegro* and *Il Penseroso*, to the confusion of Cleanth Brooks's attempt to represent the images of light and darkness as central to these poems;[7] second, that Milton's patterns are most of them classical and all of them traditional, though he allows himself considerable latitude in adapting them to his purpose, a fact not unconnected with their structural character. Thus we have the sonnet, the Messianic eclogue, the masque form and Spenserian allegory, the pastoral monody, the classical epic, the brief epic (whose perfect model Milton claimed to have found in the Book of Job), and classical tragedy. In criticizing the individual poem it is necessary to have or to acquire a clear sense of the demands, the potentialities, and the limits of the genre as Milton adapts it to his purpose; and this is at once less easy and less commonly attained than might be supposed. But to return to our classification of Milton's poems.

A second kind of poem, also encountered among Milton's earlier works, clearly finds its point of departure in an extra-aesthetic experience of some weight and carries its burden of experiential emotion, upon which an aesthetic pattern with its attendant aesthetic emotion is imposed. The effect is to confirm the initial attitude and mood by objectifying them in an ideal form, but at the same time to bring the experience under control. The process is strikingly illustrated as we shall find by *Elegy* 5 (*In Adventum Veris*) and *On the Morning of Christ's Nativity* because the attitudes affirmed and confirmed by the two poems are almost diametrically opposed: in the elegy, a glad pagan naturalism; in the ode, a joyful acceptance of Christianity, whose result is to banish forever the pagan gods. Here no problem is solved, for none is raised: the affirmation in each case is simple and unreserved; and the only effect of the poem – by no means a small effect – is to objectify the experience and, by imposing upon it an aesthetic pattern, to establish the poet's ascendancy over the emotions which it arouses. Despite the very different character of the experience and emotion, objectified, ordered, and controlled, we are justified in regarding as variants of the same simple type a number of the sonnets, early and late, which are not poems of affirmation, but of complaint, and which may issue in an *assertion* (*O Nightingale*), or in pure *negation* (*Methought I saw my late espoused Saint* – that lyric cry of unrelieved woe, which is unique), or in *invective* (*On the Late Massacre in Piedmont* and *I did but prompt the age to quit their cloggs*), or in *exhortation* (*To the Lord General Cromwell*). The burden of extra-aesthetic emotion is very evident, but the mode of dealing with it contrasts sharply with that employed in the third kind of poem.

This third kind of poem is the one most characteristic of Milton, and under it may be included the bulk of his more mature and significant verse. It likewise finds its point of departure in an extra-aesthetic experience, but of a very different sort: not a single, unambiguous attitude, to be objectified, ordered, and confirmed by the poem, but a problem to be solved or, if not solved, transcended; so that the poem embodies a development of thought, and a transformation of feeling, as it proceeds from the initial experience to a conclusion very remote from it. The earliest example of this type, and the simplest, is the sonnet *How soon hath time*, in which in December 1632 Milton sums up the results of the five months of silent self-examination that followed his retirement to Hammersmith.[8] He had by now, we may safely assume, determined that his life-work should be the service of God in poetry; and, not unnaturally, the first problem which it raised was how far his native talent warranted the choice. To his anxious gaze what he had so far achieved seemed as naught, his talent perhaps meagre, and certainly its maturing slow. This was the starting point, and this is the burden of the octave. With the sestet comes a new consideration. The poet's talent is God's gift and God's responsibility. Only the will to service is the poet's own:

> Yet be it less or more, or soon or slow,
> It shall be still in strictest measure eev'n,
> To that same lot, however mean or high,
> Toward which Time leads me, and the will of Heav'n;
> All is, if I have grace to use it so,
> As ever in my great task Masters eye.

The new consideration effects a transformation of attitude. It does not an-

swer the question about Milton's talent, but it raises the whole problem to
the level where self-regarding thoughts are simply irrelevant. It does not
solve the problem, but transcends it.

Almost identical in pattern and effect, though much more powerful, is
the sonnet on his blindness written twenty years later: *When I consider
how my light is spent.* The initial experience embraces all the despair and
bafflement of the blind man, willing but utterly unable effectively to serve
the God whom he still regards, at the beginning of the poem, as his great
taskmaster – at the beginning of the poem, but not at the end. For again
there has been a second and a better thought: God does not need any man's
service; thousands at his bidding speed; all that he requires is submission
and the will to serve: 'They also serve who only stand and waite.' But the
second and better thought could hardly have secured by itself the radical
change of attitude, and certainly could not have effected the complete resolution of emotional tension which the poem achieves. For that, it was necessary to impose upon the whole a simple aesthetic pattern, with its attendant
aesthetic emotion.

Nor is either process or effect peculiar to the sonnets. If one turns to
the celebrated passage on his blindness in the third book of *Paradise Lost,*
one will find Milton employing an adaptation of the same pattern. Running
through the whole passage of fifty-five lines is the theme of light, introduced
naturally in reference to the point reached in the progress of the poem, the
transition from the pictures of hell and chaos, the utter and the middle
darkness, to those of heaven and earth, the realms of light and day; and
the theme of light is first elaborated in its associations with heaven and
God. Then (in the circumstances just as naturally) there intrudes from the
region of extra-aesthetic experience the sad thought of Milton's blindness,
cut off irrevocably from light: (3.22–4)

> thou
> Revisit'st not these eyes, that rowle in vain
> To find thy piercing ray, and find no dawn.

But on the thought there follows hard the memory of his consolations:
poetry, classical and Christian, and above all his joy and pride in composition: (3.26–39)

> Yet not the more
> Cease I to wander where the Muses haunt
> Cleer Spring, or shadie Grove, or Sunnie Hill,
> Smit with the love of sacred Song; but chief
> Thee *Sion* and the flowrie Brooks beneath

> That wash thy hallowd feet, and warbling flow,
> Nightly I visit ...
> Then feed on thoughts, that voluntarie move
> Harmonious numbers; as the wakeful Bird
> Sings darkling ...

But these consolations are not enough. It is as though the word *darkling* brought back upon the poet's mind all that he had lost. And there follows a second and more emphatic lament for his blindness with its deprivations, and, above all, the deprivation of knowledge: (3.40–50)

> Thus with the Year
> Seasons return, but not to me returns
> Day, or the sweet approach of Ev'n or Morn,
> Or sight of vernal bloom, or Summers Rose,
> Or flocks, or heards, or human face divine;
> But cloud in stead, and ever-during dark
> Surrounds me, from the chearful wayes of men
> Cut off, and for the Book of knowledg fair
> Presented with a Universal blanc
> Of Natures works to mee expung'd and ras'd,
> And wisdome at one entrance quite shut out.

This last deprivation is the hardest to bear because in Milton's view knowledge is so necessary to a poet, and to be deprived of it cuts in upon the consolation he has emphasized, the consolation of poetry. But it also brings to mind the appropriate compensation; for the loss of outward light, the inner light, the one thing really essential for the poet of *Paradise Lost*: (3. 51–5)

> So much the rather thou Celestial light
> Shine inward, and the mind through all her powers
> Irradiate, there plant eyes, all mist from thence
> Purge and disperse, that I may see and tell
> Of things invisible to mortal sight.

The inward light is God's gift, almost God's presence. We are back at the association with which the passage commenced: the association of light with God. And we are brought back to it by the aesthetic pattern.

The mark of aesthetic pattern is similarity with difference. In the first instance the light, though associated with God, is physical light, and the darkness, introduced in contrast, is physical darkness. Now the darkness is still physical, but the light is wholly spiritual. In this passage, as plainly as in the sonnets, the content on which the pattern is imposed comes straight from Milton's extra-aesthetic experience; and the pattern, with its attendant aesthetic emotion, advances the poet's thought, helps to transform his attitude, and resolves the emotional tension which the memory of his blindness and its deprivations has produced. Poetry thus reveals its power to 'allay the perturbations of the mind and set the affections in right tune' (*Reason of Church Government*, Col. 3 [i]: 238).

The two sonnets and even the passage from *Paradise Lost* are very simple examples of this third kind of poetry because they make use of direct statement and do not resort to the complete projection of drama or the partial projection of allegory. They are poetry at all only by virtue of their clearly marked aesthetic pattern and their reinforcement of statement by imagery. But there are other poems which belong to the same general type, but which are much less simple, because, in addition to pattern and imagery, they resort to projection, and projection not only forms the basis of the pattern but replaces direct statement. Thus in these poems the initial extra-aesthetic experience is not, as in the examples just considered, directly formulated. It has to be inferred, or perhaps even discovered.

Lycidas and the *Epitaphium Damonis* take their place in the tradition of the classical pastoral monody and not only adopt its basic pattern, but employ that species of projection and of allegorical presentation which the genre permits. *Comus* stands in a roughly similar relation to the pattern of the masque and adopts, as its tradition permits, a species of allegorical projection closely allied to Spenser's. Together these poems constitute a second subdivision of the third kind of Miltonic poetry. The final development abandons allegorical projection in favour of dramatic, with a classical epic pattern in *Paradise Lost* and *Paradise Regained*, and a classical tragic pattern in *Samson Agonistes*; and these poems constitute the third subdivision, and include, of course, Milton's principal achievements, by which, in the last analysis, our hypothesis on the relation of experience, thought, and art must be justified.

III

Milton's poetry is not the sole concern of this Preface; but it is the principal concern. For only in and by his poetry does Milton rise securely to the first rank of English writers.

There have been many sounder political thinkers and better theologians; and despite some passages of undoubted eloquence there have been many greater masters of English prose. Milton was not wrong when he divined that in that medium he had the use of only his left hand (*Reason of Church Government*, Col. 3 [i]: 235. The majority of his prose works are occasional, and too their form is dictated not by Milton's superb sense of structural pattern, but by the opponent whom he is stalking chapter by chapter, and page by page. And even where he has not this excuse, he seems seldom to rise above his subject, see it in its larger aspects, and assert his control over it, as he never fails to do in his poetry. Only perhaps in the *Areopagitica* does he achieve something of this effect, and in this unspoken oration he is, significantly, working (as he does in his poetry) to a traditional form essentially structural in character, which he brilliantly adapts to his purpose.

The ideas in Milton's controversial prose, however, and in the *De Doctrina Christiana*, are worth perusing for their own sake and are rich in historical interest. But even if they were not, they would still demand our attention: first, because they represent the preoccupations of almost twenty years, preoccupations so intense that for them Milton postponed his plans in poetry; second, because they reveal experiences deeply felt, with attendant changes in outlook and temper; and, third, because the ideas and impulses of these twenty years enter into the last and greatest poems, there to be corrected or confirmed, and integrated in Milton's final philosophy of life.

This Preface makes no pretence of furnishing a biography. Its concern is with Milton's writings, but as seen in relation to his developing experience, thought, and art. Thus the scheme is, in its broad outlines, chronological. The first part (Chapters 1–3) deals with the young poet, presenting the pattern of his early development and rapidly discussing the poems in its light, while reserving for more detailed consideration the three most impressive efforts of these years, *Comus*, *Lycidas*, and the *Epitaphium Damonis*. The second part (4–6) begins by dealing in more general terms with the reformer as revealed in his controversial prose and with his developing views on ecclesiastical, political and individual liberty. It next deals with the theologian, that is, with his scheme of Christian doctrine, and in greater detail with his more distinctive views on scripture and reason, on Christian liberty, on the Godhead and the persons of the Trinity, and with his monism and his insistence upon free will, which furnish the essential basis of his ethics. With the character of his early poetry formulated in part one, and the experience and thought of the intervening years presented in part two, we are ready to consider, in part three, the mature poet, and to examine his major poems, *Paradise Lost, Samson Agonistes* (probably composed before the completion of *Paradise Lost*), and *Paradise Regained*.

2
Milton's early development

1   ur detailed survey of Milton's early development may commence with his going up to Cambridge in the year 1625; for of any English writing that he may have done in the years at St Paul's School only two metrical versions of the psalms have survived.

The common conception of the home in which he spent his childhood appears to be sufficiently accurate. It was a godly home, but not uncheerful or devoid of culture. There was music there; and there were at least some books, including Sylvester's translation of Du Bartas, and Spenser's *Faerie Queene*, the latter a rich inheritance for any poet, and if Spenser was read for edification as well as delight, it remains a question whether this is not the best way to read him and nearest to his intention. For Milton, he remained at once the bard who had sung (*Il Penseroso* 118-20)

> Of Turneys and of Trophies hung;
> Of Forests, and inchantments drear,
> Where more is meant then meets the ear,

and 'a better teacher than *Scotus* or *Aquinas*' (*Areopagitica*, Col. 4: 311), commended by his poetic art, his Christian humanist ethic, and his staunch Protestantism.

No doubt the home was intensely Protestant; for the elder Milton had been disinherited by his Roman Catholic father for adhering to the English Church, and left to make his own way in the world, which he did by becoming a successful scrivener in the city of London. But he was a conforming Puritan, who could contemplate for his son a career in the Anglican ministry. To the protestantism of the Protestant religion, he did not add, as that son under the pressure of events was destined to do, the dissidence of dissent.

In nothing did the father rise more securely above the limitations of his class and party than in his generous belief in knowledge and in liberal education, which is of the Renaissance at its best. In *Ad Patrem* Milton has thankfully recorded the provision which his father made for him; to quote Cowper's translation,

> thou never bad'st me tread
> The beaten path, and broad, that leads right on
> To opulence, ...
> But, wishing to enrich me more, to fill
> My mind with treasure, led'st me far away
> From city-din to deep retreats, to banks
> And streams Aonian, and with free consent,
> Didst place me happy by Apollo's side ...
> when I had open'd once
> The stores of Roman rhetorick and learn'd
> The full-ton'd language, of the eloquent Greeks, ...
> Thyself didst counsel me to add the flow'rs,
> That Gallia boasts, those too, with which the smooth
> Italian his degen'rate speech adorns, ...
> And Palestine's prophetic songs divine.
> To sum the whole, whate'er the heav'n contains,
> The earth beneath it, or the air between,
> The rivers and the restless deep, may all
> Prove intellectual gain to me, my wish
> Concurring with thy will.[1]

It is instructive to set beside this account Cromwell's prescription for his son: 'I would have him mind and understand business, read a little history, study the mathematics and cosmography. These things are good, with subordination to the things of God. Better than idleness ...'[2] Business and the things of God: that is the authentic note of the Puritan bourgeois tradition – the note of Defoe struck in advance. And Milton, by the wise provision of his father, escaped it. His was the cultural inheritance of Sidney and Spenser, and if, in circumstances very different, he did not manage to avoid the asperities of Puritanism, at least his Christian humanism persisted to the end.

It was fostered by St Paul's School, where the spirit of Colet still reigned, and where to expositions of Christianity and the classics Alexander Gill the elder added (like Spenser's schoolmaster, Richard Mulcaster) a zeal for the mother tongue. To these influences, and to the opportunities opened to him, Milton eagerly responded. We hear of the school boy studying till midnight, long after the family had retired, attended only by a servant; and we remember his younger contemporary, Henry More. When, says More, my tutor asked me 'why I was so above measure intent upon my studies, that is to say, for what end I was so, suspecting (as I suppose) that there was only at the bottom a certain itch or hunt after vain glory ... I answered briefly, and that from my very heart, "That I may know" ... For even at that time the knowledge of natural and divine things seemed to me the highest pleasure and felicity imaginable.'[3] So, without doubt, it already seemed to Milton: study was happiness, and it was also sanctioned by duty. (*Paradise Regained* 1.201–6)

> When I was yet a child, no childish play
> To me was pleasing, all my mind was set
> Serious to learn and know, and thence to do
> What might be publick good; my self I thought
> Born to that end, born to promote all truth,
> All righteous things ...

The words are spoken of and by Christ; but the suggestion of reminiscence is inescapable, and the passage as it continues yields a clue. For it tells of the boy Jesus talking with the doctors in the temple, and of this episode there was a representation in the schoolroom of St Paul's in Milton's day. Thus the foundations of Milton's love of learning and of his religious idealism were early laid, and together. To the Christian humanist no alliance could seem more natural, and throughout Milton's life the alliance was maintained, though to the Puritan it seemed possible that human learning might come between man and God, and this fear, as we shall see, Milton did not wholly escape. But that was at a much later date, and the confident Christian humanism of his early years, as it was fostered in his home and at school, is a fact of supreme importance. What Puritanism contributed was at this date no disruptive force, but a note of seriousness to which the natural idealism and, perhaps we must add, egoism of Milton's temper responded.

When he went up to Cambridge, it was with the intention, his parents' and his own, that he should enter the ministry of the church. Haller has argued convincingly that Milton was probably destined for a place in the spiritual brotherhood of Puritan preachers who were striving to promote their creed and way of life within the framework of the establishment, and who in the reign of James I and under the lenient rule of Archbishop Abbot made considerable headway.[4] Cambridge had been the training ground of these preachers and the nerve-centre of the movement. But when Milton was ready for the university, conditions were on the point of changing: the new reign ushered in the repressive policy of Laud, and Puritanism was first discomfited, then put upon more extreme measures. This circumstance alone would be sufficient explanation of Milton's failure to carry out the original design, and of his later assertion that he was 'Church-outed by the Prelates' (*Reason of Church Government*, Col. 3 [i]: 242). It had the momentous effect of helping him to find both himself and a better medium for God's service, of directing him (in Haller's phrase) from the rhetoric to the poetry of the spirit.

There is unassailable evidence, however, that from a very early date Milton intended, or at least hoped, to become a poet – as indeed with his endowment how could it be otherwise? We have his statement in *At a Vacation Exercise* (1628), and, what is more, his eager quest of facility and felicity in expression, which commenced some two years earlier (*Elegy* 1, spring 1626) and went on throughout the Cambridge period. Presumably his first plan, if he ever paused to formulate it to himself, was to pursue poetry as secondary to his clerical duties, after the model of the admired Giles and Phineas Fletcher. Meanwhile he must learn his craft, and the humanist tradition would leave him in no doubt of the means: by imitation, invention, conscious artistry, and, above all, practice: the result is the thirty-five poems of the Cambridge years. Some few of them recorded, and in recording realized, experiences of real importance, but even in these poems the desire of practice was probably still present as a motive.

Exactly when Milton's resolve was taken to forego holy orders and devote himself to poetry alone, we cannot with certainty determine. But three convincing factors, it is reasonable to suppose, entered into it – his sense that in the circumstances service in the church was ineligible, the realization that his talents warranted his devoting of himself to poetry, and a religious experience whose ultimate result was to transfer to the chosen medium all the sense of 'calling' that had attached to the ministry, and more. Nor are we without strong indication of the probable date. His quitting Cambridge, in the summer of 1632, would precipitate a decision. This was followed by five months given, it would seem, to silent self-examination, whose outcome was the sonnet, *How soon hath Time* (December 1632), a poem whose place in Milton's early development has not been fully understood. For it bears, as we shall see, upon two of the factors named above; it deals with the problem of Milton's native endowment and readiness for his life work, a problem which it rather transcends than solves, and by this very fact of transcendence it marks the final phase in a religious experience whose beginning is seen three years earlier in *On the Morning of Christ's Nativity* (December 1629) with what turned out to be its premature dedication to the service of God in poetry. This experience, whose beginning and end are so clearly marked, is central in the pattern of Milton's early development, and influences all his subsequent poetry. It will perhaps be useful, before entering upon more detail, to sketch the pattern of his early development in its broad outlines.

For some three and a half years (1626–9) Milton devotes himself intermittently to the writing of imitative verse, chiefly in Latin, with six of his seven elegies as his principal achievement, and notably *Elegy* 5, On the Coming of Spring. Then after a significant interval of seven months, he writes the *Nativity* and with it *Elegy* 6, an explanatory verse epistle addressed to Charles Diodati. Together they clearly mark the beginning of a religious experience which bears a very definite relation to his poetry; for in the epistle he repudiates elegiac verse in favour of heroic, which in its context plainly means religious, and of this resolve the *Nativity* is the earnest and the first fruit. But if Milton intended to give his poetry a new direction and to inaugurate a series of poems on religious themes, he was disappointed. For his next effort, *The Passion* (1630), was a failure and, alone among his poems, remains a fragment (yet a fragment which had for him some special significance since he preserved and printed it in his collected poems). Instead, he returns to love poetry, though not in the elegiac, but in the Petrarchan form, drawn thereto by the natural propensity of his age, and perhaps in response to some actual experience; for though the dating is inferential, all the evidence converges on the spring of 1630 as the time to which the first six sonnets, one English, the rest Italian, belong. If this is correct, it argues some failure of, some retreat from, the experience recorded in the *Nativity*; and with such an explanation the poetic activity of the next two years (1630–2) is perfectly consonant, for it consists wholly of poems which are in effect exercises in aesthetic patterning (as were most of those attempted before the *Nativity*) and with little experiential and no religious content, but reaching in the companion pieces and *Arcades* a new level of poetic excellence. Then with retirement to Hammersmith, in July 1632, come the months of silent self-examination to which we have already referred, and their outcome, the seventh sonnet, *How soon hath Time* (December 1632). The little poem records and realizes an experience at once religious and aesthetic, from which there is no retreat, and which leaves a permanent mark on Milton's life and work. The first result is to enable him to rectify the failure of *The Passion* by a renewed, and this time successful, application to religious verse (*Upon the Circumcision, On Time, At a Solemn Music*); the next, to launch him, with a new confidence, upon the second phase of his preparation, a period devoted no longer to practice, but to an intensified acquisition of knowledge and discipline of character; the third, and most important, to give a direction to the whole of his subsequent poetry. Almost without exception, the poems written after December 1632 are ethical and religious in theme or treatment, and rich in experiential content; they are undertaken 'as ever in my great task Masters eye'; and this is as true of the occasional pieces (*Comus, Lycidas*, and the *Epitaphium Damonis*) which fall within our present purview as of the two great epics and *Samson Agonistes*, the subjects of later chapters. So decisive is the culmination in *How soon hath Time* of the period of religious experience whose beginning is recorded in the *Nativity*.

In the *Apology for Smectymnuus* (1642) Milton has given his own account of this period, from a particular angle. While rebutting a charge of youthful incontinence, he takes occasion to speak of his developing attitude to beauty, love, and chastity, and relate it to his ideal of the poet and his office. He tells us how he delighted to read the Roman elegists, and early desired to imitate them, but with the reservation of choosing 'more wisely, and with more love of virtue ... the object of not unlike praises'; how to the elegists he soon grew to prefer Dante and Petrarch, 'who never write but honour of them to whom they devote their verse, displaying sublime and pure thoughts, without transgression'; and how these poets helped him to read aright, and to extract only profit from, the chivalric romances of the Renaissance, and, more important, contributed to shape his ideal of the poet and his office: 'long it was not after, when I was confirm'd in this opinion, that he who would not be frustrate of his hope to write well hereafter in laudable things, ought him selfe to be a true Poem, that is, a composition, and patterne of the best and honourablest things; not presuming to sing high praises of heroick men, or famous Cities, unlesse he have in himselfe the experience and practice of all that which is praiseworthy' (Col. 3 [i]: 303–4). He proceeds to recount how 'from the Laureat fraternity of poets' his studies led him to the philosophers, and notably to Plato and Xenophon, from whom he learned 'how the first and chiefest office of love, begins and ends in the soule, producing those happy twins of her divine generation knowledge and virtue'; and how, 'last of all not in time, but as perfection is last,' he pondered the precepts of Christianity on the subject of chastity, and did not slumber over the promise to those that were undefiled 'of ever accompanying the Lambe.'

Clearly this passage has its own significance and, as clearly, some points of contact with the pattern which we are tracing. But it is a mistake to forget its occasion and its context and to seek in it, as does Hanford,[5] a complete account of Milton's early development. It deals with a special problem, no doubt crucial in these years; and, like the celebrated account of Milton's prose writings offered in the *Defensio Secunda*, it interprets, and correctly, the direction taken in a period of Milton's life, when viewed from a particular angle; but it is not a complete account, and, if mistaken for such, it throws a single idea into false prominence and disturbs the critic's perspective. That the virtue of chastity was central to Milton's ideal of the poet and of the Christian admits of no doubt; and as background for *Comus* this passage, we shall see, is of the first importance. But there is evidence in these early years of a religious experience which, if it includes, also extends beyond, the ideal of chastity, and which turns on Milton's dedication of himself to God's service in poetry. Shortly before the passage in the *Apology* was penned, Milton had declared, in Book 2 of *The Reason of Church Government*, that poetic talents, 'wheresoever they be found, are the inspired guift of God ... and are of power beside the office of a pulpit, to imbreed and cherish in a great people the seeds of virtu, and publick civility, to allay the perturbations of the mind, and set the affections in right tune,' and that such poetry as he had learned to value was 'not to be rays'd from the heat of youth, or the vapours of wine ... nor to be obtain'd by the invocation of Dame Memory and her Siren daughters, but by devout prayer to that eternall Spirit who can enrich with all utterance and knowledge, and sends out his Seraphim with the hallow'd fire of his Altar to touch and purify the lips of whom he pleases' (Col. 3 [i]: 238, 241). This passage is surely of equal significance, for it bears directly on Milton's dedication of his talents to God's service, and the unmistakable echo of the *Nativity* (27–8) in the words last quoted links it with this period in Milton's life. He does not, in fact, abandon the elegiac mode in composition for the Petrarchan. He abandons it in response to an ideal of chastity becoming increasingly clear, but in order to make way for poetry of a higher kind, religious in theme and the product of a devotion truly inspired. The ideal of the poet who is himself a true poem is clearly adumbrated in *Elegy* 6, but there the image which suggests itself is that of the true priest. Only when this effort temporarily breaks down does he turn to the Petrarchan mode in composition; and it he quickly abandons. It may indeed have had the effect of directing his thoughts onward to Plato and that ideal love 'whose first and chiefest office begins and ends in the soul.' *Comus* is the evidence that he had absorbed this doctrine – and passed beyond it by virtue of Christian teaching and experience, as indeed, in the *Apology*, he says that he did. But if this was so, it was as part of a larger religious experience which included the ideal of chastity, but was not limited to it. To that experience the *Nativity* (with *Elegy* 6) and the sonnet *How soon hath Time* bear witness. It meant nothing less than an intensification of Milton's Christianity; and its outcome was the dedication of all his powers to the service of God in poetry. Without this experience, as our analysis of the poem will make clear, Milton could never have written *Comus*. On the experience the two prose passages which we have quoted both throw light; but its best and fullest record is to be read in the poetry itself.

It remains, then, to establish the pattern of Milton's early development, and to fill in its details by an analysis of the principal poems written before 1640.[6]

II

When Milton, at twenty-one, wrote the *Nativity* and *Elegy* 6, he already had to his credit, as the first fruits of his years at Cambridge, a dozen fairly ambitious Latin poems and several in English. They are all in varying degrees poetic exercises, which does not preclude the possibility that some of them embody and realize experiences important for Milton at the time of their occurrence.

He wrote them, it would seem, as ever after, with a particular audience in view: the majority of the Latin poems (as well as *At a Vacation Exercise*) for an academic audience, present with him at Cambridge; the more intimate of the Latin poems, *Elegies* 1 and 6, and perhaps also *Elegies* 7 and 5, for his friend and youthful confidant, Charles Diodati; and one English poem, *On the Death of a Fair Infant Dying of a Cough*, for the home circle. Here, and hereafter, the question of audience is not unimportant. The Romantic conception of the poet as singing to himself, not to be heard but overheard, was as foreign to Milton (despite the high proportion of subjective content in much that he wrote) as was that other Romantic notion of poetry as independent of the will, which makes the poet a sort of aeolian harp. In the home circle Milton had an audience sympathetic to his religious aspirations and to his literary ambitions. In Diodati he had one who shared more immediately his interest in learning and poetry, and participated in his youthful idealism, and who, from his age, might become the confidant, not only of these things, but of other experiences which lay outside the orbit of the home. Diodati would be able to appreciate, moreover, whatever was written with the academic audience in view; but that the bulk of Milton's verse before the *Nativity* was written for the academic audience is sufficiently evident, and its importance to him is confirmed by a fact of chronology.

In the autumn of 1626 Milton produced for this audience five ambitious sets of Latin verses, and thereafter nothing till May 1628. All that remains from this period of seventeen months is a Latin verse epistle to his earliest tutor, Thomas Young (*Elegy* 4), and the *Fair Infant*, written for his family. Now *Prolusion* 1 comments on a hostility to him which Milton has recognized among his fellow students at Christ's, and hints that it originates in differences about the prescribed studies. In the light of this suggestion, later made quite definite in *Prolusion* 6, Milton's outspoken attack on the scholastic discipline in *Prolusion* 3, in which we catch our first glimpse of the zealous reformer, becomes, *inter alia*, a provocative move in this controversy. *Prolusion* 6 (which belongs to midsummer 1628) marks the end of hostilities; for Milton has been chosen Father or leader of the revels at the vacation exercise in his college, and there can be no doubt of his eager acceptance of this return of good will. Its first sign, as Milton tells us, was apparent some months earlier: his last oration before his college (that is, *Prolusion* 4) was received, to his utter surprise, with friendly applause, when he had supposed that nothing he could write would be acceptable to them. It is highly significant that his resumption of academic verse occurs very shortly after this date, with *Elegy* 7 (May 1628); and it is reasonable to infer that its sudden cessation, seventeen months earlier, was due to a startled, and perhaps exaggerated, recognition of the alienation from his audience. Reading between the lines of *Prolusion* 6, it is easy to see that disagreement about their studies was not the only ground of Milton's feeling of isolation; the memory of his sobriquet, the Lady, still rankles; and there is further indication of his temporary disgust with Cambridge, and his loneliness there, in the studied avoidance of all reference to the university in his verse epistle to Thomas Young, and in the complaint, addressed in retrospect to Alexander Gill the younger, that he could find no one to share his literary pursuits and pleasures.[7] And the importance of his academic audience to him, at this early stage, is witnessed, not by *Prolusion* 6 alone, but by the confidences about his ambitions in poetry offered to them in the accompanying poem, *At a Vacation Exercise*, and most by his resumption of academic verse, which gave us his two best elegies (7 and 5). This is a minor episode in Milton's life, but it serves to throw some light on the poet at Cambridge.

Though Milton's eagerness in the composition of Latin verse argues his determination from the earliest date to be a poet and to become perfect through practice, the principle of imitation was, of course, at the foundation of humanistic education and the writing of Latin prose and verse was a major part of the training of every humanist. The formal test of success was the fidelity with which the classical models were imitated and the elegance of the adaptation. When the set of verses rose above mere technical virtuosity, there was no doubt another question that could be asked, namely, how far in the borrowed medium the poet had succeeded in saying something, in expressing something of himself. And to some of Milton's Latin verses this question is clearly applicable. Among the poets prescribed for reading and imitation were the Roman elegists, and especially Ovid (who received far more attention than he does today), though there were occasional protests. 'The elegiac poets,' wrote Aeneas Sylvius, 'are one and all unsuited for boys' reading: all are enervating.'[8]

The centre of Milton's early achievement in Latin verse is the *liber Elegiarum*. In the Renaissance the term *elegy* connoted a poem written (if in Latin) in elegiac metre, and (whether in Latin or in the vernacular) in the general tradition of the Roman elegists. Among them love had been the dominant theme (in the *Amores* of Ovid, in Tibullus, and in the bulk of Propertius), as it continued to be in some Renaissance elegists, in Joannes Secundus, in Campion, to a considerable extent in Buchanan, and in English in Donne. That Milton thought of love as the most characteristic subject of elegy is clear from his remarks in *Elegy* 6, in the *Apology for Smectymnuus*, and in the retraction appended to the *liber Elegiarum*. The recantation refers especially to *Elegy* 7, which Milton, breaking the chronological order, placed immediately before it. If *Elegy* 5 stood in as great (or as little) need of a recantation, it in effect had one in *Elegy* 6. There is in all this an element of convention. What was aimed at in such poetry was imitation, and this extended in measure to the attitude and tone of the pagan model: when writing in Latin one might do as the Romans did, and claim the sanction of convention; but convention also demanded that one should apologize for the imitations, though not suppress them. The conventions might be illustrated from the *Poemata* of the sombre Theodore Beza, Calvin's successor at Geneva, as well as from Milton. But if the element of convention in poem and recantation must not be overlooked, neither must it be allowed to obscure two facts: that the permitted freedom allowed Milton to express sides of his personality and experience which find little place in his English verse, and that the need for this freedom Milton outgrew. Of his seven elegies only two (7 and 5), with part of a third (1), are on erotic themes. Nor are the rest at all pagan in attitude. Two are monodies, indistinguishable in pattern and tone from the two in non-elegiac verse, and three are poetic epistles. This extension of elegy has plenty of precedent in the Renaissance: in Grotius, for example, and in English in Drayton, other subjects go near to crowding out the erotic altogether; and indeed the extension begins in the Roman elegists: in the *Amores* Ovid introduces a lament for Tibullus, and Propertius occasionally turns to mythological and other subjects, while in the *Tristia* and *Ex Ponto* Ovid inaugurates the personal epistle in elegiac form, which supplies a model for Milton and his fellows. Ovid is Milton's favourite, though he differs widely from the sophisticated poet of pleasure in attitude and tone, achieving a beauty of innocence natural to himself and very remote from his master; to Tibullus he owes nothing, and to Propertius, whose intensity and intricacy of feeling suggest Donne rather than Milton, only the trick of packing his elegies with allusions to classical myth.

With the possible exception of *Elegy* 1 (best considered in connection with *Elegies* 7 and 5), the best of the Latin poems written before Milton's temporary cessation of academic verse is *Elegy* 3, on the death of Lancelot Andrewes, and certainly it is the most characteristic example of this brief and productive period. The youthful poet was meditating on death and lamenting his many noble victims.

> But chiefly for you I grieved, good Bishop, lately the great glory of your Winchester. I melted in tears and ... thus complained: Cruel Death! ... is it not then enough that the woods should feel thy wrath, and that power should be given thee over the green things of the fields; that, touched by thy pestilent breath, the lily withers, and the crocus, and the rose sacred to Venus? Thou dost not permit even the oak to stand for ever by the stream ... To thee also succumb the birds ... though *they* give augury, and all the thousand animals that rove the dark forest, and the silent herd that the caves of Proteus shelter. Envious one! when so much power has been granted thee, why dost thou take pleasure to steep thy hands in human slaughter, sharpen thy certain arrows to pierce a noble breast, and drive from its tenement a soul half-divine.[9]

Night overtook the lament, and with night came sleep and a vision:

> ... Suddenly I seemed to be walking in a wide field ... where all things were radiant with a rosy light, like the mountain-tops flushed with the morning sunshine. Earth gleamed in a many-coloured vestment, as when Iris scatters her wealth abroad ... Silver rivers watered the green fields, and the sand shone richer than Hesperian Tagus. Through the perfumed leafage stole the light breath of Zephyr, rising from bowers of roses. Such place, men fable, is the dwelling of the lord of light, far on the shores beyond Ganges. As I stood wondering at the bright radiance and at the dense shadows of the clustering vines, lo, suddenly, Winchester's good Bishop stood before me, his countenance shining with starry light, his white vestment flowing to his golden sandals, and a filet about his saintly head. As the old man, thus venerably garbed, moved forward, the flowery earth trembled with joyful sound; hosts of angels clapped their jewelled wings, and through the air outrang the triumphant trumpet. The angels saluted their new companion with embrace and song. And with serene voice One uttered these words: Come, my son, enter the gladness of thy Father's kingdom. Here rest from thy labours for ever.

Morning returns, and the poet is left to regret the faded vision.

This is a skilfully wrought exercise in expression, with little experiential content or emotion. We may suppose that Milton felt some reverence and regret for the saintly bishop whom he had not yet learned to think of as one of the enemy (later he would speak of Andrewes in a very different and less becoming fashion); but the chief interest of the poem is literary: its use of classical convention and image to adorn a Christian theme, its simple but clearly marked aesthetic pattern, and, as essential to this pattern, a pagan complaint against death giving place to a Christian assurance of consolation and rejoicing. These things we shall meet again in Milton, but combined then with a weight of meaning and an emotion absent here.

With his resumption of academic verse in May 1628, Milton produced a very different, but certainly not less skilful, poem in *Elegy* 7. Its subject, Cupid's revenge, comes from the gay little poem with which Ovid introduces the *Amores*:

> For mighty Wars I thought to Tune my Lute,
> And make my Measures to the Subject suit:
> Six Feet for ev'ry Verse the Muse design'd,
> But *Cupid*, Laughing, when he saw my Mind
> From ev'ry Second Verse a Foot purloin'd.
> Who gave Thee, Boy, this Arbitrary sway,
> On Subjects not thy own, Commands to lay,
> Who *Phoebus* only and his Laws obey? ...
> Thus I complain'd. His Bow the Stripling bent,
> And chose an Arrow fit for his Intent.
> The shaft his purpose fatally pursues;
> Now Poet there's a Subject for thy Muse.
> He said, (too well, alas, he knows his Trade,)
> For in my Breast a Mortal Wound he made.
> Far hence ye proud *Hexameters* remove,
> My verse is pac'd and travell'd into Love.
> With Myrtle Wreathes my thoughtful Brows inclose,
> While in unequal Verse I Sing my Woes.[10]

From it sprang such variations as the Prelude to Book 1 of the *Elegies* of Joannes Secundus, the ninth Elegy of Buchanan, *De Neaera*, and, most elaborate of the three, Milton's seventh *Elegy*.

In fancied security, the poet, untouched yet by the shafts of love, thinks scornfully of Cupid and his vaunted power. Then, on a May morning, when others are abroad in celebration of love and springtime, the poet sees Cupid in a dream. The god boasts his sway over all mortals, nay, over the immortals themselves. The poet smiles in disdain and bids him to do his worst; but Cupid's revenge follows swiftly:

And now I took my pleasure, sometimes in the city parks, where our citizens promenade, sometimes at neighboring country-places. Crowds of girls, with faces like to the faces of goddesses, came and went radiantly through the walks; the day brightened with a double splendor. Surely, the sun himself stole his beams from their faces. I was not stern with myself; I did not flee from the spectacle, but let myself be led wherever youthful impulse directed. Rashly I sent my gaze to meet theirs; I could not control my eyes. Then by chance I noted one supreme above the others, and the light of her eyes was the beginning of my ills. She looked as Venus might wish to seem to mortals; lovely to behold as the queen of the gods was she. That rascal Cupid, harboring his grudge, had thrown her in my path; all alone, he had woven this plot against me. Not far off the sly god was hiding; his torch and many arrows hung as a great load from his back. Not a moment did he lose. Now he clung to her eyelids, now to her virgin face; thence he hopped upon her lips, and occupied her cheeks; and wherever the nimble archer went, ah, me! from a thousand points of vantage he struck my defenceless breast. Suddenly unwonted furies assailed my heart; I burned inly with love, I was all flame. Meanwhile she who was my only delight in misery disappeared, never to be given to my eyes again.[11]

Like *Elegy* 3, this is an exercise in poetic composition: Milton's subject is from Ovid, and he constructs a narrative pattern which shows that he has mastered in a single lesson Ovid's art of slight, but firmly handled, and rapidly unfolding story. There is, however, more of Milton himself in the poem than in *Elegy* 3. The tone is neither Ovid's nor that of his Renaissance imitators, but Milton's own: marked by a new ardour, but also, like his other early writings, by the beauty of innocence, whose source Milton correctly divined: in part from his personal temper, an innate modesty – 'a certaine nicenesse of nature' – and also from 'an honest haughtinesse, and self-esteem either of what I was or what I might be' (*Apology for Smectymnuus*, Col. 3 [i]: 304).

And it may well be that, despite the conventional character of the theme, the poem reflects Milton's experience, though heightened by poetic imagination, as it certainly suggests a growth in emotional maturity as compared with *Elegy* 1, written two years earlier, and the only poem before *Elegy* 7 to deal at all with the subject of love. Though *Elegy* 1 is a verse epistle to Diodati, and hence likely to be a more direct rendering of experience, there is, perhaps, little difference in the proportion of experience and conscious artistry which go to the making of the two poems; and it is possible that in *Elegy* 7 Milton had Diodati, as well as his restored academic audience, in view.

In the earlier poem, after referring to his rustication, Milton gives some account of his reading in drama, premonitory of *L'Allegro* and *Il Penseroso*, and continues:

> I do not always stay indoors ... I do not let the spring slip by unused. I visit the neighbouring park, thick set with elms, or the noble shade of some suburban place. And there often one may see the virgin bands go past, stars that breathe alluring flames. Many a time have I stood stupified before the miracle of some gracious form ..., many a time seen eyes brighter than gems ... and exquisite grace of brow and floating tresses, golden nets which Love casts deceivingly, and inviting cheeks, to which the hue of the hyacinth, even the blush of thy flower, Apollo, is but dull. Yield, ye Heroides, so praised of yore, and all ye loves that snared gadding Jove. And yield ye, Persian damsels ..., Grecian maidens, Trojan brides, and ye of the race of Romulus ... To the virgins of Britain first glory is due ... And London, built by the colonists from Troy, ... thou, too happy, enclosest with thy walls whatever beauty the pendant earth can boast. More than the stars of the night, ministrant troops of Endymion's goddess, are the crowds of girls that throng thy highways, bright with golden beauty, and with their radiance drawing to them every eye.[12]

Here, we have no reason to doubt, is a record of experience, though seen, of course, in the ideal light of poetry, and expressed with the aid of a clearly marked literary tradition. But the elegy does not end on this note. 'For my part,' adds Milton, 'while the blind boy grants me immunity, I make ready to leave these fortunate walls as quickly as I may. And I will avoid far off the evil halls of Circe the deceiver.' Here the premonitory note, though faint, is of *Comus*; but more important is the emphasis on innocence, whose significance is both immediate and permanent. Read in conjunction with *Elegy* 1, *Elegy* 7 would seem to carry a similar burden of experiential emotion, realized in the act of expressing it, and at the same time brought under control by being made to submit to the discipline of an aesthetic pattern.

The impression is yet stronger in the poem, written a year later (May 1629), which is the peak of Milton's early Latin verse. *Elegy* 5: *In Adventum Veris* adopts the language and the pagan spirit of the tradition in which it consciously takes its place. Not that one can point to any specific models in Ovid and his fellows or, save in the most general terms, in the Renaissance. Even in Tibullus nature plays a small part; and despite the invitation in classic myth and popular custom, the themes of love and springtime rarely come together in Roman poetry, save in a couple of Horace's odes and in the late *Pervigilium Veneris*. The development belongs rather to the Renaissance; and Milton's source has been sought in the *Maiae Calendae* of Buchanan, but there are important differences between the poems. Buchanan's chief strength lies in the vivid portrayal of individual scenes, while his relatively loose structural pattern is controlled simply by the commonplace *carpe diem* motif of Horace. Milton's firmer and more closely knit pattern turns on ideas, more interesting in themselves, whose origin is in his own experience or which he has proved upon his pulses. *Elegy* 5 is a sort of distillation of the whole body of classic myth relatable to love and the coming of spring.

Its structural pattern may be briefly set down: 1 / The first mark of spring is seen in the good green earth; 2 / the second, in the reviving poetic impulse. 3 / Poet and nightingale are respectively civic and sylvan heralds of the spring's return; and the rest of the elegy is presented as the poet's song. 4 / First, he sings of spring in the heavens, where Night retreats and, with her, 'bloodshed and fraud and violence'; next 5 / of Earth as she woos the returning sun-god; then 6 / of human kind, as rejoicing they yield to the sway of Venus, Cupid, and Hymen. 7 / Finally, through the shepherds of Arcady, and the deities of forest and field, the poet reaches the gods of high Olympus, who at this season desert the sky for earth, so that 'every grove has its deity': 'Long may every grove have its deity. Gods, desert not, I pray you, your homes amid the trees.' The prayer merges in the vain wish that the days of spring may linger, postponing the return of winter and night.

Such in briefest outline is the structural pattern. Selected quotations will give a sufficient idea of how Milton fills it in:

... Do I mistake? Doth not my strength in song also return? At the spring's gift is not inspiration here? ... Castolia swims before mine eyes, and the cloven peak of Parnassus ... My breast is moved with mysterious fervours, Madness and divine tumult stir me inly. Delian Apollo himself comes, his brows bound with Daphne's laurel: Delian Apollo himself comes ... What lofty song does my soul intend? ... The spring, the spring that gives me dower of my genius, my genius shall celebrate.

Now, Philomel, in thy bower of new leaves, begin thy modulations while all the woods are still. Sylvan and civic heralds, let us hymn the spring together ... For now the Sun flees from the Ethiopian strand ... and turns his golden chariot northward ... And murky Night goes into exile, ... and along with her Bloodshed and Fraud and Violence retreat.

Earth revives, casts off her hated age, and longs for thy embraces, O Apollo, longs for them and deserves them. For who more lovely than she when she bares her rich bosom breathing the harvests of Araby ... and the balms of the Orient and the roses of Paphos? ... Zephyrs [attend her and] lightly wave their cinnamon-scented wings, and the very birds woo thee to her ...

Headlong earth's children follow her example. For now over the whole world Cupid wanders and at the fire of the sun rekindles his torch ... Now he essays to conquer even unconquered Diana ... Venus renews her youth, and seems once more just risen from the sun-warmed sea. The youths sing hymns to Hymen ... The maidens go a-maying, each with a prayer to Cytherea for the lover of her choice. Shepherd and shepherdess pipe and sing ... Jove himself and Juno make merry in high Olympus ... And now, when the late twilight falls, fleet bands of satyrs skim over the blossoming fields, and with them Sylvanus, crowned with cypress, god half-goat, and goat half-god! The Dryads quit their wood-land shades and roam abroad over the lonely fields. Through tilth and covert riots Maenalian Pan ... Wanton Faunus pursues the Oread, while the nymph flies with startled feet ... The gods desert the skies for the woods of earth. Every grove has its deity. Long may every grove have its deity! Gods, desert not, I pray you, your homes amid the trees.

Return, O Jove! The age of gold restore! Why must you dwell in the cloudy storehouse of your thunder? Restrain, O Phoebus, the swift flight of the days and long keep rough winter from us ...[13]

Here is a note new in the poetry of Milton, and not at all character-istic of the Anglo-Saxon tradition. Indeed, the closest analogue of *Elegy* 5 comes two centuries and a half later in the lines from Swinburne's *Atalanta in Calydon* cited by Tillyard.[14] The meeting point of Milton and Swin-burne is the classics, which here in Milton facilitate an attitude of frank acceptance, the principal source of that effect of pagan naturalism met in *Elegy* 5. At the same time, the analogy can be quite misleading unless one recognizes that *Elegy* 5, in addition to being a poetic exercise which bril-liantly captures the desired tone, is a record and realization of Milton's experience and expressive of his personality, and that this is why the pagan-ism is still tempered by the beauty of innocence which is Milton's own, and very remote from anything discoverable in the decadent and exhibitive Swinburne.

The essence of the experience which the poem records, and in record-ing realizes, is Milton's recognition that the emotions whose dawning power over him is testified in *Elegies* 1 and 7, are universal in their sway. Common to all humanity, and having their counterpart in the life of nature, they not only inform much of classic myth, but are intimately connected with the poetic impulse itself: from these emotions spring the very power by which the poet gives them utterance. So much Milton clearly states. But in thus objectifying the emotions, and imposing upon them an aesthetic pattern, the poet, in a way, establishes his ascendancy over them. This Milton does not say, but he verifies it in the poem.

In the little *Song on May Morning* most of the basic elements in the pattern of *Elegy* 5 are reduced to simplicity and set, as one may say, to an Elizabethan air:

Hail bounteous *May* that dost inspire
Mirth and youth and warm desire,
Woods and Groves are of thy dressing,
Hill and Dale doth boast thy blessing.
Thus we salute thee with our early Song
And welcome thee, and wish thee long.

Fundamentally the conception and even the mood are the same, and equally remote from those of earlier poems and later, of *Elegy* 7 (1628), and the sonnets (1630). Nor need the marked contrast in the form adopted (which would weigh equally against both the earlier date and the later) make us hesitate in grouping the song with *Elegy* 5. Given Milton's interest in practice and experiment (which is a motive, primary or secondary, in all the poems of the Cambridge period), what more likely than the essaying of the same conception and mood in widely different forms?

We have chosen to analyse in some detail three of Milton's elegies, for the light which they throw on his development, and because these early examples of his art have not usually received sufficient attention. Other writings before the *Nativity* may be more briefly examined for indications of his interests and temper in these years.

His principal interest, clearly, was in the art of expression. That, every poem attests, as do also the *Prolusions*, or academic orations, which, however Milton might rebel against the barrenness of the assigned topics, gave opportunity for imitative rhetorical effects, not unlike those achieved in his Latin verse; and in two of the themes, indeed, Milton saw poetic possibilities which later prompted him to return to them: the praise of day (*Prolusion* 1) in *L'Allegro*, and the music of the spheres (*Prolusion* 2) in the *Nativity*. Though almost all his practice so far was in Latin, his interest in English verse finds striking expression in *At a Vacation Exercise*,[15] which heralds his turning to English in the rest of the Cambridge period, looks on to his ambition to write an English epic, and repudiates the eccentricities of metaphysical and other imagery, 'which takes our late fantasticks with delight.' Though Milton stands committed to English as his language, he will claim his place in the European classical tradition.

If there is scarcely any premonition of Milton the religious poet before December 1629, there is indication of the Protestant, the Puritan, and the reformer. The ambitious *In Quintum Novembris* has for its background Protestant and patriotic detestation of the plot (only twenty-one years before) to bring back the days of Mary and rekindle the fires of the martyrs. It belongs with the commemorative sermons and resembles the *Locustae* of Phineas Fletcher, which Milton may have known in manuscript. It is satire and invective cast in a narrative which is half-epic (nearer certainly to the heroic than to the mock-heroic). Its principal interest is a picture of Satan, who is still the foul fiend of mediaeval legend, but with some premonition of the terror, though not the pathos, he is to assume in *Paradise Lost*. Puritan indignation at the persecution of the saints speaks in *Elegy* 4, Milton's epistle to his earliest tutor Thomas Young, a Scot who was a good classicist and in Presbyterian orders, now chaplain to the English merchants in Hamburg, but fifteen years later to draw Milton into a defence of himself and his fellow authors, the Smectymnuans, in their war on episcopacy. In the *Elegy*, Milton writes

> Fatherland, stern parent, harsher than the white rocks beaten by the foam of your shore, does it beseem you so to expose your innocent offspring, so to drive them out, O heart of iron! into a strange land? Those whom God in his providence sent to thee, bearing good tidings from Heaven, to teach the way to the stars after the body is ashes, will you force these to seek their food in distant regions? If so, you are worthy to live forever shut in the darkness of death, and to perish with the eternal hunger of the soul![16]

In *Prolusion* 3 the reformer is seen afar off. Its subject is the scholastic discipline, and Milton beards the lion in his den. If Cicero was right and the end of the orator is to instruct, to delight, and finally to persuade, scholastic study and disputation answer none of these ends. By it 'the mind is neither delighted nor instructed, nor indeed is any common good promoted' (Col. 12: 160). Barren in matter, the scholastic philosophy is without elevation and grace of style: 'I think there never was a place for [these writers] on Parnassus, except perhaps some neglected corner at the bottom of the hill, dismal, rough and wild with brambles and thorns, covered over with thistles and dense nettles, far distant from the chorus and assembly of the

Muses ... Where the sound of Apollo's lyre shall never reach' (Col. 12: 162). Rhetoric and history, each in its way, can stir and capture the minds of men. Not so these studies, which are as fruitless as they are unpleasant. For the matters whereof they labour 'exist nowhere in the nature of things,' being mere phantoms of the mind, and if any effect ensues it is merely to make one 'a more accurate ignoramus.' Neither do they at all conduce to what is, for the individual, more precious than knowledge, namely, refinement of manners and uprightness of life' (Col. 12: 168); nor to what is the chief glory of a state, noble speaking and brave acting. In short they do nothing to foster eloquence, or teach wisdom, or incite to noble deeds. The terms of Milton's condemnation give us, by implication, his positive ideal of education. Both are in the humanist tradition. Here, and in *Of Education*, which completes the doctrine of the *Prolusion*, the influence of Bacon has been exaggerated. True, Milton advocates a study of the world around us, but he quickly reverts to Socrates to preach self-knowledge as most important of all to Christian Platonism, to advocate a contemplation of the heavenly intelligences, and (by way of appeal from the Aristotelianism of the scholastics) to the true Aristotle, who has left a scientific treatment of almost all that needs to be known. All this is humanist doctrine.

Milton's chief affinity with Bacon is his instinctive sympathy with the party of progress. This comes out not only in *Prolusion* 3, but also in the academic verses, *Naturam non pati senium*, probably written for a fellow of Christ's, to accompany his 'Determination' in the Schools in June 1628, when the subject of debate (perhaps suggested by George Hakewill's *Apology or Declaration of the Power and Providence of God*, 1627, which was his reply to Godfrey Goodman's *The Fall of Man Demonstrated to the Natural Reason*, 1616), was whether or not nature is subject to decay. Without entering far upon his argument, Milton is clearly in sympathy with the Baconian Hakewill and his assertion of the constancy of nature and the progress of knowledge.[17] But Milton is primarily a humanist, and he is also at this time a Platonist, rather than either Baconian or Aristotelian, as the similar poem (perhaps written on a similar occasion a year later), *De Idea Platonica*, makes plain.

Of specifically religious interest and idealism before the *Nativity*, the only indication is in *On the Death of a Fair Infant Dying of a Cough* (January 1628).[18] This is a grandiose memorial in the same general tradition as Donne's *Anniversaries* and Dryden's *Mrs. Anne Killigrew*, but one in which the interval between the thought and style and the occasion of the poem is even more disconcerting. Still, as the ostensible subject recedes, an opportunity occurs for the expression of Milton's youthful idealism, and in the last lines quoted below it flashes out:

Wert thou some Starr which from the ruin'd roofe
Of shak't Olympus by mischance didst fall;
Which carefull *Jove* in natures true behoofe
Took up, and in fit place did reinstall? ...

Or wert thou that just Maid who once before
Forsook the hated earth, O tell me sooth
And cam'st again to visit us once more?
Or wert thou that sweet smiling Youth!
Or that crown'd Matron sage white-robed truth?
   Or any other of that heav'nly brood
Let down in cloudie throne to do the world some good.

Or wert thou of the golden-winged hoast,
Who having clad thy self in humane weed,
To earth from thy praefixed seat didst poast,
And after short abode flie back with speed,
As if to shew what creatures Heav'n doth breed,
   Thereby to set the hearts of men on fire
To scorn the sordid world, and unto Heav'n aspire.

Such, then, was Milton when in December 1629, he wrote the *Nativity*. He had practice in the art of poetic expression, though mainly in Latin; he was skilful in the adaptation of traditional patterns, and he knew, on occasion, how to make them express his own experience and mood. He had manifested also his Puritan sympathies and his zeal for reform; and in the *Fair Infant* he had momentarily expressed something of the religious aspiration which was to find much fuller utterance in the *Nativity* and, after some hesitation and retreat, was finally to set its seal on his life-work in poetry.

III

Taken together, the *Nativity* and, three years later, the sonnet *How soon hath Time* give evidence of an experience which stands for Milton in place of what the Puritans called conversion. It differs in being closely connected with his poetry, in which it finds its chief expression. And it appears also to differ from the Puritan norm in its gradual character and in the absence of those dramatic crises and the marked self-abasement familiar to us in the lines of Puritan divines.

   An example may, perhaps, be given, from Edward Bagshaw's life of Robert Bolton, who in his earlier days, 'though he was very learned ... was a very mean scholar in the school of Christ,' and with the harvest of knowledge gathered in 'the tares of popery':

> The first news as hee heard of God was not by any soft and still voice, but in terrible tempests and thunder: the Lord running upon him as a gyant, taking him by the necke and shaking him to peeces, as he did Job; beating him to the very ground, as he did Paul, by laying before him the ugly visage of his sins which lay so heavy upon him as hee roared for grief of heart ...[19]

But authoritative writers on conversion, while outlining its stages, do not fail to recognize that the process of regeneration may be quite other than this, the gradual maturing, rather, of the seeds sown by a Christian education. 'I do not,' says Richard Baxter, 'call you to judge your state by the time and manner of your change so much as by the matter or thing itself. Find all that work upon your judgments, heart and life, that I have before laid down, and be sure it is there, and then, whensoever you came by it, you are happy.'[20] For

> the rational operation of the higher faculties (the intellect and will) may, without so much passion, set God and things spiritual highest within us, and give them the pre-eminence and subject all our interest to them ... and ... this is the ordinary state of a believer ... I ... perceived that education is God's ordinary way for the conveyance of his grace ... ; and that it was the great mercy of God to begin with me so soon and to prevent such sins as else might have been my shame and sorrow while I lived; and that repentance is good, but prevention and innocence is better, which though we cannot attain in perfection, yet the more the better.[21]

Of the same mind is William Whately, the best of all the writers on conversion. Besides those that 'did live a long time in unregeneracy,' and were suddenly and dramatically brought to a new way of life, there are, he says, others, whose conversion is gradually effected 'by favour of that great benefit of God, holy and Christian education'; and in them one work of grace may be more strongly manifested than another. 'Sometimes they find a more sensible abasement of themselves within their own hearts out of the apprehension of their sinfulness; sometimes desires and prayers are more vehement; sometimes a comfortable resolution of pleasing God doth more mightily stir them.'[22]

In expositions such as these we find the correct terms of reference for formulating Milton's religious experience. The fact that he entered Cambridge destined, as he supposed, for a place among the Puritan preachers would direct his thoughts towards experiential religion and render inevitable some consideration of his own spiritual state and development. In his circumstances, however, this would not necessarily entail a repudiation of his past life, but rather, as suggested by Whately, an intensified aspiration after spiritual things and a more conscious act of self-dedication to God's service. In Milton the dedication is, significantly, to God's service in poetry; and its first record is the *Nativity*.

A highly suggestive, although not a complete, gloss upon that poem is afforded by *Elegy* 6, an epistle to Diodati. It opens with a not too serious description of the elegiac vein, as one inspired by love and pleasure and nourished by food and wine, owing thus a threefold allegiance to Venus (with Cupid and Erato), to Bacchus, and to Ceres. Then, by way of the antithesis between elegy and epic, which was a commonplace from the days of the Roman elegists, it passes to the poet of heroic themes. Unlike the elegist, he must adopt the ascetic discipline of the Pythagoreans.

> His youth must be chaste and void of offence, his manners strict, his hands without stain. He shall be like a priest shining in sacred vestments, washed with lustral waters, who goes up to make augury before the offended gods ... Yea, for the bard is sacred to the gods ... He is their priest. Mysteriously from his lips and breast he breathes forth Jove.
> But if you would know what I am doing, ... I am singing the King of Heaven, bringer of peace and the fortunate days, promised by the holy book ... This poem I made as a birthday gift for Christ. The first light of Christmas morning brought me the theme.[23]

This sudden transition to the *Nativity* can have but one meaning. It is in no sense a heroic poem, the time for which is not yet; but it is the first earnest of Milton's resolve to become such a poet as he describes. It teaches us to read the contrast between the elegiac vein and the heroic as a repudiation of the former, to transliterate the description of the heroic poet into Christian terms as the account of a dedicated spirit divinely inspired, and to see in the ascetic discipline referred to a turning towards that moral and religious preparation for his life-work on which Milton was finally to enter after leaving Cambridge. Thus *Elegy* 6 throws light upon the *Nativity* and receives light back from it.

In the *Nativity* one recognizes three dominating ideas. The first is that of the 'birthday gift for Christ,' emphasized in the Prelude, and this conditions the temporal sequence of the hymn; for throughout the poet is approaching the stable at Bethlehem and at the end he looks back upon the scene there as, his gift presented, he withdraws. The idea is further linked with that of the Christian poet as at once dedicated and inspired, and finally the motive of the gift is love:

See how from far upon the Eastern rode
The Star-led Wisards haste with odours sweet,
O run, prevent them with thy humble ode,
And lay it lowly at his blessed feet;
Have thou the honour first, thy Lord to greet,
    And joyn thy voice unto the Angel Quire,
From out his secret Altar toucht with hallow'd fire.

In Isaiah 6:6 it is a seraph that touches the lips of the prophet with a coal from the altar; and in the traditional angelology, as Milton would remember, the seraphim betoken love of God as the cherubin betoken contemplation of his excellence. Whatever there is of simple personal religion in the *Nativity* is associated with this first idea of the birthday gift for Christ.

The second idea, though not thus fully formulated, is hinted at in the Prelude in the description of Christ as 'That glorious Form, that Light unsufferable' and in the allusion to the angel quire; and it is of equal or even greater importance, for it conditions something of the structure, and much of the imagery, of the hymn. It is the contrast between light, form, and harmony, and their opposites, darkness, formlessness, and discord. The first are epitomized by the angel quire, which is answered by the music of the spheres, and, as we observe, by the voice of the poet himself; and they triumph over their opposites, and thus symbolize the triumph of Christ over the forces of evil.[24]

Thus *symbolized*, this fact is *stated* in another way; by Christ the pagan oracles are silenced and the impure and multifarious polytheism is driven out by the single and pure faith. It is a belief based on scripture, says Ralph Cudworth, 'and agreeable to the sense of ancient doctors ... that one design of Christianity was to abolish and extirpate the pagan polytheism and idolatry.'[25] This is the third idea, essential to the *Nativity*, and at its intellectual centre, as the first is at its religious, and the second at its aesthetic centre. Together they make up the experience realized in the poem.

Each of the three main ideas thus represents a phase of the religious experience which the *Nativity* records, and each becomes in its way central in the poem, which by virtue of its aesthetic pattern combines them, and brings into relief their significance and interrelation. But to speak of the *Nativity* as a record of experience is not strictly correct. Poetry is something more than that: the experience is realized in the act of recording it. So it was in *Elegy* 5, and is in the *Nativity* and the majority of Milton's poems. In some of them elements of conflict in the experience are resolved on the imaginative plane and through the agency of aesthetic pattern. That indeed may be said to be one of the principal functions of Milton's poetry. In the *Nativity* no such resolution is required, and to that extent its pattern and function are less than typical. Only for a moment, in stanza 20, do we glimpse the possibility that to accept Christianity may mean to reject other things that are dear. In general the mood of the poem is one of simple and joyful acceptance. In this it resembles *Elegy* 5. What is accepted, however, is no longer a pagan reading of the order of nature, but nothing less than the order of grace and its supremacy over nature itself. And this it is which is symbolized by the triumphant images of light, form, and harmony.

Vastly important as is the experience recorded in the *Nativity*, it is not final. It does not turn Milton into the religious poet whom we know. It requires for its completion another experience, recorded just three years later in the sonnet *How soon hath Time*.

IV

So far, save in the case of the *Song on May Morning*, we have been dealing with poems whose date is established with some degree of probability. Of the remaining pieces only the unimportant epitaphs, *The Passion*, and the pivotal *How soon hath Time* are dated with certainty. For the rest we are thrown back upon converging probabilities. Apart from the indications of order furnished by the arrangement within groups in *Poems* (1645 and 1673), and by the Cambridge MS, our only data are the content and tone of the poems themselves, and a chief criterion is the self-consistency and significance of the scheme that one is able to work out. Accordingly, the rest of this essay may be allowed to centre on the order and approximate dates of the poems.[26]

We turn first to the problem of Milton's essays in the Petrarchan tradition, *O Nightingale* and the Italian sonnets. Smart has shown that the latter, long associated with Milton's Italian journey, actually preceded it, and that as early as 1629 Milton was buying Italian sonneteers and making or preparing to make a study of them.[27] *Poems* (1645) places the Italian sonnets after *O Nightingale* and before *How soon hath Time*, while their absence from the Cambridge MS strongly suggests that they antedate *Arcades*. The autobiographical passage in the *Apology for Smectymnuus* places Milton's Petrarchan phase after his elegiac, and without asserting that this precludes all possibility of overlapping, it is to be observed that the last of the strictly elegiac poems, *Elegy* 5, is dated with certainty in the spring of 1629. But on the evidence of the same passage, and its supposed allusion to *Elegy* 6, Hanford insists for the sonnets on a date before December 1629. The *Apology* talks first of Milton's reading in the Latin elegists, then of his learning to prefer the attitude of 'the two famous renowners of Beatrice and Laura,' and continues in words almost too familiar to quote: (Col. 3 [i]: 303–4)

> And long it was not after when I was confirmed in this opinion, that he who would not be frustrate of his hope to write well hereafter in laudable things ought himself to be a true poem; that is, a composition and pattern of the best and honourablest things; not presuming to sing high praises of heroic men or famous cities unless he have in himself the experience and practice of all that which is praiseworthy.

This Hanforth holds to refer to the doctrine of the heroic poet set forth in *Elegy* 6, and to place it as succeeding Milton's Petrarchanism in time. But his argument has the unhappy effect of forcing the sonnets back into the not less clearly distinguished period of the *Elegies*, 7 and 5, 1628–9. It seems to me possible that the passage quoted from the *Apology* refers less to the doctrine of *Elegy* 6 than to that of *Ad Patrem*, or perhaps to a telescoping in retrospect of the two. Hanford proceeds to argue that the conviction expressed in *Elegy* 6 precludes such an experience and expression of erotic emotion as the sonnets imply and contain. But this inference depends on his reading of the experience recorded in the *Nativity* and *Elegy* 6 exclusively in terms of the control or rejection of erotic emotion. And it ignores the idealism which Milton recognizes as a feature of the Petrarchan tradition. The context of the passage from the *Apology* suggests that Milton's new ideal of the poet is rather a development from his Petrarchanism than a repudiation of it. Quite clearly *Elegy* 6 implies a rejection of the type of erotic emotion found in the elegies: it is much less certain that it would necessitate the complete rejection of the idealized passion of the sonnets.[28] Lastly, it is very easy, as we have seen, to exaggerate the finality of the experience recorded in the *Nativity* and *Elegy* 6. Suppose it is granted that if the sonnets postdate these poems they represent some relapse from the high ground there attained: is such a relapse impossible or even improbable? It seems desirable, then, postponing this problem, briefly to examine the claims of each of the five years, 1628–32, to have originated the sonnets.

Against 1628 and 1629 stands the difficulty already noted, that to place the sonnets in either year would bring Milton's Petrarchanism back into the period of the elegiac eroticism represented by *Elegies* 7 and 5. Furthermore, these are May poems, and so is *O Nightingale*, and it is legitimate to ask whether the sonnet corresponds closely in content and mood to either of the elegies. It does not. It is a complaint of the absence of love, long invoked. *Elegy* 7 (1628) is a defiance of love, followed by a swift demonstration of its presence and power. Nor can much be argued from the suggestion of mediaeval reading in each work; for it is of different mediaeval poems. More divergent still is the tone of complaint in the sonnet from the buoyant, diffused eroticism of *Elegy* 5 (1629) and the *Song on May Morning*. The caution necessary in dealing with such evidence is that to the poet any mood might conceivably suggest its opposite as a subject for composition. But there is no known example of this in Milton (unless it be in the Hobson epitaphs in relation to *On Shakespeare*), and it runs counter to the intensity and singleness of his mind and to the suggestion of some genuine and moving experience underlying all the poems in question; it is a different matter from embodying the same mood in a contrasting form, as in *Elegy* 5 and the *Song on May Morning*. If I am right in my reading, to be presented below, of the years 1631 and 1632 up to Milton's quitting Cambridge, their note was one of tranquility and a certain abstraction from extra-aesthetic experience, which is quite foreign to the emotion embodied in the sonnets. One is led then to the spring and summer of 1630 as the most probable date of *O Nightingale* and the Italian sonnets. The chief argument against it is that it would make them follow hard upon the fragment on the passion; but this is not unsusceptible of explanation.

The opening lines of *The Passion* link it closely with the *Nativity*, thus dating it in the succeeding Holy Week, and suggesting that from the religious and aesthetic experience there recorded had sprung a resolve to write further specifically Christian poems, a suggestion greatly strengthened by the probability that Milton had been reading in preparation for such an effort the *Christiad*, Vida's epic on the life and death of Christ,[29] and by the religious verse which three years later sprang from the renewed self-dedication of *How soon hath Time*. But, unlike the later verse, *The Passion* is a confessed failure, breaking off after the eighth stanza, with the note: 'This subject the Author finding to be above the yeers he had when he wrote it, and nothing satisfied with what was begun, left it unfinisht.' Read in the light of the last stanza, the note tells us all we need to know:

> Or should I thence[30] hurried on viewles wing,
> Take up a weeping on the Mountains wilde,
> The gentle neighbourhood of grove and spring
> Would soon unbosom all their Echoes milde,
> And I (for grief is easily beguild)
> Might think th'infection of my sorrows loud,
> Had got a race of mourners on som pregnant cloud.

How beautiful the lines are – and how exquisitely inappropriate! It is not the touch of wit in the concluding couplet that is alone at fault (there is as much wit in the *Nativity*), but something more pervasive. It is the failure of the subject to take possession of Milton's imagination and at once to foster and express a religious and aesthetic experience, capable of subordinating everything to itself. The *Nativity* is not a complete success, but such a powerful experience is present and on the whole manages to exercise its unifying influence. In *The Passion* it is absent, and Milton's imagination lies open to every wayward fancy. One of them comes straight from the rejected world of the elegies. Unawares he finds himself once more in 'The gentle neighbourhood of grove and spring.' Where Echo is, Genius and the nymphs with flower-inwoven tresses, and all the gods of earth and heaven, may easily follow. Milton pauses just in time. The religious experience of the *Nativity* has faded and is not now renewable, by this subject at least. And so the thoughts and images appropriate to Milton's years begin to reassert their sway, as in his note he partly divines.

It would not be altogether surprising, then, if Milton should turn back to what is really an elegiac theme and write the last of his maytime poems, with its echo of *Elegy* 5:

O Nightingale, that on yon bloomy Spray
Warbl'st at eeve, when all the Woods are still,
Thow with fresh hope the Lovers heart dost fill,
While the jolly hours leads on propitious *May*.[31]

But the attitude of glad acceptance can no more be renewed than could the fervour of the *Nativity*. In its stead we have the assertion, a little anxious, and perhaps a little defiant:

Whether the Muse, or Love call thee his mate,
Both them I serve, and of their train am I.

The *Nightingale* is, in a twofold sense, introductory to the Italian sonnets, which it immediately precedes in the *Poems* (1645). Its mood is likely to be highly receptive to the experience in love, perhaps as much imaginary as actual, that evidently underlies the Italian poems.[32] At the same time it is clearly transitional, anticipating them in its form, but retaining something of the realistic attitude of the elegies; in other words, Milton's adherence to the Petrarchan tradition, which he has been studying, is here far from complete. To render it so the experience underlying the Italian sonnets is necessary. *The Passion* and the *Nightingale* in their different ways represent some relapse from the position attained in the *Nativity* and *Elegy* 6. But that position has not ceased to exercise its influence. Milton may reaffirm his allegiance to the muse and love; but confronted with an experience of love to be celebrated in verse, his instinct is to idealize the emotion. In the Italian sonnets he does this by means of the Petrarchan tradition, and in terms which are not incompatible with the ground taken in *Elegy* 6. For that poem does not contain a categorical repudiation of erotic emotion, but only of the elegiac mode of response to it and to life in general; and the later formulation of the *Apology* on the need of being oneself a true poem (if it really corresponds and alludes to the position formulated in *Elegy* 6) implies, as we have seen, no necessary repudiation of Petrarchanism.

In passing from the elegiac to the Petrarchan mode of treating love, Milton is running counter to the main movement of English poetry in his day. The Petrarchan tradition, whose naturalization in England had set the Elizabethan sonnet cycles rolling, had from the first embodied two tendencies, one towards idealization, the other towards convention, whose ultimate outcome was a convention of idealization. Thereupon a reaction had set in and manifested itself in different ways with Ben Jonson and Donne. Milton turns back to the sources of Petrarchanism and, apparently without scruple, adopts the conventions along with the idealism, as is sufficiently proved by *Sonnet* 5, whose virtuosity reminds us that here, as in the Latin elegies and indeed throughout the Cambridge period, the achievement of perfect expression by practice is a motive sometimes secondary, but rarely wholly absent. Withal Milton manages to put a good deal of himself into some of the sonnets because they spring from a real and felt experience. This is especially true of the last in the series:

> Enamoured, artless, young, on foreign ground,
>   Uncertain whither from myself to fly,
>   To thee, dear Lady, with an humble sigh
>   Let me devote my heart, which I have found
> By certain proofs, not few, intrepid, sound,
>   Good, and addicted to conceptions high:
>   When tempests shake the world, and fire the sky,
>   It rests in adamant self-wrapt around,
> As safe from envy, and from outrage rude,
>   From hopes and fears, that vulgar minds abuse,
>   As fond of genius and fixed fortitude,
> Of the resounding lyre, and every Muse.
>   Weak you will find it in one only part,
>   Now pierced by Love's immedicable dart.[33]

One cannot fail to observe that it is himself, and neither love nor the lady, that Milton is here idealizing. And one is led to ask whether he is not somewhat disquieted, as well as gratified, at the power which he discovers love to possess over his mind. This assertion of his integrity in all other respects, in terms of the Stoic, it is true, not the Christian ideal, certainly suggests as much. And its probability is enhanced when the lines are brought into relation with the conclusion of *Sonnet 3*. These Italian poems, says Milton, are new and unaccustomed plants of love's fostering:

> So Love has willed, and ofttimes Love has shown
> That what he wills he never wills in vain.
>   Oh, that this hard and sterile breast might be
>   To him who plants from heaven a soil as free!

What Milton is constrained to admit is that he finds his heart more open to love than to religion, and his hand more ready to amatory than to religious verse. Here plainly is an allusion to the religious experience of which we have a record in the *Nativity* and *Elegy 6*, in which there has been some failure and retreat,[34] but which will renew itself and achieve permanence as Milton, his decisions taken, approaches his twenty-fourth birthday.

The remainder of the year 1630 and the early months of 1631 produce nothing but the epitaphs. The famous one *On Shakespeare* is an exercise in the serious application of poetic wit; the poems on Hobson are less successful exercises in its humorous application, obviously written for an academic audience, and perhaps suggested by the *Shakespeare*; the beautiful *Epitaph on the Marchioness of Winchester* captures to admiration the very different style of the Jonsonian school with its effect of simplicity and flowing movement. These poems are then mere exercises, from which all experiential content is absent. Coming after the poems of the preceding year their insignificance is itself significant. They are to be followed, if our estimate of the rest of 1631 and 1632 is correct, by poems which bear a closer relation to Milton's inward development, the companion pieces, *Ad Patrem*, and *Arcades*; but in them too, something of the abstraction noticed in the epitaphs persists and results in a preponderance of aesthetic over non-aesthetic elements in the experience which they record.

Most readers of this study will be familiar with Tillyard's cumulatively impressive arguments for the summer of 1631 as the date of *L'Allegro* and *Il Penseroso*.[35] They turn principally on seven considerations: 1 / the absence of the poems from the Cambridge MS, where we should expect to find them if they postdated *Arcades*; 2 / the lack of all positive evidence supporting their traditional association with the period of Milton's residence at Horton; 3 / the divergence of their holiday mood from everything that we know of this time of systematic study and direct preparation for his life-work (whose character Hanford has done so much to elucidate) ; 4 / the consonance, on the other hand, of their mood with the spirit of a long vacation (as Hanford had already divined) ; 5 / the fact that they seem, especially in their openings, to presuppose an academic audience; 6 / the further link with Cambridge supplied by the evident association of *L'Allegro* and *Prolusion* 1 (in Defence of Day) ; and finally 7 / Milton's assertion in *Prolusion* 7 that during the last long vacation he had enjoyed, amid rural scenes, the highest favour of the muses. Of these arguments, 1 will bear a heavier emphasis than Tillyard gives it (any dating that conforms to the evidence of the Cambridge MS and the *Poems* enjoys the great initial advantage of having nothing to explain away) ; and 3 is susceptible of being greatly reinforced by a more adequate conception of the total pattern of Milton's career, with its decisive turning point recorded in *How soon hath Time* (December 1632), which alone will satisfactorily explain the divergence of the later mood from the moods of Cambridge, and its astonishing constancy. In connection with 7 two further considerations suggest themselves: *a* / that no poems besides the companion pieces appear to belong to any long vacation, save only the Italian sonnets, to which the terms used in *Prolusion* 7 would be quite inappropriate; and *b* / that there is a clearly traceable development of preoccupation and mood between the companion pieces, *Prolusion* 7, and *Ad Patrem*. Only in 6 does Tillyard overplay his hand by trying to show that *L'Allegro* is a poem in praise of day based upon the speech on that subject given several years before, and that *Il Penseroso* stands in the same relation to the speech in praise of night that Milton would have given had he been assigned the other side in the debate. This, however, is to confuse matter with method, and greatly to distort the subject of the companion pieces.

They are not poems in praise respectively of day and night, but poems setting forth rival conceptions of a life of pleasure, the one active and social, the other contemplative and solitary, which adopt as their scheme of presentation the ideal day. L'Allegro's commences with sunrise and the song of the lark and extends to midnight, carrying, as Tillyard happily says, the glad spirit of day into the festivities of the evening and the reading of the midnight hours; Il Penseroso's commences with curfew and the song of the nightingale, extends through a night of study, and carries its spirit into the succeeding day. It is inconceivable that *Prolusion* 1 should have suggested the subject of these poems, or even their structural pattern, which is progressive while the prolusion remains perfectly static. The debt is real, but it commences when, having designed a pair of poems on rival conceptions of a life of pleasure, and hit on the device of the ideal day as furnishing the framework within which a whole series of contrasting parallels can be presented, Milton starts work on *L'Allegro*; nor does it extend much beyond the description of dawn in that poem, and the banishments and welcomes of Melancholy and Mirth. It is clear from the evidence which Tillyard amasses that at this point Milton turns back to his first prolusion for several important suggestions in imagery. This is not the first time that he has invoked memories of his college orations: besides the example of the *Nativity* and *Prolusion* 2, there is the *Carmina Elegiaca*, which is based on an early and rejected prolusion (Col. 12: 288–91; 1: 326–7); and it is interesting to discover that the train of memory which carried Milton from *L'Allegro* to *Prolusion* 1, also carried him to the *Carmina Elegiaca*.[36]

We cannot pause to comment on the companion aesthetic patterns, woven of landscape, myth and personification, reading, music, and reverie; but our argument will not allow us to omit some subleties of differentiation between them. In *Il Penseroso* the idea of a contemplative life, though pursued for its pleasure, reaches out towards the mystical and the religious; it is recognized as involving self-discipline and as culminating in inspiration. To his invoking of Melancholy, the natural temper and proper state of the studious,[37] the thoughtful man adds:

> And joyn with thee calm Peace, and Quiet,
> Spare Fast, that oft with gods doth diet,
> And hears the Muses in a ring,
> Ay round about *Joves* Altar sing.
> And adde to these retired leasure;
> That in trim Gardens takes his pleasure;
> But first, and chiefest, with thee bring
> Him that yon soars on golden wing,
> Guiding the fiery-wheeled throne,
> The Cherub Contemplation.

These companions of Melancholy are much more than mere pieces of decorative imagery. Besides their derivation from Ezekiel 10:1, 9–19, the last four lines quoted depend on the symbolic value traditionally attached to the angelic orders. Upon this Christian humanism had been quick to seize and elaborate. The general context from which Milton lifts his image of the Cherub Contemplation can be sufficiently illustrated from the *Oratio elegantissima de dignitate hominis* of Pico della Mirandola:

> The *Seraph* burns with the fire of love; the *Cherub* shines with the radiance of intelligence; the *Throne* stands in the steadfastness of judgment. Hence if, dedicated to the active life, we undertake the care of lower things with a right weighing of them, we shall be made steadfast in the fixed firmness of the Thrones. If ... musing upon the Workman in the work, and the work in the Workman, we are busy with the leisure of contemplation, we shall flash on every side with cherubic

light. If by love we burn for the Workman alone, with that devouring
fire of his, we shall suddenly burst into flame in the likeness of a Seraph
... But how can any one either judge or love things that are unknown?
... Therefore with his own light the Cherub, in the mean position,
makes us ready for the seraphic fire and at the same time illuminates
us for the judgment of the Thrones. He is the bond of the first intelligences, the order of Pallas, the ruler over contemplative philosophy ...
Let us make ourselves one with him and be caught up into the heights.[38]

The process, as Pico goes on to make clear, while it implies a purging of the
affections and a breaking of our bondage to earthly things, nevertheless uses
a study of nature and man as a ladder of ascent to God; for through the
work the Workman is known. It would be absurd to read the whole of this
doctrine into Milton's image of the Cherub and the Throne, but not less
absurd to ignore it altogether. The doctrine is clearly present in *Prolusion* 7,
where that contemplation 'by which our mind without the aid of the body,
and as it were wrapped up in itself, copies the eternal life of the immortal
gods with an extraordinary delight,' is to be attained only after we are 'satu-
rated and perfected by knowledge and training' (Col. 12 : 254). In the light
of this scheme one glimpses a deeper meaning in Il Penseroso's studies as
they range through nature, the life of man (revealed in tragic poetry, or in
allegorical 'Where more is meant than meets the ear'[39]), the spirit-world,
and the lore of the immortal soul; one sees the propriety of the Pythagorean
asceticism, already alluded to in *Elegy* 6, and now rewarded by communion
with the gods or vision of the muses; and one understands the hope that
study and discipline may issue at last in inspiration –

> Till old experience do attain
> To something like Prophetic strain.

These things do not constitute the subject of *Il Penseroso*, which is the pleasure, not the ultimate purposes, of the contemplative life; but they furnish
some of its overtones and a hint of the direction which Milton's mind is preparing to take.

Through each of *Il Penseroso, Prolusion* 7, and *Ad Patrem* there run
two or more of these themes: leisure, learning, and poetry. In the first it is
the delight of leisure devoted to learning, with poetry represented only in the
glancing allusion to the muses and in the inference that of such a life springs
such poetry as *Il Penseroso* itself. In the prolusion it is the utility of learning
pursued at leisure that is the central theme, but in the whole account the
delight of it is implied, and while for the most part learning is considered in
relation to other ends than poetry, its place in any scheme of learned leisure

that Milton can devise is staked, and its dependence on learning is emphasized at the outset. The parallel of poet and orator is utilized to observe that in the poet 'nothing commonplace or mediocre can be allowed,' and that he 'ought to be equipped and perfected with a certain encompassing support of all the arts and all science.' In pursuit of it, says Milton, 'I am wholly afire and ablaze every day.' Leisure is necessary for learning, learning for inspiration, and this is the meaning of Hesiod's fable of a prophetic sleep. There is implicit here the whole plan of future study. But instead of continuing with a forward, Milton contents himself with a backward glance: 'I ... invoke the glades and streams and beloved elms of the villas, under which during the summer just gone by, as I recall to mind with pleasant memories, I enjoyed the highest favour of the Muses, where amid fields and remote woodlands I have even seemed to be able to grow up in a remote age' (*Prolusion* 7, Col. 12: 246–9). Thus the scene and mood of *Il Penseroso* are recalled, just after the position of *Ad Patrem*, on leisure, learning, and poetry, has been anticipated. For that poem is not adequately described as Milton's apology for poetry, which conceals its common ground with *Il Penseroso* and *Prolusion* 7. It must be described as Milton's plea for the leisure necessary to learning, and the learning necessary to poetry: his defence of poetry indeed, but also of the contemplative life which alone renders its possible: his assertion, finally, of the delight as well as the dignity of means and end – a description which immediately reveals the common ground.

No one doubts that the occasion of *Ad Patrem* was Milton's desire to forgo any other profession and give his life to poetry, and more immediately to the preparation for poetry. In the last year at Cambridge his future must have been the subject of earnest consideration, and to this year Masson, rightly, as I think, assigned *Ad Patrem*, though he made the serious mistake of associating it with *How soon hath Time*, which he dates a year too early, in 1631, and which is in every way unlike it. Recognizing a difference between the two poems, though, in my opinion, misinterpreting both of them, Grierson proposed to move *Ad Patrem* on towards the end of the Horton period. For this reason his argument must be examined. He writes:

The sonnet and the letter which accompanies it are an apology for waiting and learning; the Latin poem is an apology for poetry. Milton's father seems to have been quite prepared to allow his son ample time and opportunity for study, ready that he should make himself one of the learned men of the time, ultimately perhaps a great protestant divine and champion of the reformed faith. But when it became apparent that poetry was not an occasional bypath, but the main highway of his son's career, he seems to have been taken aback and to have demurred. This crisis can, I think, hardly have arisen till the performance and publication of *Comus* revealed both to Milton and his father whither the long-waited-for prompting of the spirit was preparing to carry him.[40]

The difference between *How soon hath Time* and *Ad Patrem* is so obvious that were Masson right in his dating of the former (but he is not), it would effectively rule out his dating of the latter. But the difference is not such as Grierson formulates or such as would justify one in placing *Ad Patrem* after *How soon hath Time*. For the sonnet is not primarily an apology for either waiting or learning: it is the record of a religious experience which adds to Milton's conception of himself as poet elements lacking in *Ad Patrem*. There Milton is urging his plan for his life-work, the plan for which he was (in Grierson's own view) abandoning divinity, and it seems impossible that after the determination to do all hereafter 'As ever in my great task Masters eye,' he should have laid no stress at all on the religious and ethical aspect of poetry and of his call thereto. For after the sonnet there is no evidence that Milton ever again wavered in his resolve; all the evidence is that he did not. Some preoccupations, with the absence of others, and the tone of *Ad Patrem* are alike foreign to the later Horton period. They seem to place the poem in the lighter air of Cambridge and with the companion pieces,[41] *Prolusion 7*, and *Arcades*. The extreme lateness of Grierson's date brings other difficulties. One is that the poem is in Latin, which Milton, save for special purposes, had abandoned soon after announcing his adherence to English in the *Vacation Exercise*. That a gifted youth should present to his father the best credentials he has, his skill in Latin verse, is understandable. That the mature Milton should indite to his father a Latin petition to be allowed to give his life to English poetry demands explanation. The connections suggested by *Ad Patrem* are nearly all with writings of the Cambridge period. He has no wealth, he states, 'except what golden Clio has given'; if the allusion is to historical reading, it reminds us of the enthusiasm for history expressed in *Prolusion 7*. When he glances at heroic poetry it is not to talk of Arthurian or other British themes, as he is to do in *Mansus* and the *Epitaphium* within a year or two of Grierson's date, but in the vague classical terms of the *Vacation Exercise* and *Elegy 6*. When he alludes to the poet as priest, it is in words reminiscent of the latter poem, and he goes on to talk of joining the angels' song, which is echoed by the music of the spheres, as in the *Nativity*. Of his poetry to date he speaks as 'my boyish verses and amusements,' whose prospect of surviving him is far from being assured. Is this the language in which Milton would speak of *Comus*, especially if its success had at last fixed his wavering choice and determined his serious pursuit of poetry? But greater than all the other difficulties is what the late date demands we should believe of Milton: that throughout the Cambridge period, and for five long years thereafter, he simply drifts, waiting till the success of *Comus* shows, not his father (that we could perhaps accept), but the poet himself, whither he is going. This is not the Milton whose deliberation and self-sufficiency have impressed and often repelled his readers, but some minor Romantic, strayed into Horton, whose favourite image for himself must be the aeolian harp.[42]

On the contrary, Milton's hopes and plans in poetry date back to his earliest days at Cambridge and appear to manifest a steady growth and clarification. In the *Vacation Exercise* (1628) he tells us something of them, but the eager practice in various poetic forms, wherein his style showed signs that it would live, began as early as 1626. In *Elegy* 6 (1629) we find him preoccupied with the character of a poet of heroic themes, and offering the *Nativity* as an earnest of his resolve to become such a poet. In *Prolusion* 7 (1631) we find his sense of the need of learning for poetry and his ardent zeal to acquire it, and in *Ad Patrem* his hope of winning at last the learned poet's crown: 'Therefore, however humble my present place in the company of learned men, I shall sit with the ivy and laurel of a victor.' Destined for the ministry, Milton must at first have relegated his poetry to a second, though still an important place, in his plans for the future. But when he made and won his plea to be allowed to retire and prepare himself for poetry, he must in his own mind have reached the determination to give his life to that activity and it alone. At first he does not seem completely to have transferred the sense of religious calling from his original destination to his new one: learning is viewed as the means to poetry, but poetry almost as a sufficient end in itself. The reason is some fading of the religious experience of December 1629, perhaps increased for the moment by this very decision that he is compelled to make. It is a temporary condition, but should be carefully observed because it accounts for the absence from *Ad Patrem* of any stress on the religious calling and ethical function of the poet. But if Milton's poetry is to take the direction which in fact it did take, the renewed dedication of himself in terms of religion is necessary; hence the importance for his poetry of the determination reached in *How soon hath Time*, though it contains no specific reference to poetry as such. Hammersmith and Horton are a preparation in mind and character, undertaken in the light of all that has gone before. After it the hopes and plans can crystallize, and Milton can speak with a new decisiveness about the great work that he intends to execute. If one places beside *Ad Patrem* the utterances of the late 1630s – the letter to Diodati (September 1637), the *Mansus* (1638), the *Epitaphium Damonis* – and, as the result of these years, the subjects in the Cambridge MS and the pronouncements on poetry in *The Reason of Church Government*, one is conscious of a great development since the poem was written.

The period between the spring of 1631 and the summer of 1632, has then, it would seem, its own character. On the one hand, it is marked by a rapid maturing of Milton's mind and art. On the other, it represents a period of tranquillity, after the very different experiences recorded in the *Nativity* and the Italian sonnets and before the self-examination that issues in *How soon hath Time*. After the Italian sonnets Milton writes little – merely the epitaphs – and that little contains hardly anything of himself. Then in the long vacation of 1631, in a setting briefly sketched in *Prolusion 7*, he produces the companion pieces. Into them goes more of himself. Here are moods that Milton has certainly experienced, with something of his favourite reading and of the scenes that have brought him delight, and, in the overtones of *Il Penseroso*, something also of his deeper feelings and thoughts. But there is a complete absence of the problematical. One has no sense, as one is later so often to have in his poetry, of Milton's *dealing with* his experience as distinct from merely recording it in terms of an aesthetic pattern. The comparison of two ways of life does not involve, as in other circumstances it so easily might have done, the posing and making of a choice between them: indeed the comparison is simply a piece of patterning, with no extra-aesthetic reference. And this in turn is rendered possible because Milton is, for the time being, able to postpone his problems, to banish 'sleepless cares and complaints' and 'walk with heart secure.' The phrases come not from the companion pieces, but from *Ad Patrem*, which, despite the momentous decision on which it depends, shows in remarkable degree the same tranquillity of spirit, the same power of abstraction from disturbing thoughts. This tranquillity and this power of abstraction are the essence of the purely aesthetic attitude which appears, not only in the companion pieces, but preeminently in *Arcades*, and establishes a kinship with them.

Arcades, which on other grounds, also, probably belongs to the spring of 1632,[43] is the most purely aesthetic of all Milton's great poems. Like the companion pieces and *Ad Patrem*, it is unvexed by any problem. Like *L'Allegro*, and to a slightly lesser degree *Il Penseroso* and *Ad Patrem*, it is undoctrinal in its utterances. And, unlike these poems, it makes, so far as can be determined, no drafts whatsoever on Milton's extra-aesthetic experience. One thing, and one only, does it tell us of Milton's state of mind at the time of its composition: it was a state of mind which permitted a sustained and joyous act of aesthetic abstraction. The companion pieces and, what is more remarkable, *Ad Patrem* approach this condition. *Arcades* securely attains it. To realize this one has only to compare it with the highly doctrinal *Comus*,[44] which makes such large drafts on Milton's experiences: a salutary exercise if it taught us not to confuse the purely aesthetic with the poetically great or interesting. But pending such a comparison the quality of *Arcades* can be illustrated by reference to a single favourite image, that of the music of the spheres. It occurs in the *Nativity*, in *Ad Patrem*, in *At a Solemn*

Music, and in *Comus.*[45] In these, as in *Prolusion 2,* the image is doctrinal, employed to convey, of course in aesthetic form, a truth which has come to Milton from his extra-aesthetic, his ethical and religious, experience. In *Arcades* the image also occurs, in lines 61–78. The Genius of the Wood has listened to the ninefold harmony, not now answering the angel choir, but existing in its own right, and holding nature in her course. And what is his conclusion? Were it not, he says, that none 'Of human mould, with gross unpurged ear,' can detect such music, it

> worthiest were to blaze
> The peerles height of her immortal praise,
> Whose lustre leads us, and for her most fit,
> If my inferior hand or voice could hit
> Inimitable sounds.

The image is divested of all doctrinal significance (for the first line quoted is not doctrinal, but part of the image itself). It is, quite properly, fitted to the Genius of the Wood, who (unlike the Attendant Spirit in *Comus*) has no moral or religious significance. Like the Genius, the image which he utters is purely aesthetic and has no implications outside the poem.

   We shall never again see Milton in precisely this mood – 'Nymphs and shepherds, dance no more!'

v

It is entirely natural that as Milton enters upon his period of conscious preparation for his life-work he should be led to renewed self-examination. For some five months after settling at Hammersmith he produced, so far as we are aware, no poetry. Then he breaks his silence in the sonnet *How soon hath Time.* Its meaning has been somewhat obscured by taking it in too close conjunction with the prose Letter to a Friend (Col. 12: 320–5), in which a copy of the sonnet was included. Grierson describes the poem as, with the letter, an apology for waiting and learning. It is nothing of the kind. It is, first, a consideration of Milton's little achievement to date, which can be assigned no satisfactory meaning unless we read it in the light of his large ambitions for the future in poetry, and second, a renewed and more decisive dedication of himself to God's service, which not only has the effect of resolving his doubts and fears, but leaves its mark on nearly all his subsequent poetry. The letter obscures the issue because, to speak quite frankly, it is a somewhat disingenuous document. The decision as between the pulpit and poetry has, it seems almost certain, already been taken, at least in Milton's mind. This, clearly, is unknown to the possibly too officious friend, and the letter does not undeceive him. Nor can he be let into the full meaning of the sonnet. It is included simply because it says quite unequivocally that Milton holds himself to be in God's hand. This the friend requires to be told, and this Milton lets the sonnet tell him. By us, however, it must be read not as part of the letter, but for itself.

It opens on the uncharacteristic note of self-distrust: How little he has so far accomplished; how immature he seems; how dubious the promise of future achievement, on which he has staked everything! Yes, but he is in God's hand. Much or little, soon or late, it will be as God has determined. All that is in the poet's power, and all that matters, is that by grace he may use his talent in God's service and with submission to his will. For

> be it less or more, or soon or slow,
> It shall be still in strictest measure eev'n,
> To that same lot, however mean or high,
> Toward which Time leads me, and the will of Heav'n.[46]
> All is: if I have grace to use it so,
> As ever in my great task Masters eye.[47]

Thus Milton renews his self-dedication and with it the clouds roll away. The thoughts in the octave are brought to a head by the approach of his twenty-fourth birthday, with its sense of the flying years. But the whole poem is the outcome of the period of silent self-examination, and records the final and decisive phase of Milton's early religious experience. The mark of a genuine religious experience is its power to change one's view of things, and of the relation of the self thereto. In the sestet Milton marshals the resources of his faith to meet the doubts and fears formulated in the octave, and the result is not strictly speaking to dispel them, but to resolve the problem by raising it to a religious level where self-regarding thoughts are simply irrelevant. This is the more remarkable when we remember Milton's unpliant egoism and his intense desire to excel.

The poem is more than a record of Milton's experience. As in *Elegy* 5 and the *Nativity*, the experience is realized in the very act of recording it. The imposition of aesthetic pattern upon the extra-aesthetic materials of experience makes the experience of the poem, which in this case is at once religious and aesthetic. In *Elegy* 5, and in large measure in the *Nativity*, there is nothing problematical; the attitude and effect are those of simple acceptance; no 'resolution' of conflicting elements occurs. Here, in *How soon hath Time*, one encounters at last, though in a simple and rudimentary form, the full Miltonic pattern and function (the resolutions of conflict by the imposition of aesthetic pattern). If one were disposed to doubt their meaning or their importance, one need only look on to *When I consider how my light is spent*, and see them repeated there, and to *Comus, Lycidas*,[48] the *Epitaphium Damonis*. In some ways – not in all – *How soon hath Time* is more characteristic than the *Nativity*. It builds upon the experience in that poem, but is in itself more decisive. The effect of Milton's renewed dedication of himself and his life-work to God's service can be traced immediately and through the years.

It is seen in the character of the poems to which he at once turns.[49] *On Time* may well have been an inscription for some elaborate timepiece, but its subject links it closely with the sonnet. There Milton has stayed by an act of Christian self-dedication the disquieting thought of time, which has stolen youth without bringing assured maturity. Now he completes the triumph over it by pointing on to the Christian hope of immortality. *Upon the Circumcision* is religious verse of another kind. The *Nativity* apparently suggested to Milton the possibility of a number of poems connected with events in the early life of Christ as these were marked in the church's calendar. The immediate result was *The Passion*, a failure. Now, under the impetus of a further religious experience, he determines, if not to continue the scheme, at least to retrieve that failure; *Upon the Circumcision* opens with a reference to the Nativity and for the rest looks towards the Passion. It is not, confessedly, one of Milton's more inspired poems, but it has the qualities of solemnity and concentration which *The Passion* so signally lacks. *At a Solemn Music* returns to the kind of *On Time*, and to its triumphal note. Whenever music is his theme Milton's thought quickens to inspiration; but in this poem the controlling ideas and their attendant emotion are religious. Some of the ideas are adumbrated in the *Nativity*, but in *At a Solemn Music* they reach a new clarification: first, there is the essential harmony, the 'pure concent' of the angel choir; second, the voice with which nature and man answered its strains

> till disproportion'd sin
> Jarr'd against natures chime;

finally, the faith that in the regenerate this harmony of nature and grace is restored and crowned at last by their union with the 'celestial consort.' Much of Milton's subsequent thought is implicit in this ideal of a harmony between nature and grace, and in the sense, so much more acute than in the *Nativity*, that in order to restore it sin must be recognized and eradicated. These are the ideas embodied in *At a Solemn Music*; but, as in the *Nativity*, and all other great poems, ideas become the basis of an aesthetic pattern and by its aid are realized, not as ideas merely, but as an experience at once religious and aesthetic. The two facts of the likeness of *At a Solemn*

Music to the *Nativity* and its immediate dependence on *How soon hath Time* are, taken together, highly significant: it is the clarification of Milton's own position in the sonnet that permits the clarification of the ideas adumbrated in the ode.

In another view the experience realized and recorded in *How soon hath Time* is complementary to that of the *Nativity* and *Elegy* 6. It does not centre at all on the control or rejection of the erotic impulse, which was a real element in Milton's early religious experience and the preparation for his life-work, but certainly not the whole of it. This the experience in the sonnet and its effects make plain. These effects are seen in Milton's conscious preparation for his life-work at Hammersmith and Horton, and in the character of the few poems that he wrote after *At a Solemn Music* (for the period of eager practice was over and he was at work now upon his own character and mind; in so far *How soon hath Time* ushers in a period of learning and waiting) ; but most of all they are seen in his maturing view of the poet's office, which sets its mark on practically all the rest of his poetry. In the *Nativity* and *Elegy* 6 there is already adumbrated the conviction that the rare abilities of the poet are, as he is later to phrase it, 'the inspired gift of God.' Now the complete transference to poetry of the sense of 'calling' will enable Milton to add that these abilities 'are of power, beside the office of a pulpit, to imbreed and cherish in a great people the seeds of virtue ... , to allay the perturbations of the mind and set the affections in right tune' (*Reason of Church Government*, 1642, 2: preface [Col. 3, i: 238]). The moral function of poetry was, as everyone knows, a commonplace of criticism in, and long before, Milton's day. In him, however, it becomes a controlling purpose precisely because it is grounded in his religion, and is part of the obligation of writing 'As ever in my great task Masters eye.'

3
Comus, Lycidas, Epitaphium Damonis

About the general character of the period which produced the three poems (*Comus*, 1634; *Lycidas*, 1637; *Epitaphium Damonis*, 1639) there can now be little disagreement. Milton's resolve to serve God in poetry had been irrevocably taken. His doubts of his own talents, or rather the tension arising from those doubts, had been resolved: his talents were God's gift; his will to serve was his own, and his sole responsibility was to bear himself 'As ever in my great task Master's eye.' But talents must be allowed to mature; and meanwhile the mind must be stored and the character disciplined: these were the tasks of the years at Hammersmith and Horton (1632–7) and those which immediately followed and included the Italian journey. In the well known letter to Diodati, dated September 23, 1637, Milton alludes to the progress of his studies, especially in history, of which his commonplace books bear further record; he speaks of his devotion to beauty ('whatever else God has bestowed upon me, he has inspired me, if ever any were inspired, with a passion for the good and fair') – the necessary and never-to-be-forgotten complement of his eager acquisition of knowledge and his rigorous effort of self-discipline; and he explains his silence ('Do you ask what I am meditating? By the help of Heaven, an immortality of fame. But what am I doing? I am letting my wings grow and preparing to fly'). In this preparation, the achieving of facility and felicity of expression by practice, so important in the Cambridge period, had no part. His decision taken and recorded in the sonnet *How soon hath Time*, Milton wrote, as a pledge of his renewed dedication, short religious poems, *On Time*, *Upon The Circumcision*, *At a Solemn Music*. The rest is silence save for the three important poems to be analyzed in this chapter, with (between *Lycidas* and the *Epitaphium*) the scanty occasional verse of the Italian journey, including *Mansus*: an astonishingly small output for six years, which can only have been the result of a fixed resolve.

The three great poems, *Comus*, *Lycidas*, and the *Epitaphium*, were all occasional: two (*Comus* and *Lycidas*) were written by request, and one (*Lycidas*) with evident reluctance, while the *Epitaphium* was drawn from Milton by the lamented death of Diodati. They have other features in common. Though occasional in origin, each becomes the vehicle for the poet's profoundly personal experience and emotion, thus confirming the return from poetry which is primarily aesthetic patterning to the poetry of experience, and the establishment, especially in *Comus* and *Lycidas*, of the typical Miltonic scheme, with tension and the resolution of tension through the application of aesthetic pattern. And in each case the pattern is adapted from traditional forms: in *Comus*, the masque or masquelike entertainment; in *Lycidas* and the *Epitaphium*, the pastoral monody.

The fortunes of the three poems have been different. Despite the diatribe of Dr Johnson and the late discovery of the poem's true subject and inwardness, *Lycidas* has been generally accepted as a perfect work of art. But this has had the effect of overshadowing the not less perfect *Epitaphium Damonis*, the least appreciated and least studied of Milton's great poems. In a degree not encountered in these, or in any of the poems so far considered, *Comus* has been and remains a problem. The purport of its argument has been the subject of disagreement and of a good deal of misapprehension, as have the closely related questions of the direction of Milton's instinctive sympathies, and of the relation of the piece to his own experience. Nor have much more agreement or accuracy been achieved in the matter of the poem's form and, specifically, of its relation to the masque. And, whether the principal fault is in the poem or its critics, all this uncertainty has, not unnaturally, raised doubts about the adequacy of *Comus* as a work of art. It will therefore require fuller examination than some of the other poems, and a more frequent challenging of current views.[1]

Comus

I

Whether *Comus* is to be classified as a masque, or whether Milton and Henry Lawes were deluded when they so described it, need not long detain us. Certainly a masque for the installation of the Earl of Bridgewater at Ludlow as Lord President of the Marches was what Milton was asked to provide; certainly, if not in strictest measure a masque, *Comus* is a masquelike entertainment; and certainly it contains all the elements found in the masque, though shaped into an individual pattern, and with some elements more emphatic and others perhaps added.

A good deal of unhelpful criticism has turned on this question of whether *Comus* is a true masque. Enid Welsford, for example, finds in the marriage masque the norm, and in Hymen the patron of the whole genre. The masque, she holds, is expressive of the forces of life and love, of youth and springtime, but of these forces as they are brought into order and harmony by Hymen, the god not only of marriage but of the social bond in all its forms; and it is these forces, thus reduced to order and harmony, that are symbolized by the dance, which becomes, accordingly, central to the masque. The only moral which the masque can convey is one which identifies goodness 'with harmony, order and, at bottom, self-expressive love,' in which 'there is no real contradiction between Hymen as leader of the Dance of Youth and Hymen as the good principle of the universe, the vanquisher of all the forces of unreason and unrest.'[2] And all this she finds very remote from Milton's theme and moral, as indeed it is.

It is perhaps almost equally remote from the facts of literary history. Essentially a masque is a social entertainment and a compliment to those in whose honour it is presented, and there appears to be no ground for asserting that the marriage masque is the norm, that Hymen is the patron of the genre, or that the dance is fraught with symbolic meaning. As social entertainment the masque gives to the dance a central place. Its business is to get the dancers eventually into position and the complimenters to the complimented. Therein lies its structural principle: a masque is an artistically retarded procession. Drama and spectacle (whether of masque or antimasque), poetry, music and song, declamation and debate, are all parts of this artistically retarded procession. One could expend pages, and not unprofitably, on the way in which *Comus* fulfils these specifications. But suppose we grant some part of Miss Welsford's large assumptions regarding the masque, we shall find that the sharpness of the antithesis between Milton's poem and the spirit of the genre depends on her misinterpretation of the piece. For she makes it expressive simply of a negative virtue and of self-assertive righteousness; she finds the climax in the Lady's successful resistance of Comus (instead of in Sabrina's freeing of her to pursue her way, which leads directly to the presenting of the children to their parents – the complimenters to the complimented – and the final dance), and, ignoring the fact that it is a dance of triumph over the forces of unreason, she complains that the dance is unintegrated with the action. How mistaken is all this, our analysis of the poem will show. But indeed Miss Welsford's preconceptions lead her into other errors of interpretation: that there is a profound cleavage between Milton the moralist and Milton the poet, that the sympathies of the latter are with Comus (as later with the Satan of *Paradise Lost*), and that this is betrayed by the response of the magician to beauty, which is indistinguishable from that of the Attendant Spirit and of the poet himself.

Other objections which circle about the question of *Comus* and the masque are less easy to bring to a focus. Greg, for example, complains of the prominence rather than the nature of the moral, of the too dramatic quality of the action by which it is conveyed, and of the forbidding virtue of the Lady, who is too much a personification of virtue to be acceptable as a character, and too much a person to be accepted or dismissed merely as an abstraction, who 'doth protest too much' and is too well aware of her danger to have the drama of innocence.[3] For those of a literary historian these opinions seem curiously uninfluenced by historical considerations. If Milton is didatic, Ben Jonson professed to follow the precept of Horace and 'suffer no object of delight to pass without his mixture of profit and ensample.'[4] If *Comus* has more of unified dramatic action and rudimentary characterization than other masques, the limits of the genre were not clearly fixed; there were masquelike entertainments as well as the masque proper, and in Italy there was the related *dramma per musica*, to whose influence *Comus* may well have responded.[5] But another and more important influence, the objection completely overlooks: that of *The Faerie Queene*, where moral allegory is combined with a good deal of action (though presented in narrative form) and a degree, not of course unlimited, of human character is added to figures like Una and the Redcross Knight, which are essentially abstractions. It is all too easy for the modern reader to forget what the poet and his original audience grasped intuitively, the potentialities and the limits of the genre; but it is the function of the historical critic to recover precisely this lost knowledge. And so with the moral prepossessions of the poet and his age, which have their effect in art as well as life and influence appreciation as well as conduct. It does not follow that, because to the twentieth century the Lady seems repellent in her inflexible and self-conscious virtue, she seemed so to the original audience, or that Milton the moralist ruthlessly sacrificed delight to instruction. It is salutary to remember the heroine of *Measure for Measure*, who is 'a thing enskied and sainted,' but productive of objections from the modern reader which seem never to have occurred to a poet far more flexible and many-sided than Milton. Nor, given Milton's action and purpose, was the charm of innocence within his reach. That, ironically enough, must be left to Byron:

> And on that cheek and o'er that brow,
> So soft, so calm, yet eloquent,
> The smiles that win, the tints that glow,
> But tell of days in goodness spent,

A mind at peace with all below,
A heart whose love is innocent![6]

Some of these reflections, it would seem, might occur to any reasonably sensitive reader of *Comus*; but it is the special function of the historical critic to urge them upon those who have forgotten or who never knew the facts on which they are based.

Comus, it is clear, finds no exact counterpart in any other masque. But we hear no complaints in the seventeenth century, or indeed until almost our own day, that it violated the conventions or the spirit of the form. The truth seems to be that, working in sufficient conformity to the genre, Milton produced a poem with an individual pattern, and one that carried a much heavier freightage of ethical thought, and entailed a more extensive use not only of drama but of allegory, than the work of any other poet. Into *Comus*, indeed, went the ideal by which he sought to live, the ideal demanded by his high conception of himself and his life-work – of a poet who must be himself a true poem, and not the ethical ideal only, but the problems which it inevitably raised, and finally the religious considerations which held for Milton the solution. This inference seems reasonable, perhaps inevitable. Nor is it simply a matter of inference. We shall quote presently the famous autobiographical passage from the *Apology for Smectymnuus*, which describes Milton's state of mind in these years and the evolution of his thought on beauty, love, and chastity, and we shall see how closely it corresponds to what we find in *Comus*. Milton is indeed at the centre of *Comus* as he is at the centre of *Lycidas*. Remembering his sobriquet at Christ's College, we wonder whether there is not a hint of this in the name selected for the central character, the Lady.

II

It is safest and most convenient to begin with something like a summary of the poem, which will at least furnish a common basis of understanding and an object of future reference.

There are three contrasting settings: I / *A Wild Wood* (1–657) ; II / *The Palace of Comus* 'set out with all manner of deliciousness' (658–956) ; and III / *Ludlow Town and the President's Castle* (957–1022). Each has its obvious symbolic value: the first representing the order of nature, the world with its possibilities of good and evil, a place of 'hard assays' and of dangers, through which, however, the good do not pass unprotected; the second representing the evil of the world, with its perversion of potential goods to evil ends, a place where danger and testing are intensified; the third representing good and security in goodness, the goal and the reward of virtue.

Within these three main divisions (which we may think of as acts) each of the clearly marked subdivisions (or scenes) has its special function in the evolving action, argument, and pattern.

I   The first act opens with i / the Prologue of the Attendant Spirit (1–92). Descending from his dwelling

> Before the starry threshold of *Joves* court ...
> In Regions milde of calm and serene Air,

he comes to 'this dim spot, Which men call Earth', where most

> Strive to keep up a frail, and Feaverish being
> Unmindful of the crown that Vertue gives,

though

> Som there be that by due steps aspire
> To lay their just hands on that Golden Key
> That ope's the Palace of Eternity;

and it is for their guidance and protection that the Attendant Spirit, the agent of providence, comes. Among the votaries of virtue are the Lady and her two Brothers (children of the Earl of Bridgewater, this day instated as Lord President of the Marches) who are coming to greet their parents through the woods made perilous by Comus (the son of Bacchus and Circe) and his rout. At the approach of Comus the Attendant Spirit conceals himself. Besides its primary function of exposition, the Prologue has its essential role in the aesthetic pattern, and, even without the fourteen cancelled lines, is rich alike in natural beauty and in symbolic value.

ii / Some part of this already begins to claim its place in the pattern in the second scene (93–168), where Comus and his rout burst upon our senses, with joyous dance and dancing speech, whose beauty is indubitable but in striking contrast with the solemn beauty of the Prologue. Not less indubitable than the beauty is the overtone of riot and excess which accompanies it and heightens the contrast. We shall have occasion to remember these things when we reach the Epilogue. *Comus* is a conflict of good and evil, and the first two scenes are appropriated by, and illustrate, the two forces respectively. At the approach of the Lady Comus conceals himself (as had the Attendant Spirit at the approach of Comus).

iii / Before the action gets under way in the third scene (169–329), the character of the scene just witnessed is underlined by the Lady, who has caught the sound of 'Riot, and ill manag'd Merriment,' like that of shepherds when

> In wanton dance they praise the bounteous *Pan*,
> And thank the gods amiss.

She has become separated from her Brothers, and images of menace begin
to fill her mind –

> Of calling shapes, and beckning shadows dire,
> And airy tongues, that syllable mens names
> On Sands, and Shores, and desert Wildernesses –

designed to call up an echo, but with a sinister difference, of Comus's 'pert
Fairies' tripping 'on the Tawny Sands and Shelves,' and to contrast with his
'dimpled Brook, and Fountain brim' peopled by the wood nymphs. But to
allay her fears she summons the allies of the virtuous mind, clear conscience,
pure-eyed faith, white-handed hope, and (significant breaking of the expected pattern) not charity, but the 'unblemish'd form of *Chastity*'.

> I see ye visibly, and now believe
> That he, the Supreme good, t'whom all things ill
> Are but as slavish officers of vengeance,
> Would send a glistring Guardian if need were
> To keep my life and honour unassail'd.

It is true, and doubly confirmed by the assurance of the Elder Brother
(below, iv) and the event (below, II.ii); yet the first effect is one of irony,
for what appears is – Comus, disguised as a shepherd. Drawn hither by the
Lady's song, he recalls that of his mother Circe, yet knows the difference;
for that

> in pleasing slumber lull'd the sense
> And in sweet madnes rob'd it of it self,
> But such a sacred, and home-felt delight,
> Such sober certainty of waking bliss
> I never heard till now. Ile speak to her
> And she shall be my Queen.

Unsuspecting, the Lady accepts the 'shepherd's' guidance, and, to heighten
the irony, dwells upon his honest-offered courtesy, a quality more often
found in 'lowly sheds' than in 'Courts of Princes, where it first was nam'd,
And yet is most pretended.' But she goes with a petition that providence
may square her trial to her proportioned strength; and the prayer is not to
be left unanswered. In *Comus* the irony is temporary and is swallowed up
in assurance.

iv / In the fourth scene (330–657) the two Brothers pause in their search for the Lady in order to debate her safety, the self-protective power of chastity and the protecting power of providence: themes already touched on by the Lady. The argument is the central exposition of Milton's doctrine of chastity, and significant in the order of its development, and to it we shall return. In the midst the Attendant Spirit appears 'habited like a Shepherd' (cf. Comus above, iii), and tells them of the herb called Haemony, the gift of a simple shepherd lad,[7] yet

> more med'cinal ... then that *Moly*
> That *Hermes* once to wise *Ulysses* gave.

Armed with this magic herb, they go to assault the necromancer's hall.

II The setting changes to Comus's palace, to which he has led the Lady. In i (658–812) she is seated in his enchanted chair, plied with his cup, which she puts aside, and with his arguments, which she rejects in scorn. The debate, which assumes everything that has been said by the two Brothers (above i.iv), completes the statement of Milton's doctrine, and will likewise require our more detailed analysis.

In ii (813–956) the Brothers break in upon the scene and put Comus and his rout to flight. But, while perfect in her resistance and unharmed in her person, such have been the protective powers of virtue and of providence, the Lady is nevertheless unable to rise, immobilized by the enchanter's spell, which he has fled without reversing. Even the Attendant Spirit cannot effect her release. Yet there is one expedient left, which the Attendant Spirit has learned of Meliboeus old – that is, our sage and serious poet Spenser: they may summon, to complete the work of rescue, Sabrina, the virgin goddess of the Severn. She comes and, sprinkling upon the Lady her drops 'of pretious cure' and robbing the chair of its enchantment, allows her to rise and, obeying the Attendant Spirit

> (Com Lady while Heaven lends us grace,
> Let us fly this cursed place),

to hasten on to her waiting parents.

III The setting changes to Ludlow, and there, in i (957–74), the children are presented to their parents and

> triumph in victorious dance
> O'er sensual Folly, and Intemperance.

Finally, in ii, the Epilogue of the Attendant Spirit (975–1022) announces his return to 'the happy climes' whence he came, thus balancing the Prologue and completing the pattern. But it does, as we shall see, much more than this.

Even in summary one can recognize, in its main outlines, the pattern of *Comus,* and can observe how that pattern is supported by a firm and clearly marked structure. But not less important than structure is concept. *Comus* is a poem with an argument; and pattern and symbol are built around a core of conceptual thought which supports them and holds the key to their interpretation. Again in its main outlines the argument of *Comus* is plain to read. But it is both clarified and enriched by being placed in its appropriate frame of reference.

This is one with which we are already familiar: the allocation of all experience, and indeed of all existence, to the order of nature or the order of grace. Within the general frame of reference, as we have observed, different degrees of connection or separation, of parallel and contrast, between the two orders may by different thinkers be assumed. To recognize the relevance of the general frame of reference is the first step in understanding. Thereafter, as the argument is read in relation to it, the particular assumptions made respecting the two orders will emerge from the argument itself.

The common opinion, correct so far as it goes, is that the argument of Comus has for its theme chastity. But more careful examination reveals that coupled with the doctrine of chastity (not identified with it as a careless reader might suppose, but coupled with it) are two others: a doctrine of temperance and continence (the 'holy dictates of spare Temperance') and a doctrine of virginity ('the sage And serious doctrine of Virginity'). When these facts are brought into relation with the intellectual frame of reference, we observe that temperance and continence are virtues on the natural level: that chastity, the central virtue of the poem, moves in an area common to nature and grace; and that the doctrine of virginity belongs exclusively to the order of grace, which in the poem it is used to illustrate and even symbolize. Or, if one may resort to a simple visual formulation, what we have is this:

1 / The *doctrine of temperance,* which, in the circumstances presented in the poem, is necessarily:

2 / A *doctrine of continence,* which to render it secure, and to translate it from a negative to a positive conception, requires to be completed by: } Nature

3 / The *doctrine of chastity,* which is thus grounded in nature. This is, moreover, elaborated, still on the level of nature, in terms of the Platonic philosophy, to the point where it can be taken over by Christianity, which sanctions the natural virtues and, by the addition of grace, carries them on to a new plane. Of chastity on this new plane, } Nature and Grace

4 / The *doctrine of virginity* becomes in the poem the illustration and symbol (but not the complete synonym). } Grace

We are concerned as yet with the argument of Comus, and not with the relation of that argument to Milton's personal experience. But it happens that we are able to test our formulation of the intellectual frame of reference as it is applied in *Comus* by comparing it with the celebrated account in retrospect which Milton gave of his experiences during the period when the poem was written. This account, in the *Apology for Smectymnuus* (Col. 3 [i]: 301ff.), was offered in rebuttal of the charge of youthful incontinence made by his adversaries, but it attaches itself to Milton's conception of the ideal poet which he sought to become, one whose life was itself a true poem. Here we find him commencing on the natural level, passing (not without aid from Plato) to the verge of the religious level, and finally moving securely thereon: we find the doctrine of continence bringing the doctrine of chastity, and at last the doctrine of virginity, in its wake, as the poet ascends from the order of nature, through an area where the two orders meet, to the order of grace. As in *Comus*, we may describe the doctrine of chastity as the central theme; and, even if we discard the reservation in the *Apology* in favour of the married state as belonging to a time after the poem was completed, we shall still recognize that the doctrine of virgnity is not regarded as coextensive with Christian teaching on the subject of chastity, though it is regarded as a doctrine specifically Christian and hence one that would be eligible as a symbol of the order of grace. Giving due weight to the direction of his 'natural disposition,' Milton tells us how he was led onward and upward, first by the writings of the poets, then by the philosophy of Plato with its 'abstracted sublimities' (a phrase we shall have occasion to remember), and to his final goal by Christianity, its plain injunctions and 'high mysteries' (another phrase to be remembered) – that Christianity which evidently confirms, while it transcends, the dictates of natural ethics and the highest wisdom of the philosophers. Milton writes in part: (*Apology*, Col. 3 [i]: 305)

> Thus from the Laureat fraternity of Poets, riper yeares and the ceaselesse round of study and reading led me to the shady spaces of philosophy, but chiefly to the divine volumes of *Plato*, and his equal *Xenophon*. Where if I should tell ye what I learnt, of chastity and love, I meane that which is truly so, whose charming cup is only virtue which she bears in her hand to those who are worthy. The rest are cheated with a thick intoxicating potion which a certain Sorceresse the abuser of loves names carries about; and how the first and chiefest office of love, begins and ends in the soule, producing those happy twins of her divine

generation knowledge and virtue, with such abstracted sublimities as these, it might be worth your listening ...

'Last of all,' he continues, 'not in time, but as perfection is last, that care was ever had of me, with my earliest capacity not to be negligently train'd in the precepts of the Christian Religion.' And these precepts confirmed and built upon 'a certain reserv'dnesse of naturall disposition, and morall discipline learnt out of the noblest Philosophy,' which alone would have been sufficient to ensure first a disdain of incontinence, then a love of chastity. But now he was able to receive the doctrine of chastity on the religious level, 'unfolding those chaste and high mysteries, ... that *the body is for the Lord and the Lord for the body.*' 'Nor did I slumber, he concludes, 'over that place expressing such high rewards of ever accompanying the Lambe, with those celestiall songs to others inapprehensible, but not to those who were not defil'd with women, which doubtlesse means fornication: For marriage must not be call'd a defilement.' Continence may be achieved on the basis of natural ethics (and be taught by those good teachers the poets, though not religiously inspired). Chastity, even in its 'abstracted sublimities,' may be learned from the wise and virtuous pagan philosophers (also poets in their way), who move likewise on the natural level but strain upward to the very verge of the religious. And these teachings Christianity by its precepts confirms. But above the natural level is the religious, and there Christian doctrine is the only guide. Such is the scheme of the *Apology*; and, broadly speaking, it is identical with that of *Comus*.

III

Chastity is the central theme of the poem, as is obvious from the emphasis that it receives. The virtues of temperance and continence are treated with brevity and subordinated to it, while the mysterious merits of the virgin state are but hinted in expounding the doctrine of chastity in its highest reaches. But that doctrine itself is set forth at large by the Elder Brother, and is symbolized by the Lady, who speaks for temperance and continence, it is true, but stands for chastity. We shall do well, however, to consider the virtues in the ascending order which we have already described.

In the temptation scene (II.i) the attack of Comus is not against chastity in the full meaning of the term, but against continence, which he derides as 'the lean and sallow Abstinence.' The solicitation that meets the Lady is identical in kind with that which meets Guyon in the Bower of Bliss, an episode immensely impressive to Milton,[8] and the real centre of Spenserian influence on *Comus*, as is quite natural, for Acrasia is Spenser's elaboration of the Circe *motif* and Comus is Milton's. The special mark of both is the prostitution of natural powers to the purposes of mere sensual pleasure. This is strongly underlined by Spenser and is symbolized by the scenery of the Bower of Bliss, where art counterfeits and even perverts nature and the beauty is as subtly false as that of the contrasted Garden of Adonis is natural and true.[9] In *Comus* there is no such elaboration of this symbol: but the wizard's palace 'set out with all manner of deliciousness' is, like the Bower of Bliss, of art, not nature, and, as we shall see, the Garden of Adonis, with its wealth of natural beauty, also finds its place in Milton's poem.

It is in another form, however, that the theme of nature chiefly enters into *Comus*. By an appeal to nature the magician seeks to undermine the virtue of continence, and this in two ways. Overtly his argument is that the natural world by the profusion of its gifts invites men to a life of unrestricted enjoyment; for this the abundance of nature was ordained, and to refuse it 'in a pet of temperance' is to manifest ingratitude and thwart nature's plan. But there is a second suggestion: the note of nature is abundance, profusion, and *a wasteful fertility*: (709–12)

> Wherefore did Nature powre her bounties forth,
> With such a full and unwithdrawing hand,
> Covering the earth with odours, fruits, and flocks,
> Thronging the Seas with spawn innumerable ... ?

Her gifts unused, Nature would be (727–35)

> surcharg'd with her own weight,
> And strangl'd with her waste fertility;
> Th' earth cumber'd, and the wing'd air dark't with plumes,
> The herds would over-multitude their Lords,
> The Sea o'erfraught would swel, and th' unsought diamonds
> Would so emblaze the forehead of the Deep
> And so bestudd with Stars, that they below
> Would grow inur'd to light, and com at last
> To gaze upon the Sun with shameless brows.[10]

'Nature,' said Renan, 'knows nothing of chastity.' It is the very contention that Comus is seeking to illustrate. And the application to humanity is not left in doubt: one should not be cozened by words, but reflect that (738–40)

> Beauty is Natures coyn ...
> and the good thereof
> Consists in mutual and partak'n bliss ...

Observe that the magician's argument ends not in the provision of life for its own replenishment, but in mere gratification. In a double sense, then, temperance, which here means continence, is, he suggests, unnatural.[11] This specious argument, says the Lady, is untrue; it is 'false rules pranckt in reasons garb': (762–7)

> Imposter do not charge most innocent nature,
> As if she would her children should be riotous
> With her abundance, she good cateres
> Means her provision only to the good
> *That live according to her sober laws,*
> *And holy dictates of spare Temperance.*

And she continues with the famous attack on 'lewdly-pamper'd Luxury' as opposed to nature's plan.

Now it is interesting and significant to observe that the Lady does not contradict the picture of nature given by Comus: she merely points out its incompleteness and repudiates his inference. Nature is marked not by abundance only, but by order and rationality. To live according to nature in the true sense is not to live riotously, prostituting her gifts to sensual gratification, but temperately and in conformity with her rational character and ends. This is plainly Stoic doctrine, and it is not for nothing that Comus is made to warn the Lady in advance against 'those budge Doctors of the *Stoick* Furr.' In the years after *Comus,* as will appear in subsequent chapters, Milton was to elaborate his doctrines of nature ('most innocent nature'), of reason and of temperance. In so doing he altered much, substituting a monistic for a dualistic philosophy and reacting, temporarily at least, against every suggestion of asceticism. I am very far from denying – indeed I insist upon – the wide interval between *Comus* and Milton's later thought. Only one must not exaggerate the differences or fail to recognize similarities where they exist. And for all the change in his metaphysic of nature, and in the tone of his ethic, the twofold aspect of nature remains and constitutes the groundwork of his no longer ascetic, though still rigoristic doctrine of temperance; and the role of reason, which is only hinted at in *Comus,* is not reversed, but confirmed and emphasized. The nature described by Comus and the Lady is the nature whose creation Milton is to recount in the seventh book of *Paradise Lost.* There creation is a twofold process, corresponding to the two complementary aspects of nature. For nature is a living whole, a vital scale, embracing life in all its profusion, and the process of creation in this aspect approximates very closely to gestation and birth. But before nature is a living, it is an ordered whole, a rationally graduated scale. And here creation does not approximate to birth; it is the imposition of form and order on chaos, the endowment of nature with a rational principle, as the other is her endowment with a vital principle. And similarly he elaborates the doctrine of temperance. It means a proper use of the gifts of nature, a proper choice made by reason among them; for 'reason is but choosing.' It is nature the vital, the abounding, that furnishes the materials of the choice, and nature the ordered, the rational, that furnishes the principle of choice. Thus Milton elaborates views of nature, of reason, and of temperance already implicit in *Comus*. There are important changes, of course: a new metaphysic of nature (but it is, in one sense, just an elaboration of the idea 'most innocent nature'), a new emphasis on the role of reason, and a more liberal content for the term *temperance*, no longer qualified by the epithet 'spare.' But it is an elaboration and modification, not a reversal: some at least of the primary intuitions on which it is grounded are already present in *Comus*.

As in Spenser, temperance is treated as a virtue on the natural level, not on the religious.[12] As in Spenser, continence[13] is coupled with temperance, and, partly as a result of this, there is a note not of asceticism, but certainly of rigorism: the Lady would not be behind Guyon in destroying the Bower of Bliss. But in Spenser's experience these virtues are not sufficient; they must be rendered secure and translated from negative to positive terms by the addition of chastity, which means not mere abstention from evil but an active pursuit of the good. To the virtue of chastity the next book of *The Faerie Queene* is devoted. And so is the next stage in the argument of *Comus*.

Having spoken for temperance, inevitably interpreted in the circumstances as continence, the Lady proceeds: (778–86)

> Shall I go on?
> Or have I said anow? To him that dares
> Arm his profane tongue with contemptuous words
> Against the Sun-clad power of Chastity;
> Fain would I somthing say, yet to what end?
> Thou hast nor Ear, nor Soul to apprehend
> The sublime notion, and high mystery
> That must be utter'd to unfold the sage
> And serious doctrine of Virginity.

Here we are brought face to face with a difficulty. It is not that the Lady fails to expound the doctrine of chastity; for that has already been done by the Elder Brother, whose exposition the reader is invited to recall – an invitation of which we shall avail ourselves. The difficulty is that here, and in the speech of the Elder Brother, there is no such clearcut distinction between the doctrine of chastity and that of virginity as there is between the doctrine of chastity and that of temperance and continence. The two seem to merge. The result has been to suggest to many readers that for Milton at this time chastity was identified with virginity and that *Comus* was really a poem in praise of the virgin state. But the intellectual frame of reference, supported as it is by the autobiographical passage in the *Apology*, indicates rather that Milton is concerned with both chastity and virginity as interdependent parts in a system which includes nature and grace, but that the central theme is the doctrine of chastity, which is illustrated *on the purely religious level* by the Christian doctrine of virginity. And this reading is verified by the fact that it clears the sense of the whole poem.

The argument as it deals generally with chastity moves in the area common to nature and grace. In the speeches of the Elder Brother (1.iv. 358–474, 583–608) the points made, and the order in which they are made, have a special interest.

1 / First the poet emphasizes the power and security of virtue in general, and in itself, without particular reference either to chastity or to anything above the natural level. 'The mind is its own place,' as Milton already knows. And virtue arms the mind, first with inward peace ('the sweet peace that goodnes boosoms ever'), and then with inward illumination:

> He that has light within his own cleer brest
> May sit i' th center, and enjoy bright day.

We are to remember this when we hear the Lady's defiance of Comus: 'Thou canst not touch the freedom of my minde'; and once more, as we shall see, before the poem closes.

2 / Then the poet suggests that chastity is in very special degree a strength and protection to the person who possesses it; a strength and protection referable, like all good gifts, to God, but still the mind's own,

> a hidden strength
> Which is Heav'n gave it, may be term'd her own.

We are still on the natural level, but the idea of virtue's – and specifically of chastity's – ultimate, though perhaps unrecognized, dependence on God's gift is suggested. Here is a point of juncture between the two orders, which permits grace to build upon nature in a way to be described below; but first,

3 / the grounding of chastity, and its power, in the order of nature is emphasized by a deliberate reference to non-Christian wisdom:

> Do ye believe me yet, or shall I call
> Antiquity from the old Schools of *Greece*
> To testifie the arms of Chastity?
> Hence had the huntress *Dian* her dred bow
> Fair silver-shafted Queen for ever chaste ...
> What was that snaky-headed *Gorgon* sheild
> That wise *Minerva* wore, unconquer'd Virgin, ...
> But rigid looks of Chast austerity,
> And noble grace that dash't brute violence ...

4 / And only now do we come to the passage to which the Lady's speech to Comus is designed to send us back:

> So dear to Heav'n is Saintly chastity,
> That when a soul is found sincerely so,
> A thousand liveried Angels lacky her,
> Driving far off each thing of sin and guilt,
> And in cleer dream, and solemn vision
> Tell her of things that no gross ear can hear,
> Till oft converse with heav'nly habitants
> Begin to cast a beam on th' outward shape,
> The unpolluted temple of the mind,
> And turns it by degrees to the souls essence,
> Till all become immortal.

Here one recognizes the Platonic tradition: the doctrine taught by Spenser,

> For of the soule the bodie forme doth take:
> For soule is forme, and doth the bodie make;[14]

the doctrine, also, accepted by Milton, of 'chastity and love, ... how the first and chiefest office of love, begins and ends in the soule, producing those happy twins of her divine generation knowledge and virtue.' To peace and freedom and illumination of mind is here added illumination of a higher order, whose note is not self-sufficiency but self-surrender, and whose communication is rapture. And, as in the passage from the *Apology*, the 'abstracted sublimities' (what the Lady calls 'the sublime notion') of Platonism lead on directly to 'those chaste and high mysteries' (the Lady's phrase is identical, 'the high mystery') of Christian teaching: for to Milton at this stage of his development Platonism marks the highest reach of thought on the natural level and its point of juncture with the divine. But here, in contrast to the *Apology*, Platonic and Christian doctrine merge, though it may well be, as we shall observe, that there is ascent within the order of grace and that more is meant by the Lady's allusion to the 'high mystery' than is contained in the Elder Brother's exposition.

5 / Finally, the recurring idea of chastity's self-protective power receives, on the religious level, its confirmation and complement in the doctrine of divine providence. Not malice, and not

> that power
> Which erring men call Chance,

but the power and providence of God reign supreme. On this the Christian stakes everything; for

> if this fail,
> The pillar'd firmament is rott'nness,
> And earths base built on stubble.

The emphasis on providence is reinforced by the presence of the Attendant Spirit, who is its minister and almost its symbol.

We have said that, like Spenser, Milton realizes the necessity of ascending from a doctrine of temperance and continence, which is in part negative, to a doctrine of chastity, which is more purely positive and dynamic. The difference is one of degree merely, and of motivation. For it will not do to regard the doctrine of temperance and continence in either poet as merely negative, issuing only in a gesture of rejection: in Guyon the doctrine is adequate to furnish a motive for heroic action, and in the Lady, to furnish a principle for the wise *use* of nature's gifts. But something more is required, and in both poets it is sought in a doctrine of chastity. Hanford goes much further, emphasizing the extent to which 'Milton has been influenced by his master's romantic allegory of chastity in the third book of the *Faerie Queene,*'[15] and finding in that book, not in the second, as we have done, the main contact of *Comus* with Spenser. But there is a very wide interval between the treatment of chastity in *Comus* and in the third book of *The Faerie Queen*. For there is no avoiding the fact that Spenser's doctrine of chastity is elaborated in closest connection with an ideal of wedded love, and that Milton's culminates in – though even on the religious level it is not co-extensive with – an ideal of virginity. If in *Comus* the ideal of chastity is coupled with love, it is with the intellectual love of the Platonic tradition as it presses forward towards a Christian conception of heavenly love. Moreover Spenser's ideal of chastity and wedded love (whatever its Christian sources) is presented purely on the natural level, without reference to religious motivation, sanction, or reward,[16] and with no hint of mystical experience, while Milton's doctrine is carried through from the natural to the religious level, and there culminates, not in Christian marriage as in *Paradise Lost*, but in 'the sage And serious doctrine of Virginity' with its aura of the mystical. Clearly, *Comus* has more in common with the *Hymne of Heavenly Love* than with the story of Britomart.[17]

Commencing with a doctrine of temperance and continence on the natural level, the argument of *Comus* ascends to a doctrine of chastity, conceived in terms derived from Plato and sanctioned by a long tradition; and chastity is the principal theme of the poem. But a further step was possible, to which the Christian poet was likewise invited by tradition: the argument might be carried on to the religious level. This step Milton plainly takes, and by the most direct road of Christian Platonism. Here the passage in Revelation 15:1–4, over which, as he tells us in the *Apology*, he did not slumber, becomes central:

> And I looked, and lo, a Lamb stood on the mount Sion, and with him an hundred and forty and four thousand, having his Father's name written in their foreheads.

> And I heard a voice from heaven, as the voice of many waters, and as the voice of a great thunder: and I heard the voice of harpers harping with their harps:

> And they sung as it were a new song before the throne ... : and no man could learn that song but the hundred and forty and four thousand which were redeemed from the earth.

> These are they which were not defiled with women; for they are virgins. These are they which follow the Lamb whithersoever he goeth. These were redeemed from among men, being the first fruits unto God and to the Lamb.

Evidence of the strong impression made on Milton by this passage is not confined to *Comus* and the *Apology*: it is seen again in 'the unexpressive nuptial Song' that welcomes Lycidas to heaven and, in much more detail, in the magnificent climax of the *Epitaphium Damonis*. We may go a step further and concede that perhaps when he wrote these poems Milton may have imagined himslf to have a vocation to such a life. But it is of the essence of the passage that it does not describe chastity as it is to be practised by the majority of Christians, but the virtue in its highest reaches to which only those with a special vocation can attain; and Christian marriage, as Milton can at no time have doubted, is likewise a vocation. Hence the reservation in the *Apology* in favour of the married state. Naturally, in such a poem as *Comus* he cannot pause upon this distinction. Nor is it necessary, surely, for any rational mind, that he should. And so this sage and serious Christian doctrine of virginity builds upon and completes the mystical doctrine of chastity advanced by Plato, and in turn becomes eligible as the symbol of chastity in the order of grace – the symbol of Christian chastity, but not its complete synonym. And the distinction that Milton could not pause to draw in the argument he could, as we shall see, symbolize in the Epilogue, where, seen from the vantage point of Christianity, all the goods of nature and grace fall into rank in an ascending scale of values. But this is to anticipate.

It is clear that Milton, unlike Spenser in the third book of *The Faerie Queene,* seeks the dynamic that is to transform chastity into a positive virtue not in nature, but in grace. This might be inferred from the whole tenor of the argument of *Comus*; but it is not left to inference. It is symbolized – almost, indeed, stated – in the episode of Sabrina (II.ii). The Lady has successfully resisted the attack of Comus. The result, however, has been not victory, but a sort of stalemate. She is defiant, but utterly immobilized, powerless to break for herself the spell which the enchanter has cast upon her; she is able, in other words, to resist evil, but not actively to practise good. Nor can the Attendant Spirit break the spell. All he can do is to summon Sabrina to her aid. She comes: (907–18)

> Shepherd, 'tis my office best
> To help insnared chastity;
> Brightest Lady, look on me,
> Thus I sprinkle on thy brest
> Drops that from my fountain pure,
> I have kept of pretious cure,
> Thrice upon thy fingers tip,
> Thrice upon thy rubied lip,
> Next this marble venom'd seat,
> Smear'd with gumms of glutenous heat
> I touch with chaste palms moist and cold,
> Now the spell hath lost his hold ...

Freedom of movement is restored, and the Lady proceeds upon her way to the Heavenly City, whose earthly image is Ludlow. The symbolism is unmistakable, as a cross reference to Spenser will show. When, during the fight with the Dragon (1.11.29–30) Spenser has the Redcross Knight stagger back into a stream of living water and come forth restored, the informed **reader** immediately recognizes not a reference to baptism (as critics have too bluntly supposed and said), but the symbol for a renewed infusion of divine grace, whose imagery belongs to the same category of Christian symbolism as finds its most familiar example in the sacrament of baptism. So with the episode of Sabrina: the sprinkling of pure water, those drops of 'pretious cure,' symbolizes an infusion of divine grace, and what is implied is the secure raising of the problem to the religious level where alone it is soluble and where alone the dynamism of true virtue must be sought.

Through the words of the Attendant Spirit, Milton introduces the legend of Sabrina by an allusion to Spenser: (819–22)

> now I bethink me,
> Som other means I have which may be us'd,
> Which once of *Meliboeus* old I learnt
> The soothest Shepherd that ere pip't on plains.

The lines have been taken to acknowledge Milton's source for the story of Sabrina, in *The Faerie Queene* (2.10.17–19);[18] and this perhaps is their surface meaning. But of the use to which Milton puts the legend, of the symbolic value which he gives to his elaboration of it, there is no hint in Spenser's story of Sabrina. For that Milton could only turn to that book of *The Faerie Queene* which moves throughout on the level of grace, and to such an episode as we have cited above.[19] That the Attendant Spirit, the agent of providence, should have been unable immediately to effect the Lady's release is also significant: his mission is to protect innocence and virtue in the natural order, like that of Arthur in *The Faerie Queene* 2.8, and to afford a measure of guidance, like that of Una in Book 1; but the operation of grace must be differentiated from protection and even guidance, as it consistently is by Spenser,[20] and must be given its own clearly marked symbols. In this likewise Milton follows his master.

The episode of Sabrina should bring home to us the character and extent of Spenser's influence on *Comus*, and the fact that, whatever else the poem may be, it is in the fullest sense Spenserian allegory, with different levels of meaning. No doubt it was the local association of the Sabrina legend that prompted its introduction, and set Milton upon his essay in Spenserian myth-making in order to adapt it first to the action, then to the deeper meaning of the poem. And lest we should fail to realize the significance of Sabrina's intervention, and his own role, the Attendant Spirit is made to exclaim: (937–44)

> Com Lady while Heaven lends us grace,
> Let us fly this cursed place ...
> Not a waste, or needless sound

> Till we com to holier ground,
> I shall be your faithfull guide
> Through this gloomy covert wide,
> And not many furlongs thence
> Is your Fathers residence ...

Like Spenser, Milton does not leave us without clues to his deeper meaning, if we will read him with sufficient attention. The spell is broken. Mobility is restored. The Lady is freed, by the operation of grace, to resume her journey and to make her way through the wild wood, which is the world, to the 'holier ground,' the Heavenly City.

IV

Whether that deeper meaning will seem to the modern reader unduly restrictive and austere will, presumably, in the last analysis, depend upon his own experiences and beliefs, with which the historical critic can have no concern. But the sense of restriction and austerity will certainly be in some degree modified by viewing the meaning of the poem in its full extent: by observing that there is an ascending scale of values, that grace builds upon foundations laid in nature, and that, in the Epilogue, the whole concludes with a symbolic summary in which, viewed from the vantage point of grace, every good falls into its appointed location in a pattern, or a vision of existence, which only the Christian can appreciate. *Comus* ends with an effort of comprehension. This is not to say that it avoids, or can avoid, some element of renunciation. Any scheme which involves a hierarchy of values, whether it proceeds to the religious level or pauses at the humanistic, will entail the rejection of evil, and also the postponement of the lower to the higher good, and thus an element of renunciation. The question is whether the dominant note is that of renunciation or of ascent and comprehension. Whatever Milton's success or failure in striking the latter note, it assuredly held a place in his intention. That the Epilogue puts beyond reasonable doubt. But before this can be made perfectly clear we must pause to consider a little more fully the attitude revealed by the poem towards the goods of the natural order, and especially its beauty.

It has been made matter of wonder that Comus shares with the Attendant Spirit (and we may add, though in lesser degree, the Brothers and the Lady) an immediate response to this beauty.[21] But there is no mystery here. The response of the good characters means that for Milton beauty is to the good a good, and one to be received with joy. Like other goods on the natural level it depends on good use and is susceptible of perversion. Almost it seems that beauty, like nature, 'means her provision only to the good.' We

have seen how, when beauty is perverted to evil ends, Spenser presents it as
art imitating and falsifying nature, and we have caught one hint of this in
Milton also. But in general Milton is quite ready to admit that the beauty
which is to the good a good is the same beauty which the evil pervert to evil
ends. This indeed is characteristic of his whole attitude to the natural order.
So with daring, and a subtlety quite wasted on his modern critics, he shows
us Comus, at his first entrance (I.ii), responding to beauty in words that
might be mistaken for those of the Attendant Spirit, but perverting it to evil
– to what Milton takes to be evil – in the very act of response. To quote the
lines in question is to prove the point, but lest it should still be missed we will
call italics to our aid: (93–144)

> The Star that bids the Shepherd fold,
> Now the top of Heav'n doth hold,
> And the gilded Car of Day,
> His glowing Axle doth allay
> In the steep Atlantick stream ...[22]
> Mean while welcom Joy, and Feast,
> *Midnight shout, and revelry,*
> *Tipsie dance, and Jollity.*
> *Braid your Locks with rosie Twine*
> *Dropping odours, dropping Wine.*
> *Rigor now is gon to bed, ...*
> *We that are of purer fire*
> *Imitate the Starry Quire,*[23]
> Who in their nightly watchful Sphears,
> Lead in swift round the Months and Years.
> The Sounds, and Seas with all their finny drove
> Now to the Moon in wavering Morrice move,
> And on the Tawny Sands and Shelves,
> Trip the pert Fairies and the dapper Elves;
> By dimpled Brook, and Fountain brim,
> The Wood-Nymphs deckt with Daisies trim,
> Their merry wakes and pastimes keep:
> *What hath night to do with sleep?*
> *Night hath better sweets to prove,*
> Venus *now wakes, and wak'ns Love.*
> *Com let us our rights begin,*
> *'Tis onely day-light that makes Sin,*
> *Which these dun shades will ne're report.*
> *Hail Goddess of Nocturnal sport*
> *Dark Vail'd* Cotytto,[24] *t'whom the secret flame*

Of mid-night Torches burns; mysterious Dame
That ne're art call'd but when the Dragon woom
Of Stygian darkness spets her thickest gloom,
And makes one blot of all the air,[25]
Stay thy cloudy Ebon chair,
Wherein thou rid'st with Hecat', *and befriend*
Us thy vow'd Priests, till utmost end
Of all thy dues be done ...
Com, knit hands, and beat the ground,
In a light fantastick round.[26]

It is the more necessary to be clear about Milton's meaning in this speech because in the aesthetic and in the intellectual pattern it was evidently intended to stand in a relation of contrast with the Prologue as originally written, and with the Epilogue, which in turn balanced each other.

On the surface the Epilogue presents a description of the Attendant Spirit's abode, as did also the cancelled lines of the original Prologue, with their allusions to the stream Ocean (and to the Atlantic, a link with the speech of Comus quoted above), to the Hesperian garden, and to hyacinth and roses. But evidently 'more is meant than meets the ear,' and the method employed is less that of allegory than of symbol. The question is, precisely what is symbolized? Hanford's answer has the merit of simplicity and definition; but it leaves too much in the Epilogue and the poem unexplained. 'Milton,' he says,

> sings of Paradise. The language is highly esoteric ... and Milton expressly calls attention in the parenthesis, 'List mortals, if your ears be true,' to the hidden spiritual meaning. The bliss proposed is that of Heavenly love as the ineffable compensation for a life devoted to the ideal of chastity ... In adopting Spenser's image of the Garden of Adonis Milton entirely changes its application ... The pagan image of the love of a mortal youth for a goddess draws insensibly nearer to the truth in the reversed symbol of the union of the God of love himself with Psyche, the human soul, and if Milton's classic taste prevents him from concluding with an allusion to the Lamb and his eternal bride it is because there is no need.[27]

If we are right in our reading of the poem so far, Milton's allusion is not merely to paradise, or to the rewards and compensations of the chaste soul hereafter. What is required in the Epilogue is some larger symbolism, which might include the reward of the chaste soul hereafter but would not be restricted to it. The Epilogue is indeed a symbolic summary of the poem's whole teaching. It presents once more the ascent from nature to grace, but viewed this time from the vantage point of grace securely achieved. It symbolizes life itself in its two orders and ascending scale, as the Christian mind, grounded in nature but illuminated by grace, alone can apprehend it.

The Epilogue commences with the order of nature, and we must understand its method. It is, broadly speaking, Platonic: what it presents is the *idea* of that order – ideal, permanent, laid up in heaven. And, that it may do so, it resorts to the ideal language of myth. Thus by means of the garden of the Hesperides is suggested the idea of whatever is fresh and beautiful in the natural world – ocean, air, and the flowering earth, where 'Revels the spruce and jocond Spring' and at the same time 'eternal Summer dwells.'

But for Milton the myth of the garden has also its special significance. In the cancelled lines of the original Prologue we hear of

> the Hesperian gardens, on whose banks
> Bedewed with nectar, and celestial songs,
> Eternal roses grow, and hyacinth,
> And fruits of golden rind, on whose fair tree
> The scaly-harnessed dragon ever keeps
> His unenchanted eye ... ;

and in a speech of the Second Brother (i.iv) the image of the golden fruit and the guardian dragon is explained by being applied: (392–6)

> beauty like the fair Hesperian Tree
> Laden with blooming gold, had need the guard
> Of dragon watch with uninchanted eye,
> To save her blossoms, and defend her fruit
> From the rash hand of bold Incontinence.

Menaced by Comus, the Lady is, as it were, her own dragon. Now in the Epilogue, however, the emphasis changes: the golden tree is still there, with and to the joy of Hesperus and his daughters; but the dragon guard is unmentioned, for a positive principle of active virtue has supplanted the negative principle of mere defensiveness. And it is with less surprise that we find the garden of the Hesperides giving place to the garden of Adonis.

There is no need to suppose with Hanford that in adopting Spenser's image of Venus and Adonis Milton entirely changes its application, or indeed that he changes it at all. On the details of Spenser's allegory of the Garden of Adonis[28] critics have not always agreed. It will be enough here to state very briefly what appears to be its main intention. In classic myth and its elaborations one recognizes three different roles assigned to Venus:

she is the goddess of wanton love (as in the opening speech of Comus) ; she is the great mother, a principle of generation in all things; and she is the celestial Venus, the symbol of intellectual or spiritual love. In the passage in question Spenser clearly has in mind the second of these roles, with no suggestion of the third.[29] It is an allegory of form and substance[30] – of material forms, represented by Adonis, the masculine principle, and material substance, represented by Venus, the feminine principle – and it sets forth the processes of decay and replenishment throughout the natural world. Further, there is, as we have remarked, a contrast between the Garden of Adonis and Acrasia's Bower of Bliss, where natural powers are prostituted, as they are by Comus, to purposes of mere pleasure, a contrast pointed in Spenser by the opposing Geniuses who guard the two portals and by the types of beauty found beyond them.[31] This allegory of Spenser's, Milton recalls in his allusion to the Garden of Adonis. It symbolizes life on the natural level: the life processes of 'most innocent nature.' And its appropriateness, once more, is found in the contrast to all that Comus stands for. There is no need to assume with Hanford that Milton alludes to the third role of Venus, the celestial Venus, or that he translates Spenser's image to a higher, even the highest, level; for, as we have shown, the natural also has its place in Milton's scheme. This is the world of nature as the chaste and religious are able to apprehend it, and only they. That is the significance of the admonition uttered just before the image of Venus and Adonis is introduced: 'List mortals *if your ears be true.*'

In Milton, as in Spenser, the myth of Venus and Adonis brings that of Cupid and Psyche in its train. To the garden of Adonis, says Spenser, Cupid (3.49–50)

> resorts, and laying his sad darts
> Aside, with faire *Adonis* plays his wanton parts.
>
> And his true love faire *Psyche* with him playes,
> Faire *Psyche* to him lately reconcyld
> After long troubles and unmeet upbrayes
> With which his mother *Venus* her revyld,
> And eke himselfe her cruelly exyld:
> But now in steadfast love and happy state
> She with him lives, and hath him borne a chyld,
> *Pleasure*, that doth both gods and men aggrate,
> *Pleasure*, the daughter of *Cupid* and *Psyche* late.

In Spenser, it is to be observed, Cupid and Psyche move on the same general level as Venus and Adonis, the natural level, represented by the garden:

the allusion is to the principle of love and generation as it applies specifically to man and in the marriage relation. In Milton Cupid and Psyche do not move on the same level as Venus and Adonis. It is here, and not in the image of Venus and Adonis, that he entirely changes Spenser's application. For he is careful to indicate that it is the 'celestial *Cupid*' of whom he sings, whose dwelling is not in, but 'far above,' the garden. Remembering the scale of ascent in the poem, and in the *Apology*, we easily recognize the level here reached: it is the point of juncture between nature and grace, where Platonic idealism is on the verge of finding its completion in Christian doctrine, and where that intellectual love whose 'first and chiefest office ... begins and ends in the soule, producing those happy twins of her divine generation knowledge and virtue,' is ready to be translated into heavenly love, with its superadded note of joy.

The note of joy is emphatic in the Epilogue, which retraces symbolically the ascent from nature to grace presented in the poem, but is able now to view each stage in the light of the last and highest. From the vantage point of grace everything falls into focus and is seen to have its divinely appointed purpose and significance, and, being thus seen, can be received with joy. For in Christian experience grace is the source of joy, no less than of peace and power and freedom. Thus it is that the note of joy sounds throughout the Epilogue, dominating the first movement which centres in the song of '*Hesperus*, and his daughters three,' crossed by sadness as Venus watches by the sleeping Adonis (but only momentarily, for he is 'Waxing well of his deep wound'), and restored in the image of Cupid and Psyche. On them Milton has bestowed not the single daughter Voluptas or Pleasure, of Apuleius and Spenser, but, with evident reference to the Platonic scheme, *twin* offspring; but these offspring he names not Knowledge and Virtue but, by a bold transposition, Youth and Joy.

It is time, however, to put this exposition to the test by quotation. The Epilogue commences with the order of nature, with the eternal *idea* of that order as it can be best expressed in the ideal language of myth, and the reader is invited to rejoice (980–1010)

> amidst the Gardens fair
> Of *Hesperus*, and his daughters three
> That sing about the golden tree:
> Along the crisped shades and bowres
> Revels the spruce and jocond Spring,
> The Graces, and the rosie-bosoomed Howres,
> Thither all their bounties bring,
> That there eternal Summer dwels,
> And West winds, with musky wing
> About the cedarn alleys fling

> *Nard,* and *Cassia's* balmy smels.
> *Iris* there with humid bow,
> Waters the odorous banks that blow ...
> And drenches with *Elysian* dew
> (List mortals if your ears be true)
> Beds of *Hyacinth,* and Roses
> Where young *Adonis* oft reposes,
> Waxing well of his deep wound
> In slumber soft, and on the ground
> Sadly sits th' *Assyrian* Queen;
> But far above in spangled sheen
> Celestial *Cupid* her fam'd Son advanc't,
> Holds his dear *Psyche* sweet intranc't
> After her wandring labours long,
> Till free consent the gods among
> Make her his eternal Bride,
> And from her fair unspotted side
> Two blissful twins are to be born,
> Youth and Joy ...

Like Knowledge and Virtue, the offspring of Cupid and Psyche are not primarily the symbol of a reward to be expected in heaven, but something that the chaste soul rises to here and now. And if this is so, their names are significant indeed. For the conclusion mitigates the austerity, though not the strictness, of Milton's doctrine. He repudiates false pleasures, but not joy; wantonness, but not the spirit of youth. The quest is arduous, he would seem to say, and demands renunciation, but among its rewards may be reckoned not only virtue and knowledge, illumination of mind, peace of mind, but the very things that the adversary would declare to be taken away: life and youth and joy. And to these the final lines of the Epilogue will add one further note: freedom.

First, the beauty of nature, with all its gracious associations, which Comus perverts; second, in the image of Venus and Adonis, the powers and processes of nature, which Comus (like Acrasia) would prostitute and thwart; third, in the image of Cupid and Psyche, ascent to the highest virtue and wisdom accessible on the natural level, indeed to the meeting point of the two orders of nature and grace. Thus far the symbolic summary has proceeded, of the whole range of life and experience on the natural level *as it is illuminated for those who have reached the vantage point of grace.* But this final step, the crown of all, remains to be recorded: (1017–22)

> Mortals that would follow me,
> Love virtue, she alone is free,

> She can teach ye how to clime
> Higher then the Spheary chime;
> Or if Virtue feeble were,
> Heav'n itself would stoop to her.

Here at last we are on the level of grace alone. For the first allusion – and it is literally the first in Milton's writings – is to a doctrine which is to be enormously important in his thinking, the doctrine of Christian liberty. It will remain for Milton a cardinal principle of specifically Christian ethics: 'Know that to be free,' he writes in the *Defensio Secunda*, 'is the same as to be pious, to be wise, to be temperate and just, to be frugal and abstinent, and lastly, to be magnanimous and brave ...'[32] One recognizes, as no doubt Milton did, the kinship with Stoic doctrine; but for him freedom through virtue, through *voluntary* obedience to the will of God, is the special mark of Christianity: it is *Christian* liberty, which gathers up into the light of revelation the experience of the freedom of mind and will already referred to in the poem. And the unmistakable allusion to a level 'higher than the Spheary chime' puts this interpretation of the lines beyond reasonable doubt. The motion and music of the spheres symbolize for Milton the perfection, the order and harmony, of nature, and parallel, on that level, the dance and song of the angels, those symbols of the higher perfection of heaven. To hear the music of the spheres indeed is given only to the pure in heart. To ascend above it is to enter the Christian heaven and 'hear the unexpressive nuptial song.'[33] And in the Epilogue the final note of all is unmistakably Christian. We have been told in the body of the poem how providence intervenes for the protection of virtue. Now this idea, too, is gathered up into the full light of Christian revelation. Here is a note not very often heard in Milton. And it might almost be called the essential note of Christianity: for it speaks to us not of God's power merely, or even of his providence, but of the Divine condescension and mercy to men who would do the will of God but are weak.

v

Like Ben Jonson in his masque of *Pleasure Reconciled with Virtue*, Milton realizes that virtue entails a degree of renunciation; but the final note is not renunciation: it is ascent and comprehension. The significant difference is that Ben Jonson pauses at the humanistic level, and presents the problem and its solution in terms of the order of nature, while Milton ascends to the religious level and seeks not only the dynamic of virtue and its final sanction, but also the principle of comprehension, in the order of grace. He does so because, in his experience, there or nowhere they will be found. To achieve his purpose Milton supplements the masque, or masquelike entertainment, by a liberal infusion of Spenserian allegory. Ben Jonson's was of course a much slighter effort, and more readily adaptable to the masque form. But there is no reason to believe that the original audience found any particular difficulty in *Comus*. Consciously or unconsciously, they accepted it for what it was: a piece of Spenserian allegory with a literal meaning more than sufficient for the entertainment at Ludlow and a deeper significance for those who cared to pursue it. Read in this light, *Comus* is perhaps more successful than many of its modern critics will allow.

Our concern, however, has not been to defend *Comus* or its doctrine, but simply to understand them: to place ourselves, so far as possible, at the poem's point of departure, and thence to pursue its pattern. Our examination has drawn attention to several features of the work: its relation to Milton's extra-aesthetic experience, a relation which is confirmed by the *Apology for Smectymnuus*; the importance of its argument, with its frame of reference and principle of ascent, likewise confirmed by the *Apology*; the individual pattern which emerges from the union of the poet's thought and experience with traditional forms; and, finally, the interdependence of thought and pattern, whereby thought directs pattern, but pattern advances thought in a poem which is no mere record, but the realization of a new experience with power to return the poet to the world of extra-aesthetic experience with emotions harmonized and vision cleared.

Comus indeed turns out to be the most important record of Milton's thought to be found in his early poetry, that is, the most important realization effected by a poem of the ideas by which he lived. But in its profounder reaches Christian thought is inseparable from religious experience, and there can be no doubt that *Comus* embodies, and in embodying advances, indeed realizes, a religious experience. Here it claims kindred with the other two poems about to be analysed, in which ideas play a less important role, but which equally embody and realize a religious experience with the same pattern of progression from the order of nature, where problems of conduct and belief emerge, to the order of grace, where they find their solution.

The Pastoral Monodies

I

Lycidas and the *Epitaphium Damonis* are the crowning achievements of Milton's earlier verse, and representative of his experience, thought, and art, and of the relation subsisting among them. There are among Milton's earlier poems partial anticipations of certain features of *Lycidas* and the *Epitaphium*. In several of them the pastoral note is heard: in the *Nativity* (which stands in easily recognized relation to the tradition of the Messianic eclogue), in *Arcades*, the companion pieces, and *Comus*. In two poems, less pastoral in character, the basic pattern of the Christian monody is employed: *Elegy 3*, on the death of Lancelot Andrewes, and *In obitum Praesulis Elienis*. But here a significant difference is also evident. Clearly these are simply exercises in the traditional pattern of the Christian monody. For the youthful Milton the death of the two bishops evoked no feeling stronger than mild regret and raised no questions which urgently demanded to be answered or transcended. In *Lycidas* and the *Epitaphium* the case is altogether different. The *Epitaphium* records a bereavement that struck home to the poet's heart, and *Lycidas,* if it embodies no such sense of personal loss, yet finds in the life and death of Edward King a focus for Milton's anxieties regarding himself and his life-work. And now the pastoralism and the traditional pattern of Christian monody, used heretofore for purely aesthetic effect, coalesce and are put to fresh use. The pastoral monody, as Christian poets had reshaped its pattern, becomes a vehicle for Milton's profoundest emotions and an instrument not indeed for solving, but for transcending his problems, and thus for achieving such a resolution of emotional tension as only poetry could effect.

To examine the pattern of *Lycidas* and of the *Epitaphium* in the light of these facts, and in some detail, is our present purpose. And because the later and less famous of the two poems bears the simpler relation to Milton's experience and to the tradition of pastoral monody, we will commence with it.

II

Nowhere is the traditional character of Milton's patterns more important than in *Lycidas* and the *Epitaphium Damonis*, which have up to a point a common background. Each takes its place in a poetic tradition still developing, though no longer very vigorously, in Milton's day. The tradition, as every one knows, goes back to the first Idyll of Theocritus, and more particularly to the third Idyll of Moschus, the famous lament for Bion:

> The wail of Moschus on the mountains crying
> The Muses heard, and loved it long ago;
> They heard the hollows of the hills replying,
> They heard the weeping water's overflow;
> They winged the sacred strain – the song undying,
> The song that all about the world must go –

When poets for a poet dead are sighing,
The minstrels for a minstrel friend laid low.
And dirge to dirge that answers, and the weeping
For Adonais by the summer sea,
The plaints for Lycidas and Thyrsis (sleeping
Far from the 'forest ground called Thessaly');
These hold thy memory, Bion, in their keeping,
And are but echoes of the moan for thee.[34]

Echoes, indeed, but each with its individual note, sounding from the particular circumstances of the poet and his subject but resounding also from the gathering tradition. Gradually the pattern of the pastoral monody was elaborated, and gradually it accumulated a store of conventions, images, and associations, which succeeding poets could adapt to their individual purposes.

Already in Theocritus we have the device of the framework, in which the shepherd sings his lament at request, and for the prize, perhaps, of some carven bowl. And this device was taken up by other poets. One of its effects is to have the poem start with common life and return to it again. In *Lycidas*, as we shall see, Milton gains this effect, with an added personal significance, by an adaptation of this framework device; while in the *Epitaphium Damonis* he boldly lifts the description of the prize out of the framework altogether and integrates it with the main body of his poem. Again, to take a few more examples, the procession of mourners, the questioning of the nymphs, the fiction that nature shares the poet's grief, the sense, nevertheless, of a contrast between man and the rest of nature, the allusions to classic myth, to Orpheus or to Hyacinthus: all these occur in Theocritus or Moschus, and all are adapted and elaborated by later poets, and, among them, by Milton. It is a cumulative tradition.

In Virgil's tenth Eclogue, that brilliant adaptation of the first Idyll of Theocritus, the Arcadian note, implicit in the Greek monodies, becomes explicit as the interval between the subject, Virgil's friend and fellow·poet, Gallus, and the pastoral life and mood is fully recognized: 'Yet ye, O Arcadians, will sing this tale to your mountains; Arcadians only know how to sing ... And O that I had been one of you, the shepherd of some flock of yours, or the dresser of your ripened grapes!'[35] This sense of interval and of regret, though seldom so decisively expressed, becomes part of the heritage of the pastoral monody. At the same time the presentation of poet and subject under the terms of shepherd life moves a long step over towards allegory. This is already fully apparent in Virgil's fifth Eclogue, whose Daphnis probably stands for the murdered Caesar, first mourned by the Roman state, then deified.

The deification of Daphnis introduces a new pattern into the pastoral monody, destined to extensive adaptation. Like tragedy and epic, the pastoral monody had naturally adopted the characteristic pagan attitude to death, viewing it as annihilation or as, at most, the mournful entrance upon a shadowy existence (hardly worth the name) in Hades. Even without a Virgilian model the Christian monodist must have abandoned this attitude, must have altered the pattern of his lament to make room for the idea of immortality and to indicate how, to the eye of faith, death is swallowed up in victory. But, by good fortune, precisely that effect is achieved in the deification of Daphnis, and Christian monodists (as, for example, Ronsard in his *Angelot*) were quick to follow Virgil's lead. Spenser, in the November Eclogue and in *Astrophel*, and Milton, both in *Lycidas* and the *Epitaphium Damonis*, progress from pagan lamentation to Christian assurance, with the former acting as foil to the latter; and the dynamic of their patterns, considered simply as pattern, is this necessary movement from the first position to the second. Such a movement, as was natural, became almost universal in Christian monody, though absent in the *Alcon* of Castiglione, the monody which in all other respects bears the closest relation to Milton's *Epitaphium*.

The *Epitaphium Damonis* is not just an inferior *Lycidas*, as is too often assumed. Adopting, like *Lycidas*, the common Christian pattern, it proceeds to its own effects and by its own means; and both are simpler and more direct than in the earlier and more famous poem. Its meaning and the source of its extra-aesthetic emotion would be plain even without the introductory note which identifies Damon as Charles Diodati and speaks of the poet's absence on foreign travel at the time of his death. Here there is no necessity to read between the lines. The burden of the poem is grief for the departed, and until the concluding movement Damon is viewed not as a type but simply as an individual. Unlike Edward King, Diodati was Milton's intimate friend. The *Epitaphium* is the memorial to their friendship, grounded in common interests, and to the bright spirit who played L'Allegro to Milton's Il Penseroso. In the digressions, if such they can be called, the poet's eye does not turn, as in *Lycidas*, to the conditions of his time, but to his own dearest concerns, in which the departed friend had been his chief confidant. It is because the poem is so personal that Milton is able, without impropriety, to speak so much and so directly of himself. The *Epitaphium Damonis* is, in effect, the last of the epistles to Diodati. But all that it has to say is at once expressed and brought under control by Milton's adaptation of a traditional pattern. Not less than *Lycidas*, the *Epitaphium* is a masterpiece of construction and decorum. And it is, as Helen Waddell has seen, the complete refutation of Johnson's surly objection to the pastoral form: 'Where there is leisure for fiction there is little grief.' 'The truth is rather,' says Miss Waddell, 'that fiction, convention, makes room for grief. The traditional language, the ancient symbols, become a kind of liturgy that releases emotion even while it controls it.'[36]

The name Damon is, of course, from the pastoral tradition; but it is not fanciful to see in it an added suggestion of the friendship of Damon and Pythias, who were, significantly, votaries of the discipline of Pythagoras, which Milton (in the sixth *Elegy*, addressed to Diodati) had adopted as the symbol of that virtue and purity essential to the poet of heroic themes. Such, he would seem to say here, was the true note also of Diodati's character and of their friendship; and the importance of this subject, the purity of Damon, becomes fully apparent at last in the triumphant final movement of the monody. But indeed the quality is diffused through the whole poem; for it was the necessary condition of their comradeship and of their common devotion to beauty and virtue, to learning, letters, and art. The friendship which the poem celebrates is, for Milton, bathed in the light of Platonic idealism, and this in turn serves to link the memory of Diodati with that of the Italian academies, and to make the friendship a symbol of Milton's receding youth. The *Epitaphium Damonis* marks the end of a chapter in Milton's life.

The poem opens with an introductory paragraph (1-17) which establishes the tradition by invoking the Sicilian Muse and the memory of the laments of Theocritus for Daphnis and Hylas and of Moschus for Bion. It tells how the poet was long held in the Tuscan city by the love of song (poetry and Italy are to be two of the poem's themes) and how he was at last drawn homeward by care of the flock (what this means the *Defensio Secunda* will inform us: the flock is nothing less than the English church and state). It tells us how, when he reached home, the full sense of irreparable loss came upon him, and how he has sought by utterance to lighten the heavy weight of woe. Here is the motive of the poem categorically stated, and it claims precedence, as the refrain reiterates, over that care of the flock which brought him home.

With this the poem proper commences. Its basic pattern is that of Christian monody, with pagan grief and despair freely expressed in the earlier movements, which act as a foil to the Christian conclusion, where these emotions are dispelled or transcended. In the *Epitaphium* the idea of immortality appears almost at the beginning, but dimly and afar off, in the pagan form simply of an immortality of remembrance, incapable of giving life to the departed or comfort to the bereaved. Midway through the poem it is repeated, this time in a form which posits remembrance by, and not merely of, the departed, but briefly, tentatively, and still to the accompaniment of regret. Finally, it swells triumphant in its full Christian form. Upon this framework Milton weaves his detailed pattern of reminiscence and reflection, the stuff of pastoral monody, turning to his own purpose its accumulated store of image and convention.

1 / In the first movement (18–34) the poet finds no help in the powers of earth or heaven which have doomed Damon to death and left his friend alone and inconsolable. (Loneliness is a dominant note through the earlier movements of the poem, though there is a point at which it will be dispelled.) Damon, it is true, cannot sink into oblivion amid the ignoble herd of the silent dead. Rather, his fame shall be honoured by the shepherds if it means anything to have kept the ancient faith and morals, to have known the arts of Pallas, and to have had a poet for one's friend. Here is the first suggestion of immortality – an immortality of fame, merely, in the memories of men.

2 / And it is wholly inadequate to bring consolation, as the second movement (35–56), whose theme is the poet's loneliness, insists. For Damon the reward of fame cannot fail. But what, cries the mourner, is to become of me? And he turns naturally to memories of his dead friend and their life together, presented in simple rural images: abroad in the fields in a summer's noon, or beside the blazing hearth on a winter's night while without the wild wind makes havoc, storming through the elm-tops. To whom now, he asks, shall I entrust my heart? (For Diodati was confidant as well as friend.) And who will restore to me thy winning ways, thy laughter, thy Attic wit, and graceful learning? (This is the Diodati who played L'Allegro to Milton's Il Penseroso.) I wander alone, he continues, through the fields and pastures, all alone now. Where the branches deepen the shades in the valley, there I await the evening. Over my head the wind, laden with rain clouds, makes a mournful sound, and the forest twilight is all astir with gleams and shadows. Thus concludes the second movement, and the first passage of reminiscence, dominated by loneliness and grief.

3 / It has almost broken through the frame of pastoral convention, to which the poem is always being brought back by its refrain. Now in the third movement (57–123) these conventions are put to novel and effective use. Not only is the flock neglected, as the refrain repeats, but all labour in field and vineyard; and from the maids and shepherds who come to enquire what ails him and to call him to their sports, the poet turns sullenly away. This is Milton's adaptation of the procession of mourners found in pastoral laments from Theocritus onward. And it leads to another brilliant adaptation. In the lament of Moschus for Bion, and commonly thereafter in pastoral monodies, man is contrasted with nature: the life of nature (that is, of each natural species) dissolves only to be renewed, but man (thought of as an individual) perishes for ever. Milton gives the contrast a new turn, and one that escapes the evident fallacy inherent in the conven-

tional form. In nature, he says, in the herd, all are companions together, of like feeling and under a common law. They are sensible of no loss or, if they are, transfer at once their affection to another. But we men are alien mind from mind, and heart from heart. Scarcely in a thousand do we find one congenial spirit; or if we do, yet in an hour when we least expect it, fate snatches him from us, leaving eternal loss behind. So it was with Thyrsis when Damon died, and he, in ignorance, far off in distant Italy, unable to clasp his friend by the hand, to close his dying eyes, or to whisper, 'Farewell, do not forget me as thou goest to the stars.'[37] Again the suggestion that for Damon death is not the end. The idea of immortality comes as it were a step nearer; but still without comfort to the bereaved. The whole context is one of mourning, intensified by regret and self-reproach for absence.

4 / And now there follows as the fourth movement (124–78) a bold digression on Milton's Italian journey and the plans for poetry which it matured: a digression, indeed, only in appearance, for it has its own justification – and it is as skilful as bold. I am the more insistent on this since the digression has been much blamed and has been declared, by so good a critic as Tillyard, to be the destruction of the poem. But it is nothing of the kind. It is bold because it *seems* to carry us away from Diodati; skilful because Diodati is ever and anon recalled, and justified because there is nothing arbitrary about it. *For in fact the seeming digression is the turning-point of the poem*: the shadows fall back and a subtle but perfectly recognizable train of associations leads on to the triumphant close.

For Milton, Italy and Diodati are indissolubly linked together. Not only was his friend of Italian race though English by adoption: Milton's Italian journey, and his gracious reception in the academies, mark the end of a chapter, the culmination of his youth, of that phase of his life so much of which is symbolized by the friendship with Diodati. In the Academy at Florence, with its Platonic idealism and its eager quest of learning and poetry, of virtue and beauty, pursued in the golden light of friendship, Milton found himself at home, and he found the spirit of Diodati irresistibly evoked. Almost a decade later, in 1647, when the rigours of Puritanism and of the Revolution were in full sway, and amid surroundings how different, Milton wrote to Dati, one of his Italian friends. He looks back fondly on his days in Italy, and with their memory comes inevitably the memory of Diodati. 'Very sad to me also was ... departure [from Florence], and it planted stings in my heart which now rankle there deeper, as often as I think with myself of ... my separation as by a wrench, from so many companions at once, such good friends as they were, and living so pleasantly with each other in one city, far off from me indeed, but to me most dear. I call to witness that tomb of Damon, ever to be sacred and solemn to me, whose adornment with every tribute of grief was my weary task – I call that sacred grave to witness that I have had no greater delight all this while than in recalling to my mind the most pleasant memory of all of you.'[38]

So in the poem, countering the self-reproach for his absence, he can say: 'Yet ... I shall never be loath to keep you in mind, Tuscan shepherds, youths devoted to the Muses; with you dwell grace and pleasantness. Thou too, Damon, wert a Tuscan ...' There, beside the murmuring Arno, while joining in their friendly contests in song and proudly hearing his own praises sung by Dati and Francini, famous for learning and poetry, he was not unmindful of his absent friend: 'Ah, how many times I said, aye, even when the urn was holding thy ashes, Now Damon is singing ... or plaiting osiers for his various uses ...'[39] And lightly changing future hope to present reality, he would imagine them by some English stream, discoursing of their chosen callings, he of poetry, Damon of the healing art. (The healing art could not save Damon, and the poetic, while it might afford him a memorial, seemed of as little power. Yet at the end, ineffectual human healing will be completed by divine, and the Christian poet will triumph over death.) This second passage of reminiscence, introduced under the guise of anticipation, is light-hearted because antedating the news of Damon's death. But the news, when received, casts a shadow back upon it: Cursed be the arts that could not save Damon, and for the poet himself, the pipes have broken in his hand. Yet will he tell his ambition and his dream.[40] It is to sing, in heroic verse, of the Trojan settlement of his native Britain and its history down to Arthur's time ...

5 / 'All these plans and dreams I was keeping for thee,' the next movement (179–97) commences (and properly; for the dead friend was Milton's confidant, and the *Epitaphium Damonis* is, as we have said, the last of the epistles to Diodati) : 'All these pleasant dreams I was keeping for thee, these and more beside;'[41] and among them the two carved cups, the gift of Manso, whose description is Milton's most brilliant adaptation of a convention of pastoral verse. In the first Idyll of Theocritus, the goat-herd offers to Thyrsis, as the price of his singing the lament for Daphnis, a deep bowl of ivy wood, newly wrought, and alive with carvings. Circled with stem and leaf, flower and fruit, it presents the picture of two suitors contending for their lady's favour in vain, and of an aged fisherman straining at his nets, and, at a little distance, of a vineyard where the watch-boy is plaiting a locust-trap of asphodel while two foxes steal the fruit and his very wallet; all of which is presented with realistic detail. This device for adding pictorial description to a pastoral poem Milton adopts, but he transposes it from the framework and makes it integral to the pattern of the lament:

About them is wrought a double brede; in the midst the Red Sea rolls, and spring scatters its odors; along the far coasts of Araby the trees drop balsam. Among the trees Phoenix, divine bird, unique on earth, blazes cerulean with multi-colored wings, while he watches the morning rise over the vitreous waters. In another place is the mighty stretch of sky where Olympus lies open to view. Yes, and Love is there, too; in clouds his quiver is pictured, his shining arms, his torch, his arrows tipped with fiery bronze. But he does not aim upon our earth at light minds, at the herd of vulgar souls. No; he rolls his flaming eyes and steadfastly sends his arrows upward through the orbs of heaven, never aiming a downward stroke. Under his fire the souls of the blessed burn, and the bodies of the gods.[42]

The pattern on the bowl described by Theocritus represents the life and loves of earth; that on the cups described by Milton, the life and love of heaven and the promise of a resurrection thereto. Thus the theme is two-fold, presented by the two pictures on the cups: first, the signs on earth which, for those smitten with the heavenly love, point to resurrection and the joys of heaven (and in so doing suffuse the themes of earth with a heavenly light); and, second, the heaven to which they point, whose motivating principle is love. The fragrant spring betokens the beauty of earth (as do all the images in the first picture), but, above all, the symbolic promise of renewal, to be reinforced by later images; the waters of the Red Sea suggest divine protection, as of God's people of old; Arabia, with its trees dropping balm, suggests divine healing, the heavenly completion of Damon's fallible earthly art, and serves to bring in the image of the phoenix, the symbol of renewal and resurrection, while the dawn rising beyond the waters reinforces this idea by yet another image, also utilized in *Lycidas*. In the second picture the sky is a general symbol of heaven, and Olympus lying open to view represents a prevision of the life of the heavenly host. That life is inspired by heavenly love, as is symbolized by the celestial Cupid as he kindles angelic natures, but also the sanctified mind in man, and this, like all the other images, points on to heaven.

6 / Then, *by a sudden return to Damon*, with no intervention this time of the refrain, the monody reaches its concluding movement (198–219). The idea of immortality (seen in the first movement, afar off, in the dim perception that Damon must not be numbered with the nameless dead, and renewed in the third movement with the metaphorical allusion to his passage to the stars) – the idea of immortality has come at last to its full Christian form: mourning is banished by triumph, and triumph includes consolation. Heaven is presented as the realization and enjoyment of the heavenly love. Milton remembers the passage in Revelation (14:1–4) describing the virgins at the throne of the Lamb. And so in the poem the hundred and forty and four thousand sing praises to the Lamb, and Damon is among them joining his according voice. The note is not that of triumph only

but of ecstasy; and abandoning his usual practice of the quiet close, certainly sanctioned by the tradition of the pastoral monody, Milton ends with the full volume of the orchestra. *It is to this conclusion that the pictures on the cups have been leading us unawares.*

> Thou also Damon (neither need I fear
> That hope delusive) thou art also there;
> For whither should simplicity like thine
> Retire, where else such spotless virtue shine?
> Thou dwell'st not (thought profane) in shades below,
> Nor tears suit thee – cease then my tears to flow,
> Away with grief! on Damon ill bestowed!
> Who, pure himself, hath found a pure abode,
> Has pass'd the show'ry arch, henceforth resides
> With saints and heroes, and from flowing tides
> Quaffs copious immortality, and joy,
> With hallow'd lips! – Oh! blest without alloy,
> And now enrich'd with all that faith can claim,
> Look down, entreated by whatever name,
> If Damon please thee most (that rural sound
> Shall oft with echoes fill the grove around)
> Or if Deodatus, by which alone
> In those ethereal mansions thou art known.
> Thy blush was maiden, and thy youth the taste
> Of wedded bliss knew never, pure and chaste,
> The honours, therefore, by divine decree
> The lot of virgin worth, are given to thee;
> Thy brows encircled with a radiant band,
> And the green palm branch waving in thy hand,
> Thou in immortal nuptials shalt rejoice,
> And join with seraphs thy according voice,
> Where rapture reigns, and the ecstatic lyre
> Guides the blest orgies of the blazing choir.[43]

In the *Epitaphium Damonis* Milton seeks in expression relief from the weight of woe. He finds it through a pattern which carries his thoughts from earth to heaven or from nature to grace. The pattern is necessary to this transition, and the pattern has its own assuaging power. It does not, as we shall find that the pattern of *Lycidas* does, return the poet to the world of extra-aesthetic experience. There is no further reference to the flock, which must, had it occurred, have given an effect of anticlimax; but it would be rash to infer that for Milton the poetic experience had no further result.

III

Of *Lycidas* a briefer analysis will suffice, since Tillyard has made clear the main purport of the poem though he has certainly not said all that requires to be said of its pattern.[44]

The real subject of *Lycidas*, he contends, is Milton himself. Or, as I should prefer to phrase it, the principal source of the poem's extra-aesthetic emotion is not grief for the loss of Edward King, but an awareness of the hazards of life and of Milton's own situation. In the *Epitaphium* (if only in appearance) Milton leaves Diodati to speak of his own concerns. In *Lycidas* (though indirectly) he is talking of himself throughout. In this sense we may say, with only pardonable exaggeration, that *Lycidas* has two subjects: an occasional and ostensible subject, which is Edward King, and a real subject, which is Milton. The relation between them is clear: Edward King's life has been one of dedication and high endeavour, and it has been cut short before he can achieve his goal and its reward. Thus he suggests a type, and his fate is also typical. But the type is far more clearly realized in Milton than in Edward King; and the fate which has overtaken him may overtake Milton also. Edward King is priest and poet. Milton is poet and priest: that is, he has changed the medium of his service to God, but not its spirit. For the poet also is a priest and prophet: all the sense of vocation is transferred to the new medium, and more. Once we recognize this, as we do from our knowledge of Milton's life and temper, we are at or near the point in extra-aesthetic experience from which the poem takes its rise, and are ready to pursue its meaning and its pattern.

We must understand, however, that this formulation – this talk of two subjects – is merely a way of bringing an important fact into relief. It must not be taken so literally as to suggest a dichotomy which the poem is unable to resolve, or lead us to minimize the importance of its occasion. Without the death of Edward King the poem would never have been written: and it was this event which made available the basic pattern of Christian pastoral monody, so brilliantly adapted by Milton. Essential to that pattern, as we have seen, is the idea of immortality and the progression from a pagan view of life and death to the transcendent view of the Christian. And in *Lycidas* this transition is not less essential to the real than to the occasional subject.

We have said that the literary background of the *Epitaphium* and of *Lycidas* are in part the same. That of *Lycidas* is in fact the more extensive. With Virgil the pastoral poem reached the form known as the eclogue, and this form was destined to a semi-autonomous development. It could on occasion detach itself from the pastoral setting, as in the *Piscatory Eclogues* of Sannazaro. But without such detachment, and already in Virgil, the eclogue manifests a capacity for extended reference not found in the earlier pastoral: by the use of allegory, or something like it, the eclogue could refer to current concerns and contemporary conditions, and could satirize, admonish, or instruct. In Petrarch, for example, in Mantuan, and in Spenser, it is employed to attract abuses in the church. Now it is clear that *Lycidas*, unlike the *Epitaphium Damonis*, looks beyond the tradition of the pastoral monody to that of the eclogue. The first digression, as it is called, is on the true poet and the nature of his reward, a subject already treated in Spenser's October Eclogue. The second digression is on the state of the church, the subject of his July and September Eclogues. These digressions depart from the pastoral tone, but not from the tradition of pastoral poetry in its wider reaches. They depend, not on the tradition of the pastoral monody, but on that of the eclogue, from which Milton lifts this feature for incorporation in his pastoral monody.

The pattern of *Lycidas* is less open and flowing than that of the *Epitaphium Damonis*: it is more symmetrical if not in reality more closely articulated; and in producing this effect the so-called digressions have an important part. Of the three movements that make up the structural pattern of *Lycidas*, the first two culminate in passages which, as Milton observes in the poem, shatter the pastoral tone, while the third does not shatter but rather transcends it. Clearly, the contrast between the unreal Arcadian world of the pastoral and the concerns of real life which break in upon it is significant at once for the content and the pattern of the poem.

Lycidas commences with a Prelude which is part of the monody but which is to be balanced by the brief Epilogue, so that together they give something of the effect of the traditional framework setting. The Prelude is heavy with the thought of death, the death of Edward King, and before it closes there is an allusion to the poet's own:

> So may some gentle Muse
> With lucky words favour my destin'd Urn.

The note of the Epilogue is life, not death: 'Tomorrow to fresh Woods, and Pastures new.' The monody proper with its three movements effects this transition.

1 / The first movement (23–84) begins with a reminiscence of the life at Cambridge presented under pastoral images, but in a manner which is a long step nearer to allegory than that employed in the *Epitaphium Damonis*. This gives place to a pastoral convention: the mourning of nature for the dead shepherd; and it, in turn, to the question (still in the direct line of pastoral monody), 'Where were ye, Nymphs [here evidently the muses]?' which culminates in the superb allusion to the death of Orpheus,

When by the rout that made the hideous roar,
His gory visage down the stream was sent,
Down the swift *Hebrus* to the *Lesbian* shore.

But the comment on the question to the Muses is significant:

Ah me, I fondly dream!
Had ye been there – for what could that have don?

as is also that later comment in the third movement:

For so to interpose a little ease,
Let our frail thoughts dally with false surmise.

The Christian poet recognizes the essential unreality of the Arcadian world and the insufficiency of its consolations, until all can be gathered up in the fullness of revealed truth. And already reality is clamouring for admission:

Alas! What boots it with uncessant care
To tend the homely slighted Shepherds trade,
And strictly meditate the thankless Muse?

or, in the hope of future fame, 'To scorn delights, and live laborious dayes'? For at any moment accident or death may supervene and rob us of the prize. ' "But not the praise," *Phoebus* repli'd.' For that is in God's gift, and

As he pronounces lastly on each deed,
Of so much fame in Heav'n expect thy meed.

Milton's words, as always, are carefully weighed. There is a distinction between tending the homely shepherd's trade and the shepherd's recreation of song, but the spirit in which the latter is pursued ('strictly meditate' the muse) prevents distinction from becoming opposition: a life of duty is the groundwork from which the song is raised, and both are a dedication, first to fame, and then to a higher end. The reference to the homely shepherd's trade is appropriate to Edward King, whose lifework was the ministry; the reference to poetry finds its full meaning only in relation to Milton, in the light of whose experience the whole passage takes on a new weight. For him at first, as for Edward King to the end, the life of duty had meant God's service in the ministry. Later it had come to mean God's service in poetry: song had become service. Because the image of the shepherd is common to pastoral poetry and the Christian tradition, it is a bridge between them.

This passage carries the image over into a Christian context, and incidentally prepares for its more overt appearance in that context in the second
movement of the monody. But the new context shatters the mood of the
classical pastoral. The first movement ends, then, with a question and an
answer, whose true purport and weight can be gauged only in relation to
Milton's conception of his own lifework and his long preparation therefor.
The question springs from experience; the answer, from faith. Both lie outside the Arcadian world, and by them its mood is temporarily shattered.

2 / In the second movement (85–131) this fact is recognized and the
mood of the classical pastoral is restored. And with the pastoral mood
comes the pastoral convention: the procession of the mourners. Triton and
Aeolus bear witness that all was calm when Lycidas perished:

> It was that fatal and perfidious Bark ...
> That sunk so low that sacred head of thine.

The lines look before and after. For this is the example of how accident may
cut short the planned life, the theme with which the first movement ended,
but if Lycidas is now sunk low, he is to rise again, as the third movement
will triumphantly proclaim. With the last of the mourners, St Peter, the
second movement culminates, once more in a question that touches Milton's
business and bosom, and shatters the mood of classical pastoral. In St Peter's
indictment of conditions in the church the tradition of the eclogue is, as we
have said, again grafted on that of the pastoral monody. The shepherd
image predominates (and there is one crucial image from the piscatory
eclogue, 'the pilot of the *Galilean* lake'), but the context is Christian and
by it the Arcadian note is silenced. The condition of the church is a theme
appropriate to Edward King, who was a faithful shepherd of Christ's flock,
and no hireling. The connection with Milton is subtler, but Tillyard is
clearly on the right track. The state of the church had implications for the
life of the nation, and the life of the nation had implications for poetry –
especially for the poetry towards which Milton's mind was turning: a national Christian epic, culminating perhaps in the wars of Arthur against the
heathen. Such a poem demanded as audience a nation united for Christ
and king, and this condition was going or gone. Milton was slow to admit
it, persisting indeed till after the *Areopagitica* in talking of his own party as
though they were the nation. But this could only be by a sort of legal fiction,
which was good enough for politics, but not for poetry; and presently Milton was to abandon the plan of a national epic. This then would seem to
be the personal bearing of Milton's digression about the state of the church:
it reveals a condition potentially as fatal to his poetry as death itself. How
nearly correct was Milton's apprehension, let the twenty years' postpone-

ment of his *magnum opus* testify. This time the question asked is answered only by implication, insofar, that is, as the concluding couplet implies confidence in God's power and the triumph of righteousness.

3 / The third movement (132–85) again commences with a recognition of the shattered pastoral tone, and its restoration, followed by a more elaborate flower passage, with nature mourning for the dead shepherd and the flowers decking his bier. But this again is a pagan fancy, a fiction of comfort. In sober reality the body is not prepared for burial, but carried far (and whither who shall say?) by the tides of ocean. But now 'false surmise' gives place to Christian truth, and with it weeping gives place to hope and consolation. Framed in the two references to the weeping shepherds ('Weep no more, woful Shepherds weep no more'; and 'Now *Lycidas* the Shepherds weep no more'), the movement develops. As the day star sinks in ocean to rise again,

> So *Lycidas* sunk low, but mounted high,
> Through the dear might of him that walk'd the waves ...

(We observe the double reference back to the fatal accident that sunk low the head of Lycidas, and to the stern pilot of the Galilean lake, whose human menace is now offset by Christ's divine mercy.) The vision of heaven, as Tillyard has observed, makes real the promise of fame therein with which the first movement concluded. But it is less intensely imagined than in the *Epitaphium*. Lycidas hears, he does not join in, 'the unexpressive nuptial Song.' There is consolation, not rapture, in the greeting of

> all the Saints above ...
> That sing, and singing in their glory move,
> And wipe the tears for ever from his eyes.

The lower intensity of the feeling has this further result, that the classical images and the Christian are blended, and not, as they are in the *Epitaphium Damonis*, fused. And so *Lycidas*, instead of ending with the full volume of the orchestra, moves to its quiet close.

> Now *Lycidas* the Shepherds weep no more;
> Henceforth thou are the Genius of the shore,
> In thy large recompense, and shalt be good
> To all that wander in that perilous flood.

The image of the Genius is not without precedent in pastoral monodies from Virgil's Daphnis onward. The perilous flood is the world. And Lycidas has already commenced to exercise his beneficent influence on those who travel through it. Of that beneficent influence the poet himself is the first recipient, as the Epilogue, to which these lines conduct us, will make plain.

The Epilogue balances the opening lines of the monody. Despite his reluctance to commence, the poet has, from morn to evening, 'with eager thought' warbled 'his *Dorick* lay.' And his poetic contemplation of Lycidas and his fate has wrought in him a transformation. With faith fortified and vision cleared, and with a mind at peace, he is returned to the world of extra-aesthetic experience, of life and labour:

Tomorrow to fresh Woods, and Pastures new.

4
The reformer

I   n his engaging letters from hell C.S. Lewis described the historical study of literature as a subtle invention of the devil to cut us off from the wisdom of the past, to make us view everything as relative and explicable by the circumstances of the age, and to prevent us from asking about the classic the one vital question, 'Is it true?' and so from correcting our thought and action by its light. The danger to which Lewis points is real. But he is quite wrong in supposing that it is the prevalent danger in criticism today. The prevalent danger, like all the devil's best inventions, is much more securely grounded in original sin – that is, in pride, self-sufficiency, and laziness. It is the temptation to bring everything for judgment to the bar of our own age and our own temperament. We magnify whatever squares with our experience and our prejudices; we discard whatever we cannot on a first reading comprehend; and for the sake of contemporaneity or of novelty or of mere emphasis in praise and blame, we often distort the writer's meaning out of all recognition. Milton has been the victim of this process from Shelley to T.S. Eliot, as no one should know better than Lewis. Historical study is not the disease, but the cure. Properly pursued, it enables us to comprehend the terms in which the author did his thinking. It is not a substitute for a judgment of value. It is the necessary preliminary if the judgment of value is itself to be valuable: you cannot assess what you do not understand. But historical study is more than a preparative and a corrective. It lets you into the mind of the past, thus, as Milton himself recognized, extending your field of consciousness – an experience in the highest degree formative. I make no apology, then, for attempting an historical treatment of Milton on liberty.

Historically Milton's doctrine of liberty was formulated in close connection with the Puritan Revolution, that epic struggle of twenty years with its succession of phases: the calling of the Long Parliament in 1640; the Puritan attack on the church led by the Presbyterians; the outbreak of the Civil War; the rise of the Independents and more extreme sectaries, with their demand for religious toleration and their effective control of the parliament's army, the New Model; the rise of the Levellers, the one group of genuine political democrats thrown up by the Revolution, to be followed later by the small but interesting body of communists, the Diggers; the purging of the parliament by the army, its judicial murder of King Charles; the establishment of the republic, soon to give place to the unconcealed dictatorship of Cromwell; the anarchy supervening on his death; the rescue of England and the defeat of Puritanism by the Restoration in 1660.

There are three ways of looking at the Puritan Revolution, and each is relevant to some part of the struggle, though taken alone each is an oversimplification. One can view the issue as primarily political, even constitutional. One can view it, on the other hand, as social and economic. Or one can insist that for the Puritans themselves it was at first religious and that their religion fixed, or where it did not fix modified, all their thinking. It is worth while to pause for a moment on these three views and ask whether and how far each is appropriate to the study of Milton.[1] Where the answer is partly or wholly negative, it may still help to clarify his position.

If one regards the issue as primarily political, one will find the chief significance of the Puritan Revolution in the assertion of the liberty, and ultimately the sovereignty, of parliament. Successfully maintained against Charles, then betrayed by the army and Cromwell, it was destined to point the way to subsequent English development. Scarcely less prophetic of the future, though happily outside England, was the repeated claim of a minority to establish the rule of justice and righteousness against the will of the majority and by violence. And also prophetic was the doctrine which had its contribution to make if not mainly to English still to Anglo-Saxon thought: the doctrine that sovereignty lay with the people, who could wisely delegate its exercise only under the strictest safeguards, that government must rest on a covenant, an agreement of the people, and that the humblest had precisely as much right to a voice in it as the most exalted, for, as Rainborough said, 'the poorest he that is in England has a life to live as well as the richest he.'[2] All this is at most collateral to the study of Milton, whose doctrine of liberty has its application to politics indeed, but is not political in origin or in its basic principles. Thus we find him progressively adopting different positions. In the *Areopagitica* (1644) he can express unbounded confidence in both parliament and people when they seem to give promise of resolution in the cause of individual liberty. In the *Tenure of Kings and Magistrates* (1649) he can invoke the sovereignty of the people against not only Charles, but the parliament, and in favour of the army which is the executant of this sovereignty, but which has also a superior mandate from God to establish justice and righteousness by the sword. In the *Defensio Secunda* (1654), through recourse to this same principle of the divine mandate, he justifies the dictatorial rule of Cromwell. And in the *Ready and Easy Way to Establish a Free Commonwealth* (1660) he contemptuously dismisses the will of the majority and proposes the paradoxical idea of forcing men to be free. Nothing is easier than to dismiss this shift of ground as mere opportunism, and indeed it was dictated by the course of the Revolution; but the correct explanation is twofold: Milton had no share in the democratic impulse of the Puritan Revolution, and his view of liberty was not primarily political.

Still less was it social and economic. A Marxist interpretation of Milton fails for utter lack of evidence. It is true that he in general concurred with the political policy of the grandees of the army and the Independent party, while pressing ahead of their religious policy. It is true that behind their policy the initiated have found the motives of the class struggle: the grandees were intent on attacking the vested interests of the crown, the church, and the landed aristocracy, while safeguarding those of the higher *bourgeoisie* against the idealism or rapacity of their allies to the left. But Milton manifests no concern with these matters, and no real interest in the parties of the left save as they espouse with him the cause of religious toleration. Nor is his outlook distinctively *bourgeois* despite his conviction that 'the most prudent men and most skilful in affairs are generally found' in 'the middle sort' (*Pro Populo Anglicano Defensio*, Col. 7: 392). Education and his subsequent pursuits largely cancelled out the influence of his social class. To his father, the successful London scrivener, Milton writes:

> thou never bad'st me tread
> The beaten path, and broad, that leads right on
> To opulence ...
> But, wishing to enrich me more, to fill
> My mind with treasure, led'st me far away
> From city-din to deep retreats, to banks
> And streams Aonian, and, with free consent,
> Didst place me happy by Apollo's side.[3]

He was critical of the education which he received at Cambridge; but his attack on it and his projected reforms do not go so deep as they are often supposed to do. They leave education still overwhelmingly literary and non-utilitarian, as one recognizes as soon as one places *Of Education* beside the writings of reformers like William Petty and the Puritans John Webster and William Dell. Unlike these, Milton was a humanist and a man of letters. In literature the *bourgeois* tradition was yet to be founded by Defoe, and Milton does not anticipate him. On the contrary, he proudly takes his place in the humanistic, the predominantly aristocratic, tradition of Sidney and Spenser. The social and economic aspects of the Revolution are still less relevant to Milton than the political and constitutional. Clearly we have not yet discovered the centre of his interests, the well-spring of his thought.

We shall find them in religion and in the Revolution in its religious aspect. To think of Milton as standing merely in the tradition of Sidney and Spenser is misleading. He is far more unequivocally committed to Christian poetry than are they, and represents indeed the grand culmination of a tradition in poetry that stretches back to Prudentius. It would be surprising indeed if the major preoccupation of Milton's poetry found no counterpart in his prose. And in fact religion is as central to his conception of liberty as to his conception of poetry. The fundamental dogmas, assumptions, and concerns of Christianity enter into the very texture of Milton's thought; and this is a chief barrier to our understanding of it. When Milton finds it necessary to justify divorce or the freedom of the press or the setting up of the English republic, on religious grounds, and to square it with scripture, this is no mere concession to his age or to an audience chiefly Puritan: it is the way in which Milton himself thought about these questions. Besides our impressive ignorance of the history of Christian thought, there are two other facts that complicate the problem for us. The first is that, owing to certain limitations in his temper and experience, and perhaps in the form of Christianity which he came to adopt, Milton sometimes seems to ignore or even to reject important parts of the tradition and spirit of the Christian religion. His lack of charity and his contemptuous dismissal of virtually the whole institutional side of Christianity are notorious. Not less characteristic is his tendency to equate religion and morality, that is, to exhaust the significance of religion in its ethical result. These limitations are undeniable, but it is absurd to infer from them, as many have done, that Milton is not a Christian at all. The second fact, which has led to the same inference, is for our purposes more important. It is the presence in Milton's thought of a large infusion of humanism and his effort to combine it with his rigidly dogmatic creed – an effort which sometimes strains the structure to the breaking point. Of Milton's heresies we shall hear again; for they are connected with his doctrine of liberty in several ways. But what we must emphasize now is Milton's Christianity and the fundamentally religious pattern of his thinking. To describe Milton simply as a Christian, however, or as a Christian humanist, is insufficient. He is a Protestant. Puritanism is the outworking of the principles of the Protestant Reformation in England, in which all their implications become apparent, and especally those implications of which Anglicanism, with its spiritualized version of the Aristotelian doctrine of the mean, stopped short. The tendency to inconoclasm, to individualism, to a sole reliance ultimately upon reason, fostered by the rejection of tradition and the wrestling of the individual mind with the manifold complexities of scripture – these and other outcomes of the Reformation are illustrated in Milton in an extreme form. In broadest terms we may say that Milton's Christianity gives him a fixed hierarchy of values, from which he is so far from seeking to free himself that he rather presents the case for liberty as a plea for freedom to realize them, but that, on the other hand, his Puritanism sharpens his sense of the impediments to their realization, among which he reckons some rules and institutions that Christians of another cast have regarded rather as principal aids.

To come, then, to Milton's doctrine of liberty and the writings in which through twenty years he sets it forth.

Looking back in 1654 on the earlier phases of the Revolution Milton tells us how from the first he saw 'that a way was opening for the establishment of real liberty; that the foundation was being laid for the deliverance of man from the yoke of slavery and superstition; [and] that the principles of religion, which were our first care, would exert a salutary influence on the manners and constitution of the nation' (*Defensio Secunda*, Col. 8: 128).[4] We observe the assumed priority of the religious issue, which is characteristic of the Puritans. Indeed at the heart of Puritanism there is an unresolved conflict: its genuine belief in liberty is accompanied, and often nullified, by its impulse to dragoon men into righteousness. Over two centuries later Archbishop Magee was to shock the descendants of the Puritans by remarking that he would rather see England free than sober. And it is now clear that the Laudian church showed more respect for the rights of the human spirit and interfered far less with the life of the individual than did most of the Puritans. But Milton is subject to no such reproach. Not only in the struggle with Charles and Laud, but in the internal conflict between liberty and reform soon to divide the Puritans themselves, he unhesitatingly aligns himself on the side of liberty. In the autobiographical passage of the *Defensio Secunda*, the passage from which I have already quoted, he goes on to speak of liberty as of three kinds, religious, domestic (or individual), and civil (or political), and briefly to assign each of his writings up to 1654 to one or other of these departments. We cannot do better in our survey than adopt his scheme, adding the remaining works, and making, of course, our own comment on all his writings.

That Milton commences with religious liberty and reform is due partly to the march of events, which conditions the order of his exposition and

something of its emphasis. But more profoundly it depends on his sense of
the priority of the religious issue. With it he launches his campaign, and in
1660, on the eve of final defeat, he can still talk of 'the best part of our
libertie, which is our religion' (*Ready and Easy Way*, Col. 6: 116). In
such early pamphlets as *Of Reformation* and the *Reason of Church Government* he shares the concern of his fellow Puritans for reform of the church,
root and branch, and allies himself with the Presbyterians to advocate it.
But the concern for liberty is also present. True liberty, which is inward,
depends, as we shall see, on true religion and sound morality, and such an
institution as he takes the Laudian church to be, by corrupting them, can
destroy this liberty at its source. Later this conviction will develop into a
distrust of institutionalism in any form. Already we observe, moreover, his
antipathy to coercion, and his anxiety to differentiate the powers and functions of church and state, later to become a demand for their total separation. And we detect the note of iconoclasm, which the Puritans learned in
their attack on the church and later applied in their dealings with the state;
Milton is impatient with the traditional and with gradualism. Change, he
declares, cannot be too 'sudden and swift, provided still it be from worse to
better' (*Of Reformation*, Col. 3 [i]: 66). Here are most of the seeds of his
final position reached in *Of Civil Power in Ecclesiastical Causes* (1659),
towards which he steadily moves in the intervening years. By 1644-5 he has
abandoned his alliance with the Presbyterians, having discovered that 'New
Presbyter is but old Priest writ large,' and in the *Areopagitica*, though it
is classed under the head of individual liberty, he is defending the cause of
liberty of conscience against them. The Presbyterians, whose interest was in
reform, not liberty, wished to establish a national church on the Scottish
model and to suppress all divergence from it. Their attitude may be not
unfairly indicated in the title of one of their pamphlets: *The casting down
of the last and strongest hold of Satan, or a treatise against toleration and
pretended liberty of Conscience.*[5] But it was easier to open the flood-gates
than to close them again, as first the Presbyterians and then the Independents themselves discovered; and there can be no doubt that the exponents
of religious toleration had much the better of the controversy. Roger Williams' *Bloody Tenent of Persecution* (1644) remains unanswerable; and to
its position Milton at last approximates, though he is never so thorough-
going, so consistent, and so effective in argument as is Williams.

Of Civil Power in Ecclesiastical Causes falls into two parts and each
involves an extreme application of a Protestant principle. The first is a
demand for the separation of church and state, which will divest the church
of all power to persecute. Here Milton makes notable use of a doctrine that
in different ways underlies the whole Puritan conception of freedom, the
doctrine of Christian liberty. He writes: (Col. 6: 28-32)

I have shewn that the civil power hath neither right nor can do right by forcing religious things: I will now shew the wrong it doth; by violating the fundamental privilege of the gospel, the new birth-right of everie true beleever, Christian libertie ... *Where the spirit of the Lord is, there is libertie. Jerusalem which is above is free; which is the mother of us all* ... For [Christ] hath not only given us this gift as a special privilege and excellence of his free gospel above the servile law, but strictly also hath commanded us to keep it and enjoy it ... *You are calld to libertie ... Stand fast therefore in the libertie wherewith Christ hath made us free; and be not intangl'd again with the yoke of bondage ... Ye are bought with a price; be not made the servants of men.* Some trivial price belike, and for some frivolous pretences paid in their opinion if, bought and by him redeemd who is God from what was once the service of God, we shall be enthrald again and forc'd by men to what now is but the service of men ... Hence it planely appears, that if we be not free we are not sons, but still servants unadopted; and if we turn again to those weak and beggarly rudiments, we are not free; yea though willingly and with a misguided conscience we desire to be in bondage to them; how much more then if unwillingly and against our conscience!

This is not merely a piece of powerful rhetoric, woven of scriptural phrases: it is an argument. If liberty of conscience is a natural right, as the Levellers had maintained, if it is essential to the peace and well-being of the civil state, as Roger Williams, among other things, had proved, it is also the special privilege of the Christian. Under the Mosaic law, indeed, men had lived in a state of tutelage, of bondage. But Christ had come expressly to abrogate the law, to substitute for forced obedience voluntary acceptance, and to raise believers to the status of sons of God. To deny them liberty of conscience is to seek to undo the work of Christ. The argument is applicable, of course, only to those whom Milton regards as true Christians, in whom alone he is interested. It assumes and perpetuates inequality by distinguishing between them and other men. The tendency of the argument is seen in Milton's denial of its benefits to Roman Catholics, to anyone indeed who will not acquiesce in his extreme reading of Christian liberty or grant to others in all circumstances the liberty of conscience which it prescribes. The failure resolutely to add equality to liberty makes Milton definitely inferior to Roger Williams as a theorist of liberty, and in other spheres besides the religious.

To the sectaries, and to those who passed with many Christians for heretics and schismatics, Milton was disposed to be more liberal, as appears in the second part of his argument, which turns on the definition of heresy.

The sole source of doctrine is the Bible; the sole interpreter of the Bible is the individual believer. Therefore nothing can be regarded as heresy, however contrary to the traditional teaching of the church, provided it be grounded in scripture and supported only by an appeal to scripture. The extent of the toleration demanded appears in the body of theology on which Milton was at work, but which remained unpublished for a century and a half after his death, the *De Doctrina Christiana*. For there, with a vast array of proof texts, he renounces the doctrine of predestination in its extreme Calvinist form, adopts a frankly Arian view of the Trinity, and rejects at once the dualism of matter and spirit and the dogma of creation from nothing. The *De Doctrina* also repeats his findings on the relation of church and state, on toleration and on free divorce (with an academic defence of polygamy thrown in for good measure); and it contains an exposition of the doctrine of Christian liberty that is fundamental to an understanding of Milton's whole position, and not least to his view on the liberty of the individual.

'Constraint and bondage,' says Milton, are 'as inseparable from the dispensation of the Law as liberty from the dispensation of the gospel' (*De Doctrina*, 1: 27 [Col. 16: 149–51]). The Mosaic law, in its three divisions, ceremonial, judicial, and moral, was a set of precepts to which absolute obedience was enjoined, in and to the letter. To demonstrate the impossibility of such obedience by man's fallen nature was the purpose of the law, and hence to bring home to him the need of a Redeemer. Christ's coming abrogated the law, its purpose fulfilled, and replaced it by the gospel. Milton insists that not the ceremonial law only, or the ceremonial and judicial, but the whole Mosaic law, including the decalogue, is thus abrogated by the gospel. For 'Paul expressly asserts that *the law is not made for a righteous man*' (*De Doctrina*, 1: 27 [Col. 16: 135]). In this interpretation Milton goes beyond most Protestant theologians, though not beyond Luther in his *Commentary upon Galatians*. Unqualified, the position would lead to Antinomianism; but it is not unqualified. It is the form of the Law that is abrogated, says Milton, not its sum and essence, which under the gospel are 'attained in that love of God and our neighbour, which is born of the Spirit through faith' (*De Doctrina*, 1: 27 [Col. 16: 141]). The outward law is abrogated, to be replaced by an inward law written by the Spirit in the mind and heart of the believer, and by the believer to be voluntarily obeyed, not in the letter, but in the spirit, 'wherever by departing from the letter we can more effectually consult the love of God and our neighbour.' 'Thus Christ departed from the letter of the law' when he said, 'The sabbath was made for man, not man for the sabbath.' 'Christian liberty,' says Milton, 'is that whereby we are loosed, as it were by enfranchisement, through Christ our deliverer, from the bondage of sin and consequently from the rule of the law and of man, to the intent that being made sons instead of servants, and perfect men instead of children, we may serve God in love through the guidance of the Spirit of Truth.' For 'truth has an essential connection with liberty' (*De Doctrina*, 1: 27 [Col. 16: 153–5]). *You shall know the truth, and the truth shall make you free.*[6]

Elsewhere in the *De Doctrina* (1: 30 [Col. 16: 273ff.]) we learn more of the inward law written by the Spirit in the hearts and minds of believers. Nothing is more obvious than Milton's reliance in argument on the text of the Bible, and on the Old Testament as well as the New. But there are, he declares, two scriptures, not one. There is the outward scripture which we call the Bible, and there is the inward scripture imprinted by the Spirit in the heart and mind, and it is by reference to this inward scripture that the outward is interpreted and judged. This inward scripture is another name for the inward law, the special privilege of the gospel; and this inward law, in turn, is none other than the law of nature given originally to Adam, obscured but not obliterated by the fall; and daily in the regenerate, under the influence of the Holy Spirit, it is being progressively restored to its original brightness. The identification of the inward law by which the Christian lives with the restored law of nature means that is is not something independent of reason but the very substance of right reason itself, and that it is to be apprehended by reason as reason is cleared and assisted by divine grace.

Such is the doctrine of Christian liberty as it finally appears in Milton. It is not to be assumed that this doctrine in its full elaboration and all its applications was present in Milton's earlier writings; but repeatedly as he faced the problems raised in his successive works, he brought the idea of Christian liberty to bear on them and was impelled to elaborate the doctrine and define its implications. At first he agrees with the majority of his contemporaries that Christian liberty is exercised only in 'things indifferent' (*Of Reformation*, Col. 3 [i]: 50), that is in matters not specifically enjoined by scripture. But ultimately for Milton the principle that the Bible itself is to be read by the Christian in the spirit and not in the letter extends the sphere of Christian liberty to all matters of faith and morals. The decisive change comes in *Tetrachordon* (the third of the divorce tracts, 1645). In *The Doctrine and Discipline of Divorce* Milton has wrestled with the question of Christian liberty, since Christ seemed to withdraw a liberty conceded by the law. Now he boldly asserts the liberty of the Christian to interpret the precepts of scripture in accordance with that charity – that love of God and one's neighbour – which Christ came to promulgate and to substitute for mere obedience to external law (*Tetrachordon*, Col. 4: 74–6). The doctrine of Christian liberty bears upon Milton's conception of liberty in different ways, some sufficiently obvious, others more subtle but not less important. At the risk of anticipating our exposition of his views on individual

and on political liberty, it will be well briefly to notice at this point some of
the ways in which Christian liberty as he conceives it influences Milton's
thinking.

1 / We have already observed the bearing of the idea of Christian
liberty on the case for liberty of conscience, which Milton himself elaborates: Christ has freed the believer from God's outward law; how much more
then from the edicts of mere men! Christ has committed the believer to the
guidance of the inner law, the law at once of faith and of reason, by whose
light even the Bible is to be read. But this inner law is that very conscience
for whose liberty Milton is pleading.

2 / We have noticed Milton's heavy dependence upon the Bible in all
his arguments, whether theological or practical. In this he is extreme even
by Puritan standards. Such dependence might well lead to a lifeless literal-
ism and to a wholly uncritical use of biblical authority. That Milton completely escapes these dangers, I will not assert. But for him Christian liberty
certainly includes the right to read the Bible itself in the spirit rather than
the letter, to judge the outward scripture in the light of the inward, in the
light of that law which is written by the Spirit in the mind and heart of the
believer; and this is no academic theory, but a right which Milton invokes.
There can be no doubt of the liberating effect of the doctrine of Christian
liberty upon Milton's own mind.

3 / But the character of this inward law by which the outward law is
abrogated and the outward scripture is read and judged must be more carefully observed. It is, as Milton conceives it, not mystical but essentially rational: it is the law of nature restored to its original brightness and apprehended by a restored reason – that is, by reason supported, not set aside, by
divine grace. Thus in dealing with the outward scripture Milton has at his
disposal all the resources of rational argument and all the resources of biblical criticism available in his day. The temper of his mind is indeed rationalistic. He is the least mystical of all great religious poets. In his poetry
this is perhaps a limitation, though there some compensating qualities come
into play, but that is not our present concern. The point is that he conceives
the inner law on which the believer finally relies as rational, not mystical, in
its character and operation.

4 / It is clear that Christian liberty has two aspects, a negative and a
positive aspect, and in both it exercises a strong influence on Milton's conception of liberty. In its negative aspect Christian liberty is conceived as the
abrogation of the Mosaic law. And in the political sphere Milton is apt to
think of liberty precisely in this way: for him political liberty means, to the
extent to which this is feasible, the abolition of outward laws.

5 / But this negative aspect of Christian liberty presupposes the positive. The outward law can be abrogated precisely because an inward law

has taken its place. The positive aspect of Christian liberty is this rule of the inward law. Milton is careful to point out that of the believer, under the gospel, not a lesser, but a greater, degree of perfection is expected than was vainly demanded under the Mosaic law. And so liberty becomes synonymous with virtue. 'Know that to be free,' says Milton, 'is the same thing as to be pious, to be wise, to be temperate and just, to be frugal and abstinent, and lastly, to be magnanimous and brave; so to be the opposite of these things is the same as to be a slave' (*Defensio Secunda*, Col. 8: 248–50).[7] In a condition of perfect freedom which is synonymous with perfect virtue, outward law is abrogated because there is no need of it. Such was the life of Eden, as we are reminded in *Paradise Lost* (9.654) : to live without external law, 'Law to ourselves' because 'our Reason is our Law'; and such also is the life of the regenerate.

6 / Liberty thus conceived is possible, then, only to the regenerate, and it is for the liberty of the regenerate alone that Milton is finally concerned. Unlike the Levellers he does not add equality to liberty; he does not make his stand for the rights of the people but, as the Puritans phrased it, for the privileges of the saints; and it is not by accident, or from the mere pressure of events, that he is ready to defy the will of the majority in order to realize his ideal. Here too the doctrine of Christian liberty has its influence. Directly, as we saw in Milton's plea for liberty of conscience, it can be made a ground for demanding the liberty of the Christian only, not the liberty of all men, and in the political sphere, at least, this is a disastrous limitation.

7 / As is apparent from the passage quoted above, in which he identifies liberty and virtue, Milton thought of the regenerate state, to which alone Christian liberty is possible, as marked less by a peculiar religious experience than by an active and voluntary condition of virtue. Nothing indeed could be more characteristic of Milton than this emphasis on morality; for the temper of his mind is not more evidently rationalistic than it is ethical. It is not surprising that his most interesting pronouncements on liberty belong to the area which he designates as domestic or individual, where the problem of liberty is most distinctively a moral problem.

8 / But everywhere in Milton the ethical emphasis is present. None can truly love liberty, he declares, but good men; the rest desire not liberty but licence (*Tenure of Kings and Magistrates*, Col. 5: 1). The antithesis is fundamental. Though Milton was sometimes carried too far by the impetus of his attack on abuses, and by a temper naturally prone to resent every form of outward restraint, to this position he always returns. The liberty which he advocates is never consciously opposed to the ideal of order; for if it were it would not be liberty, but licence. Liberty and order – an order at once rational and moral – are the twin poles of Milton's thinking, and indeed liberty as he conceives it, may be not inadequately defined as *order*

self-imposed from within. The doctrinal basis is religious – is in fact the doctrine of Christian liberty; Milton's interpretation is ethical and rationalistic; the most obvious applications, and the centre of Milton's interest, are in liberty and conscience in its widest extent.

II

Under the heading of individual or domestic liberty Milton groups *Of Education*, his pamphlets on divorce, and the famous *Areopagitica*, all of which fall between 1643 and 1645. The caption must not blind us to the religious basis of Milton's thinking on these as other subjects; but, more than in the writings on religious liberty or on political, his humanism here comes into evidence. For it is Milton's conviction that nothing can be described as for man's good unless it conduces to his benefit at once as an eternal and a temporal being.[8] Thus the end of education is twofold: to fit 'a man to perform justly, skilfully and magnanimously all the offices both private and publick of Peace and War,' but also 'to repair the ruines of our first Parents by regaining to know God aright' (*Of Education*, Col. 4: 280, 277) or more generally to supply that foundation in religion, knowledge, rationality, and virtue without which true liberty is impossible. It is for this reason that Milton classifies *Of Education* among his writings on liberty. The liberty of the student is not even mentioned. From few documents indeed will our progressive educationists derive less comfort. For Milton tacitly assumes that to minds capable of learning knowledge is irresistibly attractive and requires neither dressing up nor watering down; nor does the great individualist believe that self-expression is a substitute for knowledge.

Of Education is an educational utopia, setting forth in a single institution Milton's ideal of education through the years of school and college. It represents his reaction against Cambridge in his day with its relics of scholastic philosophy, as described and condemned in *Prolusion* 3. It is essentially a humanist and Christian humanist document and stands in the general tradition of Erasmus and of Roger Ascham. But its main emphasis falls on the content of Greek and Latin literature, which embodies the best of secular knowledge and wisdom. Languages are the key to these sources of knowledge, not something pursued for their own sake, and Milton advocates a rapid and simplified mastery of grammar, and reading from the earliest possible date. In this he resembles Comenius, who exercised a considerable influence in England. But there is little evidence of his influencing Milton's detail. Milton's debt to Bacon and his tradition, which is often exaggerated, is in fact not very great. Bacon would substitute observation for wide reading. Milton would at most have observation supplement reading. He is a humanist in putting books, and especially the classics, first.[9]

One may observe further that Milton's plan is one of general education not for the masses, but rather for the gentry and those who by social standing or ability would in Milton's day go to the university and subsequently become leaders in the life of the nation.

If we cannot get a Teachers' College out of *Of Education* we are not likely to get a Reno out of the *Doctrine and Discipline of Divorce*. Milton's plea for free divorce invokes the same twofold principle, religious and humanistic. If the terms of the argument are predominantly religious it is partly because the obstacles are religious – partly but only partly. What he is trying to establish is divorce for incompatibility of temper. Marriage was instituted for man's good. Where an insuperable obstacle occurs to the primary good proposed, there has been in effect no marriage. Such was the theoretic ground on which alone annulment had been granted. Up to a point Milton is willing to argue the case on this traditional basis, but with a difference. The primary end of marriage, he declares, citing Genesis 2:18, is companionship; the secondary end, provision for the race. Here by a characteristic appeal to scripture Milton reverses the traditional order and can then adopt the traditional principle as his own. Where some insuperable obstacle to true companionship exists, there has been in effect no marriage. Under the old dispensation provision was made for annulling such a union, at the discretion of the husband, by the Mosaic bill of divorcement. So much for the Old Testament, but what of the New? Christ came not to impose new burdens, but to set believers free; and if he appears to have withdrawn this provision, to have placed a new yoke on their shoulders and a new stumbling-block in their way, it can only be that his words have been misunderstood. The law of God and of nature are one, and by their rule nothing can bind against the good of man. If of the sabbath, though instituted for God's glory, it could be said, *The sabbath was made for man, not man for the sabbath,* how much more of marriage, which was instituted only for man's good! Thus runs the argument. Behind it lies the Protestant rejection of marriage as a sacrament and the Puritan revolt against the jurisdiction of the church. But what is characteristic of Milton is, first, the high idealism of the view of marriage on which the plea for greater freedom in its dissolution is based; then, the twofold appeal to God's intention and man's good, the invoking of the doctrine of Christian liberty, and the bold and ingenious treatment of scripture. The common assertion that he claims freedom of divorce only for the husband is specious, but untrue. 'Milton,' said Dr Johnson, 'believed that man was created only to rebel, woman only to obey.'[10] This statement is a travesty in both its parts. Milton did not regard woman as, in most cases, man's intellectual equal, though he allowed for exceptions. He recognized, however, that she had her own peculiar gifts and sources of power. We must not expect from him the enlightenment of the modern American wife, who wants it both ways.

In some other respects the *Doctrine and Discipline of Divorce* is highly characteristic of Milton. It illustrates his sense of the havoc institutions can work when accompanied by coercion, and his radical revolt against the burden of the past. Custom, he declares, always allies itself with error, never with truth; and together they would destroy all truth, justice, and human well-being, did not God from time to time raise up his servants to assail custom and error and break their fatal spell. Milton's view of history is essentially revolutionary, Platonist, and Puritan. It can best be characterized as the direct antithesis of Burke: history is not the 'known march of the ordinary providence of God'; it is a protracted wandering from the way, relieved by sudden interventions of God's *extraordinary* providence. For Milton theism does not validate the actual, does not dispose him to seek for evidences of the ideal in the actual, or in history which is the record of the actual. That, on the contrary, is the way of Burke, as Lord Acton divines, and of Burke's view he acutely adds, 'What could be more typically Anglican!' Historically, and as a light upon the Puritan mind, this is indeed significant. But most significant of all is the temporary and precarious alliance between two main impulses in Milton's thought, his Puritan radicalism and his humanistic insistence on the good of man as the ultimate criterion.

This alliance is illustrated in the *Tetrachordon*, the third of his divorce tracts (1645), which seeks to reinterpret, and in so doing to dispose of, four passages in the New Testament which seem to withdraw the concession of the Mosaic bill of divorcement and to forbid divorce. There he writes: 'For nothing nowadayes is more degenerately forgott'n, then the true dignity of man ...' It is true, he continues, that men cannot rightly claim their 'just and naturall privileges ... unless they be alli'd to inward goodnesse, and steadfast knowledge,' and that explains 'why in this age many are so opposite both to human and to Christian liberty ... while they understand not, or envy others that do; contenting, or rather priding themselves in a specious humility and strictnesse bred out of low ignorance that never yet conceiv'd the freedome of the Gospel' (Col. 4: 74). By the fall man lost his original dignity and freedom, lost his resemblance to God, in whose image he was created. (Col. 4: 74–5)

> All which being lost in *Adam*, was recover'd with gain by the merits of Christ. For ... Christ having cancell'd the hand writing of ordinances which was against us (Col. 2.14), and interpreted the fulfilling of all [the requirements of the law] through charity, hath in that respect set us over the law, in the free custody of his love, and left us victorious under the guidance of his living Spirit, not under the dead letter; to follow that which most edifies, most aides and furders a religious life, makes us holiest and likest to his immortall Image, not that which makes us most conformable and captive to civil and subordinat pre-

cepts; whereof the strictest observance may ofttimes prove the destruction ... of many innocent persons ... Although indeed no ordinance human or from heav'n can binde against the good of man; so that to keep them strictly against that end, is all one with to breake them.

This much, be it observed, was evident even to the heathen: ' "All law, [says Cicero in the *De Inventione*] ... we ought [to] referr to the common good, and interpret by that, not by the scrowl of letters. No man observes law for laws sake, but for the good of them for whom it was made." ' And even under the Mosaic law there are examples of those who are praised for departing from its precepts for due cause, and thus 'taught us on what just occasions to doe so: untill our Saviour for whom that great and God-like work was reserv'd, redeem'd us to a state above prescriptions by dissolving the whole law into charity' (Col. 4: 76).

The alliance of Puritan radicalism with the humanistic criterion of the good of man is reinforced in the *Areopagitica*, where the form, an oration modelled on Isocrates, and the noble praise of 'the old and elegant humanity of Greece' (Col. 4: 295), remind us that Milton's humanism springs from his study of the classics, and that he is the heir of the Renaissance no less surely than of the Reformation. His confidence in England is at its zenith. He is not yet disillusioned with parliament and people, nor burdened by the necessity of justifying the ways of Cromwell to men. For a moment it seems that we are listening to a potential champion of democracy, for he speaks in the spirit of faith and hope in the common man which is the indispensable spirit of democracy, and he accepts its fundamental postulate that not only truth but agreement in the truth are best ensured by free discussion. Insofar at least he is at one with those humbler liberals, the Levellers. Religion and the good of man point to the same conclusion, which is freedom. Of all those who from fear or self-interest would limit freedom he is scornful, and especially of the Presbyterians, who are reviving the Laudian and ultimately the papal practice of a censored and licensed press; but he is less violent and strident than in much of his prose. And for once he achieves in that medium what he never fails to achieve in poetry, a work of art in which he rises securely above his subject, asserts his control over its details, and realizes its wider implications. The *Areopagitica* is indeed the happiest as well as the greatest of Milton's prose works. Here, if anywhere, his individualism and his distrust of the state are legitimate: 'Give me liberty to know, to utter, and to argue freely according to conscience, above all liberties' (Col. 4: 347); and again: 'The State shall be my governours, but not my criticks' (Col. 4: 326). He recognizes the limits of legislation, the impossibility of dragooning men into righteousness. He sees that the attempt entails far more than the licensing of the press: it entails endless interference with the life of the individual, from which he recoils. Milton's feeling for the freedom of the individual is supported by his view of man's nature and situation since the fall. Truth and error, good and evil, grow up in this world together and a man must learn to discriminate between them, that he may embrace the one and reject the other. 'When God gave [man] reason, he gave him freedom to choose, for reason is but choosing' (Col. 4: 319). Underlying all Milton's belief in freedom is his belief in man's free will.

As a humanist and a Protestant he has come to distrust and despise asceticism; not its high standard of virtue, but its effort to attain its end by suppression and retreat. In a famous passage he writes: (Col. 4: 311)

> As therefore the state of man now is, what wisdome can there be to choose, what continence to forbeare without the knowledge of evill? He that can apprehend and consider vice with all her baits and seeming pleasures, and yet abstain, and yet distinguish, and yet prefer that which is truly better, he is the true wayfaring Christian. I cannot praise a fugitive and cloister'd virtue, unexercis'd and unbreath'd, that never sallies out and sees her adversary, but slinks out of the race, where that immortall garland is to be run for, not without dust and heat. Assuredly we bring not innocence into the world, we bring impurity much rather: that which purifies is triall, and triall is by what is contrary ... Which was the reason why our sage and serious Poet Spencer, ... describing true temperance under the person of *Guion*, brings him in with his palmer through the cave of Mammon, and the bowr of earthly blisse that he migh see and know, and yet abstain.

The correct description of Milton's position in this passage is that, like Spenser's, it is a blend of Renaissance humanism and Protestant rigorism. Milton is not less certain than Spenser that the Bower of Bliss must be destroyed; but he sees that it is not to be accomplished by act of parliament, for it is resident in the heart and mind of every man, who must destroy it for himself, or bring it under control. And so with the Cave of Mammon. 'They are not skilfull considerers of human things,' says Milton, 'who imagin to remove sin by removing the matter of sin ... Though you take from a covetous man all his treasure, he has yet one jewell left, ye cannot bereave him of his covetousnesse' (Col. 4: 319). It is not in their matter that vice and virtue differ, but in the form that man is able to impose upon this matter and upon his own life. To expel the matter of sin, were that possible, would be to expel the matter of virtue too: 'for the matter of them both is the same.' 'Wherefore did [God] creat passions within us, pleasures round about us, but that these rightly temper'd are the very ingredients of virtu?'

So much for Milton's ethic and its place in the argument of the *Areopagitica*. But his concern is with truth in general as well as with the virtue of the individual. Without freedom there can be no effective correction of error, no zeal for the defence and extension of truth, no progress. Here Milton anticipates several of the arguments in John Stuart Mill's chapter on 'Liberty of Thought and Discussion' in *On Liberty*. Elsewhere the terms of their argument diverge. For in the *Areopagitica*, as indeed everywhere, the basis of Milton's thinking is religious. His primary plea is for free discussion in questions of religion and ethics. His protest is against the 'crowding of free consciences and Christian liberties into canons and precepts of men' (Col. 4: 341–2). And his concern is for the progressive discovery of religious truth, a principle which he held in common with the more advanced Puritans. John Robinson had urged on the Pilgrim Fathers the duty of receiving the new truth that would from time to time break forth from the word of God.[11] John Goodwin instanced the variety of new discoveries in secular knowledge, including that of a new continent, and declared that discoveries not less important were yet to be made in theology.[12] The authors of the *Apologetical Narration* daily expected new light and refused to be bound by their present judgment, adding that they would wish to see this principle adopted by all Christian states and churches.[13] 'The Christian,' says Henry Robinson, 'ought continually to grow, not only from grace to grace but from knowledge to knowledge.'[14] 'The true temper and proper employment of a Christian,' said the author of *The Ancient Bounds*, 'is always to be working like the sea, and purging ignorance out of his understanding, and exchanging notions and apprehensions imperfect for more perfect, and forgetting things behind to press forward.'[15] Clearly it is in the spirit of these utterances that Milton writes: 'To be still searching what we know not, by what we know, still closing up truth to truth as we find it, ... This is the golden rule in *Theology* as well as in Arithmetick' (*Areopagitica*, Col. 4: 339). Milton pleads for liberty of conscience in the formation and publication of opinion as essential alike to the well-being of the individual and to the cause of truth; for 'opinion in good men is but knowledge in the making' (Col. 4: 341).

Classified by Milton as an essay on domestic or individual liberty, the *Areopagitica*, nevertheless, takes its place in the literature of religious toleration or liberty of conscience together with the works just cited and, greatest of all, the *Bloody Tenent of Persecution* written by Roger Williams in that same year. It is thus connected in a way that the divorce pamphlets are not with a principal current of the Puritan Revolution. In 1649 Milton is again caught up in its full tide. Then he turns to the political question, or to civil liberty as he calls it, and becomes indeed the official apologist, first of the army, then of the Republic, and finally of Cromwell. A movement which was more religious than political in origin has come by the inexorable logic of events to be more political than religious – not without some paradoxical results. The plea for liberty has long ago become the quest for power, and it issues at last in dictatorship. At each successive stage of the Revolution large numbers of the nation, and even of the Puritans, fell away. But Milton persists to the end. In the *Tenure of Kings and Magistrates* he defends the desperate courses of the army and its leaders, and joins to arguments about God's mandate to establish justice and righteousness by force, other arguments which come from no religious source, however mistaken, but from the secular tradition of Renaissance radicalism, the tradition represented by the *Vindiciae Contra Tyrannos*. Under the pressure of events new implications of his doctrine come into relief. It becomes increasingly evident that the doctrine is radical, but not democratic, and that it is not primarily political.

The defects of his political theory spring in part from his excessive preoccupation with the liberty of the individual. All that he asks of government is that it should guarantee the liberty of the individual – that is, of the good man – and especially his religious liberty. This done, he is content that power should be concentrated in the hands of a minority, or of a Cromwell. Of democracy as synonymous with political liberty he has no faintest conception. In the apostrophe to Cromwell in the *Second Defence of the English People* (1654), there is but one positive demand: a more adequate provision for education. The other demands are negative: Cromwell is to guarantee the separation of church and state and thereby to ensure religious liberty; and he is to allow 'the free discussion of truth without any hazard to the author' and so to thwart 'those who think they never can be free till the liberties of others depend on their caprice' (*Defensio Secunda*, Col. 8: 237–9).[16] For the rest, he is rather to abolish old laws than establish new. Laws are never in themselves beneficial: they are useful only as a restraint upon the wicked, and too often 'prohibit the innocent freedoms of the good.' 'Liberty is the best school of virtue.' And Milton adds that these demands embody the whole of political liberty: 'If there be anyone who thinks that this is not liberty enough, he appears to me to be rather inflamed with the lust of ambition or of anarchy than with the love of a genuine and well-regulated liberty' (Col. 8: 237–9). It is these same ends that, after Cromwell's death, Milton hopes to compass in the radical but undemocratic constitution of his *Ready and Easy Way to Establish a Free Commonwealth* (1660).

This work was written in the peculiar circumstances of 1659–60 when the tiny minority who held power were at odds among themselves and when public opinion in revulsion against all factions was swinging strongly to a restoration of the monarchy. Among the minority many plans were propounded; and this is Milton's. Its principal features are: 1 / the rejection of monarchy (or any form of single-person rule – such as the Protectorate) and of a hereditary House of Lords; 2 / the setting up of a Grand Council (or parliament) which shall be perpetual (no doubt he would accept the Rump) though he is willing to admit rotation; 3 / the dividing of the country into cities and surrounding territories, with their assembles, their schools, and their local grandees: these 'city states' to administer the laws, and to express assent or dissent to the laws enacted by the Grand Council, but yielding to the will of the majority of such units; 4 / a Council of State as executive. These are the principal provisions of Milton's ideal constitution.

The tract is an epitome of Milton's political thinking. We observe as its first note its radicalism, indeed iconoclasm: the complete break of his ideal constitution with the English past. And we are able to trace this to his Puritanism and see how his religion shapes the pattern of his political thought. Indeed Milton himself points the analogy. Those who would reform the state, he observes, are 'not bound by any statute of preceding Parlaments, but by the law of nature only ... to which no Parlament or people that will thoroughly reforme, but may and must have recourse; as they had and must yet have in church reformation ... to evangelic rules; not to ecclesiastical canons, though never so ancient, so ratif'd and establishd in the land by Statutes ...' (*Ready and Easy Way*, Col. 6: 113). But precisely because Milton's ideal constitution breaks with the past it is inapplicable to the present, and we detect the second note of his political thinking, its unrealism. For the English people had had quite enough of Puritan rule, and craved nothing so much as a return to the ordered procession of the traditional. But – and this is the third note of his political thinking – for the will of the English people Milton cared not at all. Of his countrymen he can write: (Col. 6: 140–1)

> [the] greatest part have both in reason and the trial of just battel, lost the right of their election what the government shall be: of them who have not lost that right [i.e., of his own party], whether they for kingship be the greatest number, who can certainly determin? Suppose they be; yet of freedom they partake all alike, one main end of government: which if the greater part value not, but will degenerately forego, is it just or reasonable, that most voices against the main end of government should enslave the less number that would be free? More just it is doubtless ... that a less number compell a greater to retain ... thir libertie, then that a greater number for the pleasure of thir baseness, compell a less [number] most injuriously to be their fellow slaves. They who seek nothing but thir own just libertie, have alwaies right to winn it and to keep it, whenever they have power, be the voices never so numerous that oppose it.

In this passage, besides the contemptuous dismissal of the will of the majority, a fourth note of Milton's political thinking appears: the fact – and here we return to our starting point – that he conceives liberty in individual and religious, but never really in political, terms. To preserve the liberty of the individual, especially his religious liberty, is the main end of government. Any government that will fulfil this end meets the demands of liberty whether it is the choice of the majority or not, and it may even impose its rule on an unwilling people; it may thus, paradoxically, force men to be free.

But on this only one judgment is possible: it is a most inadequate conception of political liberty. Even if we overlook the monstrous paradox of forcing men to be free, we must recognize that, like every other form of individualism, Milton's starves one side of the individual's nature, the social side. To meet the demands of political liberty it is not enough to have good government: you must have government in which the individual has his chance to participate, and in so doing to realize himself not as an individual in the narrower sense, but as a member of the community. Milton learned much from the Greeks. He did not learn, as he might have done from Aristotle's *Politics*, that participation in the life and government of the state is a prerequisite of the good life, is part of the good life – the lesson which only requires extension of the privilege to every man in order to issue in the full philosophy of democracy. But Milton was a Puritan and also a Platonist: in the interests of virtue and efficiency he was content to leave government to the virtuous and the efficient – if you can find them, which is not so easy as he imagines. He knew nothing of the great democratic experience, the experience of trying to persuade your fellows to be wise and, when you fail, of acquiescing in their unwisdom until you can persuade them. Outside democracy there is no such thing as political liberty. You may think perhaps that in these remarks I have abandoned the historical point of view. I have not. One group in Milton's day caught something of this vision of what democracy should and might be. That group was the so-called Levellers with their passion for equality, their faith in the arrival at truth, and agreement in the truth, through free discussion, and their readiness to bow to the will of the majority whatever that will might be. For a moment in the *Areopagitica* it looked as if Milton had caught the vision too. But he lost it. He tried, in the political sphere, to separate liberty and equality. And he acquiesced in the principle which is the negation of all democracy and destroys it at the root: the principle of *might till right is ready*, the belief that you can establish justice presently by one more act of injustice now.

Milton's doctrine of liberty and that of the Levellers sprang in part from a common source. In both can be traced the influence of Puritanism with its emphasis on Christian liberty; this is the influence which A.D. Lindsay, in his brilliant little book *The Essentials of Democracy*, describes as fostering the democratic spirit. And it is significant that in the most immediate and indisputable practical application, the demand for liberty of conscience, Milton and the Levellers are in substantial agreement. But thereafter they diverge sharply. The Levellers do not try to argue directly from religion to politics. Like Roger Williams, they distinguish between the order of nature and the order of grace, while recognizing an analogy between them. As in the order of grace there is Christian liberty, so in the order of nature there is natural liberty. As by grace all Christians as Christians have equal rights, so by nature all men as men have equal rights. As the congregation is a democracy in little, a community of equals, so is the state a democracy, a community of equals. This is part of the basic pattern of Leveller thought. Opposed to it in the Puritan mind was the rooted belief that you could argue directly from religion to politics, that Christian liberty meant liberty for the elect alone, for the converted or (as they unblushingly called themselves) the saints, that Christian equality meant their equality in special privilege or, in plain terms, their superiority to other men. The congregations are not the models of a free state, but centres of power. This was the language of Cromwell's military saints. It appears in its most extreme form in the plans of the Millennarians to inherit the earth and in Cromwell's Nominated Parliament. Here is the aspect of Puritanism which Lindsay overlooks. It must not be overlooked by us. Clearly Milton has not rid himself of the undemocratic elements in Puritanism. Even in his impassioned pleas for the liberty of the individual and for religious toleration, there is, as we have seen, some reserve. It is the liberty of the saints for which he is chiefly concerned, though naturally his definition of a saint is less crude than those which passed current in the conventicles. Only the good man, Milton's equivalent of the saint, can be truly free: the rest love not liberty but licence, and their fate is a matter of almost complete indifference to him. If this is true in the field of religious liberty, and if it is even true in the domestic or individual sphere where Milton's Puritanism enters into liberalizing alliance with his humanism, whose standard is the good of man, it is still more true in the least valuable area of his thinking, the political. There his thought derives from Puritanism not only its iconoclastic and revolutionary character, but its excessive individualism, its imperfect sense of the individual as a member of the community, the ungracious habit of dismissing opponents as unregenerate persons who have no rights, and the refusal to add equality to liberty.

III

Just before writing the *Ready and Easy Way* Milton had, it would seem, completed the *De Doctrina Christiana*;[17] besides a discussion of Christian liberty, two other subjects treated in that work have a special bearing on his theory of liberty and order.

The first is his assertion, against the extreme Calvinists in his own party, of the Arminian doctrine of man's free will. Milton readily admits that, to some, peculiar grace is vouchsafed and these no doubt are the natural, or rather supernatural, leaders to whom we must look for guidance. But to all men is given grace sufficient, and efficient too, if they will only of their own free will avail themselves of the gift. The question of liberty may be considered on different levels, and one is the metaphysical or, it may be, theological. Without some belief in free will no thorough-going doctrine of liberty is possible. It is significant that Milton, the great exponent of liberty, insists on man's free will, and that his contemporary Thomas Hobbes, the great champion of absolutism, is an unqualified determinist.[18]

The second subject in the *Doctrina*, to which I have referred, seems more remote from practical questions of liberty. It is Milton's view of the process of creation. As we shall see in the next chapter, he used his freedom of religious inquiry to argue against two traditional conceptions of orthodox theology: against the doctrine that God created the universe from nothing, and against the belief that spirit and matter are two distinct substances, with its attendant depression of matter and of the senses by which the material is known.

Creation was not from nothing, he asserts, but from an already existent 'first matter,' which only required to be reduced to form and order by the creative word of God. This first matter is the chaos of the ancients, and it is described in Genesis: it is the earth as yet without form and void, and it is the waters on which the Spirit brooded. But if this matter existed from eternity it could only exist in God whose infinity and omnipotence permit of no existence independent of him. From this it follows that matter and spirit are not distinct substances, but, as Milton puts it, different degrees of the same substance, and that matter is not something trivial or evil, as is often assumed, but 'the parent stock of every subsequent good.' Creation was the ordering of this matter and the realizing of this good by the shaping activity of the Divine Reason and the vitalizing power of God's spirit. And in man, the microcosm, a like process must be at work, reducing chaos to cosmos, and, in the elements of man's nature and the conditions of his life, realizing the potential good. 'Wherefore did [God] creat passions within us, pleasures round about us, but that these rightly temperd are the very ingredients of virtu?' (*De Doctrina*, 1 : 6 [Col. 14: 319]). The ordering of his life is the responsibility finally of the individual, and that he may discharge this responsibility he must be free.

IV

These ideas inform not only Milton's prose but his poetry; and poetry, as he himself recognized, was his true medium. There all his powers are manifested, and his doctrine, freed from the hampering and distorting influence of political warfare and the necessity of justifying the ways of Cromwell and Milton to Englishmen, shines forth with greater clarity. Yet it is in his poetry that his doctrine has been most misunderstood. Since the Romantic revival many readers have persisted in assuming that Satan speaks for Milton and is in fact the hero of *Paradise Lost*. Such an assumption distorts the true meaning of the poem and obliterates Milton's oft-repeated distinction between liberty and licence, his cherished principle that only the good can be truly free.

The first thing that should strike an unprejudiced reader of *Paradise Lost* is the emphasis placed on the principle of order; the second, the perfect compatibility of this order with true liberty. The epic as a whole presents a picture of order not less impressive than that in Dante's *Divine Comedy*. Heaven is a celestial order, hierarchical in its whole character. Only Satan and his followers (among whom we must reckon half the critics of *Paradise Lost*) suppose that such order is an infringement of liberty. For the unfallen angels and for Milton, it is the scheme within which true liberty (God's service, which is perfect freedom) is enjoyed; and for man before his fall or after his regeneration it is the model. Hell is not, as one might thoughtlessly expect, disorder. Disorder is the mark of the chaos, which is capable of being reduced to order and so of becoming 'the parent stock of every subsequent good' (*De Doctrina*, 1: 7 [Col. 15: 23]). Hell is not disorder, but something much worse: it is perverted order – with Satan enthroned, with evil in the place of good, and with a service that is perfect slavery ...

In his dealings with poor frivolous Eve Satan masquerades as the patron of liberty. The critics have proved scarcely less gullible than our first mother. But Milton's judgment on the pretended champion of freedom is summed up in a single line (6.181): 'Thyself not free but to thyself enthrall'd.' And he makes it equally clear that when Satan talks of liberty what he really means is power. 'Here,' says Satan in hell, (1.258–63)

> Here at least
> We shall be free ...
> Here we may reign secure, and in my choyce
> To reign is worth ambition though in Hell:
> Better to reign in Hell than serve in Heav'n.

Undismayed the critics retreat to new ground and discover that Satan's arguments about the Tree of Knowledge appear to be drawn in part from the pages of the *Areopagitica*. But they overlook two facts: first, that such arguments, whether uttered by Milton or by Satan, are applicable, as Milton very well knew, only in the fallen state[19] when the remnants of truth are scattered abroad and have to be collected and sifted from error, when full knowledge is indispensable to virtue and, as Milton said, to the repairing of the ruins of our first parents. Second, the critics overlook the fact that, for all Milton's devotion to knowledge and to liberty, the value which he sets upon them is not absolute: the value which he sets upon virtue, conceived as obedience to the will of God, is absolute. 'Henceforth,' says Adam, the repentant, 'Henceforth I learne, that to obey is best' (12.561). And this is not only the conclusion of *Paradise Lost*: it is the starting point of *Paradise Regained*.

Milton's doctrine is perfectly clear. And the perennial talk of the critics about Satan's standing for liberty and representing Milton's point of view is unrelieved nonsense. But there remains the question of Milton's temper; and here the matter is not quite so simple. Tillyard has remarked that if Milton had been in Eden, he would no doubt have eaten the apple and then have retired to write a pamphlet justifying his action.[20] And in that conceit there is, I think, an element of truth, just as I believe that in the heat of political controversy Milton's temper often triumphed over his principles so that he failed to distinguish accurately between liberty and the will to power, and again, in his theology, when he failed to recognize and abide by the limits of human reason or was betrayed into a tone incompatible with Christian humility. But in his poetry the defects of Milton's temper and attitude are reviewed and conscientiously corrected. This is merely a cold way of saying that the more highly integrated and organic utterance of the poet presents far more satisfactorily than the prose Milton's full and final philosophy. If Satan represents anything, it is not Milton's point of view, but the element of rebelliousness in Milton's own nature which, as Saurat rather fitfully perceived, Milton himself recognizes and repudiates. What Saurat does not perceive is that the arguments of Satan are not Milton's arguments: rather they represent erroneous or incomplete inferences from some of Milton's principles: they are what Milton's arguments might have become if he had abandoned Christianity. But he did not.

In his prose there is little, perhaps too little, self-criticism: in his poetry, for all its seeming objectivity, there is a great deal. And so the poetry becomes, among other things, the clearing house of Milton's doubts and difficulties and of the emotional tensions which they breed. Poetry, he had said, has a special power 'to allay the perturbations of the mind, and set the affections in right tune' (*Reason of Church Government*, Col. 3 [i]: 238). He was thinking of its effect upon the reader; but it is not less true, surely, of the poet himself. For what is the poetic activity as illustrated, let us say, in Milton's own poetry? It is creation: it is the imposition of form and order, of what we call aesthetic pattern, upon the materials of human experience. And it is the perfect example indeed of free activity as Milton conceived free activity. For it is unconstrained, subject to no outward control, and yet it operates in accordance with a law inward and self-imposed. Such was the music and motion of the angels (*Paradise Lost* 5.618–27)

> That day, as other solemn dayes, they spent
> In song and dance about the sacred Hill,
> Mystical dance, which yonder starrie Spheare
> Of Planets and of fixt in all her Wheeles
> Resembles nearest, mazes intricate,
> Eccentric, intervolv'd, yet regular
> Then most, when most irregular they seem,
> And in thir motions harmonie Divine
> So smooths her charming tones, that Gods own ear
> Listens delighted ...

Something like this music and rhythm of heaven is poetry for Milton at its best.

We may discuss Milton's ideas, but we must never forget that he is first of all, and best of all, a poet. This certainly does not mean, as Blake inferred, that 'he is of the devil's party without knowing it';[21] but it does mean that he has a particular feeling for both liberty and order. And of this feeling for liberty and order the result and the perfect symbol are to be found in the free and total activity of the poetic mind as this activity issues in the aesthetic patterns of *Lycidas*, of *Paradise Lost* and of *Samson Agonistes*.

5
The theologian, 1:
Milton's Christian doctrine

W e have observed Milton's steady progression to the Puritan left in matters of religion and have traced some of the influences of his religious upon his ethical and political thought. This has entailed reference to several theological doctrines, and a fuller account of some others, notably the doctrine of Christian liberty, with recourse to the *De Doctrina Christiana*, Milton's formal presentation of the positions he had reached by about 1660. It is time now to take a general view of this work and to examine more closely certain issues which recur in the major poems

I

Of the origin and growth of the *De Doctrina*, which was destined to remain unpublished till 1825, Milton has given some account. Early convinced that eternal salvation was opened only to the individual faith of the believer, he set about determining the grounds of his own faith: first, by a study of the scriptures in the original tongues; next, by setting down under the appropriate heads, in the manner of the shorter systems of divinity, the relevant texts; at length, by examining, always with the closest reference to scriptures, the arguments and counter-arguments of more copious works in theology, in which he was shocked to discover positions defended more in deference 'to custom and the spirit of party than from the authority of Scripture,' and often by resort to sophistry and 'the quibbles of the grammarians' (*De Doctrina*, 1: preface [Col. 14:7]) .[1] Thus the *De Doctrina* must have grown, with the final result of severely modifying and even reversing a number of the reputedly orthodox positions originally set down. There is reason to believe that a good deal of time was devoted to the treatise after 1655, that by 1659 it had reached its present form and substantially its present content, and that Milton was contemplating its immediate publication when overtaken by the Restoration. Such additions to the manuscript as can be proved to have been subsequent to this date are supplementary, consisting mainly of further proof texts and introduce no radical change of view. Furthermore, the doctrines assumed or advanced in *Paradise Lost* and *Paradise Regained* are entirely consonant with those reached in the *De Doctrina*.[2]

The striking difference in tone and effect between the treatise and the poems is not hard to explain. It depends, in the first instance, on a difference in purpose and form, and a consequent difference in emphasis. The *De Doctrina* is a work of systematic theology, whose appeal is to scripture and reason, and whose formulations exclude all reference to human, even to specifically religious, experience and feeling. It is, moreover, at certain points highly argumentative, not to say polemical, concerned not merely with reaching and establishing Milton's conclusions, but with exposing and demolishing the arguments brought in support of reputedly orthodox positions which he is unable to accept. This inevitably adds to the effect of remoteness and schematism, shared by many more orthodox bodies of divinity, an effect of negation almost inseparable from the rejection of recognized and long-established dogmas. The poems, on the other hand, are positive, not negative, in their effect. They contain no denials, but embody the residuum of firmly grounded beliefs after all necessary rejections are made. They do not argue: they affirm or, more commonly, assume or imply these beliefs. And neither the doctrine accepted nor the expression given to it is abstracted from human and religious experience. What the poems have to say comes to us with all the added body and power which experience can confer when its perception and expression operate in the context and through the medium of poetry.

We have said that the doctrines advanced or assumed in the poems are entirely consonant with the positions reached in the *De Doctrina*; but this does not preclude the possibility that the poems may round out and develop these positions. In certain cases, as we shall see, they clearly do so; and in considering Milton's theology it is not only permissible but necessary to draw upon the poems as well as the treatise. But one should commence with a clear impression of the scope, order, method, and tenor of the *De Doctrina*.

In scope it does not differ essentially from other Protestant works which attempt a systematic account of the essentials of Christianity, such as Archbishop Ussher's popular *Body of Divinity*, or *The Abridgment of Christian Divinity* written by Wollebius (and translated by Alexander Ross) whose topics bear a marked similarity to Milton's. The order of exposition differs from work to work; but again the similarity of Milton's to that of Wollebius (with two books, one assigned to faith or knowledge, the other to worship or works, and in the first book many chapters with common titles) is as marked as to suggest that the *Abridgment* may have furnished Milton with his starting point. A principal difference in method is that Milton is much more copious in his references to the Bible than even Ussher or Wollebius, having chosen, as he says, to fill his pages with citations 'even to redundance' (*De Doctrina*, 1: preface [Col. 14: 11]). As to the tenor, Milton's treatise differs from the more othodox bodies of divinity by introducing a number of heretical positions, and the effort to establish these leads him into the argumentative attacks on received dogmas and the note of negation, already remarked, which (though Milton, as we shall find, is no Socinian) produce a surface similarity to the Racovian Catechism or the works of John Bidle. Indeed, as one compares chapter by chapter the opinions of Milton with those of Wollebius, one is impressed by the wide divergence from his starting point in orthodoxy.

The two books of the *De Doctrina* are then devoted respectively to 'Faith, or the knowledge of God,' and 'Love, or the worship of God (1: preface [Col. 14: 23]), though Milton recognizes that, while distinct in nature, they are inseparable in practice, since 'obedience and love are always the best guides to knowledge.' Significantly, he defines faith as knowledge (it denotes not 'the habit of believing, but the things to be habitually believed') and worship as conduct ('The true worship of God consists chiefly in the exercise of good works') (2: 1 [Col. 17: 3]). Book 2 becomes in effect Milton's manual of Christian ethics. Our attention now, however, will be concentrated on Book 1, but first we must glance at the Dedication to 'all the churches of Christ, and ... all who profess the Christian Faith.'

In the Dedication, together with a running account of the origin and growth of the work and his motives in preparing it for publication, Milton annunciates three principles: that 'in common with the whole Protestant Church' (1: preface [Col. 14: 15]) he recognizes scripture alone as the source and test of doctrine (the principle which he had professed since the early ecclesiastical pamphlets); that liberty of discussion is essential to the winnowing of truth from error and to the enjoyment of Christian liberty, that it conforms to the scriptural injunction 'to prove all things' (1: preface [Col. 14: 9]), and contributes far less to the disturbance of the church than to its enlightenment (the principle basic to the *Areopagitica*) and that as the Apostles condemned for heresy nothing save what was at variance with the teaching of Christ orally delivered, so 'by parity of reasoning, ... since the compilation of the New Testament ... nothing but what is in contradiction to it can properly be called heresy' (1: preface [Col. 14: 14–15]), (the principle set forth in *Of Civil Power in Ecclesiastical Causes*). By reaffirming these principles the Dedication lays the foundation for all that follows, and by its heavy emphasis on scripture as the source and test of doctrine it allows Milton to postpone to a later chapter the formal discussion of scripture with which, following the precedent of some other Protestant bodies of divinity, he might have been expected to start.

Instead, Book 1 commences with the definition of Christian doctrine and its parts, faith and worship, and proceeds immediately to the doctrine of God (chapters 2 and following). Here Milton invokes those principles of natural religion which revelation itself assumes and on which all systems of Christian theology rely. The Deity, he says, (1: 2 [Col. 14: 25–7]

> has imprinted upon the human mind so many unquestionable tokens of himself, and so many traces of him are apparent throughout the whole of nature, that no one ... can remain ignorant of the truth ... everything in the world, by the beauty of its order, and the evidence of a determinate and beneficial purpose which pervades it, testifies that some supreme efficient Power must have pre-existed, by which the whole was ordained for a specific end. There are some who pretend that nature or fate is this supreme Power. But the very name of *nature* implies that it must owe its birth to some prior agent ... [for it] means either the essence of a thing, or that general law ... under which everything acts; [and] ... *fate* can be nothing but a divine decree emanating from some almighty power. Further, those who attribute the creation of everything to nature, must necessarily associate chance with nature ...; so that they gain nothing by this theory except that ... they are obliged ... to substitute two sovereign rulers of affairs, who must almost always be in opposition to each other.

This is the position reaffirmed in *Paradise Lost* when the Almighty says, (7.172–3)

> Necessitie and Chance
> Approach not mee, and what I will is Fate.

Milton further appeals to the universal recognition that some power, whether good or evil, 'presided over the affairs of the world,' with the comment: 'that evil should prevail over good, and be the true supreme power, is as unmeet as it is incredible. Hence it follows ... that God exists.' And, finally, 'the existence of God ... is proved by that feeling, whether we term it conscience, or right reason, which even in the worst of characters is not altogether extinguished' (1: 2 [Col. 14: 29]).

Turning then from natural religion to revealed, he continues, 'The whole tenor of Scripture proves the same thing ... Heb. 11.6: "he that cometh to God, must believe that he is" ... No one, however, can have right thoughts of God, with nature or reason alone as his guide, independent of the word, or message of God' (1 : 2 [Col. 14: 29–31]). The right thoughts which scripture enjoins are accommodated to our finite nature, for 'to know God as he really is, far transcends the powers of man's thoughts, much more of his perception' (1 : 2 [Col. 14: 31]). But in conceiving and speaking of God we cannot be wrong in following the delineation of him which he himself has vouchsafed. Thus, under the notion of accommodation, Milton finds no difficulty in accepting the anthropomorphic language of the Old Testament – a fact with important bearings on his own practice, especially in *Paradise Lost*; and the notion further serves him in developing concurrently two conceptions of the Deity, which evidently exist in his thinking, the one personal, the other metaphysical.

'It is impossible,' he says, 'to comprehend accurately under any form of definition the "divine nature" ... But though the nature of God cannot be defined, ... some description of it ... may be collected from his names and attributes' (1 : 2 [Col. 14: 39]). The names carry us little further than the basic truth of God's existence, signifying 'He who is' or 'I am that I am.' Of the attributes which Milton lists, nine describe God's 'inherent nature' ('partly in an affirmative, partly in a negative sense, inasmuch as they deny the existence of those imperfections ... which belong to created things') (1 : 2 [Col. 14: 53–5]). Thus, it can be asserted: that God is *truth*; that 'considered in his most simple nature' he is a *spirit*; and that he is further marked by *immensity* and *infinity* (significantly, treated by Milton as a single attribute), by *eternity* (having neither beginning nor end), by *immutability* and *incorruptibility* (both derived from his eternity), by *omnipresence* ('the consequence of his infinity'), by *omnipotence* (with the reservation 'that the power of God is not exerted in things which imply a contradiction'), and, finally, by *unity* (which 'may be considered as proceeding necessarily from all the foregoing attributes,' but finds also abundant separate proof in scripture). Six other attributes serve to show God's 'divine power and excellence under the ideas of Vitality, Intelligence, and Will': that he is 'the *living* God'; that he is *omniscient* (knowing even 'the thoughts and actions of free agents as yet unborn'), and, that, as regards his will, he is infinitely (*summe*) *pure and holy, most gracious, faithful and true*, and *just*. Four additional attributes may be gathered from Milton's summing up. 'From all these attributes springs that infinite excellence (*illa summa excellentia*) which constitutes the true *perfection* of God, and causes him to abound in *glory*, and to be most deservedly and justly the *supreme Lord of all things* ... It follows, finally, that God must be styled by us *wonderful and incomprehensible*.'

Though the lists of the divine attributes differ somewhat from theologian to theologian there is no attribute in Milton's that cannot be paralleled in others, and none to which the most orthodox could demur; but some of them are to be utilized in developing positions at radical variance with orthodoxy, and in two or three instances Milton's phrasing or his specific comments foreshadow the fact. The most obvious example is the frankly anti-trinitarian inference in his exposition of the divine unity, which is attributed to the Father alone. It will later appear that the emphasis on incomprehensibility as the culminating attribute bears strongly on Milton's notion of the function of the Son. Not less important, in preparation this time for his doctrine of free will, is the reference to 'free agents' introduced in the brief exposition of God's omniscience. The coupling of infinity with immensity as a single attribute serves to interpret infinity in spatial terms, while the avoidance of the word infinite as a qualitative term seems consciously to limit it to this sense, which will be found to be of pivotal importance in Milton's heterodox cosmology.

It was necessary thus to present the bases of Milton's theology. The scope of the remaining chapters may be very briefly indicated, before discussing more critically, and with reference to the later poems as well as to the treatise, the issues of special interest. Among these are Milton's Arminianism, which involves the next two chapters (3 and 4) on the divine decrees and predestination; what has been taken to be his Arian view of the Trinity, developed in the chapters (5 and 6) on the Son and the Holy Spirit; and his so-called materialism, which is expounded in the chapter (7) devoted to God's external efficiency in the creation. The next chapter (8) considers his providence or external efficiency in the government of the created world. It thus serves in some sort as an introduction to the remaining chapters, which are devoted to the working out of the divine decrees, and especially to the government of man and the scheme of salvation. Here, also, Milton makes his first attack on the redoutable problem of evil. Having rejected (as we shall find that he has done in chapter 7) the Augustinian explanation in terms of creation *ex nihilo*, he is bereft of an inclusive formula and can only refer evil to free will in the creature accompanied either by God's permissive will or by his efficient will to punish evil with evil, the whole process and its outcome being controlled, however, by his providence which from evil itself brings forth good. The bearing of these principles on *Paradise Lost*, and its avowed purpose of asserting eternal providence and declaring the justice of God's ways to men, is sufficiently evident. And the remark that, when God hardens the heart of sinners, it is not 'by infusing an evil disposition, but ... by employing such just and kind methods as ought rather to soften the hearts ... than harden them' (1: 8 [Col. 15: 81]), finds its echo in Satan's admissions in the fourth book, while 'a good temptation ... whereby God tempts even the righteous for the purpose of proving them ... [and] of exercising or manifesting their faith or patience' finds its supreme example in the Christ of *Paradise Regained*.

The chapter (9) on the special government of angels, reflecting the paucity of reference in scripture, yields little that is of use to the poet of *Paradise Lost*, or to the reader; indeed it brings home to us the degree to which Milton must there rely on his imagination. We learn merely: that 'Angels are either good or evil ... for it appears that many revolted from God of their own accord before the fall of man' (1: 9 [Col. 15: 91]), and that good and evil alike are grouped in hierarchical order, each under their prince – the good under Michael (whose name does not here stand, as is often asserted, for Christ, though he is indeed in a higher sense their head), the evil under one of various appelations, Beelzebub, Satan, etc. The only other point of interest bears rather on Milton's general view of free will and responsibility than on the poem; namely, his rejection of the opinion 'that the good angels are now upheld, not so much by their own strength, as by the grace of God' because 'it seems more agreeable to reason to suppose' that they, who are not comprehended in the scheme of redemption, 'are upheld by their own strength no less than man himself was before his fall.'

Though the three following chapters (10–12) deal with God's special government of man in the state of innocence, the fall, and the punishment of sin, and thus cover what is to be the main action of *Paradise Lost*, they throw relatively little light on its doctrinal basis, which must, in any case, be reserved for further discussion. For the rest, the chapters provide long digressions on the institution of the sabbath (interesting chiefly as an example of Milton's mode of interpreting scripture, and to be referred to in that connection below), on marriage and its dissolution (which summarizes the position taken in the divorce tracts), and on polygamy as not forbidden in scripture; they distinguish between actual and original sin, interpreting the latter as the propensity to evil derived from our first parents and hence pertaining to our generation or origin, but finding the term insufficiently inclusive since this propensity to evil was shared by Adam and Eve after their fall; and they explain the punishment of sin as subjection to 'death' of various kinds and degrees. This last leads to a chapter (13) devoted to the death of the body, which sets forth the doctrine of mortalism, that is, the death of the soul with the body, a necessary outcome, as we shall see, of Milton's monism, which does not for him, however, imply any doubt of immortal life after the resurrection.

The next three chapters (14–16) expound Christ's role in the scheme of salvation, dealing with Christ as Redeemer, his office of mediator, and his ministry (that is, the process) of redemption. Two facts are clear: first, that Milton's view of the redemption follows the pattern of Protestant orthodoxy, but, second, that it is coloured at point after point by his peculiar conception of the nature of the Son. It is thus unprofitable to enter fully upon the subject until we can bring it into relation with this prior question. But we may note, by way of anticipation: that the chapters put beyond all doubt Milton's full acceptance of the Incarnation as miraculous, indeed as a mystery and to be received by faith; that he eschews any approach to monophysitism, insisting on a hypostatic union of two natures, divine and human, in the person of the incarnate Christ; and that he unreservedly affirms the doctrine of the atonement in its most literal sense. The 'effect of Christ's satisfaction is sufficient to produce the reconciliation of God the Father with man' (1: 16 [Col. 15: 333]).

Attention now turns (chapters 17–26) to the scheme of salvation as it relates to mankind and as it achieves its end in the conversion and perseverance of the believer. In him it effects the 'renovation of man,' whereby he is 'brought into a state of grace' (1: 17 [Col. 15: 343]). The first step is man's calling to repentance and faith, which may be general and natural (as to mankind at large) or special and supernatural (as is witnessed by many examples in the New Testament and the Old). Always it is accompanied by a restoration of free will sufficient for man's intial response, but, in the nature of the case, precluding any necessity of response. 'For the power of volition cannot be wrought in us without the power of free agency ... , since it is in this power that the will itself consists' (1: 17 [Col. 15: 357]). So far the process may be described as natural; and whether the call is responded to or not will depend on the exercise of the faculty thus sufficiently restored.

In the event of genuine response, however, grace, or supernatural renovation, becomes operative. (1: 18 [Col. 15: 367]

> The intent of supernatural renovation is not only to restore man more completely ... to the use of his natural faculties, as regards his power to form right judgment, and to exercise free will; but to create afresh, as it were, the inward man, and infuse from above new and supernatural faculties in the minds of the renovated. This is called *regeneration*, and the regenerate are said to be *planted in Christ*.

'The effects of regeneration are *repentance* and *faith*' (1: 19 [Col. 15: 379]), which are to be distinguished from the natural repentance and trust which accompany any response to God's call, however transient or abortive. But, indeed, relapse is possible, if increasingly unlikely, at every later stage, since free will is still an essential element and human frailty is not wholly eliminated. And this assertion is reiterated in the definition (chapter 25) of *final perseverance*. It is 'the gift of God's preserving power, whereby they who are ... born again, and sealed by the Holy Spirit, persevere to the end in the faith and grace of God and never entirely fall away ... , *so long as nothing is wanting on their own parts, and they continue to the utmost in the maintenance of faith and love*' (1 : 25 [Col. 16: 75–7]).

Under the same condition of human responsibility (which may be general, and synonymous with conversion, or particular), *repentance* in the regenerate is the gift of God. And so likewise is *saving faith,* which, though it no doubt depends on a degree of knowledge and is the way to perfect knowledge, has, 'properly speaking, [its] seat in the will' (1 : 20 [Col. 15: 407]). The object of saving faith, Milton insists, 'is not Christ the Mediator, but God the Father' (1 : 20 [Col. 15: 403]), whence it comes that many to whom Christ was unknown 'should be saved by faith in God alone; but still through the sole merits of Christ ... given and slain from the beginning of the world ...'

Every stage reached by the believer is progressive, bringing a greater degree of illumination and freedom. Thus, after true repentance and saving faith, he may be said to be ingrafted or planted in Christ by the Father, the effects of which are 'newness of life and increase,' with 'the understanding restored in great part to its primitive clearness, and the will to its primitive liberty, by the new spiritual life in Christ' (1 : 21 [Col. 16: 5]), and with such a sense of God's love as evokes in return that special love or charity (a theological virtue coupled with faith and hope) which enables him to 'bring forth good works spontaneously and *freely,*' for, as Milton never tires of reminding us, here also 'our own cooperation is uniformly required' (1 : 21 [Col. 16: 9]).

The emphasis on the responsibility of the believer is, as we have already seen, characteristic of Milton. What will strike many readers as less characteristic is the emphasis on love in addition to faith. Yet this, too, is a recurrent, if more intermittent, note, from the *Nativity*'s grounding of dedication and inspiration in love, through the recognition that love and obedience are the best guides to knowledge and faith, on to the emphasis on Christ's love for man, and the poet's moving response thereto in the third book of *Paradise Lost*. Highly characteristic also, because it combines these two motifs of responsibility and love, and joins them to Christian liberty, is Milton's solution of the problem of *justification* (1 : 22 [Col. 16: 37]). That the believer is justified by faith alone is confuted by James 2:24: 'By works a man is justified, and not by faith only.' That he is justified by the works of the law is equally confuted by Romans 3:28: 'A man is justified by faith without the works of the Law.' He is justified then by faith, which, if it is true faith, will do the works, not of the law, but of faith, for true 'faith ... worketh by love' (Gal. 5:6); and such works are not only compatible with, they are, as Milton will explain, the very expression of, Christian liberty.

After *justification* comes *adoption*, 'whereby God adopts as his children those who are justified by faith. In one sense we are by nature sons of God, as well as the angels, inasmuch as he is the author of our being; ... But the sense here intended is that of adopted children ...' (1: 23 [Col. 16: 51]). By adoption the work of renovation is completed: 'we become sons of God ... by the assumption, as it were, of a new nature,' and enjoy the liberty befitting that state, a liberty 'not unknown to the posterity of Abraham, in virtue of their title as children of God, ... even under the law of bondage,' but 'unfolded by the gospel' in a 'clearer and more perfect light.'

'Hitherto,' says Milton, 'the increase of the regenerate has been considered in its relation to the Father alone,' though it is by virtue always of the merits of Christ. Now we are to learn of *union and fellowship with Christ,* and through this, on the one hand, 'union ... with the Father' and, on the other, that fellowship called, in the Apostles' Creed, the communion of saints, of those, that is, who constitute 'the Invisible Church whereof Christ is the head' (1: 24 [Col. 16: 57–61]). And if, by faith, we share at once in his merits and his humiliation, we shall also share in his *glorification,* imperfectly here below, perfectly hereafter, provided only we attain to *final perseverance,* which is, as we have seen, the gift of God, but still requiring our active co-operation.

The next three chapters (26–28) deal with the *covenant of grace.* In covenant theology, God is thought of as entering into a covenant with man to bless him if man for his part fulfils the obligations laid down. Two covenants are recognized: the first was a covenant of works made first with Adam, who was to obey the law of nature written in his heart and mind and also the positive command respecting abstention from the Tree of Knowledge (with, as was sometimes added, the special commands respecting marriage and the sabbath). With the fall the covenant was broken by man and its promised rewards were forfeited. This was the immediate occasion of the second covenant, given by God in his mercy, and called the covenant of grace, whereby through faith in the merits of Christ the Redeemer, mankind, or the elect among them, might yet be saved. But while the covenant of grace was operative from the time of Adam's repentance, man remained also under the covenant of works till the coming of Christ, and the terms of the covenant of works were actually written out in manifold detail in the Mosaic law, since among the deprivations attendant on the fall had been the law of nature by which man would otherwise have lived. But in his fallen state the covenant of works and its law were impossible of fulfilment by him; and a principal purpose of the Mosaic law was to convince him of the need of a Redeemer, while it also served to reveal obscurely in prophetic types the process of redemption and the perfection attainable only in the spiritual order of Christ's kingdom.

Milton's whole emphasis falls on the covenant of grace. The terms on which Adam stood in the state of innocence, he has already said (chapter 10), are (1: 10 [Col. 15: 113–15])

> sometimes called 'the Covenant of Works,' though it does not appear from any passage of Scripture to have been either a covenant, or of works. No works whatever were required of Adam; a particular act only was forbidden ... For since it was the disposition of man to do what was right, as being naturally good and holy, it was not necessary that he should be bound by the obligation of a covenant to perform that to which he was of himself inclined.

It is true that Milton speaks of the Mosaic law as implying or being a covenant of works: 'On the introduction of the gospel, or new covenant through faith in Christ, the whole of the preceding covenant, in other words, the entire Mosaic law, was abolished (1: 27 [Col. 16: 125]). 'Even under the law,' he insists, 'the existence of a Redeemer and the necessity of redemption are perceptible, though obscurely ... Under the gospel both the Redeemer and the truth of his redemption are more explicitly understood' (1: 26 [Col. 16: 99–101]). This then is the covenant of grace, now fully revealed, though in existence since God's promise to Adam after the fall; and in the privileges of the new covenant, as we have seen, Abraham and his posterity share, being made children of God, though under the law of bondage. 'The manifestation of this gratuitous covenant under the law was partly anterior to, partly coincident with Moses. Even before Moses the law was in part delivered, though not in a written form' (1: 26 [Col. 16: 103]. And when written, it had the double function generally allowed: of shadowing forth by prophetic types Christ and his ministry of redemption; and, by the impossibility of fulfilling the law or meeting the obligations of the covenant of works, of pointing to the necessity of a Redeemer and the covenant of grace. But, though Milton does not say so, this impossibility would seem to preclude it from being regarded as a covenant at all and to make it solely an instrument of the covenant of grace; hence Milton's virtual disregard of the law as a covenant of works, his treatment of it under the heading, 'Of the Manifestation of the Covenant of Grace, including the Law of God' (chapter 26), and his restriction of the Mosaic law to the children of Israel, the instrumental function being performed for the rest of mankind by the secondary law of nature, that remnant of the primary law of nature which survived the fall, and of which the Mosaic law was in part a more detailed formulation. Besides its instrumental functions, then, what Milton chooses to emphasize in the Mosaic law is chiefly its limitations: its manifold prescriptions, the curse attached to the inevitable failure in obeying it fully in every particular, the danger, almost the requirement, of reading it in the letter: all summed up in the description, 'the weak and servile rudiments of this elementary institution' (1 : 26 [Col. 16: 105]).

Contrasted with the law is the gospel: (1 : 27 [Col. 16: 113])

> The gospel is the new dispensation of the Covenant of Grace, far more excellent and perfect than the Law, announced first obscurely by Moses and the prophets, afterwards in the clearest terms by Christ himself, and his Apostles and Evangelists, written since by the Holy Spirit in the hearts of believers, ... containing a promise of eternal life to all in every nation who shall believe in Christ when revealed to them ...

That the gospel abrogates the law in some degree is asserted by all theologians – that it abrogates the ceremonial law, which is merely a prophetic type of Christ and his church, and the judicial law as it is peculiar to the commonwealth of Israel. But Milton, as we have seen, goes much further and asserts that the gospel abrogates the entire Mosaic law, that is, the moral as well as ceremonial and judicial. 'From the abrogation ... of the law of servitude, results Christian Liberty' (1 : 27 [Col. 16: 153]). For 'constraint and bondage [are] as inseparable from the dispensation of the law, as liberty from the dispensation of the gospel' (1 : 27 [Col. 16: 149–51]) : (1 : 27 [Col. 16: 153–5])

> Christian Liberty is that whereby we are loosed as it were by enfranchisement, through Christ our deliverer, from the bondage of sin, and consequently from the rule of the law ... , to the intent that being made sons instead of servants, and perfect men instead of children, we may serve God in love through the guidance of the Spirit of Truth.

In asserting the abrogation of the whole Mosaic law, Milton is not alone. He cites the theologian John Cameron, and might have found a more illustrious precedent in Luther and a less respectable one in the sectaries of sixteenth-century Europe and seventeenth-century England, those Antinomians against whom Thomas Edwards inveighs as preaching 'that the Moral Law is of no use at all to believers, that 'tis no rule for believers to walk by nor to examine their lives by, and that Christians are free from the mandatory power of the Law,' and again 'that the scriptures of the Old Testament do not concern or bind Christians now under the New Testament ... and hereupon some of them do not bind the Old Testament with the New nor read it.'[3] In the hands of the Reformers Christian liberty had been a potent weapon in attacking the corruptions of the Mediaeval church; nor did the Puritans disdain its use in their attacks on episcopacy. But for the more conservative among them Christian liberty meant no more than liberty in the use of things indifferent, and certainly did not connote the abrogation of the entire Mosaic law or much impair the authority of Israel as a model. Sensible of its possible abuses, Calvin and after him the framers of the Westminster Confession of Faith devote most of their attention to safeguarding against them and to explaining what Christian liberty is not. Luther had taken another line: he had asserted the abrogation of the entire Mosaic law, and had not confined Christian liberty to things indifferent, but had insisted that this liberty was wholly inward and spiritual and countenanced neither political revolt nor deviation in moral conduct from the Decalogue, which still furnished the rule by which the Christian must shape and test his action. And Milton's safegard, while it certainly does not limit Christian liberty to things indifferent, much less connote merely a spiritual state without implications for outward action, still forestalls the Antinomian inference.

It does so by applying the distinctions he has already drawn between the written and unwritten law of God and between the works of the written law and those of faith. 'The unwritten law,' he has said, 'is no other than that [primary] law of nature given originally to Adam, of which a certain remnant, or imperfect illumination, still dwells in the hearts of all mankind; which, in the regenerate, under the influence of the Holy Spirit, is daily tending towards a renewal of its primitive brightness' (1: 26 [Col. 16: 101]). It is in conformity with this restored inward law that the works of faith are executed. (1: 27 [Col. 16: 143])

> Therefore ... the end for which the law was instituted, namely, the love of God and our neighbour, is by no means to be considered as abolished; it is the table of the law, so to speak, that is alone changed, its injunctions being now written by the Spirit in the hearts of believers with this difference, that in certain precepts the Spirit appears to be at variance with the letter, namely, wherever by departing from the letter we can more effectually consult the love of God and our neighbour. Thus Christ departed from the letter of the law: Mark 2.27, 'the sabbath was made for man, and not man for the sabbath,' if we compare his words with the fourth commandment.

As is to be expected, Milton differentiates sharply between the nature and operation of the covenant of grace and its 'external Sealing' in the sacraments, since he defines a sacrament not as a means of grace, but simply as ' a visible sign ordained by God, whereby he sets a seal on believers in token of his saving grace, or the satisfaction of Christ; and whereby we on our part testify our faith and obedience to God with a sincere heart and a

grateful remembrance' (1: 28 [Col. 16: 165]). Under the law two cere-
monies met this definition: circumcision and the Passover; under the gospel,
two: Baptism, which signifies the regeneration of believers 'by the Holy
Spirit, and their union with Christ in his death, burial and resurrection,'
and which, as it constitutes on the part of the believer a declaration of faith,
can be administered, as it was according to scripture, only to adults; and
the Supper of the Lord, 'in which the death of Christ is commemorated ...
and the benefits of his death ... sealed to believers.' The remaining sacraments, so-called, he rejects because they are not of divine institution, 'neither
do they possess any sign appointed by God for the sealing of the covenant of
grace' (1: 28 [Col. 16: 215]). Confirmation or the laying on of hands, while
not a sacrament, may be retained 'with great propriety and advantage as a
symbol of blessing.' Penance and Orders are unexceptionable if taken merely
as 'religious symbols.' 'Marriage, inasmuch as it is not an institution peculiar
to Christian nations, ... is not even a religious ceremony, still less a sacrament, but a compact purely civil ... '

The group of chapters which follows deals with the church (29, 31, 32)
and scripture (30). The latter subject is so central to Milton's position, and
to his purpose and method in the *De Doctrina*, that it must be reserved for
discussion with his mode of interpreting scripture below.

Accepting the impossibility of making the visible church correspond in
its membership to the invisible, yet determined, like his fellow Puritans, to
make it conform as closely as is humanly possible, he defines the *visible
church* as 'the assembly of ... those indiscriminately who have received the
call [of God], whether actually regenerate or otherwise' (1: 29 [Col. 16:
219]), and its notes as, 'pure doctrine; the proper external worship of God;
genuine evangelical love, so far as it can be distinguished from the fictitious
by mere human perception; and a right administration of the seals of the
Covenant' (1: 29 [Col. 16: 221]), adding that, since Christ is the head of
the invisible church, none other can be the head of the visible. On the subject of particular churches and of church discipline, we have already noticed
Milton's steady move towards the position of the Separatists: (1: 31 [Col.
16: 285, 307, 311])

A *particular church* is a society of persons professing the faith, united
in a special bond of brotherhood, and so ordered as may best promote
the ends of edification and mutual communion of saints ... Every [such]
church ... , however small its numbers, is to be considered as in itself an
integral and perfect church, so far as regards its religious rights; nor
has it any superior on earth, whether individual, or assembly, or convention, to which it can be lawfully required to render submission ...

> Particular churches, however, may communicate with each other in
> a spirit of brotherhood and agreement, and cooperate for purposes
> connected with the general welfare.

The bond of discipline is maintained by 'a mutual agreement among the
members of the church to fashion their lives according to Christian doctrine, and to regulate everything in their public meetings decently and with
order' (1: 32 [Col. 16: 321]); and this is best ensured by a covenant entered
into at 'the formation or re-establishment of a particular church,' a covenant to be adhered to by new members at their baptism or on admission
from another congregation. The administration of discipline, including the
power to admonish and to impose ecclesiastical punishments, and known
generally as 'the power of the keys,' is confined to no ministerial order, but
belongs to the people, that is, to the congregation as a whole; and so with
the other offices, of worship, of testifying and instructing, they too may be
shared by the membership at large. There is the sharpest distinction between
civil and ecclesiastical power: the civil extending to all men, in matters
properly civil, and thus to the body and external faculties only with enforce-
ment by physical punishment; the ecclesiastical to members of the church,
and in religious matters only, which depending on the faculties of the mind
lie beyond the reach of physical punishment, and corrigible by spiritual
censures alone.

In the final chapter (33) Milton resumes the theme of glorification
(25), now made perfect, after Christ's second coming, 'with the saints [to]
judge the evil angels and all mankind' (1: 33 [Col. 16: 355]). This entails
the resurrection of the dead, believed in even before the gospel, confirmed
by Christ's testimony and by his own resurrection, and necessary to the justice and providence of God, since without it 'the righteous would be of all
men most miserable, and the wicked, who have a better portion in this life,
most happy ... ' (1: 33 [Col. 16: 351]). 'The rule of judgment will be the
conscience of each individual, according to the measure of light which he
has enjoyed' (1: 33 [Col. 16: 357]). But the judgment does not denote the
passing of sentence alone, but the exercise of dominion as in the rule of the
Judges. Here Milton decisively adopts the general pattern of Millenarian
thought. 'Coincident ... with the time of the last judgement ... will take
place that glorious reign of Christ on earth with his saints, so often promised
in Scripture ... ' (1: 33 [Col. 16: 359]). 'After the expiration of the thousand
years Satan will rage again, and assail the church ... , but will be overthrown
... and condemned to everlasting punishment' (1: 33 [Col. 16: 363]). The
'punishment of the wicked' in hell, the same place prepared for the rebel
angels and 'situated beyond the limits of the universe,' will be accompanied
by 'the perfect glorification of the righteous'; whereupon Christ will deliver

up 'the kingdom to God, even the Father ... And when all things shall be subdued unto him that put all things under him, that God may be all in all' (1 Cor. 15:24, 28). The 'present unclean and polluted world' shall be destroyed by fire – whether in its substance or 'merely by a change in the nature of its constituent parts, is uncertain, and of no importance to determine' – and shall give place to a new heaven and a new earth. 'Perfect glorification consists in eternal life and perfect happiness, arising chiefly from the divine vision [though] ... all the saints will not attain to an equal state of glory' (1: 33 [Col. 16: 375, 379]). It 'will be accompanied by the renovation of heaven and earth, and of all things therein adapted to our service or delight, to be possessed by us in perpetuity.'

This outline of the first book of the *De Doctrina* should have guarded the reader against the danger of seeing Milton's heresies out of their context in a scheme that is essentially Christian, Puritan, and scriptural; but it has, of course, been unable to illustrate Milton's constant reference to the Bible and his mode of handling its text, or in other words his reliance at once on scripture and reason. To that subject we must now briefly turn.

II

In the Dedication, as we have seen, and again in the chapter (30) 'Of the Holy Scriptures,' Milton asserts in its most extreme form the Protestant principle that the Bible, and not the church, is the sole source and test of doctrine, and rejects the whole structure of metaphysical theology, though we shall find him willing in certain circumstances to appeal to reason, and even to metaphysics, himself. In explaining the character of his doctrine the re-emphasis of the church is scarcely less important than the exaltation of scripture, for it eliminates altogether the idea of any development of doctrine from the elements in scripture by the authority of the church. This can have momentous consequences when (as, for example, in the Nicene doctrine of the Trinity) only a basis, and not the fully articulated doctrine, is found in scripture and the explicit formulation is the work of the church during the first four centuries. Milton is not, of course, alone in driving the Protestant principle to an extreme. The Reformers of the sixteenth century, who had appealed to the Bible against an unreformed church, were alarmed when others, on the same principle of the sufficiency of scripture, attacked dogmas which they regarded as among the essentials of Christianity, and notably the Nicene doctrine of the Trinity, and in Milton's day the experience was repeated with the spread of Socinianism.

It is true that many of the Puritans countenanced, and even insisted upon, a progressive revelation of divine truth, or, as they conceived it, a progressive comprehension of the truth revealed once and for all in the Bible. Not only was the development tied closely to the text of scripture, but the recipient of illumination was the individual believer, not the church; or, in Milton's phrasing: 'The rule and canon of faith ... is scripture alone. Scripture is the sole judge of controversies; or rather, every man is to decide for himself through its aid, under the guidance of the Spirit of God' (1: 30 [Col. 16: 267–9]). And 'it is evident that, since the ascension of Christ, the "pillar and ground of the truth" has not uniformly been the church, but the hearts of believers ... ' (1: 30 [Col. 16: 279]).

The promptings of the Spirit therein are indeed superior not only to the pronouncements of the church, but even to the words of scripture itself, though Milton is confident that they will be in perfect harmony with scripture if scripture is properly understood, since both are the work of God, and the believer is, like the original writer, guided and inspired. Behind his assertion of the primacy of the Spirit lies a long controversy within the ranks of Puritanism, springing from the rival claims of scriptural and experiential religion, that is, of two cardinal doctrines of the Protestant Reformation, the unconditional authority of the Bible and the possession of the gift of the Spirit by every true believer. Scripture, the more conservative insisted, was the test of spirits, whether they were from God or the devil. The Spirit, retorted the more radical, was the test, if not of scripture, at least of the interpretation put upon it. There can be no doubt that Milton takes the latter position. Its affinity with the doctrine of the inner light, associated with, but not confined to, the Quakers, is evident. But the inner light itself was susceptible of two interpretations: it might be thought of as mysterious and in effect arbitrary in its revelations, or it might be regarded as one with the rectified reason. Again, it seems certain that Milton approximates to the latter position. He writes: (1: 30 [Col. 16: 273–5])

> Under the gospel we possess, as it were, a twofold Scripture; one external, which is the written word, and the other internal, which is the Holy Spirit, written in the hearts of believers, according to the promise of God ... , as was shown above, chap. xxvii. on the gospel. ... Hence, although the extrnal ground which we possess for our belief ... in the written word is highly important, and, in most instances at least, prior in point of reception, that which is internal, and the peculiar possession of each believer, is far superior to all, namely, the Spirit itself. For the external Scripture, or written word, particularly of the New Testament ... , has been liable to frequent corruption ... But the Spirit which leads to truth cannot be corrupted, neither is it easy to deceive a man who is really spiritual.

The cross reference to Milton's treatment of the gospel is helpful, but the chapter should apparently be 26, where he distinguishes between the written and the unwritten or internal law of God. It is true that the written law is not a synonym for the external scripture, occupying only a part of the Old Testament; but the unwritten law by which, under the gospel, the believer lives would seem to be finally indistinguishable from the internal scripture, the possession of the believer under the gospel, by which likewise he must live: they are two formulations, different in content and imagery, of the same idea. And what Milton says of the unwritten law in the passage to which he refers us is significant indeed: 'The unwritten law is no other than that law of nature given originally to Adam, and of which a certain remnant or imperfect illumination, still dwells in the hearts of all mankind; which, in the regenerate, under the influence of the Holy Spirit, is daily tending towards a renewal of its primitive brightness' (1: 26 [Col. 16: 101]). But the connection of the law of nature with reason is constant and indisputable: It is by virtue of his reason that fallen man is able to apprehend the secondary law of nature, and it is by reason rectified and illuminated by grace – by 'right reason' in the Christian sense of the term – that the believer is able progressively to recover and live by the primary law of nature. If the unwritten law and the internal scripture are at bottom one, the latter is no arbitrary and individual manifestation but the pronouncement of right reason itself, progressively restored in the regenerate by the operation of the Holy Spirit. And the submission of the external scripture to the internal for interpretation constitutes the first of Milton's appeals to reason in his formulation of doctrine on a scriptural basis. What the others are will presently appear.

What, then, is Milton's view of the written scripture, the Bible, and of the proper mode of interpreting it?

His basic view of the Bible is perfectly orthodox. It consists of 'the writings of the prophets, apostles and evangelists, composed under divine inspiration' (1: 30 [Col. 16: 249]), as contained in those books commonly accepted as canonical, not on authority but by reason of their character. These 'Scriptures were not written for occasional purposes only ... but for the use of the church throughout all ages, as well under the gospel as under the law' (1: 30 [Col. 16: 251]). They contain whatever knowledge is necessary for salvation, and for the believer are 'plain and perspicuous' therein, able, as was said of Timothy, 'to make men wise unto salvation through faith'; and 'it is only to those who perish that the Scriptures are obscure ... in things necessary for salvation.' (This emphasis on the simplicity and clarity of the Bible in all that pertains to salvation is ground which Milton shares with the Anglican liberals, Chillingworth, Hales, and Jeremy Taylor.) How infatuated, therefore, are those Protestant divines who 'persist in darkening the most momentous truths of religion by intricate metaphysical comments ... , stringing together all the useless technicalities and empty distinctions of scholastic barbarism, for the purpose of elucidating those Scriptures, which they are continually extolling as models of plainness' (1: 30 [Col. 16: 261])! Yet rules of interpretation are clearly necessary, some of which Milton sets down in this chapter, while others may be collected from his comment and practice elsewhere in the *De Doctrina*. From these it is clear that, while regarding the sacred text as literally inspired, and a close knowledge of the English version, together with the gift of the Spirit, as sufficient for faith and works, he is yet prepared to employ in its elucidation all the resources of biblical criticism available in his day.

First, we must recall Milton's frank avowal of the principle of accommodation wherever the Bible speaks in human terms of God, terms safe and proper to adopt since they are of God's choosing, but not literally descriptive of him in his infinite and incomprehensible essence or activity, rather, 'accommodated' to the finite mind of man; and the degree to which this may modify his reading of the scriptural narrative is seen in his comment on the six days of creation in *Paradise Lost*: (7.176–9)

> Immediate are the Acts of God, more swift
> Than time or motion, but to human ears
> Cannot without process of speech be told,
> So told as earthly notion can receave.

Second, we must observe his emphatic recognition that the text, 'particularly of the New Testament ... has been liable to frequent corruption, and in some instances has been corrupted, through the number, and occasionally the bad faith of those by whom it has been handed down, the variety and discrepancy of the original manuscripts, and the additional diversity produced by subsequent transcripts and printed editions' (1: 30 [Col. 16: 275]). This gives point to his insistence on 'knowledge of languages' and is illustrated in his own practice (for example, in his implied rejection of 1 John 5:7, 'there are three that bear witness in heaven,' etc., because of its absence from most ancient manuscripts and its variant forms where it occurs) (1: 5 [Col. 14: 215]).

Third, in addition to knowledge of the original languages and reference to the various manuscript sources, Milton lists a number of other points. Incidents and utterances should be examined in their contexts, and with due 'consideration of cause and circumstance, of antecedents and consequents' (1: 30 [Col. 16: 265]). He has applied this method of criticism extensively in examining Christ's seeming prohibition of divorce and makes frequent use of it in the *De Doctrina*, as, for example, when arguing that while God had hallowed the sabbath to himself at the creation, its institution for the Israelites appears to date from the Mosaic law: (1: 10[Col. 15: 117])

> The most probable supposition is that Moses, who seems to have written the book of Genesis much later than the promulgation of the law, inserted this sentence from the fourth commandment, into what appeared a suitable place for it; where an opportunity was afforded for reminding the Israelites ... of the reason assigned by God, many ages after the event itself, for his command with regard to the observance of the Sabbath by the covenanted people.

Nor does such explanation contravene another of his fixed rules: 'no inferences from the text are to be admitted, but such as follow necessarily and plainly from the words themselves ... ' (1: 30 [Col. 16: 265]). One must not, however, rest content with one or two pronouncements on a subject, but must practice what Milton calls 'mutual comparison of texts,' to see how one confirms or modifies the presumed meaning of another. 'No passage of Scripture is to be interpreted in more than one sense; in the Old Testament, however, this sense is sometimes a compound of the historical and the typical.' And in all interpretations regard must be had to the analogy of faith.

Since all of these arts of interpretation require the exercise not simply of faith, but of knowledge, intelligence, and judgment, they may be thought of collectively as Milton's second appeal to reason in his formulation of doctrine on a scriptural basis.

There is a third: whenever he seeks collateral arguments in support of a position whose primary source, and for Milton its compelling authority, are in the words of scripture (as interpreted by an application of the above rules and methods), or when, in defence of what he takes to be the position thus derivable from scripture, he seeks to show the philosophical absurdity of the doctrine commonly received. Though applied to different purposes, the one of confirmation (or perhaps rather of persuasion, for Milton reiterates the sufficiency of scripture) the other of rebuttal, these appeals to reason, of which the chapter on the Son of God (5) will yield sufficient examples, are of the same kind. Here reason, whether named or not, connotes particularly, as it does in the two former kinds, the canons of logic; and the argument may approach pretty close to metaphysical reasoning, of a predominantly negative cast. It is clear, then, that Milton's protests against metaphysical theology, and his assertions of the sufficiency of scripture alone, do not preclude frequent and varied appeals to reason in support of what he takes to be scriptural doctrine and in refutation of those who go beyond it and by 'reasoning' seek to establish what is without scriptural warrant and 'in opposition to reason itself' (1: 5 [Col. 14: 213]).

On occasion, however, Milton will also attempt a line of constructive metaphysical thinking, as in the chapter on the creation (7), where, having shown, by a linguistic reference, that Genesis does not assert creation from nothing, but from some form of matter, and, by a mutual comparison of texts, that this is the constant doctrine of creation in scripture, he proceeds to inquire what creation on these terms must involve. In other words, he rounds out the scriptural doctrine by explaining the philosophical grounds and consequences of its assertion. This may be regarded as the fourth kind of appeal which Milton makes to reason.

It is clear, then, that while his theology is scriptural in basis, and drives to an extreme the Protestant tendency to exalt the authority of the Bible and minimize that of the church, it is also dependent on a high degree of confidence in human reason as such. His indeed is a form of rational theology. Confidence in reason has, of course, its limits; but only where scripture declares a mystery, as in the case of the Incarnation, or asserts a fact without explaining its mode will Milton accept the dogma on faith and abstain from further investigation. In all other instances (as in that of the Trinity, which he does not regard as an article of scriptural faith, or in that of the creation of the world by God, which he does) he will explore the subject to the limits of both scripture and reason.

There is implied throughout a sharp distinction between dogma and opinion. Where scripture makes no pronouncement, the believer is free to adopt any opinion which is consonant with reason and the analogy of faith. The question is important in view of the large imaginative elaboration of *Paradise Lost* and in lesser degree of *Paradise Regained*, but it trenches on Milton's theory of religious poetry, that is, on his aesthetics.

6

The theologian, 2:
the creation; the Son of God

Nothing is more obvious in modern Miltonic studies than the emergence of two schools, one of which is so much impressed by Milton's heresies as to lose sight of his fundamental Christianity, while the other, in not unnatural reaction, insists on the traditional character of the poet's religion and, where it cannot deny the heresies, brushes them aside as peripheral. That they are not peripheral, but central, the questions in dispute plainly indicate: the nature and place of the second and third persons of the Trinity, the problem of predestination and free will, the meaning of creation and the manner of the derivation of the cosmos from the Deity. On the other hand, Milton's positions are clearly modifications, and not denials, of the Christian scheme, and thus, at least in intention, leave his fundamental Christianity unimpaired. To adapt either of the extreme views is to falsify the end of Milton's thinking and to distort its processes. In the pages that follow I try to illustrate my contention as it bears first on his views of the creation, and secondly on his views of the Trinity.

I

Next to the essence of the Godhead and the nature and office of the Son, the subject which receives fullest and most argumentative discussion in the *De Doctrina Christiana* is creation (chapter 7), and important supplementary findings are embodied in *Paradise Lost*. Evidently Milton had thought long on this subject and regarded his views on it as more than usually important. They are in fact just as essential for an understanding of his conception of God, the cosmos, and man, or, in other words, the order of nature in its relation to God, as are his views on the Trinity for his conception of the God of revealed religion and the Christian scheme in general, or, in other words, the order of grace. It is necessary, then, to go into the question in some detail, gaining what light we may from the various traditions available to Milton, but remembering always that, while analogies may illuminate particular utterances, only his own words can point the direction of his argument or indicate what inferences he, as distinct from his critics, is prepared to draw.[1] The method here adopted does not permit us to run ahead of the evidence presented; but this much may perhaps be said. The insistent demand of Milton's religion was for the derivation of everything from God, and this was satisfied by his essentially theistic form of monism. The insistent demand of his mature ethics was for a view of man and his life which gave no foothold for mere asceticism, yet preserved a clearly marked and inviolable hierarchy of values. Such a view of man likewise demanded a monistic base, but not less imperatively required that on this base should be erected a scheme of values. Finally, the whole thing must conform to the pronouncements of scripture and submit to reason, that is, the canons of logic.

Milton's dependence on orthodox Christian doctrine illustrated

For Milton God's creation of the world was 'an article of faith' (*De Doctrina*, 1 : 7 [Col. 15: 5]); that is to say, the mode could be known only by revelation, though the fact was abundantly clear in nature and to reason. For 'everything in the world, by the beauty of its order, and the evidence of a determinate and beneficial purpose which pervades it, testifies that some supreme efficient Power must have pre-existed, by which the whole was ordained for a specific end' (1 : 2 [Col. 14: 27]).[2] The orthodoxy of his position is sufficiently attested by its agreement with Ussher's.[3]

On the question whether creation was a voluntary act or a necessary, Milton is equally orthodox. Creation was wholly voluntary: 'By his will: Ps. 135. 6: *Whatsoever Jehovah pleased, that did he in heaven and earth*' (*De Doctrina*, 1 : 7 [Col. 15: 15]). For Milton, however, as for the most orthodox, the matter is complicated by the necessitating power of God's goodness. 'We must observe,' writes John Pearson, 'that as God is essentially and infinitely good ... so is he in respect of all external actions or emanations absolutely free, without the least necessity';[4] and Milton likewise can only assert that, in creating the world, God put forth his goodness, 'which is free To act or not' (*Paradise Lost* 7.171–2). The point is of importance in differentiating Milton from a long tradition of cosmological speculation which extends from the Stoics to Spinoza, and to which in some measure he responded. For Spinoza none of the acts of God is voluntary: all are necessary, constrained indeed by no external force (for there is nothing external to the infinite God), but necessitated by the law of God's being.[5] Nothing is contingent: 'all things are conditioned to exist and operate in a particular manner by the necessity of the divine nature.'[6] There is no such thing as free will, whether in God or man: will 'cannot be called a free cause, but only a necessary cause.'[7] Accordingly, God could not have abstained from the exercise of his productive power; nor could things 'have been brought into being by God in any manner, or any order, different from that which has in fact obtained.'[8] It is easy to imagine how repugnant to Milton such determinism would be; and the final proposition he repudiates in so many words, though as an inference from Aristotle's definition of God, and not of course from Spinoza's. By it, says Milton, 'the Deity would have no choice of act, but what he did he would do of necessity, and could do in no other way, which would be inconsistent with his omnipotence and free agency' (De Doctrina, 1 : 2 [Col. 14: 49]). But the necessitating force of God's nature – that is, of his infinite goodness – remains something of a problem, as the next point in Milton's view of the creation will suggest.

In dealing with the end, or final cause, of creation. Milton is again orthodox, but with his own significant emphasis. Answering the question, To what end were all things created? Ussher writes: 'For God's glory ... How doth the glory of God appear in them? First, his eternall power ... is seen ... Secondly, his infinite wisdome is made known by them ... Thirdly, his goodnesse unto all his creatures is hereby manifested ...'[9] And Milton declares that the end was 'the manifestation of the glory of his power and goodness' (De Doctrina, 1 : 7 [Col. 15: 5]).[10] In Milton the emphasis falls at least as heavily upon God's diffusive goodness as upon his power and glory. Perhaps more heavily, for not only does he return to the idea of this diffusive goodness in his account of matter in its relation to God,[11] but in Paradise Regained he declares that God, by his Word, (3.122–6)

> all things produc'd,
> Though chiefly not for glory as prime end,
> But to shew forth his goodness and impart
> His good communicable to every soul[12]
> Freely ...

It is taken as self-evident that 'entity is good' (De Doctrina, 1 : 7 [Col. 15: 27]), an assumption common to Milton, Plato, St Augustine, and indeed Western thought in general. Existence, according to Plato, is conferred upon the creature by God's overflowing bounty.[13] Orthodoxy agrees, but stops short of regarding the created whole as existing for its own sake, and on the contrary subordinates the rest of the visible creation to man,[14] and the whole to God. And so likewise does Milton, whose subordination of the whole to God is reinforced by his view of omnipotence as including within itself every kind of cause, efficient, material, formal, and, as here, final (*De Doctrina*, 1: 7 [Col. 15: 21].[15] But Milton was not under the temptation to which Calvinism succumbed, of asserting God's free will and power at the expense of his goodness. For him the exercise of that will and power are clearly controlled by the divine nature: 'It must be remembered ... that the power of God is not exerted in things which imply a contradiction. 2 Tim. 2.13: *he cannot deny himself*' (*De Doctrina*, 1: 2 [Col. 14: 49]). Though this principle is not brought to bear by Milton directly upon the subject of the creation, it may be safely inferred that he would agree with Stillingfleet:

> We assert then so much Goodness in God, as none can be imagin'd greater; we assert that it was the communication of this Divine Goodness which gave Being to the World; but withal we acknowledg God to be an Agent infinitely wise and free, who dispenseth this Goodness of his as is best pleasing to himself, tho' ever agreeable to his Nature. As God is infinitely good in himself, so whatever he doth is suitable to this Nature of his; but the particular Determinations of God's Acts of Beneficence belong to the will of God, as he is a most free and independent Agent ...[16]

There is no tenet of orthodox belief to which Milton adheres more tenaciously than the voluntary character of the creative act.

When Milton insists that, according to scripture, God the Father is alone 'the primary and efficient cause of all things' and that the creative act was performed merely 'by the Word and Spirit, that is, by his will' (*De Doctrina*, 1: 7 [Col. 15: 5, 15–17]), we recognize that this, his first departure from orthodoxy, is primarily the result of applying to creation his doctrine respecting the Trinity (which will be explored later in this chapter). It is interesting to observe, however, what suggestion and partial support for his view he could get from orthodox theologians. Commencing with the unequivocal assertion of the Apostles' Creed, John Pearson invokes 'the paternal priority of the Deity,' and cites various passages of scripture, including 1 Cor. 8:6, *To us there is but one God the Father, of whom are all things ... , and one Lord Jesus Christ, by whom are all things,* which 'speaketh some kind of priority in action according to that of the Person,' and in this sense 'the Church did always profess to believe in God the Father, Creatour of Heaven and Earth.'[17]

In favour of a more extreme reading of the 'paternal priority,' Milton ignores what was perhaps the commoner view, that creation was the act of the Godhead without distribution to persons.[18] Yet from this view at least one contemporary reached a conclusion identical with Milton's: since, as our divines grant, 'the works of creation hold forth but one Agent, who must needs be the Principall (if not the only) Agent therein, ... therefore if Christ were an Agent, he was but an instrumentall one.'[19] And Milton disposes of the Son according to a distinction drawn in his own *Logic*: the Father alone is the efficient cause, indeed includes within himself every kind of principal cause, while the Son is 'the secondary efficient cause,' 'the instrumental and less principal cause' (*De Doctrina*, 1: 5 [Col. 14: 323]; 1: 7 [Col. 15: 7]).[20]

The points noticed in this section are very far from exhausting the dependence of Milton's theory of creation upon orthodox sources; but already they are appearing in company with ideas the reverse of orthodox, which must now claim our attention.

Rejection of creation ex nihilo *in favour of creation* de deo
It is with his categorical rejection of creation *ex nihilo* that Milton's departure from the orthodox account of the origin of things becomes decisive. On this rejection all the peculiarities of his cosmology depend.

From St Augustine onward two stages had been recognized in the creative act: the production of the matter *ex nihilo*, and the framing of the world therefrom. For the matter of a thing is logically antecedent to its form, though not necessarily antecedent in time.[21] The first stage is that recorded in Gen. 1:1, 2, where the matter is referred to by anticipation as 'the heaven and earth,' as the earth 'without form and void,' and as the abyss, or deep, and the waters. This is the unformed matter of which God made the world (Wisd. 11:18) and it is described by the Greeks as the Chaos.[22] The second stage, the imposition of form upon the matter thus created, is presented in Genesis as the work of the six days. The significance of this division is that Milton rejects the first stage as no part of the creative act, which commences with the preparation of the matter to receive form, and that for him the second stage (as described by St Augustine and his followers) becomes the whole of the creative act. Thus Milton can reject creation *ex nihilo*, but retain the scriptural account of the creation.

Milton's rejection of creation *ex nihilo* turns in the first place on the meaning of the verb *create*, the Hebrew *bara* and its Greek and Latin equivalents, which will not bear the interpretation to create out of nothing, but 'uniformly signify to create out of matter,' (*De Doctrina*, 1: 7 [Col. 15: 17]). Milton could hardly have failed to observe how much the champions of orthodoxy disagreed about the weight which could be safely placed on the verb *bara*. At one end of the scale stands Calvin who, expounding Gen. 1:1, 2 as asserting 'that the world was not perfected at its very commencement ... but was created an empty chaos of heaven and earth,' is insistent that *bara* denotes creation *ex nihilo*, whereas *yatsar* would have signified merely to frame or form;[23] at the other, Rivetus, who admits what Milton is later to assert, that *bara* and its Greek and Latin equivalents cannot bear the interpretation to create *ex nihilo*.[24] While firmly asserting the creation of all things from nothing, so that 'whatsoever entity they had when made had no existence before they were made,' Pearson will not invoke the word *bara*:

> For it is often used synonymously with words that signifie any kind of production or formation, and by it self seldom denotes a production out of nothing, or proper creation, but most frequently the making of one substance out of another preexisting ... We must not therefore weakly collect the true nature of Creation from the force of any word which by some may be thought to express so much, but must collect it from the testimony of God the Creatour, in his word, and of the world created, in our reason.[25]

It seems altogether probable, then, that here also Milton may have derived suggestion and a measure of support from writers who would have shrunk from his conclusions. But indeed, outside the pale of orthodoxy, creation *ex nihilo* was coming under sharp criticism. At the basis of such further anticipation of Milton as we find in Charles Hotham lies his assertion that *bara*, so far from denoting creation from nothing, rather signifies creation from a pre-existent matter.[26] And the opinion that Moses did not teach creation *ex nihilo*, at least in the ordinary acceptance of the term, is found in other predecessors of Milton: in the Racovian theologian Volkelius, for example, attacked by Stillingfleet,[27] and in Robert Fludd, both of whom prefer to evade, rather than reject, creation from nothing, but whose argument, different from Milton's in detail, leads to a conclusion substantially the same as his.[28]

What then was the origin of matter? As firmly as orthodoxy itself, Milton rejects the hypothesis 'that matter ... always existed independently of God' (*De Doctrina*, 1: 7 [Col. 15: 19]). The history of this hypothesis, and of Christianity's long contention against it and in favour of its own hypothesis of the creation of matter *ex nihilo*, is entirely relevant to our enquiry. The hypothesis of a pre-existent matter, as, for example, in Plato's *Timaeus*, furnished an explanation of evil which relieved God of all responsibility therefor, but at the expense of his omnipotence. To assert this omnipotence was the first purpose of the Christian doctrine of creation *ex nihilo*, and a concern which persisted to Milton's day, when Stillingfleet gives us an example of how relevant the ancient controversies still seemed by declaring that 'the eternity and improduction of Matter as the passive Principle of things' is repugnant to God's omnipotence, as well as to his independence and immensity, for it associates with him a second cause without which he cannot act, and thus subjects God to matter.[29] But to reject creation from an independently pre-existent matter was to be confronted anew by the problem of evil.[30] Yet a third hypothesis, whose affinities were with the Stoic tradition, was conceivable, namely, that creation was *de Deo*. To this hypothesis, as well as to that of a pre-existent matter, St Augustine opposes the Christian doctrine of creation *ex nihilo*. All things, he says, were created 'non de Dei natura sed a Deo ... de nihilo.'[31] And he so expounds the doctrine as also to provide a solution of the problem of evil at the cosmological level.[32]

In rejecting at once creation from nothing and from an independently pre-existent matter, Milton is driven back upon the third hypothesis, that creation was *de Deo*, for which, he writes, 'we have the authority of scripture, namely, that all things are of God: Rom. 11:36: *For of him, and through him, and to him are all things*' (*De Doctrina*, 1: 7 [Col. 15: 21]).[33] Thus scripture suggests the solution which reason demands.[34] For (*De Doctrina*, 1: 7 [Col. 15: 21, 27]])

> there are ... four kinds of causes, *efficient, material, formal*, and *final*.[35] Inasmuch then as God is the primary, and absolute, and sole cause of all things, there can be no doubt but that he comprehends and embraces in himself all the causes above mentioned. Therefore the material cause must be either God or nothing. [But] ... nothing is no cause at all ...
>
> Nor ... can it be understood in what sense God can properly be called infinite, if he is capable of receiving any accession whatever; which would be the case if anything could exist in the nature of things, which had not first been of God and in God.[36]

So far from safeguarding God's omnipotence and infinity, denied by the hypothesis of an independently pre-existent matter, as Stilllingfleet and others maintained that it did, creation *ex nihilo* was equally incompatible with these attributes, and was further convicted of logical absurdity by exalting nothing to the rank of a cause. Only the third hypothesis, that the matter was comprehended in the Deity, would safeguard these attributes.

If one hopes ever to suprise the suggestion that put Milton upon this train of thought, one must not overlok the degree to which orthodox writers like Du Bartas sometimes spoke of all things as, before their creation, comprehended in God:

> Before all Time, all Matter, Form and Place,
> God all in all, and all in God, it was.[37]

Usually nothing more is meant than that they were potentially existent in his power and wisdom; and even in Fludd[38] this idea is present and partly accounts for his language. A striking example of the derivation of the matter of all things from God, on these or similar terms, is seen in Eusebius. In a passage which also anticipates Milton's subordination of the Son to the Father, and which, further, clearly adumbrates his argument that nothing or the non-existent cannot be a cause, Eusebius writes:

> ... There is one principle of the universe [i.e, the Son], nay, one before the principle ... and greater than every name [i.e., the Father], ... the good, the cause of all, the Creator, ... the prescient, ... the one and only God, from whom are all things and for whom are all things ... Wherefore, having both the will and power, he hath ordained for himself everything ... in the visible and invisible world, making his own will and power, as it were, a kind of matter and substratum of the genesis and constitution of the universe, so that it is no longer reasonable to say that whatever exists must have come from the non-existent; for that which came from the non-existent would not be anything. For how could that which is non-existent cause something else to exist? Everything that has ever existed ... derives its being from the One, the only existent and pre-existent Being ...[39]

Again one must not ignore the suggestions to be derived from Milton's classical reading, or fail to discriminate between the different points of view represented therein, and coming down to modern times therefrom. Milton's identification of the matter with God carries him away from Platonic doctrine, at least as represented by a literal reading of the *Timaeus*;[40] for the hypothesis of an independently pre-existent matter is equally opposed to orthodoxy's creation *ex nihilo* and Milton's creation *de Deo*. Of the origin of the matter Plato gives no account, leaving it to his successors to work out a theory which should trace its ultimate origin to the Deity while retaining Plato's sense of its opposition to all that the Deity stands for by placing it at the farthest possible remove from him. Of the series of emanations by which this desired result was held to have been achieved, there is no suggestion in Milton, and indeed the doctrine of emanation would have met his needs, and squared with his principles of scriptural interpretation, no better than creation *ex nihilo*. One must not, of course, overlook the fact that Fludd, who furnishes so many striking parallels to Milton, is able to assume (though perhaps only in order to gain authority for his own doctrine) that Plato in fact derives the matter from God. He remarks that 'divine *Plato* doth seem in some sort to verify that the Chaos was God's companion from all antiquity; yet he doth intimate to us ... that though she be termed a companion to God in the Creation, yet did she issue from him by a certain eternall generation or production, and that God did afterward frame all things out of Chaos.'[41] It is conceivable that Milton may have shared this assumption, but much more probable that he turned from Plato to another classical tradition, the Stoic.

In Stoicism Milton would have found a system which commenced with logic, proceeded to cosmology, and reached its goal in a clearly defined and emphatic ethic. It was a system whose cosmology was marked by uncompromising monism, but which was at the same time theistic. It identified matter with deity: in other words, it recognized a single substance which in its passive mode or aspect was matter, and in its active, reason or, as the Stoics did not scruple to call it, God. So much Milton might have learned from a variety of ancient sources, including Diogenes Laertius and the *Epistles* of Seneca, or from such a modern compendium as the *Physiologia Stoicorum* of Justus Lipsius. If Eusebius and others could read the *Timaeus* in the light of Genesis and Genesis in the light of the *Timaeus*, it seems not impossible that Milton may have been helped towards his view of the meaning of Genesis by reading it in the light first of the *Timaeus*, then of the Stoic cosmology. The significance of this possibility (which by no means excludes the interplay of other and more nearly contemporary influences) is the aid which it gives in defining Milton's position in its broad historical relations. He rejects creation *ex nihilo*, adhering to the ancient maxim common to Pre-Socratics, Stoics, and Epicureans, *Ex nihilo nihil fit*; he rejects the idea of a matter existing independently of God as incompatible with his omnipotence and infinity, and of course he will have nothing to do with the type of monism which, tracing everything to matter and motion, eliminates the creative activity of God. What is left is the tradition of theistic monism, of which the Stoics are the ancient representatives, and Spinoza the modern. With this tradition, it seems clear, Milton has certain affinities, and it may well be partly in response to it that he attempts his re-examination of the Christian account of the origin of things.

However this may be, it is unnecessary to look beyond Milton's own day and nation to find a close parallel for the substance of his argument on the origin of matter. In the *Mosaicall Philosophy* Robert Fludd writes:

For it appeareth, as well by the infallible sense of Holy Scriptures, as the sacred Light in nature: that the first essence and matter of all things was from all eternity in God, and with God, one and the same thing ... For the Scripture telleth us, in plain terms, ... *Of him, by him, and in him, are all things* [Rom. 11:36]. And therefore, if all things proceeded from God, the Creatour, who is the highest of Entities, it followeth that they proceeded not from a negative nothing ... Moreover, if God had not produced and created all things essentially out of himself, but of a vain negative nothing, then creation would not appertain unto God, neither could it rightly be referred unto him, that is to say, if all things were not essentially of him, nor did take their beginning from him; then verily it must needs follow that all were not made by him, but would have their existence from Nothing; neither would they consist in him, but in Nothing ... To conclude, nothing ever came into being, or had its existence from any other, but onely from him, and by him, neither can any thing exist but onely in him. And therefore we may conclude, that God did beget, produce, make and create no thing, but that which was eternally in himself ...[42]

Some implications of Milton's position

Among the inescapable implications which Milton does not seek to evade is the admission of an element of corporeality in the Deity. He is content to show that on the hypothesis of creation *ex nihilo* this element would remain: 'For nor even divine virtue and efficiency could produce bodies out of nothing, according to the commonly received opinion, unless there had been some bodily power in the substance of God, since no one can give to another what he does not possess' (*De Doctrina*, 1: 7 [Col. 15: 25]). Here the parallel is astonishingly close with Spinoza, who denies the immateriality of God because, if God's nature were essentially different from that of the world, he could not be its cause: 'Things which have nothing in common cannot be one the cause of the other.'[43] 'That which has not in itself something of another thing, can also not be a cause of the existence of such another thing.'[44]

Not only so; but with the material also comes the potential. For whatever virtue the matter possesses is merely potential until actualized by the addition of form. In other words, God cannot be 'pure act,' but must include an element of potentiality. Milton does not formally admit this implication, but we find him significantly, expressing his dissatisfaction with '*actus purus* or the active principle' as an exhaustive description of God, ascribing it (truly enough, but with evident intent to depreciate it as 'metaphysical theology') to Aristotle (*De Doctrina*, 1: 2 [Col. 14: 49]). Fludd supplies a useful gloss to Milton by facing squarely the potentiality of the first matter and its comprehension in the Deity. Following St Augustine in identifying the earth 'without form and void' with the abyss shrouded in darkness, he goes on to maintain that the Originall or primary womb, from whence the waters were extracted (which were the materiall stuff whereof all things were framed) was this dark and deformed Abysse or Chaos ... That Principle which *Moses* termed ... the darke Abysse, or potentiall Principle, *Aristotle* doth call his *Materia prima* ..., which he averreth to be something in puissance, or potentially only, because it is not as yet reduced into act ... *Plato* called it *Hyle*, which is esteemed to be nothing, forasmuch as it is invisible and without form ... *Hippocrates* will have it named a deformed Chaos, or an universally troubled mass, without form or shape ...

... It was not the negative *Nihil*, but a matter that was *in potentia ad actum* ... , being destitute, neverthelesse as yet, both of any form or act ... Therefore *Hermes* tearmeth it *potentia divina* [Pimander 3] ... So that by these authorities you may discern what the first principle or potential being or beginning was, namely, the dark abysse or *terra vacua et inanis* of *Moses* [Gen. 1:2]; ... the *materia informis* or *invisa* of Solomon [Wisd. 11:18]; the *potentia divina* (of Esdras) *ante omnia creata, quae erat fons et initium omnium* [Esd.] ...[45]

And this 'first essence and matter of all things was from all eternity in God and with God ...'[46] The parallel between Fludd and Milton is striking, and the passage from the former brings into relief the consequences of Milton's position. It also directs attention to certain literary influences to which Milton was as open as Fludd. To recognize these is something very different from hurrying, as does Saurat, to the conclusion that Milton followed Fludd into the labyrinths of the Cabbala and to the association not of potentiality merely, but of evil, with God. But Fludd has more light to throw on Milton, and it serves, as we shall see, to confirm the evident meaning of Milton's words and to confute a crucial part of Saurat's startling pattern.

The mark of the potentiality of the first matter is its disorder, and a third consequence of Milton's position is thus the bringing of disorder into the presence of God. In the *De Doctrina* this receives little emphasis: the matter is simply admitted to have been 'at first confused and formless, being afterwards adorned and digested into order by the hand of God,' whereby 'it merely received embellishment from the accession of forms, which are themselves material' (1: 7 [Col. 15: 23]). In *Paradise Lost* the idea (which goes back to St Augustine and is indeed a commonplace) that the chaos of the Greeks is one with the heaven and earth of Genesis 1:1,2, opens the way for Milton's wonderful picture of the chaos with its inevitable emphasis on disorder.

The poem also restates, briefly but emphatically, the comprehension of the matter in the Deity who is infinite and omnipresent. In the *De Doctrina* God's infinity is indeed brought in, but merely to supplement the logical argument from his omnipotence (God is omnipotent: hence he comprehends within himself every cause, and therefore the material cause; God is also infinite: hence he includes everything that exists) ; and less is made of it than might be expected. In the poem, quite unmistakably, God's infinity is conceived in terms of extent; and in the treatise the same would appear to be true. While recognizing God's immensity, orthodox theology had continued to regard his infinity as primarily qualitative, that is, to associate this attribute with God's perfection. At most it was interpreted in a negative sense as 'void of all bounds of his essence.'[47] But St Augustine had written of God as containing all things, and filling them by containing them;[48] and in Milton's day critical thought was busy with the attributes of infinity and omnipresence. Henry More differs markedly from Milton in regarding God as wholly incorporeal and matter as not continuous but atomic. Coming at the question through the attribute of omnipresence, however, he thinks of the Deity as infinitely extended and as thus meeting in the attribute of infinity (and also of eternity) the definition of absolute space: God is infinite and eternal; so is absolute space.[49] Given Milton's view of God, and his view of matter as continuous, the same convergence of attributes as occurs in More between God and absolute space occurs in him between God and extended substance; and, whatever be the explanation of the fact, this is precisely the doctrine which Spinoza reached by another road.[50] In the *De Doctrina* Milton significantly groups God's infinity and immensity as a single attribute, explains his omnipresence as a result of his infinity (1: 2 [Col. 14: 43, 47]), and remarks that 'infinity and emptiness are opposite terms' (1: 5 [Col. 14: 343]). And in *Paradise Lost*, God says: (7.168–9)

> Boundless the deep because I am who fill
> Infinitude, nor vacuous space ...

In Milton, as in St Augustine, the deep is matter without form (for St Augustine so created; for Milton uncreated). Thus this first matter, whose other attributes, for Milton, all depend on its comprehension in the Deity, is nevertheless, just as it is for St Augustine, formless and unordered. Speaking of the matter (regarded by him, of course, as finite and in all its attributes opposed to the Deity) Plato describes its disorder as the state in which one would expect to find it *in the absence of God*.[51] But to Milton this expedient is closed: the matter is certainly in God's presence, as nothing can be absent from the infinite and omnipresent Deity. That Milton is not unaware of the difficulty is clear from the *De Doctrina*. There he notices the objection that in its original state 'substance was imperfect,' but can find no

better answer than to retort that the difficulty remains just as formidable if
we suppose God to have 'produced it out of nothing in an imperfect state'
(1: 7 [Col. 15: 23]), which merely removes the reproach from God as
material, to God as efficient cause. In *Paradise Lost* an answer has been
found: the matter in its disordered state is indeed in God's presence, but not
in his *active* presence. He has not chosen to put forth as yet his creative
power, but, retired within himself, has voluntarily left the matter a prey to
necessity or chance: (7.168–73)

> Boundless the Deep, because I am who fill
> Infinitude, nor vacuous the space,
> Though I, uncircumscribed, myself retire,
> And put not forth my goodness, which is free
> To act or not, Necessity and Chance
> Approach not me ...

The moment God's creative power, his active goodness, is put forth, disorder ceases: (7.216–21)

> Silence, ye troubl'd waves, and thou Deep, peace,
> Said then the Omnific Word, your discord end.

And

> *Chaos* heard his voice.

The voluntary character of the creative act, that point of orthodox
Christian doctrine to which Milton held with such tenacity, gives him his
solution of the difficulty, as it gives Fludd his.[52] And indeed on this whole
subject Fludd furnishes an invaluable gloss to Milton's meaning. Like Milton, he holds that 'all things are essentially comprehended in this eternall
and radicall Unity [i.e., God]: Forasmuch as being one, he is infinite, and
being infinite as well in his dimension and essence as power; he must of
necessity comprehend in himself all finite things whatsoever.'[53] Since the
infinite God is the source of all being, of the passive matter as of the active
creative principle,

> this eternall infinitude, this all in all, and without all, is rightly described
> first by the Apostle, and then by the divine Philosopher *Hermes*, after
> this manner ... *One God is the Father of all, who is above all, and over
> all, and in all* [Eph. 4:6] ... *Of him, by him, and in him are all things*
> [Rom. 11:36]. And *Hermes*, ... *God is an intellectuall circle whose cen-*

ter is all that which existeth, and whose circumference is without and beyond all things [Asclep. 7]. Hereupon in another place he calleth him, ... *the place in which the world is contained,* inferring thereby, according unto that of the Scriptures, that he filleth all the world, and yet remains in himself without all, in the very selfsame nature of a Unity as he was. For as he seemed in the eyes of man's weak and fragile capacity to be ... *Nihil,* before he would create any thing, yet was he both Unity and Infinity unto himself ... Also, though he shined forth of darkness, and by the revelation of his hidden wisdom or essence, made all things, as well visible as invisible, to exist formally ... , yet nevertheless, he remaineth all one in himself, and passeth not beyond the limits of his uniformity ... Even no otherwise, than we see in the mind or divine mentall beam of man, that it is all one without alteration, when it willeth and when it nilleth, namely, when it granteth or giveth, and when it denyeth. In like manner, whether the divine Infinity doth shine forth from its center towards its circumference, or centrally contracteth his acting beams within it self, yet it is all one and the same in its self, without any alteration of the essentiall identity.[54]

In another passage the image of the circle is elaborated. In the centre, which is but a point, the completed circle is implied. The centre, then, the circle yet undrawn, represents the

divinest and brightest Unity, remaining in that very estate in which it stood before the creation of the world, namely, when it reserved it self within it self and remained occult and hidden from all potentiall creatures, which it was pleased afterward by revealing of itself, or emission of its vivifying light, to inact and make manifest ...[55]

These passages confirm and explain the evident purport of Milton's lines, which is quite remote from the sense put upon them by Saurat.[56] The retirement of the Deity is not the 'retraction' found by Saurat in the *Zohar,* which is a step in, or preliminary to, the act of creation, a withdrawal by God of himself from that part of matter which he is about to frame into the world. That such a retraction was indeed held by its opponents to be a necessary expedient in a doctrine which identified God and matter, may be illustrated from Stillingfleet, who asks: If God be

in the whole [of matter] as in his adequate place, how cou'd he ever frame the World? For either he must then recede ... and contract himself into a narrower compass, that he might fashion that part of the

World which he was about, or else he might ... frame part of himself with that part of the World which he was then framing of.[57]

But by their interpretation of God's presence Milton and Fludd seek to remove this very necessity, together with other difficulties. What they are describing is not a step preliminary to creation, but the state of the matter from eternity in respect of God. It is in God's presence, for God is infinite and omnipresent; but it is not in his active presence until he wills to put forth his creative power, his 'goodness which is free To act or not.' That this is the correct reading of the lines seems to be put beyond doubt by Milton's invoking as a solvent his favourite, and perfectly orthodox, conception of creation as a voluntary act; and this conception is also involved in Fludd's explanation. So far, then, from creation's entailing the withdrawal of God's active goodness, it results quite simply and plainly from the putting of it forth. And with his active presence disorder is indeed incompatible, and is, as we have seen, instantly banished by it. That the disorder of the matter is one of the problems which Milton is here seeking to solve seems likewise to be put beyond doubt by the added statement, 'Necessity and Chance Approach not me.' In Plato the disorder of the matter is due to its domination by necessity or chance,[58] which are virtually synonyms:[59] Milton explains that while they may be permitted to dominate the matter till God puts forth his active goodness, they do not approach his essential being.

There remains to be noticed three further implications of Milton's position, which are of the highest importance.

The first is the inherent goodness of the matter, which Milton emphasizes, linking up his contention with two points of agreement with orthodoxy noticed above: creation as manifesting God's power and goodness, and the voluntary character of the manifestation. It is, he writes, (*De Doctrina*, 1 : 7 [Col. 15 : 21–37])

an argument of supreme power and goodness, that such diversified, multiform, and inexhaustible virtue should exist and be *substantially* inherent in God ... and that this diversified and substantial virtue should not remain dormant within the Deity, but should be diffused and propagated and extended as far and in such manner as he himself may will. For the original matter of which we speak, is not to be looked upon as an evil or trivial thing, but as intrinsically good, and the chief productive stock of every subsequent good. It was a substance, and derivable from no other source than from the fountain of every substance, though at first confused and formless, being afterwards adorned and digested into order by the hand of God.

And in reply to the objections that the original substance was imperfect because without form, and that to derive it from God was to derive the corruptible from incorruption, he replies: 'It is not true ... that matter was in its own nature originally imperfect; it merely received embellishment from the accession of forms, which are themselves material ... [It] proceeded incorruptible from God; and even since the fall it remains incorruptible as far as concerns its essence' (1: 7 [Col. 15: 23–5]). Milton's determined emphasis on the inherent goodness of the matter is unmistakable. Here his doctrine diverges sharply from Fludd's, who, for all his insistence on the comprehension of the matter in the Deity, attempts no such rehabilitation: despite its divine origin matter left to itself remains for Fludd the source of evil, from which it is rescued only by the operation of God's active goodness, or, in other words, there are in God two principles, a positive (his active goodness) and a negative (the passive matter), and it is less the Manichaeans' recognition of this distinction that Fludd condemns than their determined erection of the distinction into a dualism.[60] Milton's hesitant and embarrassed treatment of the problem of evil at its metaphysical level, however, suggests that he did not always succeed in maintaining the stand taken in the passage quoted above;[61] but the tendency of his argument is clear enough.

Cosmological speculation has for its first object an account of the nature and origin of things; but almost inevitably this leads to a consideration of the problem of evil, and a solution of this problem becomes in effect the second object of such speculation. A strongly marked tradition in Greek thought, whose locus classicus is the Timaeus, literally interpreted, sets up a dualism of God and an independently pre-existent matter, and finds in the matter, opposed in all its attributes to the Deity, and resistant to his design, a sufficient explanation of imperfection or evil. This explanation has the undeniable advantage of relieving the Deity, by definition perfectly good, of all responsibility for the existence of evil, physical and moral. But it is wholly ineligible for the Christian because the freedom from responsibility is purchased at the expense of God's omnipotence. Accordingly the hypothesis of an independently pre-existent matter was rejected in favour of creation ex nihilo, which traced everything to God's creative act. Historically, that was the first meaning of creation ex nihilo: it was an inevitable inference from, and indispensable support to, the dogma of God's omnipotence. But only so long as attention could be focused on the goodness of the created cosmos, or the mind could answer to that profound instinct of Western thought (which is also illustrated by the Timaeus) and regard existence as itself a good, would creation ex nihilo at this stage of its formulation seem satisfactory. For it left the problem of evil without a solution at the cosmological level;[62] and this was a fatal omission. Its result was the widespread defection of the Manichaean heresy, which reverted to the Platonic dualism, but with a new extremity of emphasis and with its own appropriate mythology. Such was the situation which St Augustine faced when he undertook to find in creation *ex nihilo* not merely a demonstration of God's omnipotence, but a solution of the problem of evil. The terms of his solution are almst too familiar to require summary, but they must be recalled because in rejecting creation *ex nihilo* Milton inevitably rejects St Augustine's solution.[63] Evil St Augustine declares to be definable only as a deprivation of good. Evil then is not a principle: it is wholly negative, and absolute evil would be absolute negation or not-being. God, who is perfect being, by the act of creation *ex nihilo* gives the creature being, draws it from not-being into being. As a result, the creature is good, but not immutable: it may direct its aspiration towards God, the perfect being, and the source of its being, or it may allow itself to fall away, to slip back towards the not-being from which it was drawn, and to which it retains, as it were, a potential inclination.

Milton rejects not only the dualism of God and matter, and the explanation of evil as derived from matter, but also the Augustinian creation of the matter *ex nihilo* and the explanation of evil in terms of not-being. He rejects the latter doctrine because, apparently, he feels that though it purports to be monistic and to cut the ground from under the old dualism by tracing everything to God while still offering a satisfactory explanation of evil, it is in reality a concealed form of dualism since in effect, and at the additional expense of a logical contradiction, it exalts 'nothing' or not-being to the rank of a principle or cause: it is, in fact, the old dualism over again, with 'nothing' cast for the role formerly held by 'matter.' And indeed, both before St Augustine and after, since being was associated with form, 'unformed matter' tended to be identified with, or closely approximated to, 'not-being' or nothing. A late example of this and of some other tendencies is seen in the résumé of Augustinian doctrine offered by the Protestant Philippe de Mornay:

> We say that making and creating are referred to natures or substances, and that all natures and substances are good, and therefore that God who is good, is the author and Creator of them. On the contrary part, we say that evil is neither a nature nor a substance, but an income or accident which is falne into natures and substances: It is (say I) a bereaving or diminishing of the good qualities which things ought naturally to have. This evil hath not any being in it selfe, neither can have any being but in the thing that is good. It is not an effect, but a default, not a production, but a corruption. And therefore to speake properly, we must not seek whence commeth the doing of evil, but whence commeth the undoing of good ... Forasmuch as evil is nothing els but a

default, want or failing of good, it is the soveraigne or chiefe default or failing, as the good is the soveraigne or chiefe being. And if it be the chiefe default, then is it not any more. For the default or failing of a thing, is a tending of the thing to not being any more the same that it was: and the failing of all, is a tending to the utter unbeing or notbeing of the whole ...

And if you aske what is then the cause thereof: ... it is the very nothing it selfe, that is, to wit, that God almightie, to shew us that he hath made all of nothing, hath left a certeine inclination in his Creatures, whereby they tend naturally to nothing, that is to say, to change and corruption, unlesse they be upheld by his power ... As in respect then that things be, they be of God: but as in respect that the corrupt and tende to not being that which they were afore; that cometh of the said notbeing, whereof they were created. And so they be good, as in respect of their bare being: and evill as in respect that they forgoe their formall being, that is to say, their goodnesse: Good on the behalfe of the soveraigne God, the Father of all substances: Evill as on the behalfe of the Nothing ... Plato, Plotin, and other great Philosophers of all Sects, are of opinion that Evill is not a thing of it selfe, nor can be imagined but in the absence of all goodnesse, as a deprivation of the good which ought to be naturally in every thing: that evil is a kind of notbeing ... That the cause thereof is in the very matter whereof God created things, which matter they termed the very unbeing, ... whereof the creatures reteine still a certaine inclination, whereby they may fal away from their goodnesse: And that in the very Soule of man, the evil that is there is a kinde of darknesse for want of looking up to that light of the soveraigne minde which should inlighten it: and through suffering it selfe to be carried too much away to the materiall things which are nothing.[64]

Such a passage, with its ominous closing of the gap between St Augustine and the dualists whom he opposed, with its emphasis on the creature's natural tendency to evil, and with its implied asceticism, might well confirm Milton in his impression that Augustinianism had failed really to derive everything from God, and had failed therefore really to rehabilitate the creature, and to cut away the cosmological foundation of asceticism.

Precisely these ends his rival theory of creation was designed to effect. He turned at once from the avowed dualism of the Platonic tradition, and the concealed dualism of the Augustinian, to a form of monism which adheres rather to the long tradition of thought extending from the Stoics to Spinoza. He asserts that there is a single substance which is the substrate of all created things, that it is good (though confessedly he finds some difficulty in quite consistently adhering to this idea) because it is of God, and he cuts away the cosmological groundwork of the natural tendency of the creature to evil and of an ascetic view of life. But in effecting these ends he inevitably sacrifices the Christian solution of the problem of evil on the cosmological level, though not on other levels, and not the possibility of working out some solution for himself.[65]

In the course of his derivation of the matter, indeed of everything, from God, he crosses the orbit of various thinkers, including Fludd and perhaps the Behmenists. But the inference which he draws from this derivation, the inherent goodness of the matter, they do not share. Rather, though in somewhat different ways, they recognize the potentiality of evil in the matter, and hence in God who comprehends the matter. Something like this is the doctrine which Saurat would have us find in Milton also. But it does not follow, because Milton crosses the orbit of other thinkers, whose views may at the point of juncture cast light upon his, that he goes with them all the way. He is nothing if not eclectic. Analogues may illuminate Milton's argument. Only Milton's own words can determine what that argument is. And the words which Saurat adduces to make good his case are in one instance simply irrelevant, and in the other diametrically opposed to the meaning which he sets upon them.[66]

The first note of Milton's cosmology is its emphatic monism; the second, his sense of its bearing on the nature and life of man. The earlier part of the *De Doctrina's* chapter on the creation concentrates our attention on the matter and the shaping of the cosmos therefrom; the latter part is devoted to the making of man and the insistence that he is (1: 7 [Col. 15: 41])

> a living being, intrinsically and properly one and individual, not compound or separable, not, according to the common opinion, made up and framed of two distinct and different natures, as of soul and body, but that the whole man is soul, and the soul man, that is to say, a body, or substance, individual, animated, sensitive, and rational ...

Man is indeed created in the image of his Maker, but he is also in another sense, and by a tradition only less venerable, created in the image of the cosmos: he is the microcosm. And Milton's view of the microcosm is as emphatically monistic as is his view of the macrocosm.

From this fact follows his adherence to the theory of traduction, or the propagation of the soul; and here we may be permitted to cite a final and rather remarkable analogue. The question of the soul's origin had been one of those debated in the Public Schools at Cambridge on 3 March 1646,[67] and the Determination pronounced by Charles Hotham, a Fellow of Peterhouse, who was a Behmenist, was subsequently published under the title, *Ad Philosophiam Teutonicam Manuductio seu Determinatio de Origine Ani-*

mae humanae ... (1648).[68] This Determination, interesting as suggesting the freedom of speculation enjoyed in the period of the Puritan Revolution, presents up to a point a very close parallel with the opinions later to be entertained by Milton. For Hotham champions traduction, declaring it to be God's method of creating souls, and in order to support his contention and give it the required cosmological basis, he rejects creation *ex nihilo* in favour of creation from the matter of the abyss, infinite in extent, eternal in duration and, while not formally identified with God, significantly described as the body of the Deity or his dwelling place; and Hotham recognized that this position necessitates a new examination of the problem of evil. But here the similarity with Milton ceases; for Hotham betakes himself to the chemico-theological terminology of Boehme, boldly derives evil, if not immediately from God, at least mediately, that is, from the abyss, and invokes 'retraction' to resolve or soften the monstrous paradox:

> And to declare my thoughts plainly, I account that part of this great Abysse from whence God shall retire himself within his own Center, to be truly Hell; but do not believe that before the fall of Lucifer it did break into its hellish actuality, but was so becalmed by the benigne effluence of the all-present Deity, that it greatly furthered the manifestation of the eternal Godhead.[69]

It was in the midst of such buffeting winds of doctrine that Milton pursued his task of thinking through for himself, with scripture and logic as his guides, the fundamental and closely interrelated questions for which over the centuries Christian theology had elaborated its answers. In Milton's England a spirit of enquiry was abroad: from philosophers (like the Cambridge Platonists who coresponded with and criticized Descartes, or Henry Oldenburg, the friend of Milton and of Spinoza and the corespondent of both), through the fellows of colleges and students of theology, down to the very sectaries whose opinion Thomas Edwards held up to execration in the *Gangraena*, and Samuel Butler to ridicule in his picture of the Independent, Ralph.[70] Contemporary analogues help to build up our sense of the immediate setting in which Milton worked. They may also in specific cases throw light on some thought of his, or some image, though they can never legitimately supply us with a train of argument of which there is no indication in his text. Nor are contemporary analogues among philosophers, Behmenists, and Cabbalists the only relevant collaterals for the study of Milton's cosmology. There are also the ancient cosmologies, Platonic and Stoic, which he encountered in his classical reading; and there is the whole body of traditional theology and commentary, especially its examples in the patristic period and in the years since the Reformation, with which his constant theological studies had made him familiar. So varied is the background of Milton's thinking on cosmology.

II

Milton's views on the Trinity present some contact with his views on the creation, and some common principles of thought, but also one important difference. The contact is seen in Milton's contention that creation is the act of the Father through (*per*) the Son, who thus has a special role, but is the secondary or instrumental, and not the primary efficient cause. This is an inevitable result of Milton's doctrine of the Trinity when brought to bear on the subject of creation, but it also, in turn, fortifies his view of the Trinity and may in part have suggested it. That view, as we shall see, is marked by an extreme of subordinationism, and not only is the role in creation which Milton assigned to the Son an example of this subordinationism, but, as I have already illustrated from Pearson's *On the Creed*, nowhere in orthodox thought is the 'subordination of persons' (Pearson's own phrase) more often implied than in the account given of the creation. The common principles of thought are seen in Milton's appeal on both subjects to two criteria alone, 'scripture and reason.' As in the account of the creation Milton refuses to go beyond the Bible either to tradition or to what he contemptuously describes as 'metaphysical theology,' so likewise in discussing the doctrine of the Trinity he insists on the letter of the Bible as the sole source of doctrine, and refuses not only the arguments of scholastic theologians, but the teaching of the Fathers and the formularies of councils, having no conception of 'the development of doctrine,' a principle peculiarly important for this central dogma of the Christian church. But the appeal to scripture is again reinforced by an appeal to reason, which means the submission of every formulation to the canons of logic. This submission Milton will waive only where the Bible declares a mystery, as it does, he is careful to point out, in regard to the Incarnation, but not in regard to the persons of the Deity. The principal difference between Milton's views on the creation and on the Trinity is that the former seem essential in order to furnish the required foundation for his ethics, while the latter stand in no such close relation to his ethical thought. Rather they are related to another of his major preoccupations, namely, purity of worship, whose first principle (as already apears in the *Nativity*) is rigorous monotheism.

To place in their proper setting Milton's views as argued in the *De Doctrina Christiana* and applied in *Paradise Lost* and *Paradise Regained,* it is necessary to recall a few historical facts. However consistent it may be with the words of scripture, however much, indeed, it may seem to be demanded by them, the complete formulation of the orthodox doctrine of the Trinity is nowhere to be found in the Bible, or in the earliest of the Fathers, but was the gradual work of Fathers and councils culminating in the Council of Nicea (325 AD), as they steered their way amid opposing errors. Of these errors two are of special importance. One, which reached its final formulation as Sabellianism, or the doctrine of a model Trinity, regarded the persons as mere modes or aspects of the one God, thus purchasing the unity of the Godhead at the expense of the distinction of the persons. The other, which reached its final formulation as Arianism, and in reaction against Sabellianism, insisted on the distinction of the persons, but declared, in order to preserve the unity of the Godhead, that the Father alone was God in the full sense while the Son (for on the second person its attention was concentrated) was the first of creatures, and so not a God by nature, but merely by the Father's gift. The Nicene formulation of the orthodox doctrine and mystery of the Trinity was designed to avoid both these errors. It triumphed, but only after a severe struggle with Arianism, which, though in some respects a new doctrine, clearly embodied and exaggerated the subordinationism found in the early Fathers and repeated in the essentially conservative, and perplexed, Eusebius of Caesarea. How far scholastic theology elaborated, and perhaps undermined, the Nicene formulation, we need not here enquire. But with the Reformation the orthodox doctrine came in some quarters again under attack: to cite a few examples, covertly in Ochino, and openly in Servetus (in the name of a revived Arianism), and in the two Socinii (in behalf of the doctrine which bears their name). Though utterly repudiated by the great reformers, such as Calvin (who testified his orthodoxy by the burning of Servetus), the movement was encouraged by the Protestant principle of scripture as the only source of doctrine and the Protestant attack on additions thereto. The practical problem of halting the operation of this principle and this attack at the point required by piety and prudence is recurrent in Protestant thought. Unitarianism, chiefly in its Socinian form, spread, and by the middle of the seventeenth century reached England in the writings of John Bidle and the translation of the *Racovian Catechism*, while to learned readers the works of Racovian theologians such as Volkelius would also be available.

That Milton was familiar with some or all of these Antitrinitarians seems probable. But certain distinctions need to be sharply drawn. Milton was no Socinian. At certain points his doctrine approximates Arianism (though how far it is Arian and how far Eusebian remains to be determined), and of Arianism in England there is, so far as I can discover, scarcely any sign till some twenty years after his death. There the first movement appears to have been Socinian rather than Arian in character, and by the 1650s John Bidle was the most vocal, but by no means a solitary, example of Socinianism. The *Racovian Catechism* was translated and printed in 1652.[71] In 1659 a group of Socinians active in Gloucester (where Bidle had for a time resided as a schoolmaster) published Παναρμωνια or *the Agreement of The People Revived*, a plea for the tolerance of Antitrinitarian opinions which cites as supporting authority Milton's *Of Civil Power in Ecclesiastical Causes*. From the fact that the Socinian tract appeared in the same year as Milton's one might perhaps conjecture some personal relation between Milton and this group, although the more cautious explanation is that the Socinians were seeking what support they could get from all the groups of the Puritan left (an explanation strengthened by their subtitle 'The Agreement of the People Revived,' which is evidently aimed at the Levellers). The position of the document is Socinian in the strict sense.

The Arian movement seems to have gathered head at a somewhat later date, about 1690, and of this movement Milton is clearly a precursor, though, with the *De Doctrina Christiana* still in manuscript, not a source. There is of course much common ground between Arian and Socinian in their attacks on orthodox Trinitarianism: it is in their positive findings that they sharply differ. The only important Arian work I have discovered which is by a contemporary of Milton is *A Friendly Debate on a Weighty Subject, or a Conference by Writing between Mr. Samuel Eaton and Mr. John Knowles, Concerning the Divinity of Jesus Christ: For the beating out, and further clearing up of Truth* (1650); here Knowles, professing his resolve no longer to see 'with other men's eyes' or to pin his faith 'on the Church's sleeve,' but to examine 'all things by the *Touch-stone* of Truth,' undertakes to scrutinize the texts brought forward by Eaton in support of orthodox Trinitarianism.[72] From this document it appears, however, that Knowles, despite his close relation with the Socinians of Gloucester, was not himself a Socinian in the strict sense but at most an Arian. Like Milton, though less categorically, Knowles marks off his own view of the Son from that of the Socinians, although on the negative side he concurs in many of their arguments against orthodox Trinitarianism.

Milton's starting point in orthodoxy is the unity of the Godhead, implied, he observes, in all the other attributes, but also proved by scripture. But it is immediately apparent that, unlike the orthodox, Milton is not concerned to reconcile the unity of the Godhead with the trinity of persons; on the contrary, he finds them incompatible. The first commandment makes it plain, and the Israelites under the law and the prophets had always held, that God is one 'in the common acceptation of numerical unity' (*De*

Doctrina, 1 : 2 [Col. 14: 51]), beside whom there was none other, much less any equal. 'For the schoolmen had not as yet appeared, who ... on arguments purely contradictory, impugned the doctrine ... of the unity of God which they pretended to assert. But as with regard to the omnipotence of the Deity, it is universally allowed ... that he can do nothing which involves a contradiction; so must it also be remembered in this place, that nothing can be said of the one God, which is inconsistent with his unity, and which assigns to him at the same time the attributes of unity and plurality.' In this statement is implicit Milton's whole position on the Trinity.

For Milton the fundamental principle of Protestantism is that 'the word of God alone [is] the rule of faith' (*De Doctrina,* 1 : 5 [Col. 14: 177]). To this assertion Ussher and other Protestant theologians would not demur. Ussher writes:

> *May it be collected by natural reason, that there is a Trinity of Persons in the Unity of the Godhead?* No. For it is the highest mystery of Divinity: and the knowledge thereof is more proper to Christians. For the Turks and Jews do confess one Godhead, but no distinction of persons in the same. *How come we then by the knowledge of this mystery?* God hath revealed it in the holy Scripture unto the faithful. *What have we to learn of this?* That they are deceived who think this mystery is not sufficiently delivered in the Scripture, but dependeth upon the tradition of the Church.[73]

But Milton, like Roman Catholic theologians on the one hand and Socinians on the other, is led to the conclusion that the received doctrine of the Trinity cannot be proved from scripture alone: it can originate only in the teaching of the church, which he holds to be insufficient. Nor will he, like Ussher, allow it to be a mystery, since it is not, like the Incarnation, asserted by the Bible to be one.

With these facts in mind we may attempt a summary of Milton's views.

Scripture speaks of the Father's having 'begotten the Son in a double sense, the one literal, with reference to the production of the Son, the other metaphorical, with reference to his exaltation' (*De Doctrina,* 1 : 2 [Col. 14: 181]). Orthodox theologians read as literal some statements that are metaphorical; Socinians (not so named by Milton) read the literal as metaphorical. (*De Doctrina,* 1 : 5 [Col. 14: 181–3])

> Certain ... it is, whatever some moderns may allege to the contrary, that the Son existed from the beginning [of time], under the name of the Logos or Word, and was the first of the whole creation, by whom

afterwards all other things were made both in heaven and earth. John 1.1–3: 'In the beginning was the word ... &c.: 17.5: '... glorify me ... with the glory which I had with thee before the world was'; Col. 1.15 ... 'the first-born of every creature'; Rev. 3.14: 'the beginning of the creation of God'; ... Heb. 1.2: 'by whom also he made the worlds.'

Here Milton categorically rejects the Socinian contention that the Son was non-existent till born on earth, that scriptural statements regarding his existence in heaven refer to his exaltation after his ascension, and that those regarding his work of creation refer to his founding of his church.[74] Equally, he repudiates the orthodox position that the Son's generation was necessary and eternal and the Son one in essence with the Father, asserting instead that it was voluntary and hence in pursuance of God's decree, which itself must have antedated its execution (*De Doctrina*, 1: 5 [Col. 14: 187–9]). (1: 5 [Col. 14: 193]).

> For when the Son is said to be *the first born of every creature,* and *the beginning of the creation of God,* nothing can be more evident than that God of his own will created, or generated, or produced the Son before all things, endued with the [i.e., the Son's] divine nature, as in the fulness of time he miraculously begat him in his human nature of the Virgin Mary. The generation of the divine nature is described by no one with more sublimity and copiousness than by the apostle to the Hebrews 1.2–3: "whom he hath appointed heir of all things, by whom also he made the worlds; who being the brightness of his glory and the express image of his person,' &c. It must be understood from this, that God imparted to the Son as much as he pleased of the divine nature, nay, of the divine substance itself, care being taken not to confound the substance with the whole essence ... This is the whole that is revealed concerning the generation of the Son of God.

Incompatible alike with developed Trinitarianism and with Socinianism, the two quoted passages are compatible with Arianism, save for the implication that the Son was created by God not 'from nothing' (the Arian contention) but 'of his own substance' (*De Doctrina*, 1: 5 [Col. 14: 187]). But this exception becomes less significant when we remember that for the Arians all creation was *ex nihilo,* for Milton, *de Deo,* so that the Arian view does not necessarily make the Son more a creature than Milton's. Further, it is evident that in respect of the Son's origin Milton makes no clearcut distinction between generation and creation: for him, as for the Arians, the Son is the first created being. Finally, though an early

Father like Novatian, writing against Sabellianism, could speak of the Son as proceeding from the Father when the Father willed,[75] it was to become a distinctively Arian contention that the Son was created at the will of God and in fulfilment of a divine decree,[76] and both these positions are clearly accepted by Milton, who writes: (*De Doctrina*, 1: 5 [Col. 14: 187–9])

> For questionless, it was in God's power consistently with the perfection of his own essence not to have begotten the Son, inasmuch as generation does not pertain to the nature of the Deity ... ; but whatever does not pertain to his own essence or nature, he does not effect ... from ... necessity ... Therefore the generation of the Son cannot have proceeded otherwise than from a decree, and of the Father's own will.

In these points of agreement with Arianism, Milton likewise agrees with Knowles, who acknowledges the Son's pre-existence in his divine or spiritual nature, but denies his 'eternal generation,' defining his 'generation' as 'that act of Creation, whereby the God of all beings did immediately and in the first place, bring forth and produce him,'[77] and who interprets such crucial texts as John 1:1–3, Rev. 3:14, Col. 1:15, Heb. 1:2–3 in substantially the same sense as Milton.

The metaphorical statements regarding the begetting of the Son refer, Milton holds, either to his resurrection or to his mediatorial office as priest and king. From Psalm 2:6–7, it appears, he says, (*De Doctrina*, 1: 5 [Col. 14: 185])

> that God has begotten the Son, that is, has made him a king: ... 'yet have I set my King upon my holy hill of Sion'; and then ... , after having anointed his king, ... he says, 'this day have I begotten thee.' Heb. 1.4–5: 'being made so much better than the angels, as he hath by inheritance obtained a more excellent name than they' ... 'for unto which of the angels said he at any time, Thou art my Son; this day have I begotten thee?' The Son also declares the same of himself. John 10.35–6: 'Say ye of Him whom the Father hath sanctified, and sent into the world, Thou blasphemest, because I said, I am the Son of God?'

It is evident that Milton does not, like the Socinians, postpone Christ's anointing to his kingly office till after the Ascension; and this fact has its important bearing on *Paradise Lost*. In Book 5 Raphael, in his accommodated narrative to Adam, describes the anointing and enthronement of the Son, with the Father's words: (603–8)

> This day I have begot whom I declare
> My onley Son, and on this holy Hill
> Him have anointed, whom ye now behold
> At my right hand; your Head I him appoint;
> And by my Self have sworn to him shall bow
> All knees in Heav'n, and shall confess him Lord ...

The episode is made to serve the action of the poem by furnishing the occasion of Satan's revolt, but is no mere transference of scriptural matter back in time as is the use of Revelation in the account of the war in heaven. It may be taken as a metaphorical statement of belief, as its conformity to the *De Doctrina* shows, and as also its bearing on Milton's answer to the question of the Son's equality with the Father.

On the nature of the Son and his relation to the Father, Milton, like Knowles,[78] dismisses the formulations of metaphysical theology as not only without scriptural warrant, but repugnant to reason and indeed meaningless. He declares the term *hypostasis* (Heb. 1:3), which is variously translated as *substance, subsistence*, or *person*, to be in its original sense the same as *essence* (*De Doctrina*, 1: 2 [Col. 14: 41–3]) as Knowles finds the terms *person* and *essence* to be indistinguishable. If the Father, says Milton, (*De Doctrina*, 1: 5 [Col. 14: 221])

> has one hypostasis, so must he have one essence proper to himself, incommunicable ... and participated ... by no person besides, for he cannot have his own proper hypostasis, without having his own proper essence. For it is impossible for any *ens* to retain its own essence in common with any other thing whatsoever, since by this essence it is what it is, and is numerically distinguished from all others. If ... the Son, who has his own proper hypostasis, have not also his own proper essense, ... he becomes ... either no *ens* at all, or the same *ens* with the Father; which strikes at the very foundation of the Christian religion.

Nor does it escape this dilemma to pretend that, whatever be true of a finite essence, an infinite essence may pertain to a plurality of persons, which merely issues in the untenable inference that there may be 'two or any imaginable number of infinite persons' (*De Doctrina*, 1: 5 [Col. 14: 223]), a line of argument closely paralleling Knowles' contention that if person and essence are distinguished it must be on the assumption that they are either finite or infinite, which in turn results in one of two inferences, that there is 'something finite in God' or that there are 'two infinites in God, to wit, the person and the essence of God, and consequently two Gods.'[79]

Such argument, however, is intended merely to expose the absurdities of metaphysical theology. For knowledge of the Son's nature and his relation to the Father, Milton's whole reliance is placed on the words of scripture; and this is equally true of Knowles, 'According to the testimony of the Son,' says Milton, 'the Father is that one true God, by whom are all things,' as may be seen, for example, from Christ's answer to the scribes (from Deut. 6:4), 'the Lord our God is one Lord' (Mark 12:29) with his words: 'it is my Father that honoureth me, of whom ye say that he is your God' (John 8:42) (*De Doctrina*, 1: 5 [Col. 14: 199]). Nor will Milton allow that whenever Christ speaks of the Father alone as God, he is speaking only 'in his human character, or as mediator' since on occasion the context shows him to be speaking in 'his filial or even his divine character' (*De Doctrina*, 1: 5 [Col. 14: 223]); moreover, 'after the hypostatical union of two natures in one person, it follows that whatever Christ says of himself he says, not as the possessor of either nature separately, but with reference to the whole of his character, and in his entire person, except where he himself makes a distinction' (*De Doctrina*, 1: 5 [Col. 14: 229]). It may be observed in passing that Knowles (with perhaps some trace of monophysitism, from which Milton is free) insists on what he calls 'whole Christ,'[80] and seems to allow no real distinction between the two natures in the one person. In perfect accord with Christ's own teaching, thus interpreted, is the doctrine of St Paul: 'Eph. 1.17: "the God of our Lord Jesus Christ"; 1 Cor. 11.3: "the head of Christ is God"; 15.28: "the Son also shall be subject unto him" ' (*De Doctrina*, 1: 5 [Col. 14: 205]). And to support these assertions Milton cites a multiplicity of other texts.

Standing athwart this appeal to scripture, however, are two passages with which Milton finds it necessary to deal in some detail. The first is John 10:30: 'I and my Father are one'; which has been interpreted as one in essence. Milton argues the Father and Son are indeed one, but not in essence, for Christ has declared in the preceding verse, 'My Father ... is greater than all,' and thereafter distinctly asserts that he claims no more than to be the Son of God whom the Father has sanctified and sent, which 'must be spoken of two persons not only not co-essential, but not co-equal' (*De Doctrina*, 1: 5 [Col. 14: 211]). He continues (*De Doctrina*, 1: 5 [Col. 14: 201–13])

How then are they one? It is the province of Christ alone to acquaint us with this, and accordingly he does acquaint us with it. In the first place they are one, inasmuch as they speak and act with unanimity ... ; John 10.38, 'believe the works; that ye may know and believe that the Father is in me, and I in him;' 14.10, ... 'the words that I speak unto you, I speak not of myself, but the Father that dwelleth in me, he doeth the works.' Here he evidently distinguishes the Father from himself in his whole capacity, but asserts at the same time that the Father remains in him, which does not denote unity of essence, but only intimacy of communion. Secondly, he declares himself to be one with the Father in the same manner as we are one with him; that is, not in essence, but in love, in communion, in agreement, in charity, in spirit, in glory.

Since Christ has thus explained the mode of his oneness with the Father, why should human reasoning, 'though in opposition to reason itself, devise another mode, which makes them one in essence'? And if the doctrine 'be proposed on the single authority of the Church, the true doctrine of the orthodox Church herself teaches me otherwise; ... it instructs me to listen to the words of Christ before all others.' Knowles, dealing at some length with this first passage, reaches substantially the same conclusions.

The second passage is 1 John 5:7: 'there are three that bear record in heaven, the Father, the Word and the Holy Ghost, and these three are one.' Here we have an example of Milton's resort to biblical scholarship as he notes the absence of the words from the Syriac, Arabic, and Ethiopic versions and from most of the ancient Greek manuscripts, and the various readings where the passage does occur. For the rest he argues that, even if authentic, it does not assert unity of essence, but, as Erasmus and Beza concede, only such unity of agreement as was proclaimed in the preceding instance (*De Doctrina*, 1: 5 [Col. 14: 215]).

To the contention that scripture ascribes to the Son 'the name, attributes, and works of God, as well as divine honours' Milton, having disposed of these two utterances, can reply that 'in every passage each of the particulars ... is attributed in express terms only to one God the Father, as well by the Son himself as by his apostles,' that 'wherever they are attributed to the Son ... they are easily understood to be attributable in their original and proper sense to the Father alone,' and that 'the Son acknowledges himself to possess whatever share of Deity is assigned to him, by virtue of the peculiar gift ... of the Father; as the apostles also testify' (*De Doctrina*, 1: 5 [14: 217–19]). From Christ's prayer in the garden of Gethsemane (Matt. 26:39), as from other passages, Milton argues that 'the Father and Son have not, in a numerical sense, the same intelligence and will' and hence 'cannot have the same esence' (*De Doctrina*, 1: 5 [Col. 14: 299–31]); and this confirms the inescapable inference from Christ's mediatorial office, namely, that if he be the one by whom we are reconciled he cannot be the God (that is, one in essence with the God) to whom we are reconciled or 'he must be a mediator between himself and us, and reconcile us to himself by himself; which is an insurmountable difficulty' (*De Doctrina*, 1: 5

[Col. 14: 207]). To the Father alone, Milton cites texts to show, the Son ascribes 'supreme dominion both in heaven and earth,' 'supreme goodness,' 'supreme glory,' and 'divine honours' (De Doctrina, 1: 5 [Col. 14: 227, 233, 237]).

To the objection that 'the Son is sometimes called God, and even Jehovah,' he replies, with citations, that 'the name of God is not frequently ascribed, by the will and concession of God the Father, even to angels and men, how much more, then, to the only begotten Son, the image of the Father' (De Doctrina, 1: 5 [Col. 14: 245]). Angels receive the title, and even the name Jehovah 'because as heavenly messengers they bear the appearance of the divine glory ... and even speak in the very words of the Deity (De Doctrina, 1: 5 [Col. 14: 249]): while the 'name of God is ascribed to judges, because they occupy the place of God to a certain degree in the administration of judgment'. (De Doctrina, 1: 5 [Col. 14: 251]). And the Son, who might claim the name as both messenger and judge, 'and indeed in virtue of a much better right,' appeals to these very facts when accused by the Jews of making himself God (John 10:34–6) '... Is it not written in your law, I said, Ye are gods? If he called them gods unto whom the word of God came ... , say ye of him whom the Father hath sanctified and sent into the world, Thou blasphemest; because I said, I am the Son of God?' Knowles makes the same point about the term god being applied to angels and men and cites Justin Martyr in his support.

EDITOR'S NOTE *This chapter is unfortunately incomplete, and the passage here reproduced gives only a fragmentary impression of the argument concerning the Trinity. Among other subjects, the author intended to explore the strain of adoptionism in Milton's belief that the Son is not the God, but a god, enjoying not a natural but a bestowed or delegated divinity. Emphasis was also to be placed on Milton's view that the primary function of the Son is to manifest the otherwise unmanifested God, acting as 'the true Image of the Father' (Paradise Regained 4.596). Attention was then to be directed to the third member of the Trinity, the Holy Spirit, and finally to the treatment of the Trinity in Milton's poetry.*

It is clear from the preceding argument that the author intended to explore both the views which Milton shared with Arians and Socinians alike, and the views he held in common with the Arians only. While admitting Arian influence, however, the author wished to stress even more heavily the influence of ante-Nicene thought as summed up by the conservative Eusebius of Caesarea. Thus the main line of argument leads back to the earlier Fathers in a manner similar to the argument concerning Milton's views on the creation. The passage which follows reveals the position in broad outline.

On the whole, it is to the Patristic period that we must look for the closest analogues, and there we shall find them not in the opinions of Arius and the original Arians only, but in the doctrine of the ante-Nicene Fathers, and very markedly in the teaching of Eusebius. It seems a reasonable inference that Milton in his quest for doctrine of scripture and the apostolic church received a good deal of suggestion from the writings of the first three centuries.

The author's notebooks reveal how eagerly he explored those early centuries for anticipations of Milton's beliefs. Eusebius is particularly prominent in these notes; his subordinationist view of the Son seems to reveal stronger affinities with Milton's doctrine than are to be found in the more strictly Arian position, while his theory of the creation is remarkably similar to Milton's.

7

Paradise Lost, 1:
theme and pattern

I We shall require at the outset a rough description or working definition of aesthetic pattern. In arriving at it, I was helped years ago by the writings of Roger Fry and Clive Bell on the sister art of painting, though I have no sympathy with their flight from the representational in art or their attempt so to define aesthetic pattern and its attendant emotion as to isolate them from content or theme and its attendant emotion. I am sure that whatever is true in the other arts, there are large areas of poetry in which this will not work. Tragedy, for example, is an imitation of an action which arouses the emotions of pity and fear, and it would be absurd to try to define the effect of *Hamlet* or *Samson Agonistes* simply in terms of pattern, though the presence of pattern profoundly modifies the emotions aroused and is a principal factor in bestowing upon them their accompaniment of pleasure. But I think that aesthetic pattern in a poem can be so far abstracted as to become an object of critical attention, which is all that our present purpose demands.

As we shall use it, there is nothing at all esoteric about the term *aesthetic pattern*. Here the primary meaning of *pattern* is formal design, and a work is said to possess aesthetic pattern when by virtue of this pattern or design it is able to make its effective and pleasurable appeal to our sense of form. At its simplest, aesthetic pattern may be illustrated in many purely decorative designs – indeed in any *good* decorative design with its grouping of elements, its sweep of line leading the eye from one feature to another, its use of parallel and contrast, or repetition with difference, its suggestion (stopping short of complete realization) of symmetry, its encompassing unity and harmony. Quite as simply, aesthetic pattern can be illustrated in many short poems. Here indeed is a very simple example, a poem by Wilfred Gibson, in which the speaker is a young country girl:

> I saw three black pigs riding
> In a blue and yellow cart –
> Three black pigs riding to the fair
> Behind the old grey dappled mare;
> But it wasn't black pigs riding
> In a gay and gaudy cart
> That sent me into hiding
> With a flutter in my heart.
>
> I heard the cart returning,
> The jolting, jingling cart –
> Returning empty from the fair
> Behind the old jog-trotting mare;
> But it wasn't the returning
> Of a clattering, empty cart
> That sent the hot blood burning
> And throbbing through my heart.[1]

Simple though this example may be, and largely visual and decorative in its effect, it has one added characteristic; it introduces a human situation and human feeling, and incorporates them in its pattern. When one is dealing with a long poem, and a classical epic like *Paradise Lost*, one must expect of course far more complicated, sustained, and subtle effects of pattern than this.

While images play their essential part in Milton's patterns, so also, and even more obviously, do ideas or themes. His patterns may be described as both structural and progressive: structural if one considers the firm framework on which they are built, progressive if one considers their movement towards an appointed end. In neither case can one come at the full character of the pattern by attending to the images alone; their role is to support the theme, to forward its progression, to fill in the framework, and to give to the whole pattern that richness and density of poetic texture without which it would remain a pattern perhaps, but a pattern in prose.

II

Paradise Lost is the outcome of Milton's deliberate effort to write a classical epic on a Christian theme, and specifically on the fall of man. Any attempt to isolate and explain the effect of the poem must seek to draw out the implications of this truism, and essay once more some comparison of *Paradise Lost* with its two great models, the *Iliad* and the *Aeneid*. It must watch the poet imposing an analogous pattern upon very different materials, and be alert to detect the modifications and extensions of the pattern which his Christian theme, outlook, and purpose demand or permit.

When full allowance is made for Milton's heresies, *Paradise Lost* remains unequivocally a Christian poem. It assumes the two orders of nature and grace and the priority of the order of grace. Its theme is man's fall from grace and it adumbrates the terms on which, by divine intervention, he will be restored. *Paradise Lost* cannot be adequately described as an epic which substitutes Christian machinery for Olympian, or even Christian legend for pagan, though it does both: it is an epic which finds its subject at the heart of Christian revelation. Implicit in the difference between *Paradise Lost* and its classical models is the whole difference between Christianity and the Graeco-Roman religions and philosophies which it replaced. The points, relevant to our discussion, at which the Christian view of things and the classical most sharply diverge, must be set down, at whatever risk of oversimplification.

The classical recognizes only one order of existence, the natural, though it acknowledges gradations within this order, whereas Christianity adds to the order of nature the superior order of grace, which alone holds the key to the enigma of life. And this addition of a second order which, in man, intersects with the first, may serve to remind us that the Christian view of existence, like every great system of thought, is itself a pattern, and consequently contains elements which can be readily incorporated in the aesthetic patterns of the poet, as Dante would illustrate and as Milton will. But let us pursue for a moment the more obvious results of the single order in the classical systems and the twofold order in the Christian. The essential naturalism of the classical systems permeates any conceptions of the supernatural they may entertain, whether in the pantheon of Homer or in the religion of Virgil, who saw 'Universal Nature moved by Universal Mind.' In Christianity, on the contrary, the supernatural dominates the natural. Though it ratifies many of the natural virtues before transcending them, Christianity will not rest content therewith, but adds its own special virtues of piety, humility, and love; and the Christian virtues combine to produce an ideal of heroism, realized in Christ, and very different from classical conceptions of the heroic, a fact which impinges directly upon epic poetry. Nor may we ignore the way in which Christianity extends what I will call the vertical range of human experience: in the classical view man may rise to the specifically human or sink to the level of the barbarian or the beast; in the Christian vision he is confronted by the dizzy alternatives of rising to heaven or plunging to the bottomless pit. I am the more insistent on this fact since Christianity is often thought merely to restrict the poet's outlook. It does not, I think, at all restrict him in his treatment of evil, but it does afford him a new orientation in several ways and with important results. Thus providence replaces the classical fate. 'Necessitie and Chance Approach not mee,' says Milton's God, 'and what I will is Fate' (7.172–3). This is something very different from fate in Homer, or even from the fate which in Virgil plays providence to the Roman race. One result is that on a total view there can be no such thing as divine tragedy, but only a divine comedy. We do not, however, always take total views, and in the divine comedy there is ample provision for tragic episodes. To prove it, one need not invoke the most moving spectacle in all history, Christ on the Cross: it will suffice to remember that as he turns to the story of man's actual fall, Milton, as he says, 'now must change Those notes to Tragic' (9.5–6). And well he may; for this tragic episode, 'with loss of *Eden*' brings 'Death into the World, and all our woe' (1.3–4). But on a total view the episode takes its place in the divine comedy as the *felix culpa*, the fortunate fall, and the lost Eden is replaced by 'a paradise within thee, happier farr' (12.587). Christianity does not eliminate the tragic from human life: it may even accentuate the tragic; but it places the tragic episode in the divine comedy, and thus invites us to take of it a double view. This Milton perfectly understood when he summed up the tragedy of Samson the man, with its human mitigations as well as its human miseries, before he permitted the Chorus to raise its eyes to the place of Samson's sacrifice in the divine scheme.

And so in *Paradise Lost* the fall is none the less tragic in its immediate impact for turning out at last to be the fortunate fall. But does not the sense of an all-encompassing providence, we may ask, reduce the human character to the dimensions of a puppet – such an Adam as, in Milton's phrase, we see in the motions? And does not the Christian epic here fall far short of Homer and even of Virgil? Not necessarily. In Homer and Virgil the individual is encompassed by the decrees of fate. And for the Christian, even Calvinism never really succeeded in eliminating free will and contingency from his life and actions; and to the attempt of Calvinism to do so, Milton is strongly opposed. He insists upon free will: 'when God gave [Adam] reason he gave him freedom to choose, for reason is but choosing' (*Areopagitica*, Col. 4: 319). The absolute decree which bestowed on man free will meant that every subsequent decree, as it bore upon the life of the individual, was not absolute but contingent on the choice he made. If there is a difference between Homer and Milton, and there is a great difference, it is not because providence leaves man's destiny less in his own hands than does fate (rather, indeed, the reverse), but because the end which providence proposes is recognized as good and because under its standard the good man does not fight alone or unsupported. In Homer the hero is by no means the master of his fate, but he is the captain of his soul. In Milton he is in some degree the master of his individual destiny, but Christ is the captain of his soul.

Nothing, indeed, in this brief preliminary attempt to isolate and appraise, in general terms, the effect upon Milton's epic of his Christian theme and outlook is intended to obscure the large degree of accommodation achievable between Christianity and classical humanism, and by the Christian humanists of the Renaissance actually achieved. It is simply intended to remind us of a certain evident difference between them, rediscovered from time to time, and clearly so in the seventeenth century under the impulse of Puritanism.

Of Milton's growing sense of this difference something may be inferred from his resolute turning to scriptural subjects in all his later poetry, from distinctively Christian judgments repeatedly expressed in *Paradise Lost*, from his changed attitude to classic myth, and from his specific rejection, in *Paradise Regained*, of the heritage of Greece and Rome when they came into competition with Christianity. At the same time, however, we find his classical humanism reasserting itself in his increasingly close adherence to ancient forms and models in epic and tragedy, with but one partial effort, in *Paradise Regained*, to implement his theoretic conviction that the Bible will yield forms and models at least comparable with the classics. In *Paradise Lost* (as also, in its different way, in *Samson Agonistes*) Milton undertakes to present a Christian theme in a classical form, and, sacrificing nothing of the purity of either, to adapt them the one to the other.

III

The terms of this undertaking Milton makes perfectly clear by implication in the opening lines of the epic. On these lines we may pause: so indispensable an introduction are they to the whole poem, so characteristic, not only of Milton's relation to his classical models, but of his spirit and of his artistry, which alone make that relation significant.

Classical precedent demands, as everyone knows, a formal statement of the subject, with some invocation of the muse, followed by a rapid bringing the reader to the point where the poet plunges *in medias res*, and then the plunge. This, precisely, the first fifty-four lines of *Paradise Lost* supply. But no sooner is the subject stated than its wide difference from the wrath of stern Achilles and the wanderings of Cytherea's son, perplexed by Juno's ire, leaps to the eye. Milton can postpone his comment of the fact till Book 9: it is sufficiently accentuated by the contrast of classical form and Chris-

tian content. The epic demands a single action of a proper magnitude, but
one with consequences beyond itself. On the consequences of his action
(other than its sending the soul of many a hero to Hades and giving his body
a prey to the vultures and the dogs, and thus fulfilling the decree of fate)
Homer indeed has nothing to say; but Virgil, on whom this feature of the
epic action chiefly depends, is sufficiently specific: 'whence came the Latin
race, and the lords of Alba, and the walls of lofty Rome.' So might Milton
have said in introducing the national epic which he did not write. As it
is, his theme is yet more universal (the *man* of his opening line – 'Of *man's*
first disobedience – is not, like Virgil's, his protagonist only, but all mankind: or if it be insisted that Virgil's *man* implies the Roman race, then
Milton's does much more than imply the human race); and its consequences are still more momentous, bringing (1.3–5)

> Death into the World, and all our woe,
> With loss of *Eden*, till one greater Man
> Restore us, and regain the blissful Seat ...

Nor is this the only contrast: Virgil's action is, for his man and the interest
which he represents, a weary struggle indeed, but culminating at last in
victory; Milton's, a defeat. Hence his first lines can echo not only Virgil's
'man,' but the ideas of woe and death so prominent in the opening words
of the *Iliad*; for *Paradise Lost* will, as Milton later remarks, turn its notes
to tragic. But now appears the one greater Man – the second reason why
Milton chose to echo Virgil's opening line – the second Adam, in St
Paul's phrase, who will turn defeat to victory. The terms of this reversal
are clearly adumbrated in *Paradise Lost* and are essential to its purpose
and effect, but they belong to the consequences, not to the action, and to
forget that this is *Paradise Lost*, and not *Paradise Regained*, is to disturb
the centre of gravity of Milton's epic, and, incidentally, to ignore the syn-
tactical emphasis (main clause and subordinate clause) of Milton's first
sentence.

In the Renaissance view of poetry, as we have already reminded ourselves, and pre-eminently in the epic, a purpose as well as an action, was
expected. In Homer a later criticism will not easily discover any purpose
beyond that of entertainment; but Virgil's purpose is plain to read. It is, by
the legend which he weaves, to inculcate the *pietas* on which the perpetu-
ation of the Roman glory will depend. Finding, however, no precedent in
Homer, he does not formulate this purpose, but leaves it to be inferred. But
Milton, drawing the correct inference, does not scruple to state his purpose categorically. It is, by his 'great Argument' (that is, the story of the
fall), to (1.25–6)

>   assert Eternal Providence,
>   And justifie the wayes of God to men.

And to ignore this purpose, or minimize its effect, is to take the first fatal step in misunderstanding *Paradise Lost*. 'The moral of other poems,' said Johnson, 'is incidental and consequent; in Milton's only it is essential and intrinsic.'[2] His purpose so dominates and controls the poem that whatever appears to the modern reader to run counter to it should at once make him suspect his own reading: this is the commonest prudence – and the rarest. It should be observed that Milton's rigorous adherence to the epic form does not preclude contact with other traditions. Properly understood, his purpose will be seen to make *Paradise Lost* not less an epic, but more than an epic; it is also a theodicy, a vindication of God's justice in permitting evil to exist, as Pope clearly recognized, when he chose, at the beginning of his own theodicy, to define his purpose in a deliberate echo of Milton: to 'vindicate the ways of God to man.'[3] But Milton's theodicy had proceeded upon a different line: not the line of natural religion, but that of Christian revelation: not concerning itself with the natural order solely or primarily, but with the two orders of nature and grace, and finding within the latter the explanation and vindication of the whole scheme. Such a purpose could no more be executed under the inspiration of the classical muses than could Milton's sacred legend be recounted, and it is, in fact, at the culmination of his prayer to the Heavenly Muse, or rather to the Spirit of God, that Milton's high purpose is uttered.

Like everything else in the opening lines, the invocation finds its precedent and point of departure in the classical tradition: in Homer's 'Sing, goddess, the wrath of Achilles,' and Virgil's 'Tell me, O Muse, the cause ... ;' and more particularly in Hesiod's description, in the *Theogony*, of the muses' dwelling place. But Milton's invocation is not of the classical muses. The Christian tradition in poetry had borrowed or invented its own muse. Urania, originally the patroness of heavenly studies, including astronomy, furnished the Christian poets with a person or at least with a name, and Du Bartas had done much, in his poem addressed to her, to make Urania the muse of specifically Christian verse. It is to Urania, then, the Heavenly Muse, that Milton's invocation is initially addressed; and, true to the tradition, and with consummate artistic skill, he parallels her with the Greek muses, while at the same time asserting her superiority. The Greek muses had three habitations in all: Olympus, where they sang before Zeus and the gods (it is to the muse of Olympus that Homer appeals for authentic knowledge of the divine causes of Achilles' wrath), the slopes of Parnassus with its cloven peaks, and Helicon, the Aonian hill, with the spring Aganippe rising beside the temple of Zeus. Milton recognizes and parallels all three.

The first, the dwelling on Olympus among the gods, he holds in reserve, as he does the name Urania, for the renewed invocation in Book 7 (where he will call upon Urania to 'descend from Heav'n,' the parallel with Olympus being underlined in the words: (7.2–3)

> Whose Voice divine
> Following, above th' *Olympian* Hill, I soare).

The second, Parnassus with its cloven peak, is remembered in the first of the alternatives presented in Book 1: the Heavenly Muse is she (1.6–10)

> that on the secret top
> Of *Oreb*, or of *Sinai*, didst inspire
> That Shepherd, who first taught the chosen Seed,
> In the Beginning how the Heav'ns and Earth
> Rose out of *Chaos*.

And the third is paralleled in the lines intended to recall the words of Hesiod, already echoed in *Lycidas*, and not without their suggestiveness for Milton, as we have seen, in forming his conception of poetic inspiration. From the muses, says Hesiod, let us begin our song, 'who hold the great and holy mount of Helicon and dance on soft feet about the deep-blue spring and the altar of [Zeus] the almighty son of Cronos.' And to the Heavenly Muse, Milton offers this alternative dwelling: (1.10–15)

> Or if *Sion* Hill
> Delight thee more, and *Siloa's* Brook that flow'd
> Fast by the Oracle of God; I thence
> Invoke thy aid to my adventrous Song,
> That with no middle flight intends to soar
> Above th' *Aonian* Mount ...

The basis of this parallelism is found in the Christian humanist tradition, and might be illustrated from the Hill of Contemplation in *The Faerie Queene*[4] which reminds Spenser of Sinai or the Mount of Olives or Parnassus, that is, of the Law, of the Gospel, and of Poetry (no doubt, of poetry in their service). But in the later Milton the distinction between the Christian and the classical is sharper, and the parallel and its limits are more clearly defined. This gives a certain firmness to his utterance, as he pursues the suggestions which the parallel offers, and bends them, with his accustomed economy, to the pattern of poem or of paragraph. A striking example of his artistic economy is seen in the former of the two alternatives here adopted, that of Parnassus-Sinai. Subordinated to the story of man's first disobedience, Milton's epic is to contain not only the story of the revolt of the angels but also an account of the creation of the world. And neither has as yet been mentioned. The revolt of the angels will find its natural place a few lines further on; but here is an opportunity to involve the subject of Book 7, and to emphasize its importance. Milton claims for his poem an inspiration analogous to that of Moses himself – when he too, in accommodated narrative, told 'how the Heav'ns and Earth Rose out of Chaos.'

But the invocation to the Heavenly Muse, rich as are the suggestions which it opens, will carry the poet only so far; and before he can voice the purpose of his poem, which is wholly Christian, he must temporarily abandon the classical parallel, and speak home: and in so doing he returns to the inspiration of Moses as he recounted the story of creation: (1.17–26)

> And chiefly Thou O Spirit, that dost prefer
> Before all Temples th' upright heart and pure,
> Instruct me, for Thou know'st: Thou from the first
> Wast present, and with mighty wings outspread
> Dove-like satst brooding on the vast Abyss
> And mad'st it pregnant: What in me is dark
> Illumin; what is low raise and support;
> That to the highth of this great Argument
> I may assert Eternal Providence,
> And justifie the wayes of God to men.

Nor may one fail to realize what the poet is here suggesting: that the desired operation of the Spirit upon his mind is itself a repetition of the creative act, bringing light out of darkness and order out of chaos, and purging, sustaining, and animating the work, as this very Spirit did the whole creation when first the world was made.

And now, having soared so high already above the Aonian mount, Milton returns to his classical models, and, in the famous formula, calls on the Heavenly Muse to 'say first, what cause' moved man, 'for one restraint,' to cast off his obedience to God and lose his paradisal state, adding significantly (for the cause will introduce the supernatural action and the revolt of the angels): (1.27–8)

> Heav'n hides nothing from thy view
> Nor the deep Tract of Hell ...

Thus Milton completes the announcement of his subject by introducing the drama in heaven and hell, indicating its causal relation to the main action, and at the same time carries the reader rapidly forward to the point at which the poem plunges *in medias res*.

In every respect these opening lines are characteristic of the whole poem. They are characteristic in the relation established with the classical epic, seeking always a precedent and a point of departure therein, and elaborating upon the Virgilian devices and effects, as Virgil had elaborated upon those of Homer, but nevertheless registering clearly the divergence from the classical epics in range and emphasis, the sense of belonging, literally, to another order. The lines are characteristic also in their artistic economy whereby one device or turn of phrase is made to serve more than a single end; suggestion is added to statement, and the true Miltonic effect of richness and density of poetic texture is achieved. Finally, they are characteristic in possessing their own patterned structure and movement, with the main action on the human level first stated and balanced by the supernatural action at the end, and between the two the double invocation of muse and Spirit, the first merging into the second, and the second repeating and making specific the double allusion to inspiration and creation. Thus the lines which announce Milton's theme are an example in little of the pattern of *Paradise Lost*.

IV

In nothing does *Paradise Lost* differ more fundamentally from its classical models than in its conception of the heroic.

Writing of his own scriptural epic, the *Davideis*, Cowley challenges comparison of the Bible with the classics as a source of heroic story, declaring many of its narratives to be better 'stored with great, heroical and supernatural actions (since *Verse* will needs *finde* or *make* such)' than 'the threadbare tales of Thebes and Troy.'[5] In the prologue to Book 9 Milton declares his own 'argument' to be (9.14–19)

> Not less but more Heroic then the wrauth
> Of stern *Achilles* on his Foe pursu'd
> Thrice Fugitive about *Troy* Wall; or rage
> Of *Turnus* for *Lavinia* disespous'd,
> Or *Neptune*'s ire or *Juno*'s, that so long
> Perplex'd the *Greek* and *Cytherea*'s Son.

It is for the action on the human level, for his 'argument' (that is, the story of man's fall), that he challenges this comparison, deliberately rejecting (9.28–9)

> Warrs, hitherto the onley Argument
> Heroic deem'd,

as (9.40–1)

> Not that which justly gives Heroic name
> To Person or to Poem,

and supplying a hint of what he regards as the true heroic in the phrase: (9.31–2)

> the better fortitude
> Of Patience and Heroic Martyrdom ...

As a statement of Milton's views, conditioned by his own experience, this is simple enough. The light which it throws upon the poem seems at first glance more ambiguous, since he has already provided the martial setting and exploits which he here decries, and since Adam at the crisis of his story no more manifests the qualities of the Christian than of the pagan heroic. It is evident that some additional consideration of the term is required.

If the basic conception can be isolated from the subtler insights of Homer's portraiture, it is a somewhat primitive form of heroism that confronts us in Achilles, whose matchless strength, unsurpassed prowess, and dauntless courage make him the very type of the Homeric hero. The others are heroic in the degree to which, like Diomede and Patroclus, they approach this ideal. Achilles' divine parentage, while conferring some added lustre in the suggested analogy with the heroes of old, is not essential. Subordinate qualities not possessed by Achilles may embellish those who possess the basic strength, prowess, and courage: the royal dignity of Agamemnon, king of men, the cunning Ulysses, even the patriotism and public spirit of Hector; but none of these is essential to the hero. And as for patience and heroic martyrdom, the first would too much resemble want of spirit, and the second would betoken defeat and hence the loss (in what precise degree circumstances alone could determine) of heroic standing. The heroic expresses itself in action and, in large measure, depends upon success in action. The primary motive is honour or personal glory. Whatever contributes to this glory is heroic. Clearly, heroism is neither a moral virtue nor an intellectual. It may subsist with overweening pride and a degree of reckless folly, and entails no regard for claims other than the hero's own, in which must be included, of course, those of his immediate followers as part almost of himself. Patriotism and public spirit are alike superfluous, or Homer would never have withheld them from his protagonist and given them to Hector alone. Milton's judgment on this pagan heroism is devastating: (11.689–99)

> For in those dayes Might onely shall be admir'd,
> And Valour and Heroic Virtu call'd;
> To overcome in Battle, and subdue
> Nations, and bring home spoils with infinite
> Man-slaughter, shall be held the highest pitch
> Of human Glorie, and for Glorie done
> Of triumph, to be styl'd great Conquerours,
> Patrons of Mankind, Gods, and Sons of Gods,
> Destroyers rightlier call'd and Plagues of men.
> Thus Fame shall be achiev'd, renown on Earth,
> And what most merits fame in silence hid.

Actually, Milton is writing of a yet earlier age, but every word is a condemnation of Homeric heroism.

In Virgil the primitive conception of the heroic has undergone drastic change. Aeneas has the requisite strength, prowess and courage, and like Achilles, is goddess-born, but these facts are accompanied and almost overshadowed by intellectual and, above all, moral qualities. Personal glory weighs with him scarcely at all, much less than with Hector, in whom, at least in its negative aspect – dread of shame – it plays a decisive and fatal role. In Aeneas the dominating motive throughout is the celebrated Roman *pietas*. It is not a simple conception, but the idea of duty, and even of self-abnegation at the call of duty, lies at its core. The first duty is to the family, ancestors, and descendants, and this form of piety Aeneas illustrates in pre-eminent degree; the next is to followers and dependents, not because one identifies their rights with one's own, but because one has contracted or inherited obligations towards them. Such an attitude, free as it is from the stultifying effects of egoism, easily expands in favouring circumstances into patriotism and public spirit. For Aeneas, Virgil provides precisely these favouring circumstances: in his family and followers are the seeds of the Roman race, and piety becomes patriotism, or even devotion to something larger than the national state. Nor is this all. Though Roman *pietas* is not Christian piety (and the common term must not be allowed to become a pitfall), *pietas* is also a religious virtue, entailing fulfilment of a duty to the gods, however conceived, which far transcends the prudential sacrifices of the Homeric heroes. Thus it is that patience is one of the virtues of Virgil's hero, as it certainly is not of Homer's; nor would it be absurd to imagine his enduring, at the call of duty, heroic martyrdom. The distance at which Aeneas stands from the Homeric hero is emphasized by pitting against him in the person of Turnus a pale reflection of Achilles.

Despite the strong inclination of Christian humanism to approximate the Virgilian and the Christian ideals, there was a point, as Dante saw, beyond which Virgil could not go. And in the particular matter of the heroic Milton is equally categorical. For him the ideal of heroism is realized once and for all in Christ. Long ago he had described Christ as 'most perfect Heroe' (*The Passion* 13), and significantly it was in connection with the heroic martyrdom of the crucifixion and the seeming defeat. The experience of the intervening years had brought home to Milton with a new urgency the idea of heroism in defeat, and this accounts for his exclusive emphasis upon it in the prologue to Book 9. But the idea does not subsist alone: the temporary defeat is part of the divine purpose which cannot fail of victory in the end, and Christian piety, yet more definitely than the Roman *pietas*, means complete submission to, and co-operation with, the divine purpose. Christ, then, is the real hero of *Paradise Lost* in the sense that, like Achilles and Aeneas, he sets the standard of heroism. It is not Christ the heroic martyr, however, that actually figures in the poem, though he is clearly adumbrated there. It is Christ the victor, clad with the Father's irresistible might, who drives Satan out of heaven, and thus performs, like Achilles, what a lesser hero could not achieve. In the successive stages of the heroic, and as it is brought under the control of morality and religion, the element of power, represented by the strength, prowess, and courage of Achilles, is not eliminated, but, by its alliance with the divine purpose, sustained and exalted. Something like this is the context in which Milton's statement on the true heroic requires to be read.

It is not only in its conception of the heroic, however, that *Paradise Lost* deviates from its classical models. At the moment of crisis, which is approaching when Milton pauses to comment on the heroic, his protagonist, as we have said, fails utterly in heroism, exhibits indeed, in Milton's earlier phrase, 'the cowardice of doing wrong' (*Of Education*, Col. 4: 288), and only after repentance, when he has learned the fortitude of patience, does he begin to approach the Miltonic standard of the heroic.

In the *Iliad* and the *Aeneid* the protagonist manifests in fullest measure the qualities, whatever they may be, which the poet recognizes as heroic; in *Paradise Lost* he does not. In Homer and Virgil hero and protagonist are, accordingly, one: in Milton they are two. This has confused the critics, who have quite rightly rejected Adam as hero and have sought another, but in their search have unfortunately stumbled on Satan. In reality Adam is the protagonist and Christ the hero, while Satan is reserved for another role, that of antagonist. To separate hero and protagonist was a bold step necessitated by Milton's theme. To have identified hero and antagonist would have been not boldness, but imbecility, since it would have wrecked that theme – as indeed in the theory of these critics it does. On Milton's plan, the qualities manifested by the hero are the criteria by which protagonist and antagonist alike are to be judged; they reveal the weakness of the one, and the wickedness, which is also the weakness, of the other.

But the strong impression that Satan, though not the hero of the poem, is still in some sense heroic will not be easily relinquished and need not be. In epic protagonist and antagonist must meet as mighty opposites, and this demands in the antagonist certain marks of heroism. Hector indeed contends for our admiration and pity with Achilles himself. And if Turnus appears less admirable it is because, as we have suggested above, he represents an outmoded form of the heroic and seems like a pale reflection of Achilles; and he is not unworthy of Aeneas' steel. But how does this affect Satan? If he had had to encounter only Adam one is tempted to say that no very high degree of heroism would have been necessary: a woman and a serpent might have made up the sum. One would of course be wrong: Adam in his innocence appears to Satan formidable enough. But, in any case, Satan has, as we shall see, much more to do than that. And to equip him for his role, Milton follows Virgil's lead, and betters the instruction. He bestows upon Satan, in the beginning, all the qualities of the Homeric hero. Satan has the strength, prowess, and daring of Achilles, the same irresponsibility and recklessness, the same egoistic desire for glory and impatience of constraint, and like Achilles, though for a different reason, the pathos of the doomed. The intended dilemma of Raleigh's question about Satan, 'Hero or fool?'[6] is no dilemma at all. He is both – like Achilles and Turnus.

It has been convenient to speak thus far as if the dichotomy of hero and protagonist in *Paradise Lost* were absolute: to speak of Adam as the protagonist and Christ as the hero; but this is to oversimplify and to give less weight than one should to the supernatural action, which is, as we shall observe, peculiarly important in *Paradise Lost*. The story of the revolt of the angels and their ejection from heaven, which stands in a causal relation to the fall of man, is told at length; and of that story Christ is not only hero but protagonist. So, in effect, Milton's epic has one hero, Christ, and two protagonists, Adam and Christ, the one defeated, the other victorious. The demanded unity is secured in several ways. In part it is secured by the causal relation between the two actions and the encompassing function of Christ, who in the preliminary action defeats Satan and hurls him down to hell, but in the predicted consequence of man's fall will descend to earth for the second defeat of Satan and the rescue and restoration of man. It is secured also by the enforced parallel (with, of course, vital difference) between the two protagonists: Adam is man whose disobedience spelled defeat; Christ is one greater Man, the second Adam, whose perfect obedience spelled victory and the fulfilment of the divine purpose. The role of protagonist in the poem is then filled by Christ-Adam, and the protagonist thus conceived includes the standard of heroism. This is the corrected and completed statement of the relation of hero and protagonist in *Paradise Lost*. And it permits two further observations.

We see now that it is because Satan is pitted against Christ, not because he is pitted against Adam, that Milton is obliged to bestow upon him marks of the heroic. But it must be a heroism compatible with folly and wickedness, that is, a pagan heroism; and for this Milton looks in the ancient epics. Such heroism Satan has in abundance at the beginning; but, as the story proceeds, and Satan sinks deeper into wickedness, he is gradually divested even of this, as if Milton were saying that without virtue, without Christian heroism, all heroism is an illusion.

We also see a little further into Milton's relation to his classical models. If the three poems be set side by side, it is evident that Achilles, Aeneas, and Christ-Adam are the protagonists in the actions and furnish, each for his own poem, the standard of heroism, and that Hector, Turnus, and Satan are the antagonists. But it is equally evident that in point of character and motive the grouping is different: Hector, Aeneas, Christ-Adam; Achilles, Turnus, Satan. Nor should one overlook a similarity, not at first glance obvious, but real and significant, between Adam and Hector. Though one is protagonist, the other antagonist, each has, and is conscious of having, a vast burden of responsibility committed to his charge, and each, though for very different reasons, fails in his charge; so that in Hector, antagonist in the *Iliad*, but protagonist of Ilium, one has some premonition of a figure without counterpart in the *Aeneid*, and peculiar to *Paradise Lost*, the figure of the defeated protagonist.

v

These special features of *Paradise Lost* – the new conception of the heroic, the new relation of hero and protagonist, the role of the double protagonist – all take their rise in Milton's Christian theme and outlook. They are the direct result of an epic action conceived in terms not of nature only, but of the two orders of nature and grace, with the order of grace, of course, claiming precedence as normative and as furnishing the key to the whole scheme of existence. So fundamental a difference must condition all Milton's borrowings from his classical models, whose centre of gravity is placed in the order of nature. Inevitably, the difference will control the whole epic pattern which he evolves. But control is not to be interpreted simply as restraint. Milton's Christian theme and outlook permit and demand extension as well, and, brought into contact with his classical models, are prolific of new suggestions.

In nothing is this more evident than in the prominence given to the supernatural action – the divine machinery – and the vital role assigned to it in the pattern of *Paradise Lost*. In the *Iliad* and the *Aeneid* the fortunes of the human actors on whom our attention is chiefly fixed are not dependent on their own actions alone, but on the conflicting purposes of the gods, who interfere to advance the interests of their favorites or thwart those for whom they have conceived hostility, though their interference is effective only within certain limits set by the superior power of Zeus-Jove and ultimately ordained by the decrees of fate. Thus a supernatural action stands to some degree in a causal relation to the main human action. This precedent Milton follows. His Messiah and the angels, his Satan and the rebel angels, are cast for the role of the Olympian gods, with the Father doubling as it were for Zeus-Jove and fate. Adam is the favourite of some of these gods, the object of the undying enmity of others, and what goes forward among the gods stands in a causal relation to the fortunes of the human protagonist. All this is made by Milton abundantly clear. Now, while Virgil had inherited from Homer the favour of Venus for the Trojans, reinforcing it by her maternal love for Aeneas, and the hostility of Juno, he had made of them only a limited use. He had not, like Homer, worked up the concerns of the gods into a drama on Olympus, with its place in the pattern of the epic and its own range of effects – including that of comic relief. Milton reverts to the Homeric principle of a drama on Olympus, with its place in the pattern of the epic and its own range of effects, but on a vastly extended plan, with a far more integral role in the pattern and effects utterly different from Homer's.

Whatever the literary form chosen by Milton for presenting the legend of the fall of man, some account must have been taken of the revolt of the angels, as the third and fourth drafts in the Cambridge MS for plays on the subject show: in one the chorus 'relates Lucifer's rebellion and fall,' while in the other the narrative is supplemented by Lucifer himself who 'appears after his overthrow, bemoans himself, seeks revenge on man.' But the epic form permits of large elaboration, and Milton, seizing the opportunity which it offers, sets forth at length and with every circumstance of heroic narrative, the events leading up to Satan's revenge. Almost one may say, the opportunity thus seized was the opportunity of writing an epic at all. Milton might describe himself as (9.27–9)

> Not sedulous by Nature to indite
> Warrs, hitherto the onley Argument
> Heroic deem'd;

but he knew that without battle scenes no epic in the traditional sense could be written, and in the supernatural action he has provided for this essential element, so abundantly present in the human action of Homer and Virgil, but necessarily absent from his own. By presenting his warfaring angels with the gods and even the human combatants of Homer in mind, Milton exploits his opportunity to the full. And not battle scenes alone, but every epic deficiency of his restricted human action, Milton is careful to supply: debates in council, embassies, the marshalling of the hosts, orations to the warriors, flytings, journeys, religious observances, ceremonial games – all the features of the classical epic for which no place could be found in Eden, Milton transfers to the supernatural action. Even the descent to the nether world, which is a feature of the *Odyssey* and the *Aeneid*, has for the reader much more than its equivalent in the scenes in hell. Thus Milton turns to account the epic possibilities of his Christian theme.

Besides bulking much larger, his supernatural action is more subtly integrated in his epic pattern than are those of his ancient models. In addition to standing, as in them, in a causal relation to the human action, it is knit to that action in other ways: by a common antagonist (Satan), by the peculiar relation, already noticed, between the defeated protagonist, Adam, and the victorious protagonist, Christ, and by the exploited parallel between the fall of the angels and the fall of man. Both fall through pride and cast off obedience to their Maker. In both disobedience brings with it loss of their happy state and gives an entry to every kind of sin and error. So far the parallel is complete. But the particular form taken by the initial sin of pride and disobedience differs in man and angels. And, unlike man, the angels fall self-tempted and remain unrepentant; so that for man there is the hope of restoration, but for the angels none. Parallelism with difference is a type of relation important in aesthetic patterns, whether in poetry, painting, or music. It is of the essence in Milton's patterning, as one can see if he casts his mind back over the earlier poems – the *Nativity*, the companion pieces, *Comus, Lycidas*, the *Epitaphium Damonis*. And the importance of its role in the pattern of *Paradise Lost* can scarcely be exaggerated.

Attached to the supernatural action also, but leading the reader back towards the life of man, is Milton's account of the creation. That this, too, was regarded as necessary to a complete presentation of the fall, whatever the form employed, reference once more to the plans for plays in the Cambridge MS, with their 'hymn of the creation,' will show. But in the extended treatment which the epic form renders possible, the poem makes contact with another tradition, that of hexaemeral literature, or those accounts of, and commentaries on, the work of the six days whose most famous example in verse was contained in the *Divine Weeks* of Du Bartas. And in its philosophical character Milton's account of the origin and nature of things seems to reach out towards yet another tradition in poetry and momentarily to challenge Lucretius on his own ground. The epic tradition was not unduly strained by being turned in these directions. In the Renaissance the epic was regarded as a work of encyclopaedic learning. By the help of allegorical interpretation the ancient tradition of Homer as master, and perhaps source, of all knowledge in his day was sustained; and he was thought, in describing the shield of Achilles, to have presented allegorically a whole cosmology. And without recourse to allegory, it was remembered that Virgil had spoken briefly but pregnantly of the *anima mundi* which generates and pervades all things. Certainly long before he turned to the theme of *Paradise Lost* Milton thought of the epic as singing not only of gods and heroes, but of things (*At a Vacation Exercise* 45–6)

> that came to pass
> When Beldam Nature in her cradle was ...

These epic precedents were at most permissive, not mandatory. It was Milton's theme and purpose that were the occasion of Book 7. How essential to them he felt it to be is testified, as we have seen, by the opening lines of the poem. By his artistry he integrates in the pattern of his poem what, less skilfully handled, might have appeared a digression. He does this by making clear its place in the chain of events leading up to the fall, by using it to set forth the cosmological basis of his ethic and the poem's, and by allowing us at once to contrast this supreme example of God's constructive goodness with the evil of Satan who only in destroying can find rest for his relentless thoughts, and to recognize, if we will, the parallel between this constructive goodness and the *reconstructive* goodness of the divine scheme of salvation.

That Milton's Christian theme immensely increases the scope and variety of his epic has been partly indicated in our reference to scenes in heaven and in hell, which become clearly defined and vividly depicted settings, contrasted with each other and with the earthly universe centring in Eden. The picture of Eden and the life of our first parents there permits Milton to work into his pattern a strain of pure idyllicism, a motif of pastoral poetry not quite without precedent in the classical epic tradition if we remember the Arcadian kingdom of Evander, but wholly unique in its detailed depiction and in the central position accorded to it. So detailed indeed is the depiction, and so central the position, that in the rather superfluous enquiry for the theme of *Paradise Lost*, good critics have insisted that this happy idyllic life and its loss are the very theme of the poem. This, of course, is to mistake a part for the whole, but it is an important part, which enabled Milton to draw on a rich tradition, classical and Christian, lying outside the ordinary orbit of the epic, and to tap one of the perennial sources of poetry.

To the three settings of heaven, hell, and the earthly universe centring in Eden, Milton adds a fourth, the chaos, that (7.211–12)

> vast immeasurable Abyss
> Outrageous as a Sea, dark, wasteful, wilde

through which Satan makes his perilous way, and which furnishes the materials of the creation. Each of the settings has its own special tone and effect and even up to a point its own technique of description. But it is not variety only, or contrast, that is thus gained. Each of the settings has its special significance in idea. Heaven represents the perfect order, perfect in itself and because it is dedicated to the highest end, God's service and glory – and God's service in perfect freedom. The earthly universe before the fall is a reflection of the heavenly order. Hell is the antithesis of the heavenly order – not disorder, as one might expect, but perverted order, whose principle Satan has phrased for all time, 'Evil be thou my Good,' and whose service is essential slavery. Disorder is the note not of hell, but of the chaos: better call it unorder, for it holds the potentiality of order, the order actually imposed upon a part of it at the creation. With the fall the earthly order relapses towards the chaos. After their sin Adam and Eve reflect in their passions its turbulent, meaningless motion. With their repentance the long and painful restoration of the lost order is begun.

These are some of the elements in the pattern of *Paradise Lost* opened to Milton by his Christian theme.

VI

As we seek to describe and define more closely the character of that pattern we may perhaps recall the results of our study of the earlier poems. We found that Milton's patterns had always a firm basis in the structure of the poem; his were essentially structural patterns. They were developed in relation to the traditional and usually well defined structure of the genre in which he chose to work: they were adaptations of traditional structural patterns. All his more serious efforts, however, had a theme to develop. And to the theme the traditional structure was adapted. Upon the supporting framework thus provided the full pattern of the poem was woven. That pattern was compacted, it might be, of specific affirmations, of statements veiled in allegory, of actions, characters and scenes, of allusions, of images with evocative power or symbolic value – of whatever, in short, was appropriate to the theme on which, and the genre in which, Milton was working. Thus there were three points of reference to bear in mind in dealing with the pattern of his poems: the traditional structure of the genre, as it was modified by the theme of the particular poem; the theme itself, that is, the developing line of conceptual thought, to which the modified structure was fitted, so that they might yield each other mutual support; and the total pattern, made up of various elements, but supported throughout by structure, and directed by theme, and conferring upon the whole work richness and density of poetic texture. There is at least a strong presumption that the same thing will be true of the pattern of *Paradise Lost*.

In its structure, as in the type of narrative effect at which it aims, *Paradise Lost* more resembles the *Aeneid* than the *Iliad*. For this there is good reason. Milton's poem and Virgil's are 'secondary' or literary epics, designed to be read with attention by individuals, relatively sophisticated, and very remote from the gatherings which first listened to the *Iliad*. As contrasted with the Homeric epic, they yield the same kind of pleasure, and to do so employ some of the same techniques. Part of the pleasure is in the poet's literary skill in imitating his model – something very different from merely copying it, since imitation allows a certain freedom and does not extinguish the hope of surpassing the model. To surpass will generally mean to elaborate upon its devices and effects, but may on occasion mean to deviate from it. Both can be illustrated from Virgil and from Milton. But Milton has two models; and he measures out, not to Homer only, but to Virgil as well, the treatment which the Roman gave to the Greek. At point after point – in the epic opening, for example, which we have examined, and in the similes, as we shall see later – Virgil elaborates upon Homer, and Milton upon Virgil. On the other hand, for Homer's flowing kaleidoscopic narrative, with its dependence upon suspense and upon such broad effects of repetition and contrast as are suited to auditory reception, Virgil substitutes a carefully articulated structure, suited to the apprehension of a reader. And so does Milton.

A typical example may be seen in their handling of the antecedent action. Though the *Iliad* plunges *in medias res*, it does not resort to the device of the single contained narrative for presenting the antecedent action. By methods more consonant with Homer's flowing kaleidoscopic style, that is, by swift and glancing references, backward and around, it contrives to tell us what we need to know of the long-drawn contest at Troy and the warriors engaged therein. The device of the single contained narrative (itself, of course, a Homeric invention, but in the *Odyssey*), was consecrated in epic usage by Aeneas' account to Dido of the fall of Troy and the events which brought him to Carthage. With supreme artistry Virgil makes the narrative of Aeneas fulfil a double function: it presents the antecedent action and it motivates the next episode by fanning the flame of love in Dido, enchanted like Desdemona by the hero's story. In *Paradise Lost* the narrative of Raphael presents the antecedent action and warns Adam of the enemy at the gate, which is indeed the ostensible reason for its introduction. If this were all we should have to pronounce Milton's art at this point very much inferior to Virgil's. But in both poems the contained narrative has a third function: it adds to their sweep and variety by introducing in effect an epic within an epic. It enables Virgil to combine in the *Aeneid* an *Odyssey* with an *Iliad*. For Milton it holds even greater possibilities: the contained narrative of the war in heaven enables him, as we have seen, to make good the deficiencies of his main action and obtain for *Paradise Lost* all the principal features of the traditional heroic poem, and further so to parallel the fall of the angels with the fall of man as to make the narrated antecedent action an essential part of his total pattern. In this his art is certainly not inferior to Virgil's.

One must not, however, exaggerate the similarity of *Paradise Lost* to the *Aeneid* in point of structure. Milton, we have said, treats Homer and Virgil much as Virgil treats Homer, adopting their devices, elaborating upon them, and when his theme and purpose demand it, departing from his models. And Milton, it would seem, actually catches up hints from Homer which Virgil misses or for which he can find no use.

The *Aeneid*, we may remind ourselves, consists of two groups of six books each. The first group is a prelude to the main action and is for the most part episodic in character: the episode of Dido (in which Virgil skilfully insinuates Aeneas' narrative of the antecedent action, itself episodic, after the fall of Troy), the episodes of the funeral games, the firing of the fleet, the visit to the nether world, with the vision and prophecy of the Rome that is to be, which fortifies the protagonist for, and thus serves as transition to, the main action, the war in Italy. The second group of six books is introduced by a prologue and renewed invocation of the muse (a mode of marking a main division in the poem which Milton observes and puts to his own use). The crisis occurs in Book 7 in the outbreak of war (Juno's last desperate throw) with the at first welcoming Latians. And the remaining books present this war in more or less continuous narrative, culminating in the slaying of the antagonist, Turnus.

Perfectly adapted to Virgil's theme and purpose, this structure would have been impossible for Milton's. But the story of the fall, as he conceived it, had possibilities of epic structure no whit inferior though utterly different. *Paradise Lost* is built up around Book 9, the account of the fall, which gives its title to the poem.

The business of the first eight books is to present the train of events in heaven, hell, and Eden, which give rise to it. Though actually composed of a series of episodes – the rousing of the Satanic host and building of Pandaemonium, the 'great consult,' Satan's journey to Eden, the visit of Raphael, in which Milton inserts the narrative of the antecedent action, etc. – they do not give an effect of episodic, but rather of sustained, narrative. The reason is twofold. The first six books have for their principal interest the revolt of Satan from his allegiance, his defeat, and his preparations for the next step in his campaign. The centring of so much attention upon the antagonist (beyond anything in Homer, and far beyond anything in Virgil) was, as time would show, not without its danger: for many modern readers, and until recently most modern critics, it has upset the delicate balance which Milton intended, and given some colour of excuse, though no solid reason, for regarding the antagonist as the hero of the epic. For here is the second reason for the impression that this is no mere series of episodes, but a continuous and directed narrative. Though Milton departs from Virgil, and in some degree follows Homer, in withholding the protagonist in the earlier books (Adam is absent until Book 4, and to the end of Book 6 receives not more than one-quarter of our attention); yet he never allows us to forget that all he is narrating is preparatory to the main action, that it stands in a causal relation to that action, and he is careful to reinforce the integration of the two actions, by the parallel between the fall of the angels and the fall of man, which we are able to apprehend in part as the former is being recounted, and fully at the end, and in other ways. From Books 7 and 8 the antagonist is withdrawn, and our attention is directed upon the earthly scene, narrowing down at last to Eden, into which the antagonist will return in Book 9.

A comparison of the crises and results of the crises of *Paradise Lost* and the *Aeneid,* and indeed of the *Iliad* too, is instructive. The crisis of the *Aeneid,* it will be observed, entails no new decision on the part of the protagonist, but simply an unswerving determination to press on despite every obstacle, by peace if it may be, by war if it must, to an end clearly envisaged and divinely appointed. And the rest of the poem carries the action, with no change of direction, to that end as denouement, though the poem concludes with the slaying of Turnus, a moment of climax, and the end itself, the founding of Rome, lies beyond its compass – a subject indeed for other epics. The crisis of the *Iliad* is of a different order, involving the decision of

Achilles to re-enter the fray, and thus changing the direction of the action, which reaches its immediate result in the slaying of Hector, with the further results, the slaying of Achilles himself and the fall of Troy, lying outside the compass of the poem. The *Iliad* does not conclude, however, with the slaying of Hector, but with an episode so foreign to Virgil's theme and purpose that he had perforce to reject it: the plea of Priam for the body of Hector.

The crisis of *Paradise Lost* differs sharply from that of the *Aeneid*. It presents to the protagonist his fateful choice. The decision which he makes is wrong and by it goodness suffers a defeat: it changes the direction of the action and it conditions the rest of the poem. Again the end, the completed denouement, man's salvation, lies beyond its conclusion; but the end is assured: the movement towards it is begun. The way lies, and can only lie, through repentance, and this entails a second crisis, a second decision, in Book 10. The two remaining books reveal in vision and prophecy the results of the fall and of man's repentance. They accomplish the reorientation of the protagonist. They set the human tragedy in the larger context of the divine comedy. And in one respect more 'classical' than the *Aeneid*, *Paradise Lost* ends on a quiet note, as does the *Iliad*.

Nor is the similarity wholly confined to these two points: a crisis which changes the direction of the action, and the quiet ending. Taught by his own bereavement and reminded of his father by Priam, pitiless Achilles learns pity: there comes to the protagonist some degree of reorientation, if not repentance, before the poem ends on its appropriately muted note. It is clear that, despite the immense chasm separating Milton's theme and outlook from Homer's, *Paradise Lost* here adopts the formula of the *Iliad* rather than that of the *Aeneid*. The change in Achilles is presented in the light of Homer's prevailing sense of the human tragedy, and a sense of human fallibility, which stops, however, very far short of a conviction of sin: there is no visible divine purpose with which to co-operate. The change in Adam posits the idea of sin – the refusal to co-operate with the divine purpose; and sin can be expiated only by repentance. This achieved, Adam's reorientation is undertaken in the full light of the divine purpose, which is also the divine comedy. In Virgil there is indeed a divine purpose in human affairs. Aeneas is enlightened by it, and increasingly, throughout the poem. Though not infallible, he never fails in his co-operation with that purpose; so there is no ground for repentance and no need for reorientation. In Homer and Milton extremes do not meet; but they seem at this point, and in their effect upon structure, to run parallel.

Yet the vast difference in theme and outlook means that the materials of Milton's pattern differ as widely as could well be conceived from Homer's, and that the pattern itself is woven under a presiding principle utterly at variance with his. The materials are not much more like Virgil's; but there is some kinship in the presiding principles, different though they be.

We may pause for a moment on two central episodes in the *Aeneid*, for which there is no precedent in the *Iliad*, but which find in different degrees their equivalents in *Paradise Lost*: the encounter of Aeneas with Dido, and his vision of the future of his race. But it is instructive to observe how different are the functions of Milton's equivalents in the development of his theme, and how different, in consequence, their place in his structural plan and in the full pattern of his poem.

The encounter with Dido, as every reader will agree, introduces a note of romantic passion in the restrained symphony of the *Aeneid*, with its intense and sympathetic portrayal of her love. This is a note altogether absent from the *Iliad*, and a long step towards the mediaeval and modern cult of romantic love. But there is no escaping the fact that in Virgil's action Dido fills the role of one of the major obstacles, and the most subtle, that Aeneas has to overcome in his execution of the divine purpose. She is the Circe of Virgil's odyssey. No doubt the love of Hector for Andromache or of Aeneas for Creusa is compatible with heroism by the Homeric standard or the Virgilian, but love itself is not a heroic passion as it became for many writers of the Middle Ages and the Renaissance. Milton knew the idealized love of the romance tradition, and in his earlier writings, as we have seen, he speaks eloquently of it. In proportion as it was a chaste love of virtue it was part of the heroic as he then conceived it. And in *Paradise Lost* he goes yet farther and makes wedded love, seen in this light, a step by which man may ascend towards the heavenly love, thus bringing it into line with his mature conception of heroism. But it is part of Adam's failure in this heroism – it is indeed the very form which that failure takes – that, put to the test, he does not maintain the ideal view of love, but relapses into a kind of romantic passion incompatible with virtue and the service of God. Thus in the circumstances Eve becomes the Dido of *Paradise Lost*; but the protagonist does not resist her entreaties, does not overcome the obstacle to virtue, to the fulfilment of the divine purpose, which she, or rather his own attitude towards her, presents. Important and memorable as is Virgil's episode, Milton moves his treatment of the motif forward to the central and most crucial moment of his action.

Whether, as he followed St Augustine in the motivation of Adam's fall, Milton wrote with the contrasting example of Aeneas and Dido in mind, must remain speculative. But no doubt attaches to the second example. The vision of his descendants and the prophecy of man's history vouchsafed to Adam as he quits Eden plainly stem from the vision and prophecy of Rome's greatness vouchsafed to Aeneas when he visits the nether world. For the visit itself, derived of course from the *Odyssey*, Milton has no place since heaven and hell are given the status of settings in his poem, though in his description of hell he is not forgetful of Virgil's sketch. But the vision and prophecy are, in their own way, as essential to his purpose and pattern as to Virgil's. In the *Aeneid* they are placed at the very centre of the poem to remind the reader of the goal of the action, the glory of imperial Rome, and to fortify the protagonist for all that must yet be done and endured. They look back to the promise of Jove to Venus in Book 1 and on to the scenes displayed in Aeneas' shield in Book 8, and are hence a focal point in Virgil's pattern. In *Paradise Lost* the object of vision and prophecy is to reorient Adam the fallen but repentant, and to fortify him by placing his tragedy and mankind's in the larger context of the divine scheme with its promise of salvation: hence their removal to the two final books of the poem. If they seem less central to Milton's pattern, it is because his theme is so different and requires a pattern of a different order. But actually their integration in his pattern is not less complete. The reorientation by Michael of Adam the fallen (Books 11 and 12) balances the orientation of Adam the unfallen by Raphael (Books 5–7). The earlier deals with antecedent events in heaven, the latter with ensuing events on earth; but the promise of salvation which illuminates the human tragedy is the promise made in heaven in Book 3.

Nothing could be more characteristic of the pattern of *Paradise Lost*, which is, like that of the *Aeneid*, a directed pattern, but directed to a different end. With the undirected pattern of the *Iliad* the contrast is inevitably sharper.

In his persuasive *Pattern of the Iliad*, J.T. Sheppard has seen in the shield of Achilles a symbol of the Homeric view of life and up to a point an epitome of Homer's craftsmanship.[7] On its panels are depicted scenes of life and death, of sorrow and rejoicing: scenes of peace, with cattle and the fruits of the earth, of industry relieved by ceremonial song and rustic merriment, of dance, courtship, and marriage, of civil life and the processes of law and order: and juxtaposed with these, scenes of war and violence, with siege of cities, ambuscades, and warriors hastening to battle, led on by the gods; and upon the scenes of peace and order, of prosperity and rejoicing, the scenes of violence, whether of men or beasts, encroach. This is the spectacle of human life on which the sun and stars look down, enacted on a stage girt round by the stream of Ocean. Its ultimate meaning is unexplained, perhaps inexplicable, and certainly little attended to; but its impact is predominantly tragic, and how the actor may bear himself heroically amid its varied scenes is the only rewarding question. It is, however, a spectacle of endless fascination, with its own kaleidoscopic pattern, or elements of pattern, made up of parallel and contrast, and of repetition with difference; and to the poet is given power to see the artistic possibilities of this pattern and to realize them in relation to the action and characters which he is presenting. The result is the pattern of the *Iliad*.

Among its elements are human characters and the clash of characters in action. No doubt in the epic, in Homer and ever after, action and not characterization, is primary. But in Homer character is revealed in action, and by the words of the actors dramatically rendered. Character, it is true, is conceived in broad general lines, as the stock epithets remind us. Nor do the characters, with the single exception of Achilles, change as a result of experience or reveal unexpected qualities. Yet Homer succeeds in creating figures which are at once typical and individuated – Achilles, Hector, Nestor, and Odysseus; and in Achilles, especially in the conclusion, he seems to transcend the limits of his age and legend. Homer's characters, then, their conflicts with one another, and even their states of mind, constitute an important part of this pattern, and of the heritage of the epic.

It is part of the heritage which Virgil did not greatly exploit. More than in the *Iliad*, indeed, action in the *Aeneid* seems to predominate over characterization, and in the characters, type over individuation. *Pius* is a more complex epithet than any applied by Homer to his figures, but it more completely exhausts the qualities of Aeneas. It is possible, of course, to exaggerate the difference; and, on any view, Dido is a shining exception. But our concern is with Milton.

In Milton characterization in the epic comes into its own. Indeed the question has been raised whether he is here dependent chiefly upon the epic tradition at all: whether he is not still influenced by his original design for a tragedy on the fall, and whether he is not responding to the achievements of drama, and not of ancient drama merely, but of Shakespeare and his fellows. Be this as it may: in *Paradise Lost*, character, the clash of characters, and their inward conflicts play a part in the total pattern much more important than in Virgil and probably, though here the account is more difficult to cast with accuracy, more important than in Homer.

This is the more remarkable because Milton's main action would appear at first glance to give no scope for characterization at all. How is one to characterize man in the idyllic state of innocence or individuate human figures when there is but one of each sex. We are told that men and women can be interesting only in the fallen state (*O felix culpa!*) and that in fact Milton's Adam and Eve becomes interesting only after their fall. The poem scarcely supports these confident statements. For Milton the unfallen is indeed an idyllic state; but it is not merely idyllic: it is also ethical: our first parents are creatures of free will, whose obedience is a free moral act, and for whom impulses, as yet innocent, may in changed circumstances give rise to a sudden crisis. In Eve's account of the first moments of her being, and more distinctly in her dream of the angel and the tree, and in Adam's perplexed admission to Raphael of his feelings for Eve, Milton, with a subtlety and precision wasted on many of his critics, takes the first bold step necessary to enrich his epic with human characters. Adam and Eve commence to emerge as individuals and as individuals they respond to the crowded experiences which fill their remaining hours in Eden. The second bold step which Milton takes is to introduce human characterization into the supernatural action, as Homer had done in a very different way. The Messiah, for good reason, is hardly characterized at all, though certain qualities are attributed to him as he successively manifests God's power, justice, and love. The angels are scarcely more individuated: they too are manifestations of God's goodness. But with the demons Milton has a free hand. So good a use does he make of it that, in Book 2, they become a group of individuals surrounding and supporting their matchless chief.

Satan is, of course, Milton's triumph of characterization. Against this truism it is idle to object that there must be ambiguity in the portrait since different generations of readers have understood it very differently. To allow the objection would be to place Hamlet outside the pale. The analogy, indeed, is striking. There is no ambiguity in these characters, but there is a degree of ambivalence, and the divergent interpretations depend on the successive recognition of elements that are really present in them, but also on their overemphasis by the critic and his wresting them from their context. The distortion depends, more obviously than usual, on changes in the commonly accepted assumptions and values which the author could not possibly foresee and provide for. But, finally, his intention is not impossible to discover if one will submit oneself to the text, and view the character as a whole, in relation to the action, and with due reference to the vehicle in which action and character are presented.

Here is a character which, contrary to usual epic practice, changes markedly with the action as it proceeds. Satan, as we have said, commences with all the qualities of the pagan heroic and ends with none of them. He is a study in disintegration – like Macbeth – and in somewhat similar fashion he is a tragic figure which may legitimately move not only terror but pity.[8] Such a character provides rich possibilities of patterned effects, which is our present concern: first, within the character itself, in the successive stages of its decline and in the contrast of the last state with the first; second, in contrast with the unchanging characters, more typical of the epic form, and essential to its pattern as fixed points (the Messiah, the faithful angels), or in comparison and contrast with characters which change indeed with the action as surely as Satan but in another fashion (Adam and Eve).

It is remarkable how evenly the interest in human character (for the characterization of Satan is essentially human) is distributed in *Paradise Lost*: in the first half of the poem, when there can be little characterization of the human pair, Satan holds the centre of the stage; when he recedes Adam and Eve come forward. No one ought to doubt, then, that character is an important element in Milton's epic pattern, as it is in Homer's, and in much greater degree than in Virgil's.

To all three poets the wide spectacle of the world lay open, with its potentialities of pattern waiting to be realized. For the epic is a representation of reality, though the form sets the spectacle at a certain distance and presents it in an impressive action and larger than life. Homer views the spectacle and weaves his pattern, to all appearance without prepossessing or with only the negative prepossession of an encompassing fatalism. The cases of Virgil and of Milton are very different. The action presented in the *Aeneid* is conceived as part of a divinely appointed plan and as moving irresistibly to an end which is meaningful and good. One cannot describe this as in itself a limitation since it confers upon the action new possibilities of patterned effects. But the pattern will be of a different order and will have a new controlling principle. The fact can be very succinctly illustrated from Virgil's imitation of the shield of Achilles. On the shield of Aeneas are depicted scenes from the history of that Rome towards whose foundation the whole action is moving, around whose assumed values the whole pattern is woven. It is a symbol, not of the human spectacle at large as the poet sees it, but of its appointed end. As such the shield takes its place in a pattern in which the prophecy and vision of Book 6 is central and is supported by the promise of Jove to Venus in Book 1, and the shield of Aeneas itself in Book 8.

From *Paradise Lost* the *motif* of the decorated shield disappears, and, as we shall see, for good reason, but not without leaving a palpable trace behind. The vision vouchsafed to Adam in Book 11 is plainly suggested by the vision of Aeneas, and, like it, directs our attention to results of the action which lie beyond the confines of the poem. But the scenes presented to Adam's view in their pictorial detail, their contrast, and their general effect of pattern are far more reminiscent of the panels in the shield of Achilles. Cain's slaying of Abel is a perfect panel, with its initial contrast of tillage and pastoral care, its scene of peaceful religious sacrifice and the sudden incursion of violence. The whole vision, indeed, is composed of clearly defined scenes each with its internal contrasts, and each in its turn contrasting with the others. One of Homer's panels presents two fair cities of mortal men:

> In the one there were marriages and feastings, and by the light of the blazing torches they were leading the brides from their bowers through the city, and loud rose the bridal song. And young men were whirling in the dance, and in their midst flutes and lyres sounded continually ... But the folk were gathered in the place of assembly; for there a strife had arisen, and two men were striving about the blood-price of a man

slain ... And heralds held back the folk, and the elders were sitting
upon polished stones in the sacred circle ... then would they spring up
and give judgment, each in turn. And in the midst lay two talents of
gold, to be given to him whoso among them should utter the most
righteous judgment. But around the other city lay in leaguer two hosts
of warriors gleaming in armour. And twofold plans found favour with
them, either to lay waste the town or to divide in portions twain all
the substance that the lovely city contained within. Howbeit the be-
sieged would nowise hearken thereto, but were arming to meet the foe
in an ambush ... Goodly were they and tall in their harness, as beseem-
eth gods, clear to view amid the rest, and the folk at their feet were
smaller. But when they were come to the place where it seemed good
unto them to set their ambush, in a river-bed where was a watering-
place for all herds alike, there they sate them down, clothed about with
flaming bronze. Thereafter were two scouts set by them apart from the
host, waiting till they should have sight of the sheep and sleek cattle.
And these came presently, and two herdsmen followed them with them
playing upon pipes; and of the guile wist they not at all. But the liers-
in-wait, when they saw these coming on, rushed forth against them and
speedily cut off the herds of cattle and fair flocks of white-fleeced
sheep, and slew the herdsmen withal. But the besiegers, as they sat
before the places of the gathering and heard much tumult among the
kine, mounted forthwith behind their high-stepping horses, and set out
thitherward, and speedily came upon them. Then set they their battle
in array and fought beside the river banks, and were ever smiting one
another with bronze-tipped spears. And amid them Strife and Tumult
joined in the fray ...[9]

The first element of dance and nuptial song, Milton has already provided
(11.556ff.) where the sons of God loved the daughters of men, and now he
proceeds to (639–71)

> Towns, and rural works between,
> Cities of Men with lofty Gates and Towrs,
> Concours in Arms, fierce Faces threatning Warr,
> Giants of mightie Bone, and bould emprise;
> Part wield their Arms, part courb the foaming Steed,
> Single or in Array of Battel rang'd ...
> One way a Band select from forage drives
> A herd of Beeves, fair Oxen and fair Kine
> From a fat Meddow ground; or fleecy Flock,
> Ewes and thir bleating Lambs over the Plaine,

Thir Bootie; scarce with Life the Shepherds flye,
But call in aide, which makes a bloody Fray;
With cruel Tournament the Squadrons joine;
Where Cattle pastur'd late, now scatterd lies
With Carcasses and Arms th' ensanguind Field
Deserted: Others to a Citie strong
Lay Siege, encampt; by Batterie, Scale, and Mine
Assaulting; others from the wall defend
With Dart and Jav'lin, Stones and sulphurous Fire;
On each hand slaughter and gigantic deeds.
In other part the sceptr'd Haralds call
To Council in the Citie Gates: anon
Grey-headed men and grave, with Warriours mixt,
Assemble, and Harangues are heard, but soon
In factious opposition, till at last
Of middle Age one rising, eminent
In wise deport, spake much of Right and Wrong,
Of Justice, of Religion, Truth and Peace,
And Judgment from above: him old and young
Exploded and had seiz'd with violent hands,
Had not a Cloud descending snatch'd him thence
Unseen amid the throng ...

Thus does Milton elaborate Adam's vision of Enoch with Homeric effect, and perhaps with memories of this very panel in Achilles' shield.

The reason why the motif of the decorated shield disappears from *Paradise Lost* is not far to seek. The Messiah has no need of defensive weapons as he goes forth to scatter his enemies before him, riding in the chariot of paternal Deity (that strange moving throne of Ezekiel's vision), armed with the thunderbolt, and with the winged Victory at his side. Satan's shield is orbed like the moon – and, like the moon, a blank. We must look elsewhere for symbols of Milton's direction and emphasis. Despite its dependence on the obviously centred vision of Aeneas, the vision of Adam will not qualify. It has its special function, the reorientation of fallen man, and thus bears upon the results of the action, but not upon its whole course. We must continue our search. And nothing perhaps is more revealing than the apparition of the Messiah to which we have just referred: (6.749–85)

       forth rush'd with whirlwind sound
The Chariot of Paternal Deitie,
Flashing thick flames, Wheele within Wheele undrawn,
It self instinct with Spirit, but convoyd

By four Cherubic shapes, four Faces each
Had wondrous, as with Starrs their bodies all
And Wings were set with Eyes, with Eyes the wheels
Of Beril, and careering Fires between;
Over thir heads a chrystal Firmament,
Whereon a Sapphire Throne, inlaid with pure
Amber, and colours of the showrie Arch.
Hee in Celestial Panoplie all armd
Of radiant *Urim*, work divinely wrought,
Ascended, at his right hand Victorie
Sate Eagle-wing'd, beside him hung his Bow
And Quiver with three-bolted Thunder stor'd
And from about him fierce Effusion rowld
Of smoak and bickering flame, and sparkles dire;
Attended with ten thousand thousand Saints,
He onward came, farr off his coming shon. ...
Hee on the wings of Cherub rode sublime
On the Chrystalline Skie, in Saphir Thron'd ...
Before him Power Divine his way prepar'd;
At his command the uprooted Hills retir'd
Each to his place, they heard his voice and went
Obsequious, Heav'n his wonted face renewd
And with fresh Flourets Hill and Valley smil'd.

These lines occur at the centre of the epic (in the final twelve-book arrangement), that is, at the end of Book 6, in the precise position of Virgil's vision and prophecy of Rome. Though less directly, they just as certainly illuminate the whole action and point to the end, beyond the limits of the poem, towards which it is moving. The first victory of Christ over Satan, clad in this splendid embodiment of power, is a symbol of the final triumph when evil shall be no more. Satan's successful attack on man, predicted but not yet accomplished, which is the subject of *Paradise Lost*, is seen by Milton, and requires to be seen by the reader, as an event in this larger action, a tragic episode indeed, but in the divine comedy. His belief in the victory of goodness, or, in other words, in the Christian scheme, is the central assumption in Milton's vision of reality and the controlling principle in the weaving of his pattern. In some respects it may limit the vision and the pattern. In other respects it leaves them free: for Christian realism – and nothing could make this plainer than *Paradise Lost* – does not question the facts of evil and of suffering, but only their finality. In yet other respects the Christian scheme extends the possibilities of pattern, being itself a patterned vision of reality.

Of some of these extended possibilities of pattern the lines quoted furnish an example. Primarily, they are an embodiment of power. (Christ, who has sought only virtue, has had power added to him; Satan, who has sought only power, and at the expense of virtue, proves impotent.) The particular power manifested is the power, if need be, to defeat and destroy. (Christ has said that he can put on God's terrors as he puts his mildness on, image of him in all things.) But with the idea of power is coupled that of reason: the chariot-throne is instinct with Spirit, but is "convoyed" (conveyed, moved and directed) by cherubim, who are symbols of reason and knowledge. And with the idea of power to defeat and destroy is also coupled the idea of power to create and restore, the principal function of the Messiah, and the scene, by him transformed, recalls and is meant to recall Eden, which is a reflection of the heavenly order and beauty. But, more than this, the passage will find its parallel in the next book when, again upborne on the wings of cherubim, and endowed with the power of God, Christ rides out on his mission of creation and reduces the chaos to order: "For *Chaos* heard his voice" (7.219).

The lines are characteristic of *Paradise Lost*, not only in their grandeur, but in their patterned effect and the integration of their pattern in the pattern of the whole, and characteristic also in their dependence upon dominant ideas which take their origin in Milton's Christian theme and outlook. There is, if I mistake not, a more constant and pervasive elaboration of pattern in *Paradise Lost* than in either of its principal ancient models; which is not to say that it is a greater poem (understanding and not evaluation is the purpose of this preface), but simply that it is different.

8
Paradise Lost, 2:
the elaboration of the pattern

1   Books 1, 2

By using Virgil's device, 'Tell me, Muse' (1.27–83), Milton rapidly indicates the point in the story where the poem is to plunge *in medias res* and presents the initial scene, Satan on the burning lake of hell, whither he and his legions have been cast on their expulsion from heaven by the Son of God (as will be narrated in the antecedent action in Book 6, lines 827–92). In Book 1 we see Satan, then, defeated, and the first emphasis falls not on his power but on the pathos of his situation: (1.54–75)

> for now the thought
> Both of lost happiness and lasting pain
> Torments him; round he throws his baleful eyes
> That witness'd huge affliction and dismay
> Mixt with obdurate pride and steadfaste hate:
> At once as far as Angels kenn he views
> This dismal Situation waste and wild,
> A Dungeon horrible, on all sides round
> As one great Furnace flam'd, yet from those flames
> No light, but rather darkness visible
> Serv'd onley to discover sights of woe,
> Regions of sorrow, doleful shades, where peace
> And rest can never dwell, hope never comes
> That comes to all, but torture without end
> Still urges, and a fiery Deluge, fed
> With ever-burning Sulphur unconsumed:

> Such place Eternal Justice had prepar'd
> For those rebellious, here their prison ordain'd
> In utter darkness, and thir portion set,
> As far remov'd from God and light of Heav'n
> As far from the Centre thrice to th' utmost Pole.
> Oh how unlike the place from whence they fell!

Against this background we have Satan's dialogue (1.84ff.) with Beelzebub, his chief lieutenant. (Beelzebub is both a pagan deity, a form of Baal, and referred to in the Bible as a prince of devils.) Satan commences to speak and at once the revelation of his mind begins. It is not a direct and simple revelation; for wherever Satan has an audience some part of his utterance is political. Only in the soliloquy can we trust what Satan says; elsewhere his speeches are designed to put the best face possible on the matter. Yet the policy to which they are attuned is the outcome of his convictions – of convictions which do not at the deepest level convince Satan himself (as the soliloquy in Book 4 makes clear) but on which he had nevertheless acted and is still determined to act. It is part of Milton's skill in characterization to let Satan utter his vaunts and only later introduce this subtler point of psychology; but there are hints given, as in the statement that Satan was 'Vaunting aloud but rackt with deep despair' (1.126). Up to a point Satan is the prey of his own propaganda, but in the depths of his being he knows that it is all wrong and he is doomed. Satan's error is among other things an intellectual error: he gets the facts all wrong. The erring will deludes the understanding. He talks, and in part thinks, of himself and God as beings of the same order (only God has more power), though in his heart of hearts he knows that God is Creator and he himself is creature.

The first note struck in the dialogue with Beelzebub is the note of pathos, the wistful remembrance of 'the happy Realms of Light' (1.85). Then comes the note of heroism – of *pagan* heroism, with its emphasis on glory, as the war against God is described as this 'Glorious Enterprize' (1.89). Later we learn (Book 5) that Satan rebelled because with the other angels he was commanded to worship and obey the Son of God, and this, he felt, was an injury, was sinking him in dignity, was not taking him at his own valuation. In Christian theology, as Milton's original audience well knew, the primal sin was pride. Satan fell through pride and, though the circumstances were different, so did Adam and Eve. How shall we define pride to cover all the cases? Pride is egoism: it is being self-centred instead of God-centred. Pagan heroism is heroism built on the basis of pride, of a sense of personal honour, of egoism. Christian heroism is built on service to God. Let us be quite clear that Satan is heroic, but with a pagan heroism: he has courage, daring, fortitude, and prowess; though even these he loses at last. Satan boasts of his own steadfastness and his refusal to repent. He is in himself, he thinks, unchanged, 'Though chang'd in outward lustre' (1.97). Actually the outward change is symbolic of an inward change – of the increasing dedication to evil. For the present, however, he seemed not 'less than Arch Angel ruind' (1.593).

Satan proceeds: (1.105–9)

> What though the field be lost?
> All is not lost; the unconquerable Will,
> And study of revenge, immortal hate,
> And courage never to submit or yield:
> And what is else not to be overcome?

Heroism indeed, but heroism mixed with and grounded in 'the study of revenge' and 'immortal hate.' It is also grounded in falsehood or delusion, since he goes on to boast that 'from the terrour of this Arm' God 'Doubted his Empire,' and further that he and his rebels are indestructible 'Since by Fate the strength of Gods And this Empyreal substance cannot fail (1.113–14). (The rebel angels like to imagine that God did not create them, but that they were self-originated or sprang by fate from the substance of heaven, and that what God did not create he cannot annihilate.) This, as we shall learn to recognize, is Satan's version – parody, one might almost call it – of Milton's standard of heroism, the 'fortitude Of Patience and Heroic Martyrdom' (9.32). Qualities in themselves indifferent (or commonly received as virtues because habitually thought of as directed to the service of good) become evil when directed to evil ends. And that his end is evil Satan freely admits. To Beelzebub's fear that strength has been left to them only to be God's thralls, Satan replies: (1.157–65, italics mine)

> Fall'n Cherube, to be weak is miserable
> Doing or Suffering: but of this be sure,
> To do ought good never will be our task,
> But ever to do ill our sole delight ...
>
> If then his Providence
> Out of our evil seek to bring forth good,
> Our labour must be *to pervert that end*,
> *And out of good still to find means of evil* ...

Here is the essential Satanic principle, the principle not of disorder, but of a perverted order; and its natural dwelling place is that hell which will later be described as (2.622–6)

A Universe of death ...
Created evil, for evil only good,
Where all life dies, death lives, and Nature breeds,
Perverse, all monstrous, all prodigious things,
Abominable, inutterable ...

It is an order which contradicts nature and defies fact. That is why Satan, though he acts upon these assumptions, cannot in his heart believe them. In his great soliloquy in Book 4 this will be made abundantly clear.

All the motifs adumbrated in Satan's opening speeches are rendered more emphatic as the poem proceeds. Some are added, and two of importance first appear in later speeches in Book 1.

Satan commences to advance the idea that the motive of his rebellion has been the desire for liberty; his words, however, betray the fact that his aim is power, not liberty. The speech in which the tell-tale phrase occurs is an interesting example of the patterned development of motifs we have already met: (1.242–63)

Is this the Region, this the Soil, the Clime,
Said then the lost Arch-Angel, this the seat
That we must change for Heav'n, this mournful gloom
For that celestial light? Be it so, since he
Who now is Sovran can dispose and bid
What shall be right: fardest from him is best
Whom reason hath equald, force hath made supream
Above his equals. Farewell happy Fields
Where Joy forever dwells: Hail horrors, hail
Infernal world, and thou profoundest Hell
Receive thy new Possessor: One who brings
A mind not to be chang'd by Place or Time.
The mind is its own place, and in it self
Can make a Heav'n of Hell, a Hell of heav'n ...
            Here at least
We shall be free ...
Here we may reign secure, and in my choyce
To reign is worth ambition though in Hell:
Better to reign in Hell then serve in Heav'n.

The thrice-repeated *reign* makes inescapable the desire for power. The final line – this is characteristic of the subtler touches in the Miltonic pattern – will take on its full significance only when Satan is confronted by Abdiel in Book 5, and by him is told that God's service is perfect freedom.

As Satan surveys his prostrate followers he feels not repentance, but pity for the disaster to which he has led them, and he sheds tears such as angels weep; but this effusion of sentiment has no influence upon his action: he prepares to lead them to yet deeper disaster. This will be paralleled in Books 4 and 9, in Eden, in his attitude to Adam and Eve.

The opening scene of *Paradise Lost* is in many ways more striking than that of either the *Iliad* or the *Aeneid*; but its remaining features are too familiar to require comment: the marshalling of the host, the catalogue of the leaders, with Milton's brilliant use of the tradition (recorded by Hooker and Burton among others) that the fallen angels became the gods of the pagan world, Satan's address to his followers, and the building of Pandae-monium, with its memories of the building of Carthage as witnessed by Aeneas. Two or three other features of Milton's artistry must not, however, go unnoticed.

Milton says (1.210–20) that Satan would never have escaped from the burning lake on which he was chained had it not been for God's per-missive will – had God not liberated him in order that Satan might com-plete his own damnation – and that God, bringing forth good from evil, manifests his goodness in mercy to mankind. We must recognize that Mil-ton's fable and his twofold purpose presented a difficulty. Viewed theo-logically, God must be recognized as omnipotent and Satan from first to last utterly within his power. But the story when given epic form demanded an adversary, doomed no doubt to ultimate defeat, but able to put up a fight, to be thought of as a worthy antagonist. This latter effect Milton achieves. He must, however, also safeguard the theological position; so he offers this explanation: Satan can resist only by God's permissive will and for the final forwarding of God's purposes. But to do so is momentarily to damage the epic effect. Milton rises to the occasion with a beautiful stroke of irony. Just after the poet's statement Satan and Beelzebub make their way to shore, (1.239–41)

> Both glorying to have scap't the *Stygian* flood
> As Gods, and by thir own recover'd strength,
> Not by the sufferance of supernal Power.

Again, Milton reinforces his depiction of Satan by an extended epic simile (for such it is though in a concealed form): Satan is seen (1.193–210)

> With Head up-lift above the wave, and Eyes
> That sparkling blaz'd, his other Parts besides
> Prone on the Flood, extended long and large

Lay floating many a rood, in bulk as huge
As whom the Fables name of monstrous size,
Titanian, or *Earth-born*, that warr'd on *Jove*,
Briareos or *Typhon*, whom the Den
By ancient *Tarsus* held, or that Sea-beast
Leviathan, which God of all his works
Created hugest that swim th' Ocean stream:
Him haply slumbring on the *Norway* foam
The Pilot of some small night-founder'd Skiff,
Deeming some Island, oft, as Sea-men tell,
With fixed Anchor in his skaly rind
Moors by his side under the Lee, whilst Night
Invests the Sea and wished Morn delayes:
So stretch out huge in length the Arch-fiend lay
Chain'd on the burning Lake ...

The point of overt comparison is Satan's gigantic stature, but the beings to whom he is likened are not only huge but are also the enemies of God, defeated and subjected to punishment: Briareus who, according to Virgil, *strove against the thunderbolts*; Typhon the *serpent* so huge that he reached the stars, but *Zeus overcame and imprisoned him*; Leviathan, called by Isaiah the *serpent and dragon* that is in the sea and said to *be reserved for God's special vengeance*, but more commonly thought of (and by Milton) as the whale. Nor is the adventure on the Norway foam introduced merely for amplification or the addition of variety and picturesqueness to the epic narrative; Satan is the arch-deceiver and those who trust to him, angels or men, are like the deluded mariners anchored in the lee of a monster and courting destruction unawares.

Since we shall not again have occasion to refer to Milton's art of the simile we may so far digress as to glance at two other examples from Book 1. The first, a compound epic simile descriptive of Satan's followers as they lie prone on the fiery lake, finds its point of departure in the *Aeneid*, and furnishes a clear instance of Milton's elaboration upon his model; and since his other sources are equally evident it offers an excellent opportunity of watching Milton at his work. (1.300–13)

　　　　he stood and call'd
His Legions, Angel Forms, who lay intrans't
Thick as Autumnal Leaves that strow the Brooks
In *Vallombrosa*, where th' *Etrurian* shades
High overarch't imbowr; or scatterd sedge
Afloat, when with fierce winds *Orion* arm'd

> Hath vext the Red-Sea Coast, whose waves orethrew
> *Busiris* and his *Memphian* Chivalry
> While with perfidious hatred they pursu'd
> The sojourners of *Goshen*, who beheld
> From the safe shore thir floating Carkases
> And broken Chariot Wheels, so thick bestrown
> Abject and lost lay these, covering the Flood,
> Under amazement of thir hideous change.

Of the souls waiting passage to another state Virgil had written: (*Aeneid* 6.309–12)

> Hither rushed all the throng ... *thick as the leaves of the forest that at Autumn's first frost dropping fall,* and thick as the birds that from the seething deep flock shoreward, when the chill of the year drives them overseas and sends them in to sunny lands.[1]

To the suggestion in the first half of this compound simile Milton adds the memory of a leafy scene visited a quarter of a century before, allowing himself this one image of pure beauty in a series whose note is not beauty, but desolation rising to terror. The second comparison turns on one of the Hebrew names for the Red Sea, the Sea of Sedge, and the weed on its margins mangled in the storms heralded by Orion (Virgil's stormy Orion, thought of by Milton as still a giant and armed with wind and wave, driving through the waters of the Red Sea). But the Red Sea has other associations, and it is by a process of aggregation through association that Milton builds his effects; so he is led to a third and more telling comparison, though implied, not directly stated. The rebel angels lie there thick as the scattered carcasses and broken chariot wheels of Pharoah's engulfed army.

> And the waters returned and covered the chariots and the horsemen and all the host of Pharoah ... But the children of Israel walked upon dry land in the midst of the sea.

Thus Exodus 14:28–9; and the unforgettable touch of ruin and desolation, the broken chariot wheels, is from the same chapter, where the Lord 'took off' the wheels of their chariots; while the sounding Busiris and Memphian (as a synonym for Egyptian) were available in such sources as Raleigh's *History of the World* and Sylvester's translation of Du Bartas. But more is conveyed by the final and implied comparison than a crescendo of ruin and desolation. The Satanic host, like the host of Pharoah, are engaged in the service of God's implacable enemy and against his people: and this is their fate. The suggestion is completed by a touch of irony; for it is not God's people that from the safe shore survey the smitten army, but Satan, who has brought them to this pass, and the 'safe shore' is hell.

Very different from this example of close co-ordination and mounting effectiveness is the simile with which Milton concludes the book. Its point is merely the minute size to which the common rout of Satan's followers is reduced in order that they may crowd within the walls of Pandaemonium, and Milton, with an eye to contrast only, allows himself to follow associations seemingly remote from the confines of hell – yet not wholly so (1.777–90)

> Behold a wonder! they but now who seemd
> In bigness to surpass Earths Giant Sons
> Now less then smallest Dwarfs, in narrow room
> Throng numberless, like that Pygmean Race
> Beyond the *Indian* Mount, or Faerie Elves
> Whose midnight Revels, by a Forrest side
> Or Fountain some belated Peasant sees,
> Or dreams he sees, while over-head the Moon
> Sits Arbitress, and neerer to the Earth
> Wheels her pale course, they on thir mirth and dance
> Intent, with jocund Music charm his ear;
> At once with joy and fear his heart rebounds.
> Thus incorporeal Spirits to smallest forms
> Reduc'd thir shapes immense ...

The 'Pygmean Race Beyond the *Indian* Mount' is a memory of Pliny. The alternative of 'Faerie Elves' leads us straight into the world of *A Midsummer Night's Dream*: but strangely blended with it is an echo – from epic and from the nether world – of Aeneas' doubtful encounter with Dido among the shades: (*Aeneid* 6.450–4)

> Among them ... Dido was wandering in the great forest, and ... the Trojan hero ... knew her, a dim form amid the shadows, as, even in the early month, one sees or fancies that he has seen the moon rise amid the clouds.[2]

A moment more the poet lingers. Then the contrast: (793–6)

> in thir own dimensions like themselves
> The great seraphic Lords and Cherubim
> In close recess and secret conclave sat
> A thousand Demy-Gods on golden seats.

And therewith 'the great consult began.'

It is necessary for our sense of the continually elaborated pattern thus to descend on occasion and watch the weaving of its minuter parts. There is one further idea of general significance which must be emphasized. We have spoken of hell as a perverted order, and so it is. It is dedicated to evil; it is based on false assumptions: but it achieves all the outward marks of a genuine order, and up to a point it is terrifyingly efficient. Here two passages on which we omitted to comment come to view: the marshalling of the Satanic host and the building of Pandaemonium.

Both are examples of disciplined activity and ordered co-operation. Roused from their trance by Satan's voice, his followers form into ranks and, under their banners, (1.549–67)

> move
> In perfect *Phalanx* to the *Dorian* mood
> Of Flutes and soft Recorders; such as rais'd
> To hight of noblest temper Hero's old
> Arming to Battel, and in stead of rage
> Deliberate valour breath'd, firm and unmov'd
> With dread of death to flight or foul retreat,
> Nor wanting power to mitigate and swage
> With solemn touches, troubl'd thoughts, and chase
> Anguish and doubt and fear and sorrow and pain
> From mortal or immortal minds. Thus they
> Breathing united force with fixed thought
> Mov'd on in silence to soft Pipes that charm'd
> Thir painful steps o're the burnt soyle; and not
> Advanc't in view, they stand, a horrid Front
> Of dreadful length and dazzling Arms, in guise
> Of Warriors old with order'd Spear and Shield,
> Awaiting what command thir mighty Chief
> Had to impose.

The music sounds authentic, and the order which it symbolizes seems a real order. This music can support a pagan heroism, and temporarily assuage the pains and regrets of hell. But we are not permitted to forget that the scene is hell or that the service to which this order is dedicated is Satan's, whose words still linger in our memory: (1.159–60)

> To do ought good never will be our task,
> But ever to do ill our sole delight.

We must pause for a moment on this unexpected presence of music in hell.

It is there because hell has a sort of order, though perverted because dedicated to an evil end. But as the poem proceeds we understand it better. In Book 2 the gates of hell open with thunderous discord to let Satan pass out on his mission of destruction, while in Book 7 the heavenly gates open with 'harmonious sound On golden Hinges moving' (1.206–7) to speed the Messiah on his mission of creation. It would seem that while hell has its *internal* order as well as heaven, its influence on all without, since it is a perverted order, is wholly destructive, as that of heaven is everywhere beneficent and constructive. The *gates* of hell and of heaven represent the *external* relations and influences of the two orders respectively. Furthermore, music in hell itself appears to be a temporary manifestation. We hear nothing of it after the second book, where the fallen angels sing their own exploits. In Book 8 Raphael reports that long ere one reaches the gates of hell he hears (243–4)

> Noise, other then the sound of Dance or Song,
> Torment, and loud lament, and furious rage.

In the strict chronology of events this comes of course early, but in the poem – in the information given to the reader – later. (One must allow for a certain element of double time in *Paradise Lost*.) Also, Milton has recognized troubled thoughts, anguish, and pain in the fallen angels which music can only assuage, not banish. And at the end the only sound in hell is the universal hiss of serpents. The perverted, the self-centred order disintegrates. It loses its symbol of harmonious co-operation long before it loses its efficacy for evil. But that efficacy itself is ultimately doomed.

Within hell, however, and at the point which we have reached, the walls of Pandaemonium rise to music, like those of another Troy. Willing workers are not lacking nor materials, including gold, 'that precious bane'; and Mammon is there to direct operations and gloat upon the sight – Mammon who in heaven had eyes only for the golden pavement, and for the beatific vision none. Mulciber, who once built in heaven, is the architect now of a structure rich in barbaric splendours (fit dwelling for those whom the chaste beauties of heaven could not charm) and illuminated from the bowels of hell with counterfeited light. (1.717–30)

> Not *Babilon*,
> Nor great *Alcairo* such magnificence
> Equal'd in all their glories, to inshrine
> *Belus* or *Serapis* thir Gods, or seat
> Thir Kings, when *Egypt* with *Assyria* strove
> In wealth and luxurie ...

> from the arched roof
> Pendant by suttle Magic many a row
> Of Starry Lamps and blazing Cressets fed
> With *Naphtha* and *Asphaltus* yielded light
> As from a sky.

Just as it parodies the light of heaven, and the magnificence, so hell, though founded in rebellion against the very idea of due subordination, substitutes its own for the heavenly scale where, under God, the angel princes (1. 736–7)

> rule,
> Each in his Hierarchie, the Orders bright.

The terms on which Satan rules his orders dark are revealed in the great consult. This famous scene, occupying the first half of Book 2, is in a different key, more resembling the first book of the *Iliad*, with speeches in council dramatically rendered, and with little of epic ornament, as if, having outdone Virgil in Book 1, Milton now turns his attention to Homer. This is pardonable virtuosity. But the serious business of Book 2, besides advancing the action, is to complete the presentation of hell and its principles. This it does first by showing the leaders in debate, and Satan, not perhaps the first whig, but certainly the first politician, as the skilful manipulator of assemblies, operating in part through his agent Beelzebub, who has already, in the dialogue of Book 1, shown himself Satan's perfect echo.

We are given a glimpse of Satan on his throne, his parody of God's state, his barbaric, nay, oriental splendour, and are told that he was 'by merit rais'd To that bad eminence' (2.6). Satan's ability and his heroism (in a pagan sense) are unquestioned. But he feels himself insecure, the fate of rebels, and commences by asserting his title to rule by every known sanction (some of them ironic enough): birthright in heaven, free election, merit in counsel and in battle, the consent of the governed; and who would envy the pre-eminence in pain and danger which is the throne of hell? This is the best security of union. For the principle of hell is the darkness of enlightened self-interest. And now to the question of a new offensive, 'Whether of open Warr or covert guile?' (2.41).

On this pivot the great consult turns – with recurrent questions: Is God omnipotent and omniscient? Can he annihilate the rebels, and will he if he can? Could any state, or extinction itself, be worse than their present plight? Is there a chance of regaining heaven, or at least of avenging themselves upon their enemy? Would it not be better, on the contrary, to keep the ills they have, and even attempt to build an empire in hell? Towards an

affirmative answer to this last question the decision is moving when Beelzebub intervenes with the plan of an attack on God through his favourite
creature, man, in appearance a compromise solution, but the one Satan
has determined on from the first. In the course of the debate four characters,
besides Satan, clearly emerge. Nowhere in epic poetry is there a more concentrated effort of dramatic characterization.

Moloch speaks in the character of 'the strongest and the fiercest Spirit'
that fell. He is the exponent of brute force: 'My sentence is for open Warr.'
He would bomb God out of heaven – God who 'reigns by our delay': (2.
60–70)

> let us rather choose
> Arm'd with Hell flames and fury all at once
> O'er Heav'ns high Towrs to force resistless way,
> Turning our Tortures into horrid Arms
> Against the Torturer: ...
> he shall hear
> Infernal Thunder, and for Lightning see
> Black fire and horror shot with equal rage
> Among his Angels; and his Throne itself
> Mixt with *Tartarean* Sulphur, and strange fire,
> His own invented Torments ...

And this at least will be reprisal, 'Which if not Victory is yet Revenge.' The
dominant note is fierce strength and brutality. But this is not all: there is
also a minor note of pathos and a kind of perverted heroism – qualities
shared with Satan. Moloch repines at imprisonment in 'this opprobrious
Den of shame.' On the great question of whether God can annihilate them,
he has his word – of impatient dismissal: either he can or he can't, and in no
case can they be worse off than now. But it is not pathos and perverted heroism alone that Moloch shares with Satan: there is a touch – one can hardly
mention it without exaggerating – of aspiration, which for a moment gives
a sort of lift to the lines: (2.70–81, italics mine)

> [To some] perhaps
> The way seems difficult and steep to scale
> With upright wing against a higher foe.
> Let such bethink them ...
> *That in our proper motion we ascend*
> *Up to our native seat*: descent and fall
> To us is adverse. Who but felt of late
> When the fierce Foe hung on our brok'n Rear

> Insulting, and pursu'd us through the Deep,
> With what compulsion and laborious flight
> We sunk this low?

It is not true (as we shall learn at 6.864) ; but it is magnificent: indeed Satan corrects it in this book (2.432ff.), emphasizing after Virgil (Book 6) the ease of descent, the difficulty of ascent.

There is no such note in the contrasting character of Belial, who replies. He knows all the debater's tricks, and the orator's too, relying on tone as well as on argument, undermining heroism by pretended realism, and sapping determination by resort to the pathetic. His range is, of course, limited: he can compass pathos because he feels self-pity; he could never compass aspiration. His realism is not all pretended. He has intellectual distinction, and repeatedly we feel that he is less deluded than Moloch or Satan. He recognizes God's omnipotence and omniscience, but only to argue the danger of heroism and the folly of heroics. He is right, but basely so. This is the mark of the fallen state: everything is perverted, the heroism of Satan, and the intellect of Belial, whose (2.115–17)

> thoughts were low:
> To vice industrious, but to Nobler deeds
> Timorous and slothful.

He and Mammon are the only figures in *Paradise Lost* with no touch of heroism: the one given over to ignoble sensuality, the other to the ignoble greed of wealth. In the heroic tradition – not the Christian heroism of Milton, but that which he allows his devils to exemplify – heroism can subsist with a degree of both vice and folly. The hero can exhibit (as Johnson says of Dryden's Almanzor) 'a sort of majestic madness and illustrious depravity.'[3] The heroic tradition in its more sober form, as also in its later and more extravagant developments with the Byronic hero, yields plenty of examples; and in this general tradition Milton's Satan clearly stands. Two things, however, are beyond the pale: sensuality so habitual as to be one with effeminacy and sloth, and greed of wealth. Here Spenser offers a good commentary: in *The Faerie Queene* the votaries or victims of sensuality are always, though sometimes only temporarily, unheroic, disarmed, and relaxed; and no one will forget the knightly Guyon's contempt for Mammon.

Belial protests that, in other circumstances, he too would be 'for open Warr ... as not behind in hate' (but actually he has no heart for fighting). Then with a graceful compliment to Moloch, but intentionally damaging ('he who most excels in fact of Arms'), Belial proceeds to rebut his argument for war as grounded in doubt and despair and better fitted to dissuade. And as for the promised revenge: could we, he says, break through the angel guard, (2.135–42)

> and at our heels all Hell should rise
> With blackest Insurrection, to counfound
> Heav'ns purest Light, yet our great Enemy
> All incorruptible would on his Throne
> Sit unpolluted, and th'Ethereal mould
> Incapable of stain would soon expel
> Her mischief, and purge off the baser fire
> Victorious.

This is the truth, which only Belial sees. To the great question of God's power to annihilate them, Belial adds the question of his will. The insight is characteristic. So also is the rejection of annihilation as in any circumstances a relative good. The sense-bound creature can imagine no worse fate. Milton's Belial is a great and subtle portrait of a sensualist, which recognizes that the hallmark of sensualism is not the denial of an intellectual being but the inability to conceive it apart from sense: (2.145–51, italics mine)

> And that must end us, that must be our cure,
> To be no more; sad cure; for who would lose,
> Though full of pain, this intellectual being,
> Those thoughts that wander through Eternity,
> To perish rather, swallowd up and lost
> In the wide womb of uncreated night,
> *Devoid of sense and motion*?

Again, the tell-tale phrase. But, he continues, it is false to say that, annihilation apart, we cannot be worse off. Pursued by God's active vengeance, hell itself seemed a refuge; and worse fates Belial can easily imagine – in terms, characteristically, not of degradation, but of physical pain: what if (2.175–86)

> this Firmament
> Of Hell should spout her Cataracts of Fire,
> Impendent horrors, threatning hideous fall
> One day upon our heads; while we perhaps
> Designing or exhorting glorious warr,
> Caught in a fierie Tempest shall be hurl'd

> Each on his rock transfixt, the sport and prey
> Of racking whirlwinds, or for ever sunk
> Under yon boyling Ocean, wrapt in Chains;
> ... this would be worse.

Belial alone recognizes God's omniscience and its inevitable result:
(2.192–3)

> Not more Almighty to resist our might
> Than wise to frustrate all our plots and wiles.

(We are meant to recall Satan's 'to be weak is miserable, Doing or Suffering.') Belial's realism goes a step further yet, and admits the justice of their punishment: (2.200–1)

> nor the Law unjust
> That so ordains.

His purpose is certainly not to justify the ways of God to devils, but to remove the incentive to action which injustice, real or imaginary, provides. And he accuses the bolder spirits of lacking not only realism, but, fine touch of irony, the courage to suffer with dignity. He had started by complimenting Moloch; he ends with an open sneer: (2.204–8)

> I laugh, when those who at the Spear are bold
> And vent'rous, if that fails them, shrink and fear
> What yet they know must follow, to endure
> Exile, or ignominy, or bonds, or pain,
> The sentence of thir Conqueror.

But there are limits to Belial's realism. Perhaps, if they are quiet, God will relent. Or is this mere sophistry? Milton sums it all up: (2.226–8)

> Thus *Belial* with words cloath'd in reasons garb
> Counsel'd ignoble ease, and peaceful sloath,
> Not peace.

Mammon supports him. Like Belial he is utterly unheroic, but unlike him, quite stupid. He is your practical man, with one idea of his own (all the rest are stolen): to forget heaven and exploit the undeveloped resources of hell. He will make a heaven of hell: no nonsense (like Satan's) about compassing this by thought; it will take action. Hell's inverted parallel to heaven is plain to every reader. Mammon thinks that they are really alike,

or may be easily made so. As God counterfeits darkness, they may counter-
feit light (he got this idea from the lamps in Pandaemonium) ; there is no
lack of gold and gems, as he has seen, (2.272–3, italics mine)

> Nor want we skill or Art from which to raise
> Magnificence; and *what can Heav'n shew more?*

This question is the measure of Mammon's obtuseness. Hell may be made
not only magnificent but comfortable if they can become acclimatized:
'Our torments ... Become our Elements ... our temper chang'd Into their
temper.' This hope is the symbol of his degradation. Actually it is taken
over from Belial. Another idea seems at first less congruous, till we recognize that it also is not his own: who would return to heaven, if he could,
there (2.241-3)

> to celebrate his Throne
> With warbl'd Hymns, and to his Godhead sing
> Forc't Halleluiahs ... ?

Better to live in hell, (2.255–7)

> Free, and to none accountable, preferring
> Hard liberty before the easie yoke
> Of servile Pomp.

This is the Satanic doctrine, but there is irony in its likeness to Milton's own
and double irony when it is uttered by Mammon.

His speech is greeted with applause. The low thoughts of his auditors,
whether of desire or fear, meet his halfway. Seeing the danger, Beelzebub
intervenes and voices Satan's policy. He resembles Satan who, we have been
told, still seemed not 'less than Arch Angel Ruind.' For Beelzebub, (2.
304–5)

> Princely counsel in his face yet shon,
> Majestic though in ruin.

By the terms of his address he seeks to recall the assembly to themselves:
(2.310–14)

> Thrones and Imperial Powers, off-spring of heav'n
> Ethereal Vertues; or these Titles now
> Must we renounce ... for so the popular vote
> Inclines ...

Then in a powerful speech: it is idle to suppose that God will abate their punishment or suffer them to build in hell an empire to match and out-match his own. Granted that open war is too perilous, and impossible of success, still there is another way. As Beelzebub describes it, it seems easy and safe and he pauses to hear their ready assent. But it asks an initial feat of skill and daring. Who shall be chosen for the first desperate mission to the earth? The devils gaze at one another in consternation.

This is the moment (2.430ff.) for which Satan has waited. Emphasiz-ing the dreadful hazard of the task, he assumes it as the duty and the right of his eminence and rule. Thus at the end as at the beginning of the scene, Satan fortifies his position; and lest any should belatedly volunteer, 'Cer-tain to be refus'd,' and seek to share his glory, he suddenly dismisses the assembly. But they, fearing his anger as much as the task itself, yield him worship who seemed (2.509–11)

> Alone th' *Antagonist of Heav'n*, nor less
> Than Hells dread Emperour with pomp Supream
> And God-like *imitated* State ...

The words are significant, and so are those in which Milton comments on the seeming solidarity of hell's perverted order: (2.482–3)

> neither do the Spirits damn'd
> Lose all thir virtue.

And the reason – (2.483–501)

> least bad men should boast
> Thir specious deeds on earth, which glory excites,
> Or clos ambition varnisht o'er with zeal ...
> O shame to men! Devil with Devil damn'd
> Firm concord holds, men onely disagree
> Of Creatures rational, though under hope
> Of heavenly Grace: and God proclaiming peace,
> Yet live in hatred, enmity, and strife ...

In the midst of this passage is set a single and relatively simple epic simile, but one full of suggestion: (2.486–95)

> Thus they thir doubtful consultations dark
> Ended rejoycing in their matchless Chief:
> As when from mountain tops the dusky clouds

Ascending, while the North wind sleeps, o'erspread
Heav'ns chearful face, the lowring Element
Scowls ore the dark'nd landskip Snow, or showre:
If chance the radiant Sun with farewell sweet
Extend his ev'ning beam, the fields revive,
The birds their notes renew, and bleating herds
Attest their joy, that hill and valley rings.

The simile describes the joy, revived hope, and unison with which the
devils adopt Satan's policy and acknowledge his leadership: it is like the
sudden breaking of the evening sun through storm clouds, and the response
of nature's creatures to it. Hope is symbolized by light, unison by music.
But the whole simile is shot through with the suggestion that this is a last
manifestation, that it is transient and even delusive. The shadows of night
and storm will soon descend. And the suggestion of the delusive is heightened when we reflect that the light of hope comes not from the sun which
sinks to rise again, but from Satan.

While Satan commences his hazardous journey, and the lesser fiends
are free to follow their own pursuits, Milton takes the opportunity to complete the picture of hell. Starting (2.528ff.) with epic games (like those in
the fifth book of the *Aeneid*), he adds other diversions. Every detail is made
to count. The games and martial exercises take on a note of Typhoean rage,
as the devils instinctively re-enact (for the reader anticipates) the war in
heaven; not only rage, but pain, intrudes upon their recreations (as a simile
of Alcides and the envenomed robe suggests). Others, more contemplative,
sing their own heroic deeds, praises, and hapless fall (not God's glory as in
heaven); or, reasoning 'Of Providence, Foreknowledge, Will and Fate'
(the subjects on which the reader is to be enlightened by divine revelation
in the next book) 'found no end, in wandring mazes lost. ... Vain wisdom
all, and false Philosophie' (2.599–65). But not all the active spirits spend
their energies in mock-battle. Some explore the remoter reaches of hell, with
its four infernal rivers emptying into the fiery lake, and beyond the fifth
river, Lethe, a continent of ice. There are echoes of Virgil and of Dante;
but everything is on a gigantic scale (a continent of ice, instead of Dante's
circle, is characteristic): (2.618–28)

through many a dark and drearie Vaile
They pass'd, and many a Region dolorous,
O'er many a Frozen, many a fierie Alpe,
Rocks, Caves, Lakes, Fens, Bogs, Dens, and shades of death,
A universe of death, which God by curse
Created evil, for evil only good,

> Where all life dies, death lives, and Nature breeds,
> Perverse, all monstrous, all prodigious things,
> Abominable, inutterable, and worse
> Than Fables yet have feign'd or fear conceiv'd,
> *Gorgons* and *Hydras*, and *Chimera's* dire ...

At the gates two yet more dreadful figures await Satan. Sin and Death are his own offspring, unrecognized; Sin sprang from his head in heaven, Death from their subsequent embraces. 'For lust when it hath conceived bringeth forth sin, and sin when it is finished bringeth forth death' (James 1:15). Milton dramatizes the statement with a description of sin based on Ovid's picture of Scylla, and one of death, whose technique, but not its detail, more resembles Spenser: (2.666–72)

> The other shape,
> If shape it might be call'd that shape had none ...
> Or substance might be call'd that shadow seem'd ...
> black it stood as Night,
> Fierce as ten Furies, terrible as Hell,
> And shook a dreadful Dart.

Satan, who is yet to lose his heroic virtue of courage, stands his ground, and asks how such a hell-born monster dares assail a spirit of heaven: (2.688–96)

> To whom the Goblin full of wrauth reply'd,
> Art thou that Traitor Angel, art thou hee,
> Who first broke peace in Heav'n and Faith, till then
> Unbrok'n ...
> And reck'n'st thou thyself with Spirits of Heav'n ... ?

(How all occasions inform against Satan!) It is part of the pathos, the significance, and the irony of Satan and the nobler among his followers that they have rebelled against their own natures and still think of themselves as sons of heaven. But Sin intervenes to pacify, to tell the sordid tale of her begetting, and Death's, and to glory in a dream of the future: (2.866–70)

> thou will bring me soon
> To that new world of light and bliss, among
> The Gods who live at ease, where I shall Reign
> At thy right hand voluptuous, as beseems
> Thy daughter and thy darling, without end.

Satan, Sin, and Death, as this and other touches proclaim, are the infernal trinity, a grim embellishment of Milton's pattern.

Now (2.890ff.) the gates of hell open with thunderous discord, and Satan pauses to look out upon the chaos, that

> dark
> Illimitable Ocean without bound ... ;
> The Womb of nature and perhaps her Grave.

Then dwarfed by its mighty, inchoate, and meaningless forces, but still undaunted, he battles his way through its storms to the presence of the great anarch, Chaos himself. Him he deludes with the false promise that he goes to the new-made earth in order to restore it to his rule. (Actually he has far other plans: not to restore it to the unorder of chaos, but to incorporate it in the perverted order of hell.) And so he pursues his way to within sight of the battlements of heaven and of the pendent earthy universe linked in a golden chain.

Though but briefly described in comparison with hell, the chaos is vividly presented, and it is an essential and recurrent part of Milton's pattern. The chaos has a double source, poetic and philosophic. It figures in most of the Pre-socratics and in the *Timaeus* of Plato; it is also described by the poets, and notably by Ovid in the *Metamorphoses*. In *Paradise Lost* the chaos has, correspondingly, a double role: in Book 7 primarily philosophic; here poetic, but with a forward look to its other function. The chaos is undetermined. It is imperfect because order is a good; but it is not, like the perverted order of hell, committed to evil. The great anarch may say 'Havoc and spoil and ruin are my gain' because, reduced to order, the chaos is no longer chaos. But this is something very different from Satan's 'Evil be thou my good.' Man's sin and folly, as we shall see, destroy the reflection of the heavenly order, and man and nature relapse towards chaos; but grace accepted can restore the divine order. It is only if grace is refused and Satan preferred, that man commences to reflect not the unorder of chaos but the perverted order of hell. But this is to anticipate.

II (BOOKS 3, 4)

Having established two of his symbolic settings in the utter and the middle darkness, and carried his action to the required point, the poet ascends to the realms of light, and, contrary to epic precedent and Aristotelian rule, now speaks in his own person, in the famous invocation to light – itself a perfect piece of patterning of the lyric order, and one that looks back to the first invocation of the Heavenly Muse (1.10–12) and of the spirit (1.19–23) and on to the fond description of the muse's 'nightly visitation unimplor'd' (9.22). This passage of fifty-five lines is a comment on the point reached in the poem: we have made our way through hell and chaos, the utter and middle darkness, up to the realms of light, and around the ideas of light and darkness, and the triumph of light over darkness, the pattern is woven.

1 / Light, though not yet distinguished into physical and spiritual, is from the first associated with God and heaven: (3.1–6)

> Hail holy Light, offspring of Heav'n first-born,
> Or of th' Eternal Coeternal beam
>   ... since God is light,
> And never but in unapproached light
> Dwelt from Eternitie, dwelt then in thee,
> Bright effluence of bright essence increate.

and so on to the created light with which God invested, at its first appearing, 'The rising world of waters dark and deep.'

2 / Thus the idea of physical darkness is introduced, but introduced with the accent on the triumph of light over darkness, as at the creation, so in the poet's journey, here described, through the utter and the middle darkness up to the realms of light. 'Thee I revisit safe,' the poet cries, but adds, significantly, (3.22–6)

> And *feel* thy sovran vital Lamp; but thou
> Revisit'st not these eyes, that rowle in vain
> To find thy piercing ray, and find no dawn;
> So thick a drop serene hath quencht their Orbs,
> Or dim suffusion veild.

3 / So we are brought to the blind man's physical darkness, over which light cannot triumph. But Milton does not repine. Rather he chooses to think of his consolations: his memories of classical poetry (called 'sacred song' because all poetry is the gift of God), then the poetry of the Bible, and, best of all, the joy of poetic composition: (3.26–40)

>   Yet not the more
> Cease I to wander where the Muses haunt
> Cleer spring, or shadie Grove, or Sunnie Hill,
> Smit with the love of sacred Song; but chief
> Thee *Sion* and the flowrie Brooks beneath
> That wash thy hallow'd feet, and warbling flow,
> Nightly I visit ...

Then feed on thoughts, that voluntarie move
Harmonious numbers; as the wakeful Bird
Sings darkling, and in shadiest Covert hid
Tunes her nocturnal Note.

4 / But *darkling*! The word is like a bell to toll the blind poet back to
his affliction, and the sense of it floods over him again: (3.40–50)

> Thus with the Year
> Seasons return, but not to me returns
> Day, or the sweet approach of Ev'n or Morn,
> Or sight of vernal bloom, or Summers Rose,
> Or flocks, or heards, or human face divine;
> But cloud instead and ever-during dark
> Surrounds me, from the chearful wayes of men
> Cut off, and for the Book of knowledg fair
> Presented with a Universal blanc
> Of Natures works to mee expung'd and ras'd,
> And wisdome at one entrance quite shut out.

This final deprivation, we are meant to recognize, menaces the very consolation on which he has chiefly relied, his poetry; without knowledge and
wisdom there can be for Milton no poetry, and how can the blind man gain
knowledge and wisdom?

5 / Yet there is a way: (3.51–5)

> So much the rather thou Celestial light
> Shine inward, and the mind through all her powers
> Irradiate, there plant eyes, all mist from thence
> Purge and disperse, that I may see and tell
> Of things invisible to mortal sight.

Thus the passage concludes, and with it the pattern. Once more, as in the
beginning, light is associated with heaven and God: it is celestial light.
Once more light triumphs over darkness. But now spiritual light is distinguished from physical; for only spiritual light can triumph over the
physical darkness of the blind poet.

Further analysis would bring into relief other elements in this pattern,
both general and particular. For example, the distinction of physical light
and spiritual turns on the Christian conception of the two orders of nature
and of grace, itself a conception with an implicit pattern. In utilizing it
Milton never fails to accord full recognition to the beauty and worth of
the natural order while maintaining always its subordination to the higher

order. So it is in this passage, with its images of natural beauty. Among them some of the particular elements of the pattern reside: the recurrent images of flower and stream, of mist and the light breaking through mist, of the return of the seasons and the alternation of sun and shade. Again, coming to a focus in the image of the nightingale, there is the recognition that night may be the hour of poetic inspiration; and this, I suppose, might be construed as one of those paradoxes dear to modern criticism; for what it suggests is that darkness, the enemy, may turn out to be a friend in disguise.

Thus Milton prepares to speak in accommodated narrative of God and heaven. What follows has been much criticized for the baseness of its versified theology ever since Pope complained that 'God the Father turns a school divine.'[4] It is pertinent to remark, however, that the knowledge conveyed – the firm assertion of man's free will – is essential to a comprehension of the poem, that decorum would hardly permit the poet to introduce images and similes into the speech of God, that an epic must be read as a whole and that the pattern of the whole can be relied upon to gather up and neutralize passages which, taken by themselves, might appear unduly prosaic, and, finally, that this passage clearly has its function, not merely in conveying information, but in the pattern of the whole.

In the words of God to the Son, as he observes Satan's approach (3.8off.), we hear the same view set forth of man's free will, and of decrees necessarily contingent, despite God's foreknowledge, as is argued in the *De Doctrina Christiana*. This is necessary to be explained because it is the basis on which Milton will – and the only basis on which he can – justify the ways of God to men. But since foreknowledge apprehends that man will fall, a decree contingent upon that event must also be registered at this point if Milton is to fulfil his second purpose and 'assert Eternal Providence.' The doctrine of the atonement held by Milton and formulated here strikes something of a chill by its hard legality, but the defect, if there is one, is in religious sensibility, not in epic propriety, and anyway this impression is certainly mitigated by the terms of the Son's offer of himself as sacrifice and its simple motivation in love (3.227ff., 41off.).

It is on the offer of the Son that the place of this scene in the pattern of the epic mainly depends. The council of God balances in the pattern, and contrasts with, the council of demons in Book 2. The Son shares the throne of God not in rivalry, but in perfect submission, raised to that good eminence by merit more than birthright. And this throne he will leave for earth on his mission of salvation, the offer, which only he dares make, motivated by no form of self-assertiveness but by submission to the Father and love and pity for mankind. Later we shall find Satan momentarily expressing love and pity for Adam and Eve, but immediately the thought is crossed by remembrance of his hatred of God and converted to malice.

The contrast with Satan is patent at every point. Nor is Christ's role as the second Adam, so important for the pattern of the poem, forgotten.

The opportunity for a full description of heaven, the third setting, is not taken at this point; but the spirit of the heavenly order is clearly indicated in the filial obedience of the Son and the joyous service of the angels (3.344ff.). Their loud hosannas at the word of peace contrast with the martial shout of the Satanic host; their glittering harps, hung at their sides like quivers, contrast with the clashing arms. Their music is of another order, a sacred song, with power to 'waken raptures high' and symbolize the perfect concord of heaven. And there is not only this backward look, but a forward. Heaven is the prototype of Eden. Here is the River of Bliss and growing beside it are 'Celestial Roses,' and by the Fount of Life Immortal *amarant*, transplanted thence to grow in Eden beside the Tree of Life, but at the fall lost, like it, to men. The angels weave its blossoms in their golden crowns. With such significant suggestions given, the fuller account of heaven can await Raphael's narrative of Satan's revolt against its order.

The rest of Book 3 completes Satan's odyssey. With no very important role in the pattern, its episodes keep the pattern in mind, as when the future inhabitants of the paradise of fools (those 'who in vain things Built thir fond hopes of Glorie' (3.448–9), and Empedocles, 'who to be deemd A God leap'd fondly into *Aetna* flames') are an ironic comment on Satan. More important, the way from heaven to earth will later be balanced (if balance is the right word for anything so significantly asymmetrical) by the bridge built by Sin and Death to earth from hell. Satan's close view of the sun, with his deception of Uriel, its guardian, after introducing a brief preliminary account of the creation (the subject of Book 7) furnishes the occasion of the great soliloquy with which Book 4 opens.

The soliloquy commences as Satan's address to the Sun: (4.32–9)

> O thou that with surpassing Glory crownd,
> Look'st from thy sole Dominion like the God
> Of this new world ...
>   to thee I call,
> But with no friendly voice, and add thy name
> O Sun, to tell thee how I hate thy beams
> That bring to my remembrance from what state
> I fell ...

Thus the soliloquy is Satan's apostrophe to light, which unexpectedly balances Milton's great invocation at the beginning of the preceding book, and to our surprise we discover that they deal in part with the same subject: the speaker's affliction and his relation to God; but the blind poet gratefully accepts the gift of grace, spiritual light, and Satan rejects the light and gives his allegiance to darkness. By this device of oblique patterning, as we may call it, Milton further integrates his personal digression in the pattern of the poem, and sharpens the line of cleavage between himself and the antagonist with whom later criticism has supposed him to sympathize. It is a vague word. If it connotes any degree of approval, Milton certainly does not sympathize with Satan. If it connotes merely the imaginative insight that permits the putting of a point of view and the moving portrayal of a personality, he certainly does.

Whether or not this great soliloquy was originally conceived as part of a projected dramatic treatment of the fall, it successfully adapts the technique of drama to the epic. Like a soliloquy by Shakespeare it presents the thoughts passing through the mind of the character. It does not require to be discounted, as do all Satan's speeches to followers or opponents. There is no deception here save self-deception. In the soliloquy Satan rises to his full stature as a tragic figure, and at the same time stands forth completely self-condemned. If this seems paradoxical, it is also entirely characteristic of Milton's attitude towards his greatest creation.

Here Satan himself strips away all his pretences – pretences by which he has imposed upon others, and half imposed upon himself. He admits that 'Pride and worse Ambition' were the causes of his fall (contrast the self-justification of his political speeches and the pretence of being the champion of liberty), that he owes his being and every gift to God, to whom he has been guilty of the basest ingratitude (contrast his stubborn refusal to acknowledge elsewhere the relation of creature to Creator), that he had 'free Will and Power to stand,' as God had averred, and that he alone, and neither God nor fate, is responsible for his fall. And he is equally realistic about the result: (4.86–92)

> Ay me, they little know ...
> Under what torments inwardly I groane;
> While they adore me on the Throne of Hell,
>   ... onley Supream
> In miserie.

This indeed he had not altogether denied – had even in the great consult made political capital out of his eminence in pain and danger. Other thoughts now cross his mind, but only to be rejected: (4.58–60)

> O had his powerful Destiny ordaind
> Me some inferior Angel, I had stood
> Then happie ...

But still he would have rebelled, as follower instead of leader. (4.79–81)

> O then at last relent: is there no place
> Left for Repentence, none for Pardon left?
> None left but by submission ...

And submission he has publicly rejected: 'For who can think Submission' (1.661). But suppose it were possible, it could not last. Freed from pain, and restored, he would rebel again: (4.95–6, italics mine)

> how soon unsay
> What *feign'd submission* swore.

This is a deft stroke: Satan rightly recognizes that feigned submission is the most he could achieve, but tacitly assumes that it would suffice to readmit him to heaven: Satan who has half-convinced himself that you can beat the Omnipotent sees no particular difficulty in deceiving the Omniscient. But, unlike the Satanic school of critics, Satan does not here blame God, does not, as he does in his public utterances, accuse him of arbitrary will. He admits God's goodness and his love, though (4.48–113)

> all his good prov'd ill in me,
> And wrought but malice ...
> whom hast thou then or what to accuse,
> But Heav'ns free Love dealt equally to all?
> Be then his Love accurst, since love or hate,
> To me alike, it deals eternal woe.
> Nay curs'd be thou; since against his thy will
> Chose freely what it now so justly rues.
> Me miserable ...
> Which way I flie is Hell; myself am Hell;
> And in the lowest deep a lower deep
> Still threatning to devour me opens wide ...
> So farewel Hope, and with Hope farewel Fear,
> Farewel Remorse: all Good to me is lost;
> Evil be thou my Good; by thee at least
> Divided Empire with Heav'ns King I hold,
> By thee, and more then half perhaps will reigne.

The soliloquy is the keystone of Milton's characterization of Satan, and a masterpiece of dramatic revelation and artistic economy. It should remove forever the impression that in Milton's conception Satan is foredoomed to evil, and not simply to defeat in his evil. It makes clear that, like man, he was created 'Sufficient to have stood, though free to fall' (3.99), and presents his initial act of rebellion as one freely chosen. This was essential if there was to be any effective characterization of the antagonist, or indeed any real antagonist to characterize, and equally essential to that part of the pattern which turns on the parallel between the fall of the angels and the fall of man. After the initial choice some element of compulsion enters, the compulsion inherent in the evil choice itself; and Satan becomes, like Shakespeare's Macbeth, a study in the deteriorating effects of evil upon character: a study which rings true to the profoundest *human* experience, and not least in the virtual impossibility of retreat and the gathering momentum of ruin. This Milton achieves within the limits imposed by his subject and by the epic form, but beyond the demands of either.

In the soliloquy he also takes occasion to complete, in one memorable phrase, the formulation of the perverted order of hell: *Evil be thou my good* (for does not Satan carry hell with him wherever he goes?); and further to suggest that it is an order grounded in despair because it entails, at every point, a defiance of God and of fundamental facts.

In arresting contrast with this perverted order, there breaks upon us the vision of Eden, exposing (4.207–8)

> In narrow room Natures whole wealth, yea more,
> A Heav'n on Earth.

These are the two aspects of Eden. It represents unfallen nature in all her perfection as she first came from the hand of God, with no need of art to supply deficiencies, real or imagined, and with every gift a good because enjoyed in innocence and subject as yet to no abuse. This aspect opens to the poet all the resources of the idyllic. At the same time, and with perfect consonance, Eden is the reflection on earth of the heavenly order. Here nature and grace are one: the fatal cleavage between them attendant on the fall of man has not yet appeared.

Eden is 'a happy rural seat', with flowers which (4.241–3)

> not nice Art
> In Beds and curious Knots, but Nature boon
> Powrd forth profuse on Hill and Dale and Plaine.

They grow beside the streams that water Eden, and among them 'without Thorn the Rose.' Gold is not (as already in hell, and later for man) 'that precious Bane,' but (as in heaven) a thing of beauty; and in Eden it is represented by 'fruit burnisht with Golden Rinde ... *Hesperian* Fables true, If true, here only.' 'The mantling vine' and 'purple Grape' are still innocent and so is the myrtle, the poet's symbol of love. There is music in Eden. Birds supply it with the wind among the leaves; and to its notes dance the not yet banished figures of classic myth: (4.264-68)

> The Birds thir quire apply; aires, vernal aires,
> Breathing the smell of field and grove, attune
> The trembling leaves, while Universal *Pan*
> Knit with the *Graces* and the *Hours* in dance
> Led on th' Eternal Spring.

In this fair natural setting it is our first parents, at one with God, and so with nature and with themselves, who specially reflect the heavenly order: (4.291-5)

> in thir looks Divine
> The image of thir glorious Maker shon,
> Truth, wisdome, Sanctitude severe and pure,
> Severe but in true filial freedom plac't;
> Whence true authoritie in men...

Behind this last phrase lies Milton's doctrine of the heavenly order which alone can reconcile freedom and submission, liberty and authority. In the unfallen state, as again in different conditions under the gospel, the heavenly order is imitated. It entails the acceptance of God's rule by creatures endowed with free will: not a mechanical obedience under compulsion like that of a slave, but a voluntary obedience, with love and gratitude, and with the consent of reason and of the whole being, like that of a son; so that the act of obedience is itself an exercise of liberty, and God's service is found to be indeed perfect freedom. And only those who freely submit to authority in this way can in their turn justly exercise authority. This, as will appear more fully in the two succeeding books, is the principle of the heavenly order. It is the principle against which Satan has rebelled in heaven and which he has now come to Eden to attack.

For Satan is there the while, perched like a cormorant on the Tree of Life, and devising thoughts of death. Nor are we permitted to forget his shadow: among the haunts of natural beauty which cannot compare with Eden, the poet includes (4.268-71)

> that fair field
> Of *Enna*, where *Proserpin* gathering flours
> Herself a fairer Floure by gloomie *Dis*
> Was gather'd ... :

lines to be remembered when we come to the temptation of Eve. But now
Satan soliloquizes on what he sees. Though he has beheld 'undelighted all
delight' (for Eden, able to charm all sorrow but despair, had no power
upon him), he is moved to admiration by Adam and Eve, (4.362–4)

> whom my thoughts pursue
> With wonder, and could love, so lively shines
> In them Divine resemblance.

Nothing in Milton's portrayal of Satan is subtler than the lingering attrac-
tion which he feels and the unconscious, and unconsciously ironic, tributes
which he pays to the divine against which he has rebelled. This soliloquy,
though narrower in range than the first, is not less revealing. Love, mingled
with pity for their helplessness against his attack, is Satan's first spontaneous
response to the human pair; then the momentary illusion that he comes,
not as an enemy, but to seek their alliance; then, with the memory of his
own predicament, a note of conscious irony enters and with the fixed idea
– his hatred of God – love and pity are suppressed, (4.373–81)

> yet no purpos'd foe
> To you whom I could pittie thus forlorne,
> *Though I unpittied*: League with you I seek,
> And mutual amitie so straight, so close,
> That I with you must dwell, or you with me
> Henceforth; my dwelling haply may not please
> Like this fair Paradise, your sense, yet such
> Accept your Makers work; he gave it me
> Which I as freely give ...

Once more Satan's better feelings end in feeling, with no influence upon
action (there is an incipient sentimentalist in Satan), but presently the
feelings themselves perish before the stronger passion of hatred for God.
'The Tyrant's plea' necessity, as Milton calls it, is the merest excuse. When
next Satan speaks the love and pity for Adam and Eve have changed to
envy and cruel hate.

It is the spectacle of their perfect felicity in each other, the innocent
and therefore uninhibited love of Eden, that completes this change. Love
affords one of the principal motifs woven into the pattern of *Paradise Lost*.
In Adam and Eve, the unfallen, the perfect marriage is depicted. (It is
introduced but not completed at this point and requires Raphael's admonition in Book 8 to round out and safeguard its doctrine.) And in Adam and
Eve the fallen we are to see marriage as it is. From Raphael we are to learn

(not without surprise) that sexual love exists among the angels, and, from Satan, that its unfulfilment is one of the major miseries of hell. A third time he soliloquizes: (4.505–11)

> Sight hateful, sight tormenting! thus these two
> Imparadis't in one anothers arms
> The happier *Eden*, shall enjoy thir fill
> Of bliss on bliss, while I to Hell am thrust,
> Where neither joy nor love, but fierce desire,
> Among our other torments not the least,
> Still unfulfill'd with pain of longing pines.

From his observation Satan might have gathered a hint for his attack on Eve and on Adam through Eve, since his devotion to her is so patent. On Eve because her fond account to Adam of her earliest memory plainly reveals absorption in self (before drawn to Adam instead), and as she gazes at her image in the lake we are meant to remember Narcissus. Like Eve's dream and Adam's account to Raphael of his feeling for Eve, this is an indication, innocent as yet, of the weak place in their armour. What Satan indubitably gains is his first intimation of the prohibition attendant on the Tree of Knowledge which grows hard by the Tree of Life ('So neer,' Milton repeats, 'grows Death to Life'). Satan continues: (4.512–26)

> Yet let me not forget what I have gain'd
> From thir own mouths; all is not theirs it seems:
> One fatal Tree there stands of Knowledge call'd,
> Forbidden them to taste: Knowledge forbidd'n?
> Suspicious, reasonless. Why should thir Lord
> Envie them that? can it be sin to know,
> Can it be death? and do they onely stand
> By Ignorance, is that their happy state,
> The proof of thir obedience and thir faith?
> O fair foundation laid whereon to build
> Thir ruin! Hence I will excite their minds
> With more desire to know, and to reject
> Envious commands, invented with designe
> To keep them low whom knowledge might exalt
> Equal with Gods ...

No one can miss the anticipation of the stratagem by which the attack is to be made or fail to recognize its importance in the pattern. But the attentive reader is meant further to realize that here Satan is expressing his own genuine doubts about the prohibition, his sense of its injustice or its absurdity, and that in the temptation scene it is these that he exploits. Given only the temptation scene, we might have put it all down to sophistry. This soliloquy, which represents his undisguised thoughts, shows that it is something much subtler: sophistry building upon a misconception egregious but sincerely entertained.

The brief interlude that follows, of Uriel's arrival to warn Gabriel at the gate of paradise of Satan's proximity, reminds us briefly that this is an epic struggle. 'Now came still Eevning on' and we are again with our first parents in their idyllic retreat. We learn more of Eden and of ideal marriage.

Though nature reigns in the garden, not 'curious art,' man's yet pleasant because voluntary labour is asked, says Adam, (4.625-7)

> to reform
> Yon flourie Arbours, yonder Allies green,
> Our walk at noon, with branches overgrown;

indeed more hands are needed – the hands of the children they ardently desire. 'Meanwhile, as Nature wills, Night bids us rest.' Eve replies in a speech whose submissiveness echoes Milton's earlier formulation, 'Hee for God only, shee for God in him': (4.635-7)

> what thou bidst
> Unargu'd I obey; so God ordains,
> God is thy law, thou mine.

Eve's words motivate the relation in perfect love, but they will contrast strongly with her later attitude; for there is domestic drama as well as heroic action woven into the pattern of *Paradise Lost*, and pastoral poetry and a lyric note beside. Of the uniting of genres Eve's speech is an example. Starting with her loving submission to Adam, it goes on to the pleasant order of their day, each hour with its appropriate accompaniment of natural beauty, from sunrise 'With charm of earliest Birds' to (4.647-8)

> silent Night
> With this her solemn Bird and this fair Moon;

and closes again on the note of love. It is a lyric rhapsody based on the simple epic device of repetition: all the phrases in the first half are repeated in the second: (4.651-6)

But neither breath of Morn when she ascends
With charm of earliest Birds, nor rising Sun
On this delightful land, nor herb, fruit, floure,
Glistring with dew, nor fragrance after showers,
Nor grateful Eevning mild, nor silent Night
With this her solemn Bird, nor walk by Moon
Or glittering Starr-light without thee is sweet.

This (with Adam's talk of the stars and how they declare the glory of God, and of other music in Eden besides the birds, unseen spirit voices hymning the Creator) brings them to their bower and their own evening devotions, and the reader to Milton's famous 'Haile wedded Love.'

As Book 4 opens with Satan, so it closes, and in an epic battle of words. Surprised by the angel guard, 'Squat like a Toad, close at the eare of *Eve*' (4.800), and seeking to work upon her imagination in sleep, Satan starts up in his own shape though with diminished glory (a recurrent theme). In the hostile dialogue with Gabriel, two or three important hints are given for the interpretation of Satan's character and action. When Satan accuses Gabriel of lacking his usual wisdom if he is surprised that one should flee the pains of hell, the latter retorts: (4.904–5)

O loss of one in Heav'n to judge of wise,
Since *Satan* fell, *whom follie overthrew.*

Folly (the defiance of facts) is not less a mark of Satan's fall than sin (rebellion against God). Accused in turn of having escaped from hell himself and left his followers in the lurch, Satan indignantly replies that like 'a faithful leader' he (4.935–7)

alone first undertook
To wing the desolate Abyss, and spie
This new created World;

and Gabriel: (4.947–52, italics mine)

To say and straight unsay, pretending first
Wise to flie pain, professing next the Spie
Argues no Leader but a lyar trac't,
Satan, and couldst thou *faithful* add? O name,
O sacred name of faithfulness profan'd!
Faithful to whom? ...

This is yet more important because it crystallizes in a phrase one of Milton's fundamental assumptions. It is an assumption consonant alike with classical ethics, with Christianity, and with common sense, but not always remembered or accepted today: namely, that not only possessions (as Plato recognized) but qualities, and even what are commonly called virtues, are in themselves indifferent until we know the end for which they are employed. They are good only as the end is good, and evil if they are prostituted to evil ends. Thus it is with Satan's courage, his constancy, and his indomitable will. And thus it is, as we are now told, with his fidelity to goodness and to God; but to give such sentiment and action the name of faithfulness is to profane the word. Finally we have Gabriel's comment on Satan's posing as 'patron of liberty' – Satan whose service to God before his rebellion was tainted with servility because it was not the spontaneous offspring of love and reverance which would have made it perfect freedom: (4.957–61, italics mine)

> And thou sly hypocrite, who now wouldst seem
> Patron of liberty, who more than thou
> Once fawn'd, and cring'd, and *servilely ador'd*
> Heav'ns awful Monarch? wherefore but in hope
> To dispossess him, and thyself to reign?

Such words seemed but the prelude to combat, had not the heavenly scales been weighted against it. (Milton enriches the epic device from the *Iliad* and the *Aeneid* by description based on the Bible.) Satan looking up, as he had at the sun, saw the sign in the sky, and (4.1014–15, italics mine)

> fled
> Murmuring, and *with him fled the shades of night.*

III (BOOKS 5, 6)

Morning in Eden, and Eve confides to Adam the dream which Satan has inspired. Foreshadowing as it does Satan's temptation of Eve, the dream fulfils more than one function. It is Milton's adaptation of an epic device, the dream of ill-omen or the dream sent to betray the dreamer to destruction. As a dream it has the psychological realism, the genuine dreamlike quality, achieved by Chaucer and by Spenser, with its blended memories (some of them distorted) of Adam, his words of love and praise, his reference to the one prohibition under which they live, his talk of the stars. The dream introduces the pattern and prepares for Raphael's warning and for the temptation itself. Most important, it serves to motivate, or, more strictly, to suggest the weakness which will cause, Eve's fall. This is a delicate task for the poet. The epic form (only less than the dramatic) demands some preparation for what is to come. Here, and in the revelation of Eve's initial self-centredness (4.449–80) and of Adam's feelings for Eve (8.528–59), Milton's preparation has troubled Tillyard: it is, in effect, too good, so that Adam and Eve seem to have lost their 'innocence' before the fall. But this is, I think, a mistake.[5] Tillyard is tacitly assuming St Augustine's view of the state of innocence, which excludes the greater part of human experience. Milton's view is quite different, and there is no contradiction between his beliefs and the demands of his poem. In the state of innocence as Milton conceives it, the play of contrary impulses could be experienced. One cannot well understand in what sense a being without such experience could be described as possessing free will. An impulse of love and gratitude to the Creator is clearly experienced by Adam and Eve; and it is evidently Milton's contention that impulses which might in some circumstances come into conflict with this could also be experienced. The problem is how to indicate the latent existence of these impulses without the sacrifice of innocence. Milton's answer here is Eve's dream and the other examples we have mentioned. In Eve's dream the impression left upon the reader is that of a degree both of vanity and curiosity counteracted for the time being by fear and horror of the deed of disobedience as such. And Adam's account of the aberrations of the imagination in sleep and his conviction that (5.117–19)

> Evil into the mind of God or Man
> May come and go, so unapprov'd, and leave
> No spot or blame behind,

are designed to make clear Milton's view as well as to reassure Eve, and us, of her unimpaired innocence.

Their morning orisons, as their evening on the preceding day, we are privileged to hear: (5.145–9)

> Orisons, each Morning duly paid
> In various style, for neither various style
> Nor holy rapture wanted they to praise
> Thir Maker, in fit strains pronounc't or sung
> Unmeditated ...

Thus our first parents imitate the praises of the angels, at once spontaneous and perfect in their order and harmony, and anticipate the inspired songs of religious poets, as they call on all God's works to join them in his praise, the angels first, and next the stars (5.177–8)

> that move
> In mystic Dance not without Song ... ,

and so down to the humblest of his creatures, of whose making we are presently to hear.

So they turn to their last day of pleasant labour together, to be contrasted with the next when Eve will work in the garden alone.

To them Raphael descends like Mercury, a messenger from heaven. After a discourse which takes its rise in the much-criticized explanation of how he, an angel, can partake of human food, but which extends in its sweep to a monistic account of everything as originating in God and returning to him at last 'If not deprav'd from good' (5.471) (if not, that is, wilfully rebellious to the heavenly order and self-dedicated to the perverted order of hell), and which ends in the admonition the archangel was sent to utter: after this discourse which looks back to God's pronouncements on free will and on to the account of the creation, Raphael commences, at Adam's request, the narrative of the antecedent action. Here we have further light on heaven and the heavenly order, and here, as we said, Milton develops the parallel, with difference, of the fall of the angels and the fall of man so important for his pattern, and provides the martial element, so necessary for the epic, which his human action will not afford.

Raphael is an effective narrator. He commences with the necessary proviso that he must accommodate his story to the human auditor, (5.571–4)

> and what surmounts the reach
> Of human sense ... delineate so
> By lik'ning spiritual to corporal forms,
> As may express them best,

but he adds – and here Milton insinuates the relation of the earthly to the heavenly order: (5.574–6)

> though what if Earth
> Be but the shadow of Heav'n, and things therein
> Each to other like, more than on earth is thought?

This understood, Raphael fixes the time in words that echo the opening lines of Ovid's *Metamorphoses* and plunges into the narrative of Satan's

revolt in heaven. Again the problem of motivation arises, though in a somewhat different form. What was the *occasion* of Satan's revolt? Milton finds
the answer in his own peculiar view of the relation of the Son to the Father.
The occasion of revolt was the declaration of divine honours to be paid to
the Son. (5.577–87)

> As yet this world was not, and Chaos wilde
> Reignd where these Heav'ns now rowl, where Earth now rests
> Upon her Centre pois'd, when on a day
> (For time, though in Eternitie, appli'd
> To motion, measures all things durable
> By present, past, and future) on such day
> As Heav'ns great Year brings forth, th' Empyreal Host
> Of Angels by Imperial summons call'd,
> Innumerable before th' Almighties Throne
> Forthwith from all the ends of Heav'n appeerd
> Under thir Hierarchs in orders bright ...

To them, ranged orb within orb around the throne, (5.596–606)

> the Father infinite,
> By whom in bliss imbosm'd sat the Son,
> Amidst as from a flaming Mount, whose top
> Brightness had made invisible, thus spake ...
> This day I have *begot* whom I declare
> My onley Son, and on this holy Hill
> Him have anointed, whom you new behold
> At my right hand ...

The theology of this passage we have already discussed. It refers not to
the production of the Son, nor to any addition to his nature, or status: already (as we learn later) he has exercised divine functions and been the
agent of his Father's creative power in the production of heaven and of the
angels, from whose nature and status his are perfectly distinct. What we
here witness is the manifestation, the ceremonial confirming, of the Son's
place and power, the *enthronement*, which is the essential symbol for Milton
of the Son's delegated divinity. This it is which occasions Satan's revolt.
Envious of the Son's newly proclaimed honours, and regardless of the fundamental fact that they differ totally in nature, he 'felt himself impair'd.'
Satan's initial revolt, like all his subsequent conduct, is motivated by egoism
and grounded in a fallacy, is a revolt against the facts.

It is in essence a revolt against the whole of the heavenly order. And of that order we are given a symbolic summation in the rejoicings of the angels: (5.618–27)

> That day, as other solemn dayes, they spent
> In song and dance about the sacred Hill,
> Mystical dance, which yonder starrie Spheare
> Of Planets and of fixt in all her Wheeles
> Resembles nearest, mazes intricate,
> Eccentric, intervolv'd, yet regular
> Then most, when most irregular they seem
> And in thir motions harmonie Divine
> So smooths her charming tones, that Gods own ear
> Listens delighted.

The song and dance of the angels symbolize the perfection of the heavenly order, as the stars 'that move In mystic Dance not without song,' symbolize its reflection in the order of nature. But the heavenly order, as it is realized in the praises of the angels, is not only perfect, but free, because it is the voluntary tribute of free intelligences; and so also the natural order, as it is realized in the praises of our first parents at their morning devotions, which we are intended at this point to recall. Nothing of this will Satan allow.

God can afford to hold the rebel in derision; and so far this rebel's reading of the situation shall be allowed: at the hands of the Messiah, the divine protagonist against whom he has chosen to come forward as antagonist, he shall receive his defeat. This is the foundation of the whole epic conflict which Raphael proceeds to relate. Of its successive events to the end of Book 5 – Satan's withdrawal of his command to the north under pretence of preparing for the Messiah's coming, his successful insinuation of revolt on the pretext of innovations in the heavenly order and infringement of established liberties, and Abdiel's exposure of Satan's argument – of these events, only the last requires comment.

The role of Abdiel is to confront Satan with the facts. It is significant that Abdiel is a seraph. The seraphim symbolize love of God. At first glance it might have seemed most natural to make Abdiel one of the thrones (action) or one of the cherubim (contemplation). What Milton is saying, however, is that love is the basis of perfect obedience and of superior insight. Satan's contention is that the angels enjoy their existence and their privileges not by God's gift, but by their native right as gods and self-originated beings. This contention (the origin of those questions about whether God can destroy the rebels, destroy what he has not created, which we have already heard discussed in hell) meets from Abdiel a stern denial, anticipated for the reader by Satan's own admission in the first soliloquy of Book 4. The angels are creatures and owe their existence and their godlike state to the Almighty's power and goodness. The instrument of their creation was none other than the Messiah, greater in himself than 'all Angelic Nature joind in one' (5.834), at whose honours they now repine. In those honours God intended no abatement of his angels, but the exalting rather, by placing the Son at their head, to take on, as it were, the angelic nature (as he was later, we are intended to reflect, to take upon himself and thereby to exalt the nature of man). Let Satan repent while there is yet time, but if he will not, then, says Abdiel: (5.894–6)

> Then who created thee lamenting learne
> When who can uncreate thee thou shalt know.
> So spake the Seraph Abdiel, faithful found –

faithful to God and faithful to fact. This is true faithfulness, contrasted with the faithfulness that Satan boasts. It is impossible for us as we read of Abdiel not to think of Milton in the Restoration, and impossible that this should not also have been in Milton's mind.

So ends Book 5, but Abdiel's confronting of Satan has a sequel. Dawn breaks in heaven as Abdiel returns. (Thus Book 6, like its three predecessors, opens with a reference to light, as it is to close in the triumph of the Messiah and the forces of light.) The Almighty sends forth Michael, Gabriel, and their legions to battle and with them goes Abdiel. Between the hosts drawn up in battle array (6.109–11)

> *Satan* with vast and haughtie strides advanc't,
> Came towring, armd in Adamant and Gold;
> *Abdiel* that sight endur'd not ...

And he continues his insistence on facts. He rebukes Satan: (6.135–6)

> fool, not to think how vain
> Against th' Omnipotent to rise in Arms ... ;

points to the hosts who now stand ready to defend the right (though God does not need their service), hosts, he adds, (6.145–6)

> To thee not visible, when I alone
> Seemd in *thy World erroneous* to dissent ...

To Satan's angry retort (this is where Mammon learned his doctrine), (6.166–9)

> I see that most through sloth had rather serve,
> Ministring Spirits, traind up in Feast and Song;
> Such hast thou arm'd, the Minstrelsie of Heav'n,
> Servilitie with freedom to contend ... ,

Abdiel replies with one more inexorable fact: (6.172–84)

> Apostate, still thou errst, nor end wilt find
> Of erring, from the path of truth remote:
> Unjustly thou deprav'st it with the name
> Of *Servitude* to serve whom God ordains,
> Or Nature; God and Nature bid the same,
> When he who rules is worthiest, and excells
> Them whom he governs. This is servitude,
> To serve th' unwise, or him who hath rebelld
> Against his worthier, as thine now serve thee,
> Thyself not free, but to thyself enthrall'd ...
> Reign thou in Hell thy Kingdom, let mee serve
> In Heav'n God ever blest ...

With this echo of Satan's 'Better to reign in Hell, than serve in Heav'n,' the refutation of the Satanic doctrine of liberty is completed.

The first day's battle is deliberately reminiscent of Homer. Satan seeks out Michael in the centre of the fray, and in the words which are the prelude to their duel a phrase of Satan's underlines his acceptance of the Homeric standard, the pagan ideal of heroism: (6.289–90)

> The strife which thou call'st evil, but wee style
> The strife of Glorie ...

The Satanists especially are a blend of Homer's heroes and his gods. Like the gods they are vulnerable and subject to pain (sin has made them so) but still immortal – or rather, as the poet significantly says, subject not to death by wounds, but only to annihilation. Vulnerability and subjection to pain Satan proves in his person, as, struck down by Michael, he is rescued by his fellows and borne on his shield to his chariot, like some stricken hero on the windy plains of Troy. After many another combat, the Satanic host, (6. 394–8)

> Then first with fear surpris'd and sense of paine
> Fled ignominious, to such evil brought
> By sin of disobedience, till that hour
> Not liable to fear or flight or paine.
> Far otherwise th' inviolable Saints ... ,

as the evening falls, are left in possession of the field.

Satan calls his leaders in council. (Such scenes are briefer than in the main part of the epic but still revealing.) He addresses them as (6.420–2)

> Found worthy not of Libertie alone,
> Too mean pretense, but what we more affect,
> ... Dominion, Glorie ...

At last Satan avows, perhaps only now discovers, his real aim. True, they have met with some disadvantage and with pain unknown before. But, he argues, God threw in forces which he deemed sufficient for their decisive defeat and failed: where, then, is his omniscience? And as for pain, the experience but proves their (6.433–5)

> Empyreal form
> Incapable of mortal injurie,
> Imperishable ...

As always with Satan, an errant will gives rise to a disastrous misreading of the facts. Better armed, they will succeed, and he divulges his invention of artillery.

Brought into use on the second day of battle, it lends to the epic narrative at least variety, and brings to the angelic forces a temporary setback. If this episode, and the angelic reply by hurling whole mountains clad with pines, fail of the intended effect of sublimity, no such failure is present in the closing scene of the war in heaven. Again the divine counsel balances the Satanic council, and once more the Father addresses his true image, the Son: (6.680–703)

> Effulgence of my Glorie, Son belov'd
> Son in whose face invisible is beheld
> Visibly, what by Deitie I am,
> And in whose hand what by Decree I doe,
> Second Omnipotence, two dayes are past ...
> Since *Michael* and his Powers went forth to tame

> These disobedient; sore hath been thir fight,
> As likeliest was, when two such Foes met arm'd;
> For to themselves I left them, and thou knowst,
> Equal in their Creation they were form'd,
> Save what sin hath impaird, which yet hath wrought
> Insensibly, for I suspend thir doom ...
> Two dayes are therefore past, the third is thine;
> For thee I have ordain'd it, and thus farr
> Have sufferd that the Glorie may be thine
> Of ending this great Warr, since none but Thou
> Can end it ...

This is the prelude to that scene of the Messiah's going forth to battle in the chariot of paternal Deity (whose central position in the pattern of the poem we have already sought to explain and whose details we have already analysed). Arrived at the place of battle, the Son alone drove the terror-struck beings before him to where heaven's wall opened to disclose 'the wasteful Deep': (6.862-92)

>   the monstrous sight
> Strook them with horror backward, but far worse
> Urg'd them behind; headlong themselves they threw
> Down from the verge of Heav'n, Eternal wrauth
> Burnt after them to the bottomless pit.
>   Hell heard th' unsufferable noise, Hell saw
> Heav'n ruining from Heav'n and would have fled
> Affrighted; but strict Fate had cast too deep
> Her dark foundations, and too fast had bound.
> Nine dayes they fell; confounded *Chaos* roard,
> And felt tenfold confusion in thir fall
> Through his wilde Anarchie, so huge a rout
> Incumberd him with ruin: Hell at last
> Yawning receavd them whole, and on them clos'd ...
> Disburd'nd Heav'n rejoic'd, and soon repaird
> Her mural breach, returning whence it rowld.
> Sole Victor from th'expulsion of his Foes
> *Messiah* his triumphal Chariot turn'd:
> To meet him all his Saints who silent stood
> Eye witnesses of his Almightie Acts,
> With Jubilee advanc'd; and as they went,
> Shaded with branching Palme, each order bright,
> Sung Triumph, and him sung Victorious King,

Son, Heir, and Lord, to him Dominion giv'n,
Worthiest to Reign: he celebrated rode
Triumphant through mid Heav'n, into the Courts
And Temple of his mightie Father Thron'd
On high: who into Glorie him receiv'd,
Where now he sits at the right hand of bliss.

Thus Raphael concludes the antecedent action proper, the epic within the epic, which brings us to the point where the story was taken up in Book 1.

IV (BOOKS 7, 8)

There remains, however, something more to be told, antecedent to the human action, namely the creation of the earthly universe and the placing of Adam and Eve in Eden. The elaboration of this subject is not without purpose. When we first encounter Adam, in Book 4, he is saying, (4.412–15)

needs must the power
That made us, and for us this ample World
Be infinitely good, and of his good
As liberal and free as infinite ...

That, essentially, is the theme to which the poet returns in Book 7. We have seen the Messiah, God's perfect image, put on his wrath and terror to expel the enemies of the heavenly order. We now see him the agent of God's creative power, his constructive goodness, as it produces a new world which reflects the heavenly order. On his mission of creation the Messiah comes from heaven as Satan on his mission of destruction comes from hell. All this is obvious, but it is only a part of the function of Book 7 in the pattern of the whole. In the event, Satan is to turn the new world into a second battle-field, attacking by guile, force having failed, the crown of the new creation, man. This time Satan is to succeed, but only to call forth the promise of the Messiah's mission of salvation, of reconstruction, the completely counter-vailing parallel of Satan's mission of destruction; nor is even that the end, as Book 12 will reveal.

From the beginning of Book 7 onward we are moving towards, and finally centring our attention on, the earthly scene; and this is the reason for the new invocation with which the book commences. Like the invocation at the beginning of Books 1 and 3, it is in itself a piece of lyric patterning; and this time the pattern is enriched by memories of its predecessors. As in the initial invocation the poet addresses the heavenly muse, here identified as Urania ('the meaning, not the Name'), and her dwelling is fixed in heaven itself, thus completing the parallel with the Greek muses, who are sometimes thought to dwell on Olympus with the gods. Following her voice divine the poet has soared (7.3–4)

> above th' *Olympian* Hill ...
> Above the flight of *Pegasean* wing,

and has entered the very heaven. For there, and not on Olympus, the Heavenly Muse has dwelt since before the world was made, dwelt there and with her sister Wisdom has played before the Almighty, well pleased with their celestial song. The overt reference is to the books just completed, whose scene is heaven. But the allusion to the famous passage in Proverbs about Wisdom's presence at the creation links the invocation with the subject-matter of Book 7 and makes the transition to the second half of the poem. May Urania, the poet prays, conduct him back in safety to his native element, lest he suffer the fate of Bellerophon, flung from the back of Pegasus to wander, erroneous and forlorn, on the Aleian field. In this native element, 'More safe I Sing ... ' Safety and achievement are the motifs of the second half of the invocation, introduced by this contrast with Bellerophon, who failed of both. The safety which the poet desires is safety from error, but he cannot forget the more material dangers that surround him, the hostility of his countrymen which menaces him and threatens to bereave his poetry of an audience. So, as in the invocation to Book 3, the thoughts of his own predicament crowd upon him. But this time it is not the thought of his blindness that is uppermost: he mentions it, but now he can speak of the light of dawn without a pang; he is reconciled. No, it is the sense of alienation and isolation that is uppermost, intensified no doubt by his darkness. And once more he turns for consolation, for support, for the possibility of achievement, to poetry – poetry inspired by the Heavenly Muse: (7.24–39)

> More safe I Sing with mortal voice, unchang'd
> To hoarce or mute, though fall'n on evil dayes,
> On evil dayes though fall'n, and evil tongues;
> In darkness, and with dangers compast round,
> And solitude; yet not alone while thou
> Visit'st my slumbers Nightly, or when Morn
> Purples the East; still govern thou my Song,
> *Urania*, and fit audience find, though few,
> But drive farr off the barbarous dissonance
> Of *Bacchus* and his revellers, the Race
> Of that wilde Rout that tore the *Thracian* Bard

In *Rhodope,* where Woods and Rocks had Eares
To rapture, till the savage clamor dround
Both Harp and Voice; nor could the Muse defend
Her Son. So fail not thou, who thee implores:
For thou art Heav'nlie, shee an empty dreame.

The myth of Orpheus in the second half balances the myth of Bellerophon
in the first, and at the same time recalls the invocation to Book 3, where the
poet says that 'With other notes than to th' *Orphean* Lyre' he sung, 'Taught
by the heav'nly Muse.' The parallel with the pagan classics, and the difference from them, is a constantly recurring motif in the pattern of *Paradise
Lost.*

As in Book 3, the fundamental postulate of free will and its place in
the divine counsels is communicated by the Father speaking to the Son, so
in Book 7 the purpose and meaning of creation is similarly revealed. To
make good the loss of the rebel angels from heaven ('if such it be to lose
Self-lost,') God will create a new race, and for them a world in which to
dwell till (with another reference to the motif 'raised by merit') – (7.157–
73)

till by degrees of merit rais'd
They open to themselves at length the way
Up hither, under long obedience tri'd,
And Earth be chang'd to Heav'n, and Heav'n to Earth,
One Kingdom, Joy and Union without end ...
And thou my Word, begotten Son, by thee
This I perform, speak thou, and be it don:
My overshadowing Spirit and might with thee
I send along, ride forth, and bid the Deep
Within appointed bounds be Heav'n and Earth,
Boundless the Deep, because I am who fill
Infinitude, nor vacuous the space.
Though I uncircumscrib'd myself retire,
And put not forth my goodness, which is free
To act or not, Necessitie and Chance
Approach not me, and what I will is Fate.

The theology of these last lines we have already discussed. It is not
without its importance for a complete understanding of *Paradise Lost*; but
it is clearly not so essential to the central meaning of the poem as is the
postulate of free will. In this respect it is like the precise relation of the Son
to the Father, and like that, it constitutes a major departure from orthodox
Christian doctrine. Consequently, Milton is content to be true to his con-

victions without obtruding them too emphatically upon the reader, and indeed to remain as close as he conveniently can to the language of orthodoxy and especially to the language of the Bible, which he and the orthodox share in common. Presumably he expected the percipient reader to bring together the lines just quoted and Raphael's assertion that all things are produced from one first matter, proceed from God, and up to God return 'unless deprav'd from good.' The account given of the creation is consonant with this expression of monism. Its bearing upon the main contention of the poem is that it presents the creature as entirely good in substance, and hence presents man as capable of exercising free will with no inherent bias towards evil. That this is Milton's contention the least percipient reader can hardly fail to apprehend, and the contention, rather than the metaphysical reasons supporting it, is what every reader must apprehend.

Accordingly, after the lines quoted, Milton is free to develop his account of the creation with reference to other ideas germane to the pattern of the poem. Once more Raphael warns that this is an accommodated narrative, 'So told as earthly notion can receave.' Then he allows the chorus of the angels to emphasize the points with which we commenced: the contrasting aspects of the Messiah in this and the preceding book, and, in this, God's diffusive goodness in creation: (7.184–91)

> Glorie to him whose just avenging ire
> Had driven out th' ungodly from his sight,
>   ... to him
> Glorie and praise, whose wisdom had ordain'd
> Good out of evil to create, instead
> Of Spirits malign a better Race to bring
> Into thir vacant room, and thence diffuse
> His good to Worlds and Ages infinite.

The contrast is further emphasized by the description of the Son's setting forth on his mission of creation; and a second contrast is immediately introduced with Satan as we remember him to have set forth on his mission of destruction, the gates of hell opening with thunderous discord, his standing on the verge of chaos to look out upon its wild waste, his bold venturing into it. The Son sets forth, (7.194–221)

> Girt with Omnipotence, with Radiance crown'd
> Of Majestie Divine, Sapience and Love
> Immense, and all his Father in him shon.
> About his Chariot numberless were pour'd

Cherub and Seraph, Potentates and Thrones,
And Vertues ...
          Heav'n op'nd wide
Her ever during Gates, Harmonious sound
On golden Hinges moving, to let forth
The King of Glorie in his powerful Word
And Spirit coming to create new Worlds.
On heav'nly ground they stood, and from the shore
They view'd the vast immeasurable Abyss
Outrageous as a Sea, dark, wasteful, wilde,
Up from the bottom turn'd by furious windes
And surging waves, as Mountains to assault
Heav'ns highth, and with the Center mix the Pole.
    Silence, ye troubl'd waves, and thou Deep, peace,
Said then th' Omnific Word, your discord end:
Nor staid, but on the Wings of Cherubim
Uplifted, in Paternal Glorie rode
Farr into *Chaos*, and the World unborn;
For *Chaos* heard his voice ...

And as the work of creation commences, yet another echo is heard, this time of the heavenly order whose essence is light, and of the poet's invocation to light at the beginning of Book 3: (7.243-6)

Let ther be Light, said God, and forthwith Light,
Ethereal, first of things, quintessence pure
Sprung from the Deep ...

But already another aspect of creation, which is central to Milton's view of nature, and is to be central to the pattern of this book, has been introduced. Nature is an order, *a rational scale of being*; and this order, this rational scale, is produced through the instrumentality of the Word, the Logos. But nature is not less prolific than rational: *a vital scale of being*; and this aspect is, from the first, associated with the Spirit or power of God: Before the divine fiat, 'Let there be light,' (7.233-7)

          Darkness profound
Cover'd th' Abyss: but on the watrie calme
His brooding wings the Spirit of God outspred,
And vital vertue infus'd, and vital warmth
Throughout the fluid Mass ...

And in the whole subsequent account images of gestation and birth abound. Even as the Word speaks, naming the kind, defining the form, the earth or the waters give birth to examples without stint. The 'Waters generate Reptile and Spawn abundant' (7.387–8). Earth not only brings forth grass and herb, bush and tree, but (7.454–66)

> Op'ning her fertile Woomb teem'd at a Birth
> Innumerous living Creatures, perfect formes ..
>   now half appear'd
> The Tawnie Lion, pawing to get free
> His hinder parts, then springs as broke from Bonds,
> And Rampant shakes his Brinded mane ... ,

and so with all the other living things, of animal and vegetable. This is that 'nature boon' which we have viewed in Eden, whose impulse of growth and reproduction has set Adam and Eve to their pleasant garden labour. This too is that nature which, not in its rational order only, but in its abundant life, glorifies the Maker. God looks upon it all and sees that it is good and bids all living things increase and multiply, and man among the rest: man 'the Master work, the end Of all yet don.'

In man the vital principle and the rational achieve their full realization and perfect harmony, for in man the earthly order which reflects the heavenly reaches the consciousness of so doing. Thus man is (7.506–16)

>   not prone
> And Brute, as other Creatures, but endu'd
> With Sanctitie of Reason, ...
>   self-knowing, and from thence
> Magnanimous to correspond with Heav'n,
> But grateful to acknowledge whence his good
> Descends, thither with heart and voice and eyes
> Directed in Devotion, to adore
> And worship God Supream, who made him chief
> Of all his works,

and gave him to rule the rest. In man's unfallen state the rational principle rules the vital, without conflict or struggle, finding its support and sanction in voluntary and filial obedience to God, whose every gift is good. And this filial obedience in its turn qualifies man to rule. This, as we have said, is the reflection of that scheme and pattern in heaven against which Satan has rebelled and which he now seeks to destroy on earth.

Man is created by a special act of God, and in God's own image, but he too is a single being. There is no word of body and soul as separate and opposed entities, but only of a creature at once corporeal, vital, and rational. In the foregoing account the word soul connoting life, but not reason, has been applied repeatedly to all living things, and now Raphael says: (7. 524–8)

> he formd thee, *Adam*, thee O Man
> Dust of the ground, and in thy nostrils breath'd
> The breath of Life; in his own Image hee
> Created thee, in the Image of God
> Express, and thou becam'st a living Soul ... :

only, as we have already learned, reason is the 'being' of the human soul, and the express image of the Maker. Thus the creature, man, is linked on the one hand with nature, on the other with divinity. And the emphasis already thrown upon the Son as the true and perfect image of the Father gives an added significance to the creation of man in God's image: in this too the second Adam parallels and completes the first.

The angel chorus which celebrates the return from the mission of creation starts with God's constructive goodness, involves some of the other motifs, and ends, as do also Books 6 and 8, with an admonition to man to preserve the state which God has bestowed upon him to keep or lose at will. (7.602–32)

> Great are thy works, *Jehovah*, infinite
> Thy power ... ;
>   greater now in thy return
> Then from the Giant Angels; thee that day
> Thy Thunders magnifi'd; but to create
> Is greater than created to destroy ...
>   Who seekes
> To lessen thee, against his purpose serves
> To manifest the more thy might: his evil
> Thou usest, and from thence creat'st more good.
> Witness this new-made World, another Heav'n ...
>   Thrice happie men,
> And sons of men, whom God hath thus advanc't,
> Created in his Image there to dwell
> And worship him, and in reward to rule
> Over his Works ...
> And multiply a Race of Worshippers
> Holy and just: thrice happie if they know
> Thir happiness, and persevere upright.

The eighth book completes the antecedent action, the warning, and the archangelic visit, and brings us back to Eden, the scene of the crisis.

As Adam continues to question the archangel (whose answers at once complete the picture of the earthly order and gently admonish man to think first of what pertains to God's service and his own happiness) Eve retires to tend her fruit and flowers, not unnoticed by the poet, who takes occasion to comment on her beauty and on the perfect harmony of her relations with Adam, so soon to be disrupted. (8.52–8)

> Her Husband the Relater she preferr'd
> Before the Angel, and of him to ask
> Chose rather; hee, she knew would intermix
> Grateful digressions, and solve high dispute
> With conjugal Caresses, from his Lip
> Not Words alone pleas'd her. O when meet now
> Such pairs in Love and mutual Honour join'd?

This at the beginning of the book.

Invited by Raphael, Adam takes up the tale and recounts the life of Eden since his creation. His opening words are significant: (8.250–1)

> For Man to tell how human Life began
> Is hard; for who himself beginning knew?

They are a partial echo of Satan's words when contemptuously dismissing Abdiel's reminder that by the Son God had created the angels: (5.856–8)

> who saw
> When this creation was? rememberst thou
> Thy making ... ?

Satan had continued: (5.859–64)

> We know no time when we were not as now;
> Know none before us, self-begot, self-rais'd
> By our own quick'ning power, when fatal course
> Had circl'd his full Orbe, the birth mature
> Of this our native Heav'n, Ethereal Sons.
> Our puissance is our own ...

But Adam from the instant of his creation knows that he came not of himself and appeals to the sun and earth (we remember by contrast Satan's address to the sun at the beginning of Book 4): (8.278–82)

Not of myself; by some great Maker then,
In goodness and in power pre-eminent;
Tell me, how may I know him, how adore,
From whom I have that thus I move and live,
And feel that I am happier than I know.

The beginning of the answer is in Adam's dream, divinely inspired, and in this also contrasting with Eve's dream inspired by Satan, that he awakes to find it true. In the dialogue that follows Adam asks for a meet companion and in his insistence wins his Creator's praise, who finds in him self-knowledge, expressing, as he says, 'well the spirit within thee free, My Image ...' (8.440–1). So Adam's account proceeds through the creation of Eve, their first encounter (complementing Eve's memories of her earliest moments and her first sight of Adam – Book 4), their marriage and the epithalamion, provided, not by an angel chorus (as in Milton's dramatic drafts and in Vondel's *Adam in Exile*), but by the whole natural order, as if in this event it reached its own consummation. And Adam seeks to explain to the angelic visitant, and to himself, his feelings for Eve.

The passage that follows has no doubt offended many later readers, brought up in the Romantic tradition (that outcome of the fall, for which Milton made insufficient allowance!); but it is essential, not only to the poet's doctrine, but to the poem's action. Adam is completely conscious that, by God's decree and nature's law, he is Eve's superior in wisdom and authority; and we are expected to remember, 'Hee for God only, shee for God in him.' Yet, says Adam, (8.546–54)

> yet when I approach
> Her loveliness, so absolute she seems
> And in herself compleat, so well to know
> Her own, that what she wills to do or say,
> Seems wisest, virtuousest, discreetest, best;
> All higher knowledge in her presence falls
> Degraded, Wisdom in discourse with her
> Loses discount'nanc't, and like folly shewes;
> Authority and Reason on her waite ...

And his own bafflement has come out in the admission, (8.530–2)

> here passion first I felt,
> Commotion strange, in all enjoyments else
> Superior and unmov'd, here onely weake ... ,

and in the surmise, (8.534–7)

> Or nature faild in mee, and left some part
> Not proof enough such Object to sustain,
> Or from my side subducting, took perhaps
> More then enough ...

Again Milton faces the problem of dramatic motivation: while Adam is yet sinless, and without the sacrifice of his free will, we must somehow be prepared for the form which his sin will take. The archangel sees Adam's danger and the necessity of warning him and he improves the occasion by completing, partly with a reservation, partly by an extension, the Miltonic doctrine of love, which we have already discussed: (8.561–92)

> Accuse not Nature, she hath done her part;
> Do thou but thine, and be not diffident
> Of Wisdom, she deserts thee not, if thou
> Dismiss not her, when most thou needst her nigh ...
> In loving thou dost well, in passion not,
> Wherein true Love consists not; love refines
> The thoughts, and heart enlarges, hath his seat
> In Reason, and is judicious, is the scale
> By which to heav'nly Love thou maist ascend ...

For once the archangelic answer does not completely clear Adam's mind: (8.596–606)

> Neither her out-side formd so fair, nor aught
> In procreation common to all kindes
> (Though higher of the genial Bed by far,
> And with mysterious reverence I deem)
> So much delights me as those graceful acts,
> Those thousand decencies that daily flow
> From all her words and actions mixt with Love
> And sweet compliance, which declare unfeign'd
> Union of Mind, or in us both one Soule;
> Harmonie to behold in wedded pair
> More grateful then harmonious sound to the eare.

Love, it is said, leads up to heaven. Do not the angels then also love? Raphael admits that they do, and can only repeat his warning, not solve a problem which, more than any other touched upon, is peculiarly Adam's own.

If there is any deficiency here it is not due to oversimplification, and it does not reside in the dramatic handling of the episode. Within the limits of his doctrine and his sensibility, Milton presents it with singular truth and insight. If it be objected that Adam's perplexity too much suggests that of the fallen state, the difficulty is not of Milton's making. It inheres in the legend, in the action for which he has to provide adequate motivation. The problem is rendered peculiarly acute by the dramatic presentation required of epic narrative. As a problem in theology and psychology it is attacked on the theoretic level by St Augustine, who asserts that before creatures endowed with perfect freedom of will could knowingly disobey a command of God the will must already have become corrupted:

> Our first parents fell into open disobedience because already they were secretly corrupted; for the evil act had never been done had not an evil will preceded it ... if the will had remained steadfast in the love of that higher and changeless good by which it was illuminated to intelligence and kindled into love, it would not have turned away to find satisfaction of itself ... ; the woman would not have believed that the serpent spoke the truth, nor would the man have preferred the request of his wife to the command of God.[6]

In other words, the corruption of the will has already commenced in the state of innocence, that is, before the sudden crisis and the overt action which terminate that state. The problem which St Augustine raises rather than solves, Milton cannot avoid. But with it he takes a different way. Evil, he has said, into the mind of man may come and go and, so long as it is not approved by the will, may be no evil to him. This is Milton's postulate. And if it is granted in the case of positive incitements to evil such as Eve's dream inspired by Satan, how much more must it be of attitudes which in certain circumstances may lead – though they have not yet led – to a breach of God's command. Such an attitude is revealed in Adam's words to Raphael; and the archangel rebukes it, not as sinful, but as dangerous. Motivation is supplied; yet the state of innocence is preserved. The essence of the state of innocence is a will not yet corrupted, not yet turned decisively and by a conscious choice from God to other objects. And in Milton's view the will is not corrupted until the crisis, the moment of choice, arrives; but the forces are already present which, at that moment, will contend with, and overcome, the impulse of obedience and lead the will to approve an evil course. Whatever one may think of the two positions, Milton's and St Augustine's, as philosophy and theology, one must admit that for epic poetry Milton's offers a possible motivation, St Augustine's none. They differ also on the relations of Adam and Eve in the state of innocence. St Augustine holds that in Eden their marriage would have been consummated for the sake of children only and without passion, but that actually they fell before this could be accomplished. Milton, on the contrary, assumes that the marriage was consummated for the sake of children indeed, but also of their completed union, and not without passion though without that concupiscence which was the first result of the fall. And he boldly and effectively makes this complete union, with the yet innocent element of passion, part of the ground of Adam's perplexity as it is later to supply the weight that tips the scale of Adam's free will against obedience to God.

That Adam should have felt perplexity does not contradict Milton's conception of the state of innocence, which is idyllic indeed, but not merely idyllic, and whose essence is a free will not yet seduced and corrupted. The state of innocence is not a state of thoughtlessness, and where there is thought there may be perplexity. Its position with regard to good and evil is the reverse of that which marks the fallen state: in the latter good is known only by, or as opposed to, evil; in the former, evil is known only as something opposed to the good. From the discourse of the archangel, compact of information and warning, Adam has learned to think more acutely. Things have fallen into focus, problems have occurred to him, but none so intimate or so acute as this of his attitude towards Eve. It is a mark of Milton's dramatic insight and propriety and consistency that, while the relations of Adam and Eve have not changed since we first saw them together in the garden in Book 4, there was at that point no hint of the perplexity which Adam now so plainly feels.

This element of drama, like the dramatic characterization of Satan, takes its place in the pattern of the poem. For Eve no such perplexity exists as assails Adam. Her temptation will take another form, but not less certainly than his it will disrupt the harmony which she now so much values, and which only their joint repentance will be able to restore. Book 8 starts with Eve's sense of the perfect harmony. It ends with Adam's sense of the problem inherent in his part therein. This is the basic pattern of Book 8. It is even more carefully calculated than one might suppose. For on it is based, in part, the pattern of Book 9, the crisis of the poem, when Eve is first to fall and then to become, by virtue of the ascendancy already established over Adam, the Dido of *Paradise Lost*, but a Dido whom Milton's Aeneas is unable to resist, unwilling to abandon.

Nor is this all. Adam's perplexity springs from the very nature of his union with Eve, and it is this union which furnishes the ground in nature of his fall. Adam's perplexity the archangel can not dispel, but he can indicate that the bond of nature offers two opposing possibilities. If it can on occasion come into competition with man's duty to God, with that impulse of love and obedience which is the only sure foundation of wisdom and hence commands the absolute sanction of reason, it can also, rightly tempered, lead upward towards God and become 'the scale By which to heav'nly Love thou maist ascend' (8.591-2). That it may do so requires not the complete transcending of earthly love as in the Platonic scheme, not its abandonment as the higher steps in the ladder of ascent are achieved, but the carrying of the natural union upward, with submission to God, and into his very presence, whereby, like all else in the natural order, it is gradually transformed and transfigured – (5.475-6)

> more refin'd, more spiritous, and pure,
> As neerer to him plac't or neerer tending.

One will not understand Milton's view of marriage in Eden, or thereafter, unless one reads it in the context of his total view of reality.

With perfect dramatic propriety, the archangel takes his stand at the point reached in the action of the poem. He assumes the innocent union of Eden and is concerned only to point to the ladder of ascent which it offers and to warn against the danger, as yet only potential, which besets the way. Almost immediately now we are to see these potential dangers realized, but before the action is completed we are to receive yet further light on the natural union and the possibilities which it embraces: are to recognize that it can play its humble yet essential part in leading our first parents to repentance and thus become a ladder of re-ascent towards God and the heavenly love. Thus the archangel's discourse fulfils a threefold purpose: it completes Milton's exposition of marriage in Eden; it foreshadows the imminent crisis in Book 9; and by formulating the doctrine of ascent from natural to heavenly love it prepares for the dramatic development, and the doctrinal significance, of the last three books – a development and significance which may also be stated in terms of pattern, since they depend upon Raphael's account of the relation subsisting in the state of innocence between natural and heavenly love, but present that relation as it realized under the very different conditions of the fallen state. Nothing is more essential in the pattern of *Paradise Lost* and nothing is more subtly woven into that pattern. But first we come to the crisis.

v (BOOK 9)

The approaching crisis asks a pause and the last of the prologues. Milton now must turn his notes to tragic as he records the defeat of the human protagonist. But not for that is his subject less heroic. The *tragic* and the *heroic* are the pivotal points on which the pattern of this prologue turns. Of the absorption of the tragic episode in the larger pattern of the divine comedy Milton wisely says nothing at this point. It will become sufficiently apparent in Books 11 and 12. For heroic style his dependence is still on the Heavenly Muse: (9.21-4)

> my Celestial Patroness, who deigns
> Her nightly visitation unimplor'd,
> And dictates to me slumbring, or inspires
> Easie my unpremeditated Verse ...

(We remember what he has already told us about her, and perhaps also the inspired and *unpremeditated* devotions of our first parents.) Blindness and a hostile environment are not again mentioned: they have been mastered. Increasing years, possibly too the old age of the world, and a cold northern climate are impediments; but still the answer is the Heavenly Muse.

In the general pattern of the poem Book 9 sends us back in memory to Book 4; the setting is Eden; the characters, Satan, Eve, Adam; the mode of presentation, soliloquy and dialogue. The idyllic surroundings are unchanged, but the situation and the characters are altered. Even before the fall the rift in the perfect harmony of the human pair has appeared, but it is the merest shadow. And in Satan, now first seen since Book 4 (for the rebel of Books 5 and 6 is an earlier Satan), the resolution then taken, 'Evil be thou my good,' has done its dreadful work. Now the plan which he then conceived is to be put in execution. Now Eve's prophetic dream, inspired in Book 4, though not narrated till Book 5, is to have its fulfilling.

To escape detection by Uriel a second time, Satan has flown with the night, and now, in darkness, steals into paradise by way of the subterranean river and shrouded in mist. He speaks, and his soliloquy, expressive in its main purpose of his character and state of mind, is fraught with echoes: 'O Earth, how like to Heav'n ...' It is indeed a terrestial heaven, danced round by other heavens, whose lights shine only for its behoof. It is a centre to receive from all, as God in heaven is a centre to give forth all. The stars in their influence are productive not in themselves, but only here: (9.111-30)

> Productive in Herb, Plant, and nobler birth
> Of Creatures animate with gradual life
> Of Growth, Sense, Reason, all summ'd up in Man.
> With what delight could I have walkt thee round,
> If I could joy in aught, sweet interchange
> Of Hill, and Vallie, Rivers, Woods and Plaines,
> Now Land, now Sea, and Shores with Forrest crownd,
> Rocks, Dens, and Caves; but I in none of these
> Find place or refuge; and the more I see

Pleasures about me, so much more I feel
Torment within me, as from the hateful siege
Of contraries; all good to me becomes
Bane ...
For onely in destroying I find ease
To my relentless thoughts ...

(As good is in its nature creative, evil is in its essence destructive.) Not earth only, but heaven itself would be a hell unless he could master 'Heav'n's Supreme.' And so his thoughts run on with malice to God and desire to betray man to a misery like his own, while he seeks for the serpent and, not without compunction, enters into it: (9.163–6)

O foul descent! that I who erst contended
With Gods to sit the highest, am now constraind
Into a Beast, and mixt with bestial slime,
This essence to *incarnate* and imbrute ...

(The word incarnate is deliberately chosen to suggest the inverted parallel with Christ – incarnate to save.)

Dawn breaks, and Adam and Eve come forth and render vocal the praises of all creation, then fall to talk of the day's task. And here the pattern of Book 8 commences to repeat itself, with difference. For Eve withdraws, from Adam this time, and the harmony emphasized before in the poet's comment now manifests its first rift, and is presently to be shattered. The dialogue is essentially dramatic in its natural revelation of character. Intent at first only on speeding their work, Eve suggests that each should pursue it alone. Mindful of the warning of a foe at hand, Adam demurs: (9.267–8, italics mine)

The Wife, where danger or dishonour lurks,
Safest and seemliest by her Husband staies,
Who guards her, *or with her the worst endures.*

(We catch the unconscious irony of the last phrase.) Eve is quick to sense the doubt of her strength and constancy, which Adam has carefully *not* expressed: (9.279–81)

But that thou shouldst my firmness therefore doubt
To God or thee, because we have a foe
May tempt it, I expected not to hear.

While emphasizing the danger, and the malice and subtlety, of one who could seduce angels, Adam tries to remove this impression. In vain. Eve (9.319–20)

> thought
> Less attributed to her Faith sincere

than was her due and 'her reply with accents sweet renewd': (9.322–7)

> If this be our condition, thus to dwell
> In narrow circuit strait'nd by a Foe ...
> How are we happie, still in fear of harm?
> But harm precedes not sin ...

Then wherefore should the encounter be feared or shunned? And again, (9.340–1)

> Fraile is our happiness, if this be so,
> And *Eden* were no *Eden* thus expos'd.

So Eve, though still innocent, prepares to meet Satan half way. Already we recognize the faint shadow of the Satanic outlook: Eve feels herself impaired by Adam's attitude, and she is, if unconsciously, half-critical of God's provision for them. It is to this, and not to the thwarting of his own better judgment and authority, that Adam somewhat 'fervently' replies: (9.343–68)

> O Woman, best are all things as the will
> Of God ordain'd them, his creating hand
> Nothing imperfet or deficient left
> Of all that he Created, much less Man
> Or aught that might his happie State secure,
> Secure from outward force; within himself
> The danger lies, yet lies within his power:
> Against his will he can receave no harme.
> But God left free the Will, for what obeyes
> Reason, is free, and Reason he made right,
> But bid her well beware, ...
> Least by some faire appeering good surpris'd
> She dictate false, and misinform the Will
> To do what God expressly hath forbid ...
> Seek not temptation then, which to avoide
> Were better ...

> Trial will come unsought.
> Wouldst thou approve thy constancie, approve
> First thy obedience.

But farther than this he will not urge her; and he will not use constraint. If she will go she may: if she thinks that trial unsought may find her less prepared than now – (9.372–86)

> Go; for thy stay, not free, absents thee more;
> Go in thy native innocence, relie
> On what thou hast of virtue, summon all,
> For God towards thee hath done his part, do thine.
> So spake the Patriarch of Mankinde, but *Eve*
> Persisted, yet submiss, though last, repli'd.
> With thy permission then, and thus forewarnd ...
> The willinger I go ...
> Thus saying, from her Husbands hand her hand
> Soft she withdrew ...

This final statement we shall have occasion to remember.

Thus Eve 'like a Wood-Nymph light,' but still with the port of goddess, 'Betook her to the groves' (always in Milton's golden world a symbol of the pagan and idolatrous: here, of course, still innocent – but nevertheless ominous). With no sacrifice of high seriousness, Milton has added his gratuitous touches of domestic drama. Under his hand Adam and Eve become fully alive and individualized. And now he dwells upon Eve's beauty and her pathos and humanizes her situation (like Ralph Hodgson after him) by presenting Satan as seducer and Eve as victim, but without vulgarizing the episode. And for Adam (9.397–411)

> Her long with ardent look his eye pursu'd
> Delighted, but desiring more her stay,
> Oft he to her his charge of quick returne
> Repeated, shee to him as oft engag'd
> To be returnd by Noon amid the Bowre,
> And all things in best order to invite
> Noontide repast, or afternoons repose.
> O much deceiv'd, much failing, hapless *Eve*,
> Of thy presum'd return! event perverse!
> Thou never from that houre in Paradise
> Foundst either sweet repast, or sound repose;

> Such ambush hid among sweet Flours and Shades
> Waited with hellish rancour imminent
> To intercept thy way, or send thee back
> Despoild of Innocence, of Faith, of Bliss.

And to Satan she appears (9.425–33)

> Veild in a Cloud of Fragrance, where she stood,
> Half spi'd, so thick the Roses bushing round
> About her glowd, oft stooping to support
> Each Flour of slender stalk ...
>   mindless the while,
> Herself, though fairest, unsupported Flour,
> From her best prop so farr, and storm so nigh.

Satan, who has heretofore viewed undelighted all delight, is momentarily vanquished by Eve's beauty and innocence and tastes the idyllic charms of paradise: (9.463–6)

>   the Evil one abstracted stood
> From his own evil, and for the time remaind
> Stupidly good, of enmitie disarm'd
> Of guile, of hate, of envie, of revenge ...

bereft, in other words, of the whole principle on which his life and action had been grounded since his fatal resolution, 'Evil be thou my good,' and supplied with no new and better principle – hence 'stupidly,' not intelligently, good. (9.467–71)

> But the hot Hell that alwayes in him burnes,
> Though in mid Heav'n, soon ended his delight,
> And tortures him now more, the more he sees
> Of pleasure not for him ordain'd: then soon
> Fierce hate he recollects ...

and 'stupidly good' would now be his own description of his former state.

From flattering words which 'Into the Heart of Eve ... made way,' through the serpent's explanation that he owes the gift of speech to a tree, and on to Eve's unwary consent that he show her the wonder-working growth, are easy steps. But on pointing out the Tree of Knowledge, the tempter encounters resistance: Eve, 'yet sinless,' rehearses the prohibition concerning it, and ends: (9.652–4)

God so commanded, and left that Command
Sole Daughter of his voice; the rest, we live
Law to ourselves, our Reason is our Law.

Now Satan strikes a new note: he appeals to reason, and (9.665–6)

with shew of Zeale and Love
To Man, and indignation at his wrong.

It is show merely, but woven into the argument are the genuine doubts and
objections which he has felt on first hearing of the prohibition (4. 514ff.)
and his reiterated, though not altogether genuine, doubt of whether God is
indeed the fount and origin of things. His speech is a masterpiece of sophistry and suggestion which owes part of its power to this incorporating of
the speaker's real or at least habitual sentiments. (9.684–730)

Queen of this Universe, doe not believe
Those rigid threats of Death; ye shall not Die:
How should ye? by the Fruit? It gives you Life
To Knowledge. By the Threatner? look on mee,
Mee who have touch'd and tasted, yet both live,
And life more perfet have attaind then Fate
Meant mee, by ventring higher than my Lot, ...
          or will God incense his ire
For such a petty Trespass, and not praise
Rather your dauntless virtue, whom the pain
Of Death denounc't, whatever thing Death be,
Deterrd not from atchieving what might leade
To happier life, knowledge of Good and Evil;
Of good, how just? of evil, if what is evil
Be real, why not known, since easier shunn'd?
God therefore cannot hurt ye, and be just;
Not just, not God; not feard then, nor obeyd ...
Why then was this forbid? Why but to awe,
Why but to keep ye low and ignorant,
His worshippers ...
The Gods are first, and that advantage use
On our belief, that all from them proceeds:
I question it, for this fair Earth I see
Warm'd by the Sun, producing every kind,
Them nothing ...
          and wherein lies

> Th' offence, that Man should thus attain to know?
> What can your knowledge hurt him, or this Tree
> Impart against his will if all be his?
> Or is it envie, and can envie dwell
> In heav'nly breasts?

The irony of this last question's coming from Satan! And throughout we observe the impeccable logic – impeccable if we omit the essential fact that the prohibition is the test merely of obedience and that reason itself dictates obedience to God. And we observe, as we said, the lacing of Satan's sophistries with his genuine or at least his habitual sentiments.

Eve is dazzled by the Satanic logic, but not too much so to try her own hand at it in the soliloquy which is prologue to her fall: (9.758–76)

> In plain then, what forbids he but to know,
> Forbids us good, forbids us to be wise?
> Such prohibitions binde not. But if Death
> Bind us with after-bands, what profits then
> Our inward freedom? ...
> How dies the Serpent? He hath eat'n and lives
> And knows, and speaks, and reasons, and discerns ...
> What fear I then, rather what know to feare
> Under this ignorance of good and Evil,
> Of God or Death, of Law or Penaltie?
> Here grows the Cure of all ...

As in her dream, a strange exhilaration seizes on Eve, but there are other results. The apple is in itself a thing indifferent; the prohibition, the simple test of an obedience grounded at once in reason, faith, and love. But the sin of disobedience, as Eve's soliloquy enables us to infer, carries with it or includes among its immediate consequences folly upon folly and sin upon sin: pride ('expectation high Of knowledge, nor was Godhead from her thought'), intemperance ('Greedily she ingorg'd without restraint'), scepticism ('Though others envie what they cannot give'), self-delusion ('I perhaps am secret ... and other care perhaps May have diverted from continual watch Our great Forbidder ...'), selfishness, breaking of the natural order, adoption of the false Satanic view of liberty (Eve questions whether to reveal the secret to Adam or 'keep the odds of Knowledge ... Without Co-partner,' so to become more nearly his equal and even perhaps his superior, 'for inferior who is free?'), jealousy, and a love for Adam fatal to him (she thinks of herself as dying and Adam 'wedded to another Eve' to 'Live with her enjoying,' and she resolves that at all costs he shall share with herself in 'bliss or woe'), finally idolatry (her reverence, at parting, to the tree). The tale of sin and folly will be completed in Adam's fall. The poet has no more pity to waste on Eve.

But Adam is still unfallen, and the pathos of his situation as he awaits Eve's return is not unnoticed. The first shadow of disagreement has fallen between them and Adam, who was not the offender, has brought a peace-offering of flowers, into whose description is infused, for the last time, the idyllic note of life in Eden: (9.838–48)

> *Adam* the while
> Waiting desirous her return, had wove
> Of choicest Flours a Garland to adorne
> Her Tresses, and her rural labours crown
> As Reapers oft are wont their Harvest Queen.
> Great joy he promis'd to his thoughts, and new
> Solace in her return, so long delay'd;
> Yet oft his heart, divine of something ill,
> Misgave him; hee the faultring measure felt,
> And forth to meet her went, the way she took
> That Morn when first they parted ...

No sooner met than Eve commences her explanation and apology, ending with the announcement that what she did she did for Adam, who must now make proof of the fruit's wonderful power lest their fates be disjoined and she too late renounce deity for his sake. Adam's amazed dismay is fittingly symbolized: (9.892–3)

> From his slack hand the Garland wreath'd for *Eve*
> Down drop'd, and all the faded Roses shed.

Far otherwise the roses shed their petals on this human pair sleeping in their bower. The dropped and faded garland is a symbol also of the end of the idyllic life in Eden, now become 'these wilde Woods forlorn.' Adam is aghast at Eve's crime and its consequence; but in those consequences he quickly determines, in the soliloquy which is the prologue to his fall, that he must share: (9.900–16)

> How art thou lost, how on a sudden lost,
> Defac't, deflourd, and now to Death devote? ...
> And mee with thee hath ruind, for with thee
> Certain my resolution is to Die;
> How can I live without thee, how forgoe

> Thy sweet Converse and Love so dearly join'd,
> To live again in these wilde Woods forlorn?
> Should God create another *Eve*, and I
> Another Rib afford, yet loss of thee
> Would never from my heart; no no, I feel
> The Link of Nature draw me: Flesh of Flesh,
> Bone of my bone thou art, and from thy State
> Mine never shall be parted, bliss or woe.

The deliberate echo of the phasing of Eve's jealous fears points the contrast and the irony. Eve's jealousy and Adam's self-immolation spring alike from love. As love, Adam's is of the higher order; yet both are culpable as entailing rebellion against God. Of that the poet leaves us in no doubt. He does not oversimplify the problem. He takes full account of the dilemma in which Adam finds himself – of the way in which the forces of nature that supported the perfect union in the state of innocence now motivate the imperfect union, the union which in a moral and religious view Adam ought to have renounced. Those who will not agree with Milton's judgment should still have the candour to admit his realism and the superb artistry with which it is integrated in this pattern.

Adam does not seek to mitigate Eve's fault. But perhaps moved by the desire to comfort her, he questions whether the penalty will really be death, and this leads him on into a piece of Satanic logic. For God to destroy them would be to uncreate; to create others in their place would give the adversary cause for triumph. But like Satan himself he is only half convinced by his own logic; at a deeper level he is undeceived: (9.952–62)

> However I with thee have fixt my Lot,
> Certain to undergoe like doom; if Death
> Consort with thee, Death is to mee as Life;
> So forcible within my heart I feel
> The Bond of Nature draw me to my owne ...
>   So *Adam*, and thus *Eve* to him repli'd.
> O glorious trial of exceeding Love,
> Illustrious evidence, example high!

Eve, clearly, is the first of the romantic critics! Whether she is really moved by Adam's attitude or is still playing a part; whether her desire, if death be the penalty, to die alone is sincere, the reader is left to judge for himself. If it is indeed a spontaneous expression of her better feeling, it remains a feeling only. Her action is to urge Adam on to eat of the fruit. The parallel with the good feelings of Satan is obvious and ominous.

Eve's situation, however, not anything she says, motivates Adam's action, – Eve's situation and 'the Bond of Nature' between them,

So forcible within my heart I feel
The Bond of Nature draw me to my owne.

It is the very same bond which might have furnished the base for that ladder of ascent leading to the heavenly love, and the same bond as will later become the starting point of repentance and of re-ascent. Thus drama, doctrine, and pattern focus in a single phrase. But the bond of nature is merely one potent fact: it is not the only fact, or the supreme fact, which is the overriding duty of obedience to God. The bond of nature motivates Adam's choice: it does not condone, much less justify, that choice.

In his fall Adam is not, like Eve, a victim of Satan's wiles. He is not deceived, but 'fondly overcome with Femal charm,' and determined, at whatever cost, not to be parted from her. Like Satan, he is a rebel against facts – the facts of the natural order which place him above Eve. Yet more fundamentally, he offends against the spiritual order by preferring Eve to God. The sins of Satan, of Eve, and of Adam, despite the different forms which they take, and the different circumstances which accompany them, have a common root in pride: in their being self-centred instead of God-centred. The particular form which Adam's sin takes is uxoriousness. In this Milton agrees with St Augustine; but he is more dramatically convincing because, unlike St Augustine, he does not eliminate sexual emotion from the state of innocence and consequently permits us to infer, what indeed the words of Adam to Raphael have put beyond doubt, that sexual emotion is an element in, though not synonymous with, the uxoriousness which is Adam's undoing.

It is upon this aspect of their relation that the fall has its first disastrous effect. Again Milton agrees with St Augustine that concupiscence is a result and not the cause of the fall. It is instantly manifested. In St Augustine's view it is a new experience; in Milton's the corruption of an experience formerly enjoyed in innocence. The difference is no doubt grounded in religious and ethical considerations but it serves Milton's pattern well. For at this point he intends us to remember the innocent relation, the description of the marriage bower, and nature's epithalamion (4.738–75; 8.500–20). The lines 'her hand he seized,' etc. (1037ff.) have their place in Milton's pattern, a pattern here of action. The gentle 'hand in hand' which had marked their perfect and innocent union and from which Eve had voluntarily withdrawn (Book 9) is now replaced by the union, impetuous, forcible, and transitory, of lust. The true marital union on the foundation of the fallen will, as we have said, he restored and symbolized by the 'hand in hand' with which they quit Eden in the last lines of the poem: the bond of nature is restored but only after their repentance. Further, in the words now ascribed to Adam, who begins to talk like a gallant, with a strong suggestion of the rake, there is an echo of words addressed by Zeus to Hera in *Iliad* (14.292–353). This carries with it for the poet, and the reader who recognizes the echo, a suggestion of the pagan. But we are to contrast the reference to the account of the same gods – Jupiter and Juno – at 4.499–501, where in the state of innocence the figures of classic myth itself are still innocent.

The next result is perturbation of mind, described in terms calculated to suggest the meaningless turmoil of the chaos: (9.1121–31)

> They sate them down to weep, nor onely Teares
> Raind at their Eyes, but high Winds worse within
> Began to rise, high Passions, Anger, Hate
> Mistrust, Suspicion, Discord, and shook sore
> Thir inward State of Mind, calm Region once
> And full of Peace, now lost and turbulent:
> For Understanding rul'd not, and the Will
> Heard not her lore, both in subjection now
> To sensual Appetite, who from beneath
> Usurping over sovran reason claimd
> Superior sway ...

They have forfeited the peace of Eden (mind and not place is what counts) with its reflection of the heavenly order. They have relapsed towards the unorder of the chaos. In this image there is indeed a concealed element of hope. Adam and Eve have sinned, but they have not committed themselves to the perverted order of hell. Their allegiance to God may be renewed; the reflection of the heavenly order may be recovered: but only after repentance. And repentance is not yet.

But now neither will confess a fault. Each blames the other. Adam laments Eve's folly and her weakness and the train of events which started with her wilful desire to work alone. And Eve, 'soon mov'd with touch of blame,' replies with more fervour than logic, returning the blame to Adam: (9.1153–89)

> Was I to have never parted from thy side?
> As good have grown there still a liveless Rib.
> Being as I am, why didst not thou the Head
> Command me absolutely not to go ... ?
> Hadst thou been firm and fix'd in thy dissent,

> Neither had I transgress'd, nor thou with mee ...
> Thus they in mutual accusation spent
> The fruitless hours, but neither self-condemning,
> And of their vain contest appeer'd no end.

The book opened with a shadow of disagreement. It closes with complete, though not final, rupture.

VI (BOOKS 10–12)

The last three books are essential to Milton's theme and purpose. The central theme is, as the title indicates, the fall of man. The fall, however, must be seen in perspective to be recognized for what is is, a tragic episode in a divine comedy. The account of the fall declares the justice of God's way to men. But only by viewing it in this larger context, where justice and mercy meet each other, can the poet fulfil the second half of his purpose and assert eternal providence. The last three books form, then, part of Milton's pattern which he is careful to integrate with the pattern of the whole: balance is maintained; earlier themes recur, and we are repeatedly aware of parallel with differences.

Book 10 is principally divided into four episodes, each an immediate result of the fall: the sending of the Son to pronounce judgment upon man, where justice is tempered with mercy; the eruption of Sin and Death from hell to claim the earth as their inheritance; the execution of justice upon Satan and his crew; and the bringing of Adam and Eve to that repentance which is necessary if the divine scheme of salvation is to include them. The final episode is, then, in the nature of a second crisis, with this time the right choice made and the action redirected towards life and salvation.

The Son's mission of judgment parallels his going forth to expel Satan and his legions (Book 6) and to the creation of the world (Book 7), the one to judge and destroy evil, the other to produce and extend good. The third mission combines judgment and mercy, since what is to be judged is not irrecoverably evil. Again the Son goes as true image of the Father: (10.65-7)

> he full
> Resplendent all his Father manifest
> Express'd ...

The hosts of angels accompany him only to the gates of heaven, which open slightly this time; this mission, like his defeat of Satan, he must execute alone. We are intended not only to look back to his earlier missions, but on to the promised incarnation. When they are judged, Adam and Eve are not yet repentant. Adam, though reluctantly, accuses Eve, and Eve the serpent. In Adam's words there is an echo of his confession to Raphael which casts a light back upon his fall: (10.141–2)

> And what she did, whatever in itself,
> Her doing seem'd to justify the deed.

And the reply of the Son casts an equal light back upon the true nature of Adam's sin: (10.145–9)

> Was shee thy God, that her thou didst obey
> Before his voice, or was she made thy guide,
> Superior, or but equal, that to her
> Thou did'st resigne thy Manhood, and the Place
> Wherein God set thee ... ?

The sentence of death in confirmed, but accompanied by the promise that Eve's seed shall bruise the serpent's head. Neither sentence nor promise is explained; but God's compassion is as evident as his justice. And the Son returns to intercede with the Father.

Meanwhile, with sympathetic intelligence of their father's success, Sin and Death issue where the still open gates of hell belch flames into chaos, and swiftly build a causeway to the earth. It is a final example of cooperative and constructive effort by and for the perverted order of hell – construction whose end is destruction; and it is a parody of the creation in Book 7: (10.282–8)

> Then Both from out Hell Gates into the waste
> Wide Anarchie of *Chaos* damp and dark
> Flew divers, and with Power (thir Power was great)
> Hovering upon the Waters; what they met
> Solid or slimie, as in raging Sea
> Tost up and down, together crowded drove
> From each side shoaling towards the mouth of Hell.

When completed the causeway is a path from hell to earth as the path through the spheres gives access to earth from heaven. It is an asymmetrical completion of the universe because evil and a result of the fall, just as from the same cause the earthly universe itself is thrown off balance. Sin and Death now encounter Satan, returning from Eden where he has hidden, cowering, at the voice of the Son, finally bereft of courage, his last heroic quality, but still glorying in being 'Antagonist of Heav'n's Almighty King.' From them he accepts the work as his own, as the creation by the Son and Spirit was God's indeed.

Nor does the infernal parody cease there. Having sent on Sin and Death as vice-regents in his earthly kingdom, Satan makes his way to Pandaemonium, ascends his throne, and in 'permissive glory,' as at the great consult, addresses his followers, narrating rapidly the hazardous voyage through chaos and the happy outcome. Man (10.485–90)

> by fraud I have seduc'd
> From his Creator, and the more to increase
> Your wonder, with an Apple; he thereat
> Offended, worth your laughter, hath giv'n up
> Both his beloved man and all his World
> To Sin and Death a prey, and so to us ...

Voltaire could not have bettered Satan's derision. As to the judgment on himself, 'A World who would not purchase with a bruise'! Then, as he expects their applause, he is greeted by hisses, and sudden retribution overtakes him and his followers, 'in the shape he sin'd,' transformed to serpents and forced to eat apples of dust and ashes. Having wilfully parodied God's state, Satan is now compelled unwillingly to parody his own boasted action, whether the boast was true or a lie, and eat the apple himself, his followers as always following docilely in his wake.

Before the final episode of Book 10, the repentance of Adam and Eve, there is a brief account of the changes in the heavenly bodies resultant upon the fall: a passage recalling by contrast the account given of these bodies in Book 8, as the fabrication of the causeway by Sin and Death recalled the account of creation in Book 7. In both cases the first effect is to disrupt the pattern of the universe, to thrust the element of asymmetry upon God's works, fit symbol of the disruptive force of sin. But the power which produced the first order can restore it, and upon one condition will, that man shall repent and willingly accept the proffered gift of grace.

At the crisis of the poem Adam and Eve have made the wrong choice, and, after the madness of sin, they have awakened to behold in terror and sullen resentment their ruin. They have not yet learned to repent the sin itself. They do so now in a scene which is to be re-enacted, with variations, to the world's end. And nowhere is Milton's touch surer or his sympathy more deeply engaged.

The note of Adam's musings is despair, and the vague memory of

Satan's great soliloquy in Book 4 which has haunted us, suddenly crystallizes in the words: (10.837–44, italics mine)

> what thou desir'st
> And what thou fearst, alike destroyes all hope
> Of refuge, and concludes thee miserable
> Beyond all past example and future,
> *To Satan only like both crime and doom.*
> O Conscience, into what Abyss of fears
> And horrors hast thou driv'n me; out of which
> I find no way, from deep to deeper plung'd!

But their states of mind present significant differences. Without self-pity, Adam can realize the extent of his loss: (10.860–2)

> O Woods, O Fountains, Hillocks, Dales and Bowrs,
> With other echo late I taught your Shades
> To answer, and resound farr other Song.

Nor is it his own loss alone that he thinks of: his betrayal of his descendants yet unborn is the bitterest drop in his cup, and the blessing 'increase and multiply' has become a curse. Like Satan's his thoughts, as they twist and turn, lead him inexorably back to his crime and to God's justice: (10.828–31)

> Him after all Disputes
> Forc't I absolve: all my evasions vain,
> And reasonings, though through Mazes, lead me still
> But to my own conviction ...

This conviction, however, and its attendant despair are in Adam really the first step towards repentance, not yet recognized as such, but when recognized embraced with hope, not like Satan's 'O, then, at last repent,' instantly rejected and issuing in yet deeper despair.

The next step, again not recognized as such, is reconciliation with Eve. It is significant that this precedes conscious repentance and the hope of forgiveness. It is achieved, not perhaps without grace, but certainly on the basis of that strong natural bond which had led Adam to prefer death with Eve to life without her. Adam's fortunes are inextricably interwoven with Eve's and his sin and his repentance spring in part from the same root. We have watched their alienation from its first foreshadowing in Eve's wilful desire to work alone. Now the movement is reversed, and we watch their gradual reconciliation. Again, significantly, the first motion is Eve's, whose repentance has commenced with bitter regret for the wrong done to Adam. He repels her, 'Out of my sight, thou Serpent,' reminding her and us of her first offence, (10.873–80)

> But for thee
> I had persisted happie, had not thy pride
> And wandring vanitie, when least was safe,
> Rejected my forewarning, and disdain'd
> Not to be trusted, longing to be seen
> Though by the Devil himself, him overweening
> To over-reach, but with the Serpent meeting
> Fool'd and beguil'd, by him thou, I by thee ...

But Eve, persistent as ever, is not to be repulsed. She confesses her fault and pleads her double misery. Adam has sinned against God only, she against God and him. (The echo of 'Hee for God only, shee for God in him' seals Eve's acceptance of the inequality against which she has rebelled.) She will pray, and this time there is no pretence, that she may bear the full weight of the punishment alone. And Adam is moved to love and commiseration. He too, 'if Prayers Can alter high Decrees,' would bear all the punishment himself. But since this cannot be, (10.958–61)

> let us no more contend, nor blame
> Each other, blam'd enough elsewhere, but strive
> In offices of Love, how we may light'n
> Each others burden in our share of woe.

Then again the thought of their descendants afflicts him, and the curse, 'to our Seed (O hapless Seed!) deriv'd.

Eve's counsel of abstention from offspring and suicide if need be (she has submitted to Adam but not yet to God) Adam firmly but gently rejects. Undeceived as ever, he recognizes what such counsel implies, defiance of God; and already his thoughts are commencing to move in a very different current, towards submission and reconciliation.

He is reconciled to Eve, has in effect forgiven her, and manifests in his gentleness a new tolerance for her weakness, intolerant only of his own. The bond of nature has begun to reassert its beneficent influence – without waiting for the work of grace to be completed, to be more indeed than silently and unrecognizedly begun. And now Adam, and after him Eve, are ready for the next step, without which their reconciliation itself is incomplete, because unsanctified: they are ready to turn to God with an admission of their sin and a prayer for forgiveness. Adam and Eve have

been prepared for this in different ways – Eve by her movement of repentance towards Adam, Adam by his forgiveness of Eve, but both on the
basis of the natural bond. So Adam, remembering 'with what mild And
gracious temper' God had pronounced his judgment upon them, proposes:
(10.1086–98)

> What better can we do, then to the place
> Repairing where he judg'd us, prostrate fall
> Before him reverent, and there confess
> Humbly our faults, and pardon beg, with tears ...
>   So spake our Father penitent, nor *Eve*
> Felt less remorse ...

We notice the contrast with the conclusion of Book 9:

> Thus they in mutual accusation spent
> The fruitless hours, but neither self-condemning,
> And of their vain contest appeer'd no end.

We observe that the first result of the natural bond as it re-asserts its sway
is to give effect to the common resolve of repentance. They go together,
but, though the significance of this will perhaps come home to us only
at the end of the poem, *not* hand in hand. That seal of completed reunion
must wait upon repentance, though the impulse towards reunion, the
renewed expression of the natural bond, may antedate repentance and
lead on to it.

A light is thrown back upon the movements of Book 10 by the opening
lines of Book 11; for the poet tells us that the resolution of repentance
had not been reached without the silent interposition of grace: (11.2–5)

>   for from the Mercie-seat above
> Prevenient Grace descending had remov'd
> The stonie from their hearts and made new flesh
> Regenerate grow instead ...

This is precisely what we have seen happening. Before the fall nature
and grace could work in perfect unison; and still it is in aid of nature
that grace is sent, and not in simple opposition to it.

The resolution of repentance redirects the action of the poem and
opens the way to restoration, the long, painful road back. But it does not
stay the consequences of the fall, which we are now about to witness.

In Book 11 the change is signalled by the appearance of the Messiah in a new role: as the Mediator he presents to the Father the first prayer of penitent man; and God sends Michael to conduct Adam and Eve from the garden, but at the same time to instruct them touching the future: (11.113–16)

> Dismiss them not disconsolate; reveal
> To *Adam* what shall come in future dayes,
> As I shall thee enlighten, intermix
> My Cov'nant in the womans seed renewd;
> So send them forth, though sorrowing, yet in peace.

Adam, sensible already of inward peace, comments on the strange efficacy of prayer, and his thoughts turn again to the still cryptic promise of the bruising of the serpent's head. Eve, pathetically, hopes that they may be allowed to live out their appointed days in Eden. But already the signs of change in nature are apparent. The bird of Jove stooping upon its prey is at once an example and an epic omen.

Then Michael descends with the angelic guard. The contrast with the coming of Raphael, in archangelic form but 'sociably mild,' is pointed. Michael presents himself to Adam in human form, but stern and stately. We are to recognize that his coming to reorient the fallen Adam balances Raphael's coming to complete the illumination of Adam the innocent, and are to reflect on man's altered state. At the word of dismissal from Eden, Eve breaks into lamentation for her 'native soil,' 'these happy walks and shades,' the flowers she rejoiced to tend, and the 'nuptial bower' by her adorned. Her words are like a look back over the life in Eden. The angel's words to Eve recall us to another motif: (11.290–1)

> Thy going is not lonely, with thee goes
> Thy Husband ... ;

and his words to Adam point yet another parallel: (11.366–9)

> Ascend
> This Hill; let *Eve* (for I have drencht her eyes)
> Here sleep below while thou to foresight wak'st,
> As once thou slepst while Shee to life was formd.

The parallel is closer than we at this point imagine; for as Adam's eyes were closed, but not the cell of fancy, his internal sight, so Eve in a dream is made aware of what it behooves her to know. There are glances forward, as well as backward – the hill which Adam ascends is likened to that (11.382–4)

> Whereon for different cause the Tempter set
> Our second *Adam* in the Wilderness,
> To shew him all Earths Kingdomes and thir Glory ...

Adam is to be shown the effects of his original crime in the series of visions of man's life and conduct from the fall to the flood, on whose literary relations, dependent at once upon the vision of Aeneas and the shield of Achilles, and upon whose artistry we have already sufficiently commented. These visions reveal the incursion of the perverted order of hell upon the pale relics of the heavenly order left on earth, but the heavenly order is not without its witnesses in Abel, in Enoch (who reminds us of Abdiel), and in Noah.

In Book 12 vision gives place to summary narrative by Michael with much less of pictorial detail and more of doctrine. Pattern is not neglected. Nimrod, for example, is intended to recall Satan, as Enoch in the preceding book recalls Abdiel. More important, Michael's narrative had a dominant and recurring theme, the cryptic promise of the bruising of the serpent's head, which is gradually elucidated as the archangel proceeds through Abraham and the inheritance of the chosen people, Moses and the giving of the law, David and his royal house, to the coming of Christ, his death and resurrection, and his second coming in judgment. The basic pattern is that of the Christian scheme itself. The fall is recognized as a tragic episode in what is in its whole extent a divine comedy: it is indeed the fortunate fall.

At the same time there is emphatically stated the stern Puritan version of the Christian view of history, which refuses to minimize the reality of evil, and is vividly conscious of the effects of original sin and the antithesis of the two cities. In this version history presents a spectacle of recurrent wanderings from the way relieved by interventions of God's extraordinary providence. Thus the old world grew progressively worse till God destroyed it in the flood. Thereafter for a time men dwelt together simply and in the fear of the Lord, but corruption set in anew. Again, with the earthly ministry of Christ and the accomplishment of man's redemption a new start was made, but after the age of the apostles abuses quickly grew up in the church itself, with persecution of those who would truly follow Christ. And this process, here merely illustrated, will continue till the last judgment. Though the divine purpose cannot fail, Satan is the prince of this world, and in it repeats the spectacular, if finally hollow, victory won by him in Eden. Progressively he extends in the realm which he has invaded the perverted order of hell, so that at the last the Messiah comes, not only to judge, but to dissolve (12.547–51)

> *Satan* with his perverted World, then raise
> From the conflagrant mass, purg'd and refin'd,
> New Heav'ns, new Earth, Ages of endless date
> Founded in righteousness and peace and love
> To bring forth fruits, Joy and eternal Bliss,

in other words, to end the tragic consequences of the fall and restore the movement of the divine comedy, and in so doing to inaugurate the new paradise, the eternal reign of the heavenly order, this time unchallenged and unimpaired. This version of the Christian view of history is also patterned, and its pattern Milton incorporates in the last two books of his poem.

But the drama of history is epitomized in the life of the individual. Heaven and hell are objective realities indeed, but also states and habits of mind. Adam has learned his lesson: (12.561–73)

> Henceforth I learne, that to obey is best,
> And love with fear the only God, to walk
> As in his presence, ever to observe
> His providence, and on him sole depend,
> Mercifull over all his works, with good
> Still overcoming evil, and by small
> Accomplishing great things, by things deemd weak
> Subverting worldly strong, and worldly wise
> By simply meek; that suffering for Truths sake
> Is fortitude to highest victorie,
> And to the faithful Death the Gate of Life;
> Taught this by his example whom I now
> Acknowledge my Redeemer ever blest.

Among other things, Adam has learned the secret of the true heroic and thus can utter the final word on the recurrent theme of heroism, pagan and Satanic, Christian and true. All this he has learned from the second Adam, and now he is ready for the promise: So thou (12.586–7)

> shalt possess
> A paradise within thee, happier farr.

For if heaven and hell are not places only but states of mind, so also is paradise.

Adam and his descendants have much to suffer before the appointed order of events has run its course and the triumph of good over evil is completed: that is the first purport of Michael's narrative. But that the end is not in doubt is the second. And for those who will accept God's offered grace there is progression in truth and goodness: an inward light to guide, an inward power to sustain, and this is the 'paradise within thee, happier farr,' which transforms lives and human relations.

It is fitting and significant that the light of this inward paradise should first shine upon Adam's relations with Eve. Ideal in the paradisal state, though even there, as Adam learns to his cost, fraught with the possibility of evil as well as of good, they have been utterly disrupted by the fall. Yet now, under the conditions of man's darker lot in a fallen world, they are on the way to being restored and are the first feature of his new life to be illuminated by the light of grace.

Eve has renounced her rash desire for solitude and a life independent of Adam. Perhaps we may catch the contrast with an earlier scene in her words: (12.614–17)

> but now lead on;
> In mee is no delay; with thee to goe,
> Is to stay here; without thee here to stay,
> Is to go hence unwilling.

Whether or not we catch here the contrast intended, it will be reinforced by a key phrase a few lines further on.

He must be a careless reader who fails to recognize how much of the pattern of *Paradise Lost* is rounded out and completed in the quiet close of the epic as our first parents quit paradise, and especially in the two concluding lines. (12.641–9)

> They looking back, all th' Eastern side beheld
> Of Paradise, so late their happie seat,
> Wav'd over by that flaming Brand, the Gate
> With dreadful Faces throng'd and fierie Armes:
> Som natural tears they drop't, but wip'd them soon;
> The World was all before them, where to choose
> Thir place of rest, and Providence their guide:
> They hand in hand with wandring steps and slow,
> Through *Eden* took their solitarie way.

The inexorable fact of the fall is not obscured by repentance or by promise. It is symbolized by the gate of paradise now angel-guarded, not for but against the human pair. We distort the poem if we forget this or try to make its subject other than paradise lost; only, the loss is not irreparable. The wrath of God is as much a fact as his mercy – as much a fact, but not as potent a force. The pathos of 'so late their happie seat' reminds us of the pathos of Satan's 'Farewell happy fields,' but also of the essential difference between the banishment of the human protagonist and of the superhuman antagonist. The 'natural tears' remind us perhaps, by contrast, both of Satan's 'tears such as angels weep' and the first tears of Adam and Eve after the fall: 'they sat them down to weep ...'; but these tears tell us of the new world which they are entering, with its natural succession of deprivation and grief, but also its mitigating challenge: 'The World was all before them ...': hope and the lure of the future are likewise part of the natural order. But to the aid of nature comes grace, 'and Providence their guide.' There lurks here a not insignificant analogy with the conclusion of *Lycidas*. Like that conclusion these lines represent tranquillity after suffering and contribute the quiet close that Milton prized; but tranquillity is not the only note: 'The World was all before them where to choose ...' – 'Tomorrow to fresh woods and pastures new.'

Of the concluding lines another key phrase is *hand in hand*. It sends us back in memory to the first rift in the paradisal union of Eve and Adam ('from her husband's hand her hand soft she withdrew'), and, beyond this, to all that has since transpired, not forgetting the intoxication which followed upon Adam's fall, 'Her hand he seiz'd,' and the loveless and desecrating union, 'of thir mutual guilt the Seale.' That false union is followed, we remember, by total alienation, and a solitude different from that which Eve had perversely and frivolously desired and worse than that from which Adam had recoiled into sin. The memory of this the second key word of the concluding lines, *solitary*, is intended to invoke. If the bond of nature and dread of solitude determined the form of Adam's sin, they also commenced the work of restoration ('let us no more contend nor blame Each other ...'), and this was a step, not in, but still towards, repentance. Milton's sense of paradox in human experience is nowhere more subtly affirmed than in the relations of Adam and Eve. In the unfallen state they held not only the possibility, as Raphael said, of ascent to heavenly love, but equally the possibility of disaster. In the fallen state, though the problem is complicated, the two possibilities yet remain; and this fact also Milton has woven into his pattern. Nor does he seek to oversimplify the interdependences of nature and grace. If the beginning of the renewal of true union was a step towards repentance, the union required repentance to complete it. Adam and Eve sought forgiveness together, but not hand in hand.

Now, as they quit paradise, it is hand in hand once more, and if their road is solitary they share it together.

VII

Our analysis of the poem will not have been undertaken in vain if it has suggested something of the density and richness of the poem's pattern, and if in
so doing it has indicated a mode of examination susceptible of being profit-
ably applied in much greater detail. Certain other facts it must also have
made plain.

Milton's adoption of the classical epic form was no arbitrary choice,
no example of mere virtuosity in grafting a set of conventional devices and
effects upon a subject matter radically different from that of Homer or of
Virgil. On the contrary the choice was reasoned and evidently preceded by
such a study of the *Iliad* and the *Aeneid* as revealed their true inwardness,
a study which never obscured the essential difference of pagan from Christian, and the result is that the dependence of *Paradise Lost* on its ancient
models is not less real, but far subtler and more varied, than the industrious
listers of epic conventions often suppose. The choice, once made, entailed
no doubt submission to the demands of the traditional form; but nothing in
Paradise Lost finds its *raison d'être* solely in these demands. Everything is
made to answer also the more imperative demands of Milton's subject,
theme, and purpose.

His subject centres in a simple and relatively primitive legend: the
story of the Man, the Woman, and the Serpent in the Garden. But the
legend comes to poet and audience already incorporated – already occupying a pivotal position – in a complete and divinely authenticated account of
man, his world, and their destiny. Milton must preserve the basic simplicity
of the legend and at the same time bring into relief the typical and universal
character of its figures and the limitless significance for mankind of their
actions and of the chain of events which they set in motion. Here the epic
form serves him well. For it enables him, first, to set his figures at a distance
and present them larger than, and remote from the conditions of, ordinary
life; and, second, to give them their place in that vast drama of existence
which involves the whole cosmos and, beyond that, the chaos, heaven, and
hell. Though neither Homer nor Virgil attempts (or in the nature of the
case could attempt) anything so vast, Milton recognized that their form,
and perhaps their form alone, was susceptible of extension to compass the
great argument with which he was resolved to deal. More than this, however, was required. Somehow these figures and their actions must be
brought home to us; and that could never be accomplished simply by setting
them at a distance and displaying their relation to the total drama of existence. But here another potentiality of the epic came to Milton's aid. The
epic formality does not preclude – paradoxically it rather serves to permit –
the progressive humanizing and individualizing of the figures of the legend.

Precisely because the epic formality does not demand it, every touch of individual humanity appears gratuitous and is emphasized by contrast. Their stature once established, and the significance of their actions, the poet may, if he will, diminish the distance at which his figures stand and allow us to perceive in them human beings like ourselves. This occurs progressively in Homer's portrayal of both Hector and Achilles; it occurs, though intermittently and less effectively, in Virgil's portrayal of Aeneas; and it dominates the later phase of Milton's Adam and Eve.

But before this the significance of our first parents and their place in the whole drama of existence have been made, as we have said, abundantly clear. Milton is building, on the one hand, on his own version of the whole Christian scheme and, on the other, on the accepted possibility of a supernatural action in the epic. To include in his poem the vast yet clearly ordered Christian scheme, he provides a supernatural action totally different, of course, and treated in a spirit as remote as could be well conceived from Homer's, yet preserving by the device of 'accommodated' narrative, a varying and appropriate degree of human reference in the different figures of his supernatural action, and pre-eminently in Satan who, incidentally, presents this contrast with Adam and Eve, that he becomes less human and individualized as the poem proceeds. Milton's striking and original adaptation of the traditional supernatural action to meet the necessities of his theme and purpose entails the invoking of a sustained relation of parallel and contrast with the human action, of which this is indeed a minor example. It also entails, as we have seen, the extension of Homer's double setting (Troy and Olympus) to a quadruple: earth, centring in Eden, but set in the whole cosmos, heaven and, in contrast to it, hell, and finally in contrast to the cosmos, the chaos, each setting symbolic of an idea and each related to all the rest and to the life of man. And here, as indeed at every turn, we are confronted with pattern and the role of pattern in the poem.

Of pattern in *Paradise Lost* three characteristics may be confidently affirmed. It is in its foundation a structural pattern, firmly drawn, and presenting massive examples of parallel and contrast. Quite as fundamentally, it is a philosophic pattern, depending on the ideas, traditional or original, which constitute Milton's interpretation of the legend and its significance, the ideas appearing in various forms, as explicit statements, dramatic projections, poetic symbols. But not less important, it is a pervasive pattern. We are continually being reminded of something that has gone before or are being unobtrusively prepared for something yet to come. Character, action, and setting, speeches and epic similes, besides preserving parallels and contrasts with others of their kind, have commonly a strong effect of pattern in their individual development, and it is here perhaps that the element of pattern which pervades the whole poem can best be isolated and studied in detail. There is indeed some analogy with the method and effect of Milton's blank verse. It is commonly and truly said that his verse paragraphs are complex units of sound. They are patterns of tone and rhythm which supply the absence of stanza and rhyme by a curious and subtle lacing of dominant sounds, and thus achieve an effect of unity, continuity, and integration. And so it is with the patterns of idea and of image which unfold as the paragraph or larger unit is read. They support the basic structural pattern; they bring under control the vast range of materials with which Milton is working; they lend to the parts of the poem, and cumulatively to the whole, that same effect of unity, continuity, and accomplished integration.

VIII

EDITOR'S NOTE *The following essay, which is incomplete, was to have formed a separate chapter entitled* 'Paradise Lost, 3: experience, thought, and pattern.' *Enough of the study exists to enable the reader to perceive the main line of the argument.*

Among the individual passages which yield or contribute to this effect of unity, continuity, and accomplished integration, none is more striking than those in which the poet speaks in his own person. These at once reveal their kinship in pattern with, on the one hand, the earlier poems and, on the other, the rest of the epic. For example, the prelude to Book 3, Milton's invocation to light, looks back to such intensely personal patterns as that of the sonnet on his blindness, but also on to Satan's address to the sun at the beginning of Book 4. Thus it serves in some sort to bridge the interval between Milton's subjective and his dramatic use of pattern, and may be allowed to raise once more the question of the relation subsisting between the dramatic patterns and the poet's extra-aesthetic experiences. In dealing with Milton the question can be avoided only by setting an arbitrary limit to one's enquiry. Among the earlier poems, as we have seen, those which resort to direct statement render the relation explicit, and others as unmistakably reveal it by means of the semidramatic projection of allegory. Hence the question becomes insistent, whether this relation, evidently so characteristic of Milton, does not also employ for its expression the more fully dramatic projection of the later poems.

The question is easier of formulation, and of tentative solution, with reference to either *Paradise Regained* or *Samson Agonistes* than to *Paradise Lost*. For, like all Milton's other poems save the great epic, each of these is short enough to be read at a sitting and thus to have its total pattern brought under the reader's eye at one time. And the difference in length and relative complexity encountered when we turn to *Paradise Lost* inevitably reflects a different mode of composition, and a different *aesthetic* experience on the part of its author. Poe's assertion of the impossibility of a long poem remains an important half-truth, confirmed by the innumerable pieces of perfect and self-contained patterning in *Paradise Lost*, the short poems of which the critic insists every long poem is made up; but the theory is at fault in refusing to concede full poetic standing to the containing pattern of the whole and to the activity which produced it and which envisaged the relation of the contained patterns thereto. This, by the way. The bearing of Poe's half-truth on our present enquiry is that, if *Paradise Lost* stands in some discoverable relation to Milton's experience, if some process analogous to that found in the other poems is here too at work, if some element of extra-aesthetic experience furnishes the point of departure for an aesthetic experience realized in an aesthetic pattern, it need not be confined to – it perhaps need not, for we will not prejudge the issue, even extend to – the pattern of the whole, but may reside in the self-contained patterns with which the epic abounds; and the pattern of the whole may concern itself with no single extra-aesthetic experience at all, but solely with bringing the various aesthetic patterns of the poem, and their attendant aesthetic experiences, into order and focus.

If for the moment, then, we leave aside the containing pattern of *Paradise Lost*, we recognize a series of subordinate themes which become the pivotal points of more or less self-contained patterns within it. One is the nature of true liberty and the relation which it bears to order and due subordination as illustrated in the heavenly hierarchies. A second is the reflection of this heavenly order in the life of man, as seen in Eden in the relation of Adam and Eve to their Creator and to each other, the latter relation developing into the semi-autonomous theme of marriage, its ideal, and its potentialities and pitfalls. A third theme is the intrusion of pride and self-assertiveness and the character of the revolt against the heavenly order, and its reflection, which this entails, as illustrated in Satan pre-eminently, but also in Adam and Eve. A fourth is the enigma of human history, explicable only as the result of the fall, its place in the divine comedy, and the operation of providence in and through history. There are other themes: the nature of the Son and his role in the divine economy, the unity and essential goodness of all substance with their implications for the nature of the creative process and for the problem of evil, the existence of free will in rational beings and the element of contingency which it injects in the scheme of things. That these themes take their origin in Milton's extra-aesthetic thought and experience is indubitable since they are canvassed at length in *De Doctrina Christiana*. But the four that we have selected for special mention, and which, if no less central in Milton's theology, are yet more central to *Paradise Lost*, will sufficiently test the dependence of the poem on the extra-aesthetic experience of its author.

The first of these themes, the nature of the true liberty and the relation which it bears to true order and due subordination, we recognize as one of the fundamental and recurrent issues of all Milton's prose writings. Only there, except for the *De Doctrina*, it has always to be dealt with in the context of change and controversy; and this controls, and in measure thwarts, the clear formulation of his ideal of liberty, in which nevertheless Milton places all the importance of his prose works. Here, in *Paradise Lost*, freed from these limitations and with all the additional resources of poetry at his command, he is able to present his ideal perfectly in the heavenly hierarchies, where the voluntary service of God is at once the definition of liberty (cf. that Christian liberty which the gospel opens to the believer) and the resolution of the antinomy of liberty and order; and the presentation, significantly, culminates in an aesthetic pattern as the hierarchies move 'about the sacred hill' in 'mystical dance' whose figures are 'regular then most when most irregular they seem.' In the poem this heavenly order is not isolated: it is reflected in the order of nature. The movement of the angelic dance, as Raphael tells Adam, resembles most the movement of the stars and planets – the movement, but not the motivation, for the essence of the heavenly order is the *voluntary* service of *rational* beings, and it is only in Adam and Eve, in paradise, that the full reflection of the heavenly order shines. Here too it culminates in an aesthetic pattern in their spontaneous acts of worship, and not in these alone, but in all their mutual intercourse till sin commences to invade their lives and obscure the reflection of the heavenly order.

This brings us to the second theme as it develops into a treatment of love and marriage. Again, the subject has engaged Milton in his controversial prose, and with specific reference to our first parents in Eden as establishing the norm of wedded love; but, through force of circumstances, it had to be presented in the incongruous setting of a plea for free divorce: the practical necessity is plain enough, and the logic of the argument is sufficiently satisfactory, but the juxtaposition remains nonetheless incongruous. No one can doubt the deep implications of Milton's experience for the divorce tracts. Nor can there be much more question about the theme of love and marriage in *Paradise Lost*. And if it is entirely legitimate to recall Mary Powell in connection with the former, it seems not less so to remember her and Katharine Woodcock in connection with the latter. The poetry is not less poetry for drawing into its aesthetic pattern elements of experience and transforming them by so doing. It is unnecessary, and of course quite impossible, to isolate the experiential element *in the poem* since it has been, as we have said, transformed. But it is idle to suppose that one has argued this element out of existence simply because one has demanded a kind of documentation which, in the nature of the case, cannot be supplied. The proper questions surely are these: Is there not independent evidence of Milton's deep concern with this issue of love and marriage, its ideal, its potentialities and its pitfalls, evidence likewise of a direct connection with Milton's personal experience and of a high degree of emotional tension issuing therefrom? Did not there intervene between the divorce tracts and *Paradise Lost* a second experience of a very different order in the short-lived union with Katharine Woodcock, his 'late espoused saint,' which must certainly have had its effect on Milton's view of the whole problem, enriching but at the same time complicating the issue? Is it not true that there is a degree of insight, of sympathy, even of tenderness, in dealing with Adam and Eve, wholly absent in the divorce tracts, and this without unsaying anything which had previously been maintained? And is not the most reasonable explanation some accession of experience coupled with the transforming effect of poetry itself? For the power of poetry to transform is of the essence in our contention: poetry, as we have said, is no mere record of an experience, much less of an extra-aesthetic experience; on the contrary, poetry is the realization of an aesthetic experience which transforms whatever of extra-aesthetic experience may furnish its starting point, and of this final aesthetic experience one can only say that the poem *is* the experience.

None of the contributing themes in *Paradise Lost* receives fuller treatment than this of love and marriage. The relation dramatically projected in Adam and Eve is carried from the original and ideal union which is a reflection of the heavenly order, through sin and its attendant disorder and disunion, to repentance and the possibility of an order and a union restored, with the promptings of nature cleared and fortified, as we have seen, by the operation of grace, but still in their first manifestations prior to it. Nowhere does the extension of the story beyond the fall more evidently complete the pattern than in the treatment of love and marriage. The promised paradise within casts its anticipatory light on the reunion of Adam and Eve.

But before that point is reached, before the tragic episode of the fall can be placed in the divine comedy, the fall itself, in its various aspects, must be explored and the parallel, with difference, between the fall of man and the fall of the angels, developed. The central action of the poem is the rebellion against the heavenly order, with the obscuring of its reflection on earth and the setting up in hell of a perverted order which struggles with the heavenly order for the possession of man and his allegiance.

In this action of rebellion Satan is the prime mover, the very type of rebellion, and of the pride and self-assertiveness from which it springs. But the insight and vividness with which Satan is portrayed have created in innumerable readers the impression that somehow at bottom the antagonist has the poet's sympathy. This impression is far too widespread to be simply dismissed. On the other hand, it encounters the greatest difficulties from within the poem; and if the impression manages to survive a frank facing of them, it can only be at the expense of the poem as a work of art, in the tacit admission that it is marred by divided aims and countervailing effects. If such indeed is the truth, then the admission had better be made explicit. But it is the duty of the critic to try first every reasonable hypothesis that will cover the phenomena and save the poem. The rudiments of such an hypothesis have been advanced by Saurat, who seeks them in Milton's extra-aesthetic experience. Satan, he suggests, embodies elements in Milton's own character which he has come to recognize: hence the insight and vividness of the portrayal; but they are elements which he has also come to condemn, hence the vindictiveness (as Saurat says in his unguarded way) with which Milton pursues his creation.[7] We need not adopt this hypothesis in its entirety or follow Saurat in his contention that Milton is himself the real hero of *Paradise Lost*, defeating Satan singlehanded. What is valuable is the suggestion that the insight and vividness have a ground other than sympathy, and one perfectly compatible with those features of the poem and of the portrayal which act so strongly against it. Nor does the suggestion lack confirmation. No one can read his controversial prose without recognizing that pride and egoism were marked features of Milton the natural man. The *doctrine* of liberty there propounded is sufficiently different from Satan's, but it is accompanied by a scornful impatience of every outward restraint which requires all the doctrinal emphasis on inner restraint to balance it. Nor is the plea for liberty wholly unvitiated by the will to power, which manifests itself, not crudely, but in the subtle form of an insistent desire to impose, by argument and exhortation, his will upon his countrymen, all the more insidious because his will is identified in his mind with the will of God. A repeated effect of the experience, at once religious and aesthetic, realized in the earlier poems is the disciplining and transcending of Milton's pride and egoism. It is not perhaps too much to see in *Paradise Lost*, and especially in the character of Satan, a similar effect being produced by a very different method ...

The centrality of the Son in the epic pattern of *Paradise Lost* has been sufficiently illustrated. He is the poem's hero (in the sense of affording the standard of heroism, Christian and Miltonic) and one of its two protagonists; he expels Satan from heaven and, in his role of the second Adam, so essential to the pattern of the epic, will defeat him again on earth. The Messiah is presented, as in the *De Doctrina*, as the true image of the Father, his perfect manifestation, and the principal instrument of his power, but far more effectively and in bolder relief. Milton retreats from no essential position assumed in the *De Doctrina*; but he dwells, not as there upon the argumentative and negative aspects of his doctrine, but upon the large residuum of positive belief which survives argument and negation. That he should present this residuum in language largely derived from Scripture, and common to him and the orthodox reader, is a necessity of his poetic treatment; but, more than that, the effort to place his doctrine and belief in relation to a whole poetic vision of existence brings out implications of which he may have been imperfectly aware as he penned the systematic formulations of the treatise ... We have hazarded the suggestion that Milton thought more freely, more organically, and in consequence more satisfactorily, under the impulse of poetic composition than at other times. Certainly his monism has a larger significance in the poetic narrative of the creation than in the corresponding chapter of the *De Doctrina*. While itself not quite free from difficulties, the narrative removes anomalies in this chapter, recognizes the wider implications of Milton's position and places his special view of creation in the context of his poetic vision of existence by giving it a role in the pattern of his poem, with its fourfold setting of heaven, the earthly universe, the chaos, and hell. Milton's view of creation, as we have seen, entailed the abandonment of St Augustine's metaphysical explanation of evil and threw him back upon the earlier emphasis on free will as the only available explanation of evil in angels and men. In *Paradise Lost* he reaffirms the position of the *De Doctrina*, and reinforces it by making the free will of the rational creature, human or angelic, with the attendant contingency, central to his whole poetic vision and to the action of the epic ...

9
Last published poems, 1 :
Samson Agonistes

I   ilton's last volume of verse, *Paradise Regain'd, a Poem in IV Books, to which is added Samson Agonistes,* bears the date 1671, and was listed for publication on 2 July 1670. There is almost conclusive evidence that *Paradise Regained* was conceived and written after the publication of *Paradise Lost.* It is so dated by Edward Phillips, and even if we question Thomas Ellwood's naïve claim to have suggested to Milton a sequel to the first epic, a poem on 'paradise found,' we have no reason to doubt that some such conversations as he reports actually took place, and hence no reason to reject the confirmation which he offers of Phillips' date. This external evidence, as we shall see when we turn to the poem, is strongly supported by internal evidence and by every reasonable inference. In the dating of *Samson Agonistes* no such certainty is possible.

Phillips professes himself wholly unable to say when *Samson Agonistes* was composed, having evidently heard nothing of its existence till 1670, when he seems to have read it in manuscript.[1] We know, though apparently Phillips did not, that the subject of this poem, unlike that of *Paradise Regained,* had long been in Milton's mind. For while neither in the Cambridge MS nor elsewhere is there any evidence of attention to the theme of the temptation in the wilderness before the writing of the second epic, the death of Samson finds its place in the list of subjects for possible dramatic treatment, in the brief notation 'Dagonalia (Jud. 16)' – and there are various references to the episode in Milton's prose. There seems, however, to have been no special interest in the theme; for the Dagonalia is not one of the subjects for which the Cambridge MS furnishes an outline or argument, and of the incidental references in the prose, only one, in the *Pro Populo Anglicano Defensio* (Col. 7: 219), seems to bear any very significant relation to the play as we have it. For *Samson* we have, then, a *terminus ab quo,* 1642, and a *terminus ad quem,* 1670, and for the rest are wholly dependent on internal evidence.

Masson was content to place the tragedy with *Paradise Regained* in the years 1667–70, indeed to regard it as Milton's last poem,[2] and until quite recently this view has been accepted without question. But, in fact, the dating of *Samson* with or immediately after *Paradise Regained* presents very serious difficulty, so divergent are the two pieces in doctrine, temper, and tone. Though the critics of Masson make nothing of this fact, they are intent on thrusting the tragedy back to a point well before the Restoration, and in one instance almost to the *terminus ab quo.* This is to carry the flight from Masson too far, and their arguments, as it seeems to me, leave the internal evidence for a date subsequent to the Restoration wholly un-impaired.

W.R. Parker has argued persuasively for composition at two separate dates, 1646–8 and 1652–3, largely on the ground that the tone and temper of the tragedy are similar to those revealed in the Psalms (80–8, and 1–8) which Milton translated in April 1648 and August 1653. Rightly rejecting Masson's tendency to regard *Samson* less as a tragedy than as concealed autobiography and a conscious allegory of contemporary politics, he admits, however, a relation to Milton's life and experience. 'It is not difficult to see,' he writes,

> how Milton came more and more to look upon Samson as a moving symbol of man's weakness and strength. In 1646–8 when he realized that blindness threatened him, when the clergy were still damning his views on marriage and divorce, when he felt lonely and miserable and frustrated in his life's work, he may have wondered how Samson managed to rise above his troubles and fulfil at last his great purpose. The moment at which the poet first considered the mental process that led to Samson's regeneration was the moment at which the drama was conceived ... We cannot say, of course, just when the moment of creative insight came; but we can believe that Milton felt little personal interest in Samson's attitudes until he, too, was a rejected champion facing the grim fact of blindness ... The working out of the drama was in a sense the working out of his own problem. And as the drama grew ... we may be sure that Milton's varied experience more and more determined the tone and emphasis of the composition. The dark mysteries of God's providence, the incredible stupidity of 'the common rout," the terrible responsibility of the chosen ones, ... the danger and dazzling power of intuition, the certainty of final triumph whatever the cost – all these products of Milton's disillusion and stubborn faith combined to make ... a profoundly moving drama touched with prophecy.[3]

This is admirably said. It makes, however, the strongest possible case not for the years 1646–8 or 1652–3, but for the time when Milton's grounds for disillusion were far more complete, and his stubborn faith put to its severest test: for the time when political disaster, utter and irredeemable, and personal peril, were fresh upon him, and when he may well have seemed to have spent his strength and light in vain: the year following upon the Restoration, between May 1660 and May 1661. I suggest that in this year when disaster overtook his cause and sent him into hiding, a fugitive from the vengeance of his enemies, Milton may well have turned or returned to the theme of Samson as the perfect vehicle for his emotions.

If *Samson Agonistes* were the literary solace of Milton's months of hiding, there would be reason enough for its tone of bitterness and despair, for the apparent immediacy of its political allusions to Restoration England, and incidentally for the absence of Edward Phillips when it was composed. On this view Milton would be seen as writing *Samson Agonistes* before completing *Paradise Lost* or dreaming of *Paradise Regained* and perhaps as achieving by means of the tragedy the partial tranquillizing of his spirit necessary before he could do either. Nor, considering the intimacy of the experience which it embodied, would it be at all surprising if Milton, discoursing freely to his nephew of his other writings, should keep the secret of *Samson* till time, and a new vantage point reached, had made him willing to disclose it to all the world.

This is the hypothesis which I would advance, and it appears to me to cover all the principal phenomena, and to be called in question by no known evidence, internal or external. As against Parker's dates, it appears to offer an occasion wholly adequate to call into being the profound passions of the play; and it saves, and accounts for, those scarcely veiled allusions to the lords of the Restoration and the leaders of the Puritan parties, which Parker would sacrifice. As against Masson's date, it avoids the difficulty of the wide interval between the doctrine, temper, and tone of *Samson Agonistes* and *Paradise Regained*, and the startling contrast between the mood from which *Samson* takes its rise and the tranquillity, and even cheerfulness, which Milton, by universal testimony, manifested in his later years.

It is true of course that, despite their divergence, *Samson Agonistes* and *Paradise Regained* have some features in common. With *Paradise Lost* they treat a series of ideas which evidently much occupied the older Milton: temptation, disobedience, repentance, obedience, restoration; and while the two epics divide the series between Adam and Christ, the tragedy, as if to complete the theme, runs through the whole in the person of its hero. Again, in their relation to Milton's experience, *Samson* and the brief epic appear to be in marked degree retrospective as well as introspective. And, finally, as contrasted with *Paradise Lost,* the two are written in a plain style (or, rather, plain styles, for they are very different), the invention, it has been argued, of Milton's latest years, when he had divested himself of traditional 'royalist' imagery and achieved a form of expression wholly consonant with his republican sentiments.[4] These facts should warn us against setting *Samson* at too great a distance in time from the two epics. They militate more strongly against the years 1646–8 and 1652–3 than against 1660–1, when the style of *Paradise Lost* was fixed beyond recall, and when Milton was commencing to manifest the characteristics of his final period.

Though Masson recognized no such necessity, it is, indeed, possible to devise an hypothesis which would permit us to regard *Samson* as Milton's last poem: namely, that unlike *Paradise Regained*, it was the product, not of Milton's normal state of mind, but of one of those periods of depression, of retrospective and introspective brooding, which must, as old age came on and physical powers waned, have beset any man in Milton's situation: his world in ruins about him, and himself old and ailing, blind and essentially alone. In such a mood the certainties of *Paradise Regained* would recede and the paradise within have to be struggled for again.

I do not advance this second hypothesis because I believe that the first, which places *Samson Agonistes* in 1660–1, covers all the phenomena, and explains more simply the intensity of feeling embodied in the tragedy, and the tragedy's relation to the two epics. But one should not, I believe, reject the possibility that this first hypothesis, attractive as it is, may be wrong, and that *Samson Agonistes* may indeed be, as has long been assumed, Milton's last poem. In that case it will be necessary to fall back upon my second hypothesis; for without some such explanation the difficulty of grouping *Samson* in time with *Paradise Regained* is formidable. The date assigned to a poem inevitably has a bearing upon its interpretation. In deciding upon the meaning of *Samson Agonistes* considered in itself, and in interpreting its allusions, the difference entailed by the two dates, 1660 and 1670, is not perhaps very great. But the difference entailed in one's conception of the pattern of Milton's final years, and the place of the poem therein, is considerable.

We will deal with *Samson Agonistes* on the assumption that it was written in 1660–1, and finally return, very briefly, to this question.

II

When Milton set down the subject of Samson in the Cambridge MS, and when he returned to it during or immediately after the year of the Restoration, he was not dependent simply on the bare narrative in the Book of Judges, not without a tradition to suggest his interpretation of it. Christian exegesis and commentary had transfigured the barbaric tribal hero in various ways. They had extracted from his story the obvious moral that unchastity is a sin and punished by God with afflictions. But, more than this, they had read into Samson himself what is wholly lacking in the Old Testament account, a sense of sin, repentance, and the desire for forgiveness and restoration to God's service. The Epistle to the Hebrews had numbered Samson among the saints, among those elders who by faith had obtained a good report (Heb. 11:2, 32), but evidently from the account in Judges Samson, a Nazarite and dedicated to God's service from the womb, had fallen away, and it could only have been by faith and repentance that he had been restored. Thus the latest experiences of Samson become a study in regeneration, and his act of fierce revenge the seal of his repentance and restoration. This interpretation, as we shall see, is fundamental to Milton's conception of Samson. Other interpretations which were evolved were ignored by the poet. The question, debated by commentators, of the righteousness of Samson's revenge troubles Milton not at all. They decide that it was indeed righteous since its motive was not the destruction of Samson's enemies merely, but of God's and since God deigned to use him as an instrument. To Milton this seems self-evident: at least he assumes it in silence. Here his only concern is to demonstrate after St Augustine that, being impelled by God's prompting to an act of service entailing his own death, Samson was not guilty of the sin of suicide.[5] Nor does he, like Peter Martyr, seek a justification in Samson's public character, presenting him as a magistrate who might redress his nation's wrongs by action against its *de facto* rulers when a private citizen might not. To Milton Samson continued to be, as he had been to Josephus, a national hero, and also, as he was to Christian commentators, a saint who, before his fall and after his repentance, enjoyed the gift of the Spirit and acted by divine impulsion. But he was not by Milton presented as a type of Christ, a view which inevitably directed attention away from Samson's sin, whose reality is central to Milton's whole conception of the character and action.

One of the things given, then, is the Samson story as it reaches Milton, modified by various traditional explanations, among which he is free to make his own selection. A second is the traditional form into which he decides to cast the story as he conceives it: classical tragedy in its strictest sense, whose models are the Greek tragic poets, and which has for its effect what Aristotle described, and Milton accepts, as *katharsis*.[6] The choice of form conditions the style and the management of the plot, 'which is nothing indeed but such economy or disposition of the fable as may stand best with verisimilitude and decorum' (Col. 1 [ii]: 333) : it does not, we must assume, itself alter Milton's interpretation of his scriptural theme.

Misled by Milton's prefatory emphasis on his Greek models, an emphasis entirely justified if properly understood, critics have assumed that the poet intended not only to follow them in structure and convention but to reproduce their spirit and effect, and that hence the only possible criterion for judging *Samson Agonistes* is Greek tragedy. Opinions on his success have differed.[7] Jebb, to take a famous example, vigorously defends Milton against Johnson's charge that *Samson Agonistes* has a beginning and end but no middle, that nothing occurs to precipitate the catastrophe. But he goes on to condemn the drama as not truly tragic, as not Hellenic at all in spirit and effect, but thoroughly Hebraic. It does not, like Greek tragedy, pit the hero against superior powers before which he goes down to inevitable defeat, yet demonstrating his heroism even in his defeat. On the contrary, Samson is an instrument of the supreme power, and the only possible conclusion is that 'All is best.' Nor, in the most vigorous and effective defence against Jebb, does Parker question the assumption that Greek tragedy furnishes the sole and sufficient criterion. But it is precisely this assumption that I would question.

In *Paradise Lost* Milton follows his classical models every whit as closely as in *Samson Agonistes*; yet no one supposes that he is trying to reproduce the spirit and effect of Homer, or even of Virgil. His purpose is to adapt the classical epic form to a Christian content and outlook, and to achieve thereby a new but still genuinely epic effect. And I would ask whether *mutatis mutandis* the same thing may not be true of *Samson Agonistes*. The only way to find out is to re-examine the drama from this point of view, that is, with two questions in mind: What is the effect actually achieved? And is it one that can be legitimately described as tragic?

To attempt an answer, however tentative, to these questions we must establish a proper understanding of the theme and action, and on the way thereto may comment on the insufficiency of Jebb's. He recognizes that 'Samson's will is the agent of the catastrophe' and that everything which 'helps to determine his will and define his purpose' leads on to it. But he proceeds: 'The force which is to produce the catastrophe is the inward force of Samson's own despair, not an external necessity pressing upon him.' On the contrary, as I have heretofore argued, and D.C. Allen has further demonstrated, it is not Samson's despair that produces the catastrophe, but his gradual rising out of his initial state of feeling, in which indeed the last heroic act would have been quite impossible.[8] Again, it is true that Samson voluntarily precipitates the catastrophe, for Milton never surrenders his robust belief in man's free will within God's providential scheme, and could not possibly achieve the effect at which he aims if he did so here. But if there is 'no external necessity,' there is still an overruling power: there is God who controls the outcome: and this fact, pardoxically, Jebb later insists upon in order to explain Milton's failure to achieve the Greek tragic effect. In his reading of the poem Jebb altogether misses the interplay of these two forces, Samson's will and God's, because while he oversimplifies the conception of God as providence, he ignores the intense religious experience undergone by Samson as he comes to a realization that God's 'ear is ever open; and his eye Gracious to re-admit the suppliant' (1172–3). When Jebb insists on the Hebraism of *Samson Agonistes*, he does not ask himself how much of this adheres inevitably to the legend with which Milton is working, or whether the religion which permeates the poem is not in fact Christian, and whether it is not the Christianity, far more than the Hebraism, that differentiates it in effect from Greek tragedy. The problem of *Samson Agonistes* is part of the problem of Christian tragedy – of the problem and Milton's solution of it.

Act I, as we may call it (1–331: Samson, Chorus), gives us Samson's situation and initial state of mind. He has sinned and been most dreadfully punished. But the punishment, be it noted (for this is characteristic of Milton's whole presentation), is the natural and inevitable outcome of Samson's actions, just as the sufferings of Oedipus are the natural and inevitable outcome of his. Blinded now, enslaved, the mockery of his enemies, Samson knows that all these evils have come upon him through his own weakness.[9] He experiences bitterest remorse; but this is not repentance: it is too entirely self-centred for that, and it has issued in a degree of despair, itself a sin in the Christian view, which can entertain no thought of forgiveness, no ray of hope. Yet Samson's foot is on the path that leads to repentance, though it will first lead him yet deeper into the slough of despond: he has acknowledged that the fault is wholly his. I can find, he says, (18–46)

> Ease to the body some, none to the mind
> From restless thoughts, that like a deadly swarm
> Of Hornets arm'd, no sooner found alone,
> But rush upon me thronging, and present
> Times past, what once I was, and what am now ...
> Why was my breeding order'd and prescrib'd
> As of a person separate to God,
> Design'd for great exploits; if I must dye
> Betray'd, Captiv'd, and both my Eyes put out,
> Made of my Enemies the scorn and gaze? ...
>
>   Promise was that I
> Should *Israel* from *Philistian* yoke deliver;
> Ask for this great Deliverer now, and find him
> Eyeless in *Gaza* at the Mill with slaves ...
> Yet stay, let me not rashly call in doubt

Divine Prediction; what if all foretold
Had been fulfilld but through mine own default,
Whom have I to complain of but myself?

Doubts momentarily assail him, and complaints of providence mingle with
his self-reproach, so that the Chorus is fain to counsel, 'Tax not divine
disposal' (210), though this is only the submission which Samson himself
acknowledges as God's due, and indeed echoes his own words: (60–2)

But peace, I must not quarrel with the will
Of highest dispensation, which herein
Happ'ly had ends above my reach to know.

Taken in conjunction with Samson's full admission of his personal responsibility, these lines give us our first clue to the inner tension between man's
freedom and God's providence which only the final words of the poem will
resolve.

From the conviction of his own responsibility Samson never wavers.
Even of Dalila, 'That specious Monster, my accomplisht snare,' he can aver,
'She was not the prime cause, but I myself' (230, 234). Still Samson is far
from true repentance. His remorse, as we have said, is in large measure self-
centred: (198–205)

[I] like a foolish pilot have shipwrack't,
My Vessel trusted to me from above,
Gloriously rigg'd; and for a word, a tear,
Fool, have divulg'd the secret gift of God
To a deceitful Woman: tell me Friends,
Am I not sung and proverbd for a Fool
In every street, do they not say, how well
Are come upon him his deserts?

These are the words of wounded pride, and pride has its issue in religious
despair. Conformable to the truths of moral theology, this is also the fruit
of Milton's imaginative insight. To the Chorus, Samson appears (120–1)

As one past hope, abandon'd
And by himself given over.

The principal purpose of this mainly expository first act is, then, to
underline Samson's remorse, not yet repentance, and his religious despair:
to give us the starting point of the movement back to God – and on to the

catastrophe. Second, we already recognize the character and function of the Chorus: it is Hebrew in its outlook and offers at is were a Hebraic commentary on the story which the poet will present, consistently though unobtrusively, from a Christian standpoint, and thus it serves the purposes of historical realism; it is not the mouthpiece of the poet: it does not run ahead of events, but like the audience follows them step by steep and learns from them what it can.

Less simple is the role of Manoa, whose entrance marks the beginning of Act II (332–709: Samson, Manoa, Chorus). True to his classical models Milton subordinates his people to the action and to the central figure of the hero, but Manoa's functions are varied and more than the others he gives the impression of a self-motivating character. Here, as again in the final act, he supplements the Chorus, now joining in Samson's lament, now criticizing his 'marriage choices,' even, like Samson and like the Chorus, seeming to question the ways of providence, rebuked this time by Samson himself: (373–5)

> Appoint not heavenly disposition, Father,
> Nothing of all these evils hath befall'n me
> But justly; I myself have brought them on,
> Sole Author I, sole cause ...

In his main endeavour Manoa is deluded: his effort to ransom his son is a counteraction wholly ironic. Yet his words have an effect on Samson beyond, and sometimes contrary to, their intention. They bring home to Samson the offence against God and against Israel: (448–59)

> Father, I do acknowledge and confess
> That I this honour, I this pomp have brought
> To Dagon ... ;
>   to God have brought
> Dishonour ... ;
>   have brought scandal
> To *Israel*, diffidence of God, and doubt
> In feeble hearts ... ;
> Which is my chief affliction, shame and sorrow,
> The anguish of my Soul, that suffers not
> Mine eie to harbour sleep, or thoughts to rest.

This is a step forward, though for the time being it only deepens Samson's despair. More subtly still, in the course of his mistaken argument Manoa puts his finger on the insufficiency of Samson's remorse: it turns too much on the offence against himself. God, says Manoa, (510–15)

> evermore approves and more accepts
> (Best pleas'd with humble and filial submission)
> Him who imploring mercy sues for life,
> Then who self-rigorous chooses death as due;
> Which argues over-just, and self-displeas'd
> For self-offence, more than for God offended.

Rejecting his father's proposal and his optimistic inferences, Samson fastens on these words: (521–2)

> His pardon I implore; but as for life,
> To what end should I seek it?

To conceive the possibility of pardon is of course to take another step forward; but to conceive it in this context is not immediately to lighten the burden. Indeed, in this act, Samson reaches his lowest depth of despair; (606–32)

> O that torment should not be confin'd
> To the bodies wounds and sores ...
> But must secret passage find
> To th' inmost mind ...

> Sleep hath forsook me and giv'n me o're
> To deaths benumming Opium as my only cure.
> Thence faintings, swoonings of despair,
> And sense of Heav'ns desertion.

And from the Chorus, orthodox though it be, Samson's misery wrings the impassioned cry of bafflement: (667–91)

> God of our Fathers, what is man!
> That thou towards him with a hand so various,
> Or might I say contrarious,
> Temperst thy providence through his short course,
> Not evenly, as thou rul'st
> The Angelic orders and inferior creatures mute,
> Irrational and brute.
> Nor do I name of men the common rout ...
> But such as thou hast solemnly elected,
> With gifts and graces eminently adorn'd,
> To some great work, thy glory
> And peoples safety ...

> Nor only dost degrade them, or remit
> To life obscur'd, which were a fair dismission,
> But throw'st them lower than thou didst exalt them high,
> Unseemly falls in human eie,
> Too grievous for the trespass or omission ...

The Chorus itself will correct this judgment in its final comment, but not so as to dispel the whole of the mystery. Meanwhile it makes its powerful contribution to the darkness, through which a gleam of light is presently to break. But first must come the two crucial encounters, with Dalila and with Harapha. For the first, if it is to have its due effect, the essential preparation is Samson's repentance; for the second, the conviction already voiced by Samson *de profundis*, that if with him the strife is over, God is still God and in his own good time and way will triumph over Dagon (460–71).

In Act III (710–1074: Samson, Dalila, Chorus) the coming of Dalila is described with incomparable vividness by the Chorus; but her motives are left by Milton obscure. They do not matter: she is there for the sake of Samson and the action, not in her own right. The primary function of the scene is to demonstrate by Dalila's powerlessness to reassert her sway the completeness of Samson's repentance. Only obedience, Milton believes, can remit the sin of disobedience – Christ's obedience for Adam's disobedience, Samson's for his own – and what is remitted is the sin, not all its consequences. But this is no mere demonstration or for the audience alone. It has its effect upon Samson himself and hence upon the action. He has won his first victory, over himself; and, though he does not realize it, he approaches his next decisive encounter with new possibilities of emotional response.

Act IV, if the divisions were marked, would fall into two scenes. The first (1075–1307: Samson, Harapha, Chorus) presents this encounter with the champion of the Philistines. It will precipitate the summons to appear before the lords, the occasion of the final catastrophe; but, more important, it is just what is needed to rouse Samson, and draw him on to form and utter, almost unawares, a hope – the first in the whole action. Harapha jeers: (1156–9)

> Presume not on thy God, whate're he be,
> Thee he regards not, owns not, hath cut off
> Quite from his people, and delivered up
> Into thye Enemies hand –

to be bound, blinded, imprisoned and set to labour, companion of the slave and ass. It is only what Samson himself has said before. Nor does he seek now to mitigate his fault or deny the justice of his punishment; but in his mounting anger at Harapha he gives back for insult defiance: (1168–77)

All these indignities, for such they are
From thine, these evils I deserve and more,
Acknowledged them from God inflicted on me
Justly, yet despair not of his final pardon
Whose ear is ever open; and his eye
Gracious to re-admit the suppliant;
In confidence whereof I once again
Defy thee to the trial of mortal fight,
By combat to decide whose god is god,
Thine or whom I with *Israel*'s Sons adore.

Nothing surely could be psychologically more true, or dramatically more effective. Samson, we remember, has reasserted his confidence in God; his remorse has become repentance, and he has sued for God's forgiveness; and but now, in the encounter with Dalila, he has stood firm: a deed has sealed his repentance and given a basis for returning confidence in himself. All this was necessary before the hope could be born that Samson might be indeed forgiven and, for one final exploit, be restored to God's service and the communion of his own people; but it was all latent, as it were, unrecognized by Samson himself. Till the hope was uttered, he did not dream that it existed: and utterance was born of the perfectly natural union of repentance and indignation.

Here, at length, is dawning the resolution necessary for Samson's last heroic act. The change is not too sudden or complete; but now to the passive desire for death is joined an active and more powerful motive. Harapha will seek vengeance for the scorn heaped upon him. Let him, says Samson, for (1262-7)

come what will, my deadliest foe will prove
My speediest friends, by death to rid me hence,
The worst that he can give, to me the best.
Yet so it may fall out, because thir end
Is hate, not help to me, it may with mine
Draw thir own ruin who attempt the deed.

And this new resolution the Chorus instantly recognizes: (1268-71)

Oh how comely it is and how reviving
To the Spirits of just men long opprest!
When God into the hands of thir deliverer
Puts invincible might ...

Samson, they feel, is once more doubly armed (and this is of crucial signi-

ficance, as we shall see) – doubly armed with 'celestial vigour' and with
'plain Heroic magnitude of mind' (1279–80).

In the second scene (1308–1444: Samson, Officer, Chorus), the summons arrives, and Samson, knowing his presence at a heathen festival unlawful, refuses: 'I cannot come'; and then with mounting anger at the in-
dignity designed him, for all thoughts of self have not been quenched: 'I
will not come,' and again, 'I will not come' (1321, 1332, 1342). But before
the Officer returns, better thoughts have prevailed: the inner voice, so long
silent, has spoken once more – the seal of Samson's restoration: (1381–4,
1423–5)

> I begin to feel
> Some rouzing motions in me which dispose
> To something extraordinary my thoughts.
> I with this Messenger will go along ...

> Happ'n what may, of me expect to hear
> Nothing dishonourable, impure, unworthy
> Our God, our Law, my Nation, or myself ...

And the Chorus replies: (1427–8)

> Go, and the Holy One
> Of *Israel* be thy guide ...

In Act v (1445–1758: Manoa, Messenger, Chorus) the futile counteraction, Manoa's effort to ransom his son, provides an overtone of pathos and
a sustained note of irony, his narrative punctuated, from the main action,
by shouts and the noise of ruins. The Messenger enters to recount the catastrophe; and Manoa and the Chorus comment antiphonally on Samson and
his end.

It is of the first importance to observe that Samson's tragedy is considered, and the effect summed up, on the purely human level (1660–1744)
before the Chorus is permitted to raise its eyes to the larger issue of the place
of his sacrifice in God's providential plan, before it can determine that 'All
is best, though we oft doubt ...' (1745–58). For this dual reference is not
confined to the comments on the catastrophe. It extends to the whole situation and action. In an earlier reference to Samson's exploits, in the *Pro
Populo Anglicano Defensio*, Milton had presented the alternative, 'whether
he acted in pursuance of a command from heaven or was prompted by his
own valour' (Col. 7: 219). In the poem, the Chorus, as we have seen, recognizes Samson as doubly armed, with 'celestial vigour' and 'plain Heroic magnitude of mind.' The poet has found a way not to choose between the two

views, but to combine and harmonize them. And of this we are reminded by Samson's attitude just before the last heroic effort: he stood 'as one who pray'd Or some great matter in his mind revolv'd' (1637–8) : he was in fact doing both. Granted that the outcome is controlled by God's overruling power, and that his grace is operative from the first, though overtly so only as the catastrophe approaches, yet Samsons' responses are at every point natural and humanly intelligible. If he is an instrument of providence, he does not cease to be an individual, fallible, though corrigible, heroic – and by his own action doomed.

The effect of the final comments is at once to magnify Samson and to reconcile us to his fate: and this raises a problem. A common feature in all tragedies is a sense of disaster. A feature of very many is, at the end, some mitigation of this sense of disaster, some reconciling of the audience to the experience which they have witnessed and shared. This is true of many tragedies, but certainly not of all. We remember, for example, the grim closing words of the *Oedipus Tyrannus* ('Let no man be accounted happy till he has carried his happiness with him down to the grave'), nor could anyone, perhaps not Sophocles himself, foresee the consummation that awaited Oedipus at Colonus. Again, we remember how little of mitigation may attend the intervention of the god *ex machina*, as for example in the *Medea* of Euripides. In a word – despite some exceptions, such as Aeschylus' conclusion of the *Oresteia* – Greek tragedy generally leaves us with small ground for consolation or reassurance. But Greek tragedy, as we observed at the outset, is not necessarily the norm to which alone we should refer; and in Shakespeare the mitigation of our sense of disaster plays a larger part in the final effect, though it differs in kind and degree from play to play. There is the sense of a moral order vindicated and restored (*Macbeth*), of the task accomplished at whatever cost (*Hamlet*), of the transforming effect of suffering, as well as of death the deliverer (*Lear*), of a human heroism somehow greater than the entangling fate to which the hero succumbs (*Othello*, and indeed *Hamlet*) ; and finally there is a sense of life as something that goes on chastened by these experiences (the four tragedies). And of all these means, explicity or by implication, Milton avails himself on the human level before invoking the providential: (1660–7, 1687–1724)

> O dearly-bought revenge, yet glorious!
> Living or dying thou hast fulfill'd
> The work for which thou wast foretold
> To *Israel*, and now ly'st victorious
> Among thy slain self-kill'd
> Not willingly, but tangl'd in the fold,
> Of dire necessity, whose law in death conjoin'd
> Thee with thy slaughter'd foes ...

But he though blind of sight,
Despis'd and thought extinguish't quite,
With inward eyes illuminated
His fierie virtue rouz'd
From under ashes into sudden flame ...

So virtue giv'n for lost,
Deprest, and overthrown, as seem'd,
Like that self-begott'n bird
In the *Arabian* woods embost,
That no second knows nor third,
But lay e're while a Holocaust,
From out her ashie womb now teem'd,
Revives, reflourishes, then active most
When most unactive deem'd,
And though her body die, her fame survives,
A secular bird ages of lives.

Come, come, not time for lamentation now,
Nor much more cause, *Samson* hath quit himself
Like *Samson*, and heroicly hath finish'd
A life Heroic ...

To *Israel*
Honour hath left, and freedom, let but them
Find courage to lay hold on this occasion,
To himself and Fathers house eternal fame;
And which is best and happiest yet, all this
With God not parted from him, as was feard,
But favouring and assisting to the end.
Nothing is here for tears, nothing to wail
Or knock the breast, no weakness, no contempt,
Dispraise, or blame, nothing but well and fair,
And what may quiet us in a death so noble.

This reconciliation, this mitigating of the sense of disaster, is restricted to
the human level, the level on which tragedy commonly moves, for the reference to God is in relation less to the outcome than to Samson's personal
experience and feelings, and the image of the phoenix, which so often in
Christian symbolism represents immortality, is carefully confined to the immortality of Samson's fame; and these considerations lead on to a first formulation of the tragic *katharsis* as Milton conceives it.

Only when this is accomplished is the Chorus allowed to raise its eyes to God's providential purpose and the place of Samson's sacrifice therein, and to correct, though not to deny, the doubts which have assailed it and Manoa and Samson himself. And since God's ways are just but also mysterious, acceptable by faith but often baffling to reason, the effect of the larger view is less to cancel than to confirm and complete the narrower, or so at least Milton's treatment would seem to say: (1745–58)

> All is best, though we oft doubt,
> What th' unsearchable dispose
> Of highest wisdom brings about,
> And ever best found in the close.
> Oft he seems to hide his face,
> But unexpectedly returns
> And to his faithful Champion hath in place
> Bore witness gloriously; whence *Gaza* mourns
> And all that band them to resist
> His uncontroulable intent,
> His servants he with new acquist
> Of true experience from this great event
> With peace and consolation hath dismist,
> And calm of mind, all passion spent.

And as if to confirm this reading of the lines, they again culminate in a formulation – perhaps the most famous in all literature – of the Aristotelian *katharsis*. Clearly Milton supposed that, with his basic Christian assumptions, he had still produced a genuinely tragic effect. Nor will the reader who clears his mind of prepossessions, and allows the poem to have its full effect, be likely to demur.

III

To say that *Samson Agonistes* is Milton's attempt to write a Christian tragedy is not to deny all relevance to his Greek models. It simply means that we must not expect divergent assumptions to issue in identical effects and must be willing to extend our terms of reference. Though many critics have followed Macaulay in asserting that Euripides is Milton's principal model, there seems to be singularly little ground for this opinion. In spirit his closest affinity is with Aeschylus, whose ethical and theological emphasis Milton can hardly have failed to appreciate, and who, in the *Oresteia*, re-reads an ancient and barbaric legend with all the insight of a profound moral and religious sensibility. In form, on the other hand, as Jebb recognizes (though his choice of the *Trachiniae* is not the happiest example), Sophocles is the chief model; and this is confirmed by Parker, who rightly chooses the *Oedipus at Colonus* as the closest of all Greek analogues. But the similarity in form, and up to a point in content, serves to underline the difference in spirit and effect.

Though standing somewhat apart from Sophocles' other works, and modifying the inferences to be drawn from them, the *Oedipus at Colonus* is his deliberately chosen conclusion, which supplies the mitigation wholly lacking in the *Oedipus Tyrannus*; and it must be read in the light of the whole story and of the Sophoclean outlook. That outlook, if we follow H.D.F. Kitto, posits a cosmic order encompassing and governing the life of man. It is not a moral order such as Aeschylus presented as progressively realized; at most it subsumes such an order. Whoever runs athwart this cosmic order, whether wilfully or, like Oedipus, without intent, is, in Kitto's vivid image, like one who interrupts the flow of a powerful electric current, which destroys him and flows on. The gods have predicted, they have not decreed, the fate of Oedipus. Now he reaches Colonus, conscious that there he is to be released from suffering and the final prediction fulfilled. The prelude to this event is a series of encounters, much as in *Samson Agonistes*. The effect of these encounters is to magnify the figure of Oedipus from the blind and helpless wanderer of the opening scene to one of heroic proportions once more, with power to confer benefit and doom. In so far there is a parallel effect in Samson. But Oedipus' determination is not formed by these encounters: it is merely exhibited. Though, to steal a phrase from Dryden, it seems like treason in the court of Apollo to say it, the *Oedipus at Colonus* lies much more open to Johnson's charge than does *Samson Agonistes*: the action does not precipitate the catastrophe, as in Milton's tragedy it plainly does. Oedipus' reliance on divine prediction, and his determination to await its fulfilment at all hazards, had already been reached in the long interval since the ghastly revelations of the *Oedipus Tyrannus*, and especially in the year of wandering that had led at last to Colonus. Milton has chosen the much more difficult task of displaying in the first four acts a gradual change of mind in his hero comparable in extent to the whole development of Oedipus from the time when he stood before the palace blinded and desperate. The catastrophes, when at last they come, present some similarities: each hero goes to meet his end willingly and with a sense of fulfilment. But the effect in the two cases is very different. It must be so for dramatic reasons as well as philosophical – in the light, that is, not merely of the outlook of the two poets, but of the prior experiences of the two heroes. Oedipus has erred unwittingly: contemplating his deeds he has known an abyss of horror, but not remorse of conscience: his *hubris* perhaps supplied the trigger of the

weapon that destroyed him, but certainly not the charge: and now he
awaits release, as Samson has also done. But Samson's experience has been
of a different order: he has sinned, been punished, and repented, and he
has been miraculously restored to God's service. The *Oedipus at Colonus*
ends in mystery, and, partly because the known reality is so intolerable, mystery is relief. *Samson Agonistes* ends in the transcending of mystery, and in
something that is more like triumph than mere relief: death is indeed relief
– but death is swallowed up in victory. Both plays announce an end to
weeping and lamentation; but to realize to the full the difference, one has
only to place beside Milton's final chorus the final chorus of Sophocles (as
it is movingly rendered by a modern translator) :

> This is the end of tears:
> No more lament.
> Through all the years
> Immutable stands this event.[10]

It would be hard to imagine any comment more noncommittal.

Since ours is a purely inductive study, let us try a comparison with
Shakespeare. At first glance no two tragedies could be more unlike than
Samson Agonistes and *Hamlet*. In form, at least in the narrower sense of
the term, they have nothing in common, and in content little enough. Each
has as its basis a barbaric legend and a folk hero (as indeed have many of
the great tragic themes including the *Oresteia* and the Oedipus plays), and
in both *Hamlet* and *Samson Agonistes* (as also in the *Oresteia*) a dominant
motive in the legend is revenge, which, as Bacon reminds us, is 'a kind of
wild justice.' These legends and heroes the poets by their superior insight
transform, so as to bring into relief a profounder and subtler human significance without wholly eliminating the basic primitive elements. It is when
we come to the pattern of the action in *Hamlet* and *Samson Agonistes* that
we strike what may turn out to be a clue. For without confusing poet with
philosopher, or art with life, one may, and I think must, concede that the
imagined action in such serious works of literature as these does in some
way represent the poet's intuition of what life is, or on occasion may be,
like. Now the common factor in the action of *Hamlet* and *Samson Agonistes*
is that each hero is moving, however hesitantly or unwittingly, towards the
fulfilment of his task and, for they are conjoined, towards his own doom.
Not that the task (Hamlet's execution of justice or Samson's service of
God) necessarily of itself entails the destruction of the hero. It does so because of the hero's own conduct, because, that is, of the interplay of free
will and circumstances which together weave a web of necessity no less inexorable than that in which Oedipus is entangled. The heroes do not, like

Oedipus in the *Tyrannus*, unconsciously run athwart the order of things; they do not, like Macbeth, defy the moral order or, like Edmund, call its mandate in question. On the contrary, they perish at last in giving effect to it. They are on the side of the power – the overruling power – which destroys them. Irony is of the very substance of tragedy; and this is the element of irony common to the two plays. In *Samson Agonistes* the power is frankly identified as providence. In *Hamlet* we detect at least in the hero a growing sense of a providential order: 'There's a divinity that shapes our ends ...'; 'There's a special providence in the fall of a sparrow.' Even if we interpret this as a purely subjective response on his part, it is apt to have some influence upon us; and even if it has not, there remains the pattern of action and the tragic irony which is inseparable from it.

These common features, which condition the kind of tragic effect achieved, spring from a common source, namely, the assumption, for the most part implicit in *Hamlet*, but much more explicit in *Samson Agonistes*, of a Christian view of man and the world. In *Hamlet* it is a Christian view of man in the order of nature, with no specific reference to grace: one could not, with any show of propriety or probability, speak of Hamlet's undergoing a religious experience. In *Samson Agonistes*, on the other hand, to miss the presence and purport of Samson's religious experience, and the silent operation of grace therein, is but to half read the play, and thus to throw it out of focus.

The greater precision, the more specific religious reference, in *Samson Agonistes* has a twofold result. First, it heightens the tragic irony of the catastrophe and, in retrospect, of the steady movement on towards it, for that movement is the very same as Samson's movement back towards God. Second, it supplies the ground of a more complete resolution, a stronger mitigation of the sense of disaster than is common in tragedy. In *Hamlet* the sense of disaster, though mitigated, is still predominant at the end; and Shakespeare does here what he does nowhere else: he looks, if only fleetingly, beyond the earthly scene, where the tragic action has worked itself out, to some resolution beyond it ('Good night, sweet Prince, And flights of angels sing thee to thy rest'). From any such reference Milton has abstained, and critics have guessed at various explanations, including his mortalism; but the all-sufficient explanation is that tragic precedent was against it, and anyway it would have been superfluous.

The question has often been asked whether a Christian tragedy is really possible. No doubt on a total view Christianity presents the drama of existence as a divine comedy – or at most a divine tragicomedy – in which the overruling power is the supreme goodness and whatever or whoever opposes it is finally eliminated. Whether their fate is in any negotiable sense tragic is a question that need not detain us: it no more arises than does the question whether in *Samson Agonistes* the fate of the Philistines is tragic. If such a subject were ever given tragic treatment, it would have to be in a pagan, not a Christian, context. If a Christian tragedy is possible, then its subject will be the saved, or those on the way to being saved, not the utterly lost. And clearly in the ample confines of the divine comedy there is plenty of room for tragic episodes. 'I now must change Those Notes to Tragic,' writes Milton, as he introduces the subject of the first sin, and the first repentance, and their consequences. Christianity never denies the power of sin and suffering, though it envisages a final escape from them. In suffering, indeed, it discovers a new dimension. 'Prosperity,' said Bacon, 'is the blessing of the Old Testament; adversity is the blessing of the New.' This idea has entered deeply into the Christian consciousness, and not with the theologically minded alone: it receives its recognition not only in *Samson Agonistes*, but also, for example, in *Lear*, and even Cleopatra can say, 'My desolation does begin to make A better life.' This is not theology: it is a profoundly true apprehension of one of the possibilities of human experience, on which Christianity has seized, and it is pregnant with drama, as Shakespeare knows and so does Milton.

Suffering may be the lot of either sinner or martyr, and Samson is both. He has sinned, and through suffering he has progressed to self-knowledge and repentance, the necessary prelude to re-admission to God's service. But now God's service is martyrdom, if not precisely the usual kind. Patience, as the Chorus observes, (1287–91)

> is most oft the exercise
> Of Saints, the trial of thir fortitude,
> Making them each his own Deliverer,
> And Victor over all
> That tyrannie or fortune can inflict.

This, however, is not the way of tragedy, and Samson is called upon to play a more active role: to be his own deliverer in a more literal sense and to achieve therewith a victory that dwarfs all his former triumphs. But suffering, though it may be a means of grace, is suffering still, and death, though it be the price of such a victory, and though it even come as a release from suffering, is still death. Thus some of the ingredients of tragedy are certainly available; and it only remains to be asked what the poet has been able to do with them. What Milton has done in respect of the action we have seen: he has made the way of repentance and restoration, the way back to God, also the way that leads inevitably to the catastrophe, and has thus achieved at a stroke the only kind of irony that is at once compatible with a Christian outlook and as potent as any to be found in tragedy anywhere. Moreover, he has shown the necessity which thus conjoins Samson's salvation and victory with his death to be no arbitrary imposition of the overruling power, but the outcome of Samson's conduct – of his sin and of his subsequent repentance. That his repentance is achieved under the impulsion of divine grace does not alter the fact that it is Samson's own. If God is present and operative in the tragedy, as he must be in a Christian view, at least he does not operate arbitrarily – or from a machine!

So much for the poem, if it stopped short with the catastrophe. It does not. The conclusion, as we have also seen, is directed wholly to reconciliation, to mitigating the sense of disaster: first on the human level, and, when that is completed, by invoking the overruling power, showing the place of Samson's sacrifice, of his whole experience, in the providential order of God, who does not force men's wills but nevertheless controls the event. The emphasis of this comment is justified not only on doctrinal but on artistic grounds. The very strength of the element of tragic irony in the action both permits and demands it. And the irony and the resolution of irony alike depend on the fact that this is a Christian tragedy: that is to say, a tragedy which, however scrupulously it adheres to classical conventions, is written unfalteringly from a Christian point of view.

Christian exegesis of the Samson story had developed different and sometimes mutually incompatible interpretations. Samson had been regarded as a repentant sinner who, by God's mercy, had been restored to his service. He had also, like Moses, Joshua, David, and others, been regarded as a prophetic type of Christ, and his sacrifice as a type of Christ's on the cross. There can be no doubt that Milton builds his drama wholly on the former conception; and we need not complicate the question of the possibility of a Christian tragedy by introducing the latter view.

In that possibility Milton clearly believed; but his artist's intuition taught him that it could be realized only under certain conditions. The first was the provision of a strong element of tragic irony in the pattern of the action. The second was a resolution of that irony by a final appeal to God's providential order, to the rhythm as it were of the divine comedy. Nor was this all. If one was to achieve an effect truly tragic, one must focus attention on the hero, and must so present his response to the outward pressures of circumstance, and the inward impulsions of grace, as to render that response intelligible in purely human terms. And here Milton's former sense of a dichotomy in Samson's motivation came to his aid; only now it presented itself not as a pair of alternatives but as two forces working to a common end: 'celestial vigour' *and* 'plain Heroic magnitude of mind.' The sense of Samson as heroic individual does not stop short with the catastrophe: it extends to the comment. The reconciliation, the mitigating of the sense of disaster, is worked out in purely human terms before the larger rhythm of the divine comedy is invoked, lest that rhythm should not only resolve the tragic irony of the action, but dissolve the whole tragic effect.

Since I have been considering *Samson Agonistes* as a Christian tragedy, I have inevitably dwelt upon the view of life implied as conditioning the kind of tragic effect achieved. This does not mean that I am overlooking, or relegating to second place, the distinguishable, though inseparable, contribution of the poem's form. I have in fact been silently taking it into account in every statement made and every line of the poem quoted. But it is proper that this element of poetic form should receive overt recognition. Kitto remarks that the form which Sophocles imposes upon the Oedipus legend is a reflection and reinforcement of the whole Sophoclean view of life. And what is true of Sophocles is no less true of Milton. Every great poet adapts form to content in his own way. But the basic classical structure common to Milton and Sophocles is peculiarly effective because the framework which it supplies for every subtlety of insight and modification still retains its beautiful clarity and its insistent suggestion of inevitability. Here the true importance of Milton's adoption of his Greek models finally lies. It is not that he is seeking to reproduce their spirit and effect – far from it – but that he is adapting their means to present and produce his own. To say that *Samson Agonistes* is a classical tragedy with a Christian theme and outlook does not completely define the effect or the means used to attain it; but it puts us, I think, on the right track. It gives us a point of view from which to read and judge the poem.

IV

Samsons Agonistes is, of course, perfectly comprehensible and deeply moving without any attempt whatsoever to relate it to Milton's experience. But the critic is legitimately concerned with the source of a poem's power, with the place of the poem in the whole body of its author's work, and with what the poem did for the poet. And here – in this context of a general understanding – the question of the relation of art and experience is insistent.

That life is one thing and art another is a truism, but that there can be no connection between them is a *non sequitur*. We may agree that *Samson Agonistes* is tragic poetry and neither veiled autobiography nor political allegory. But this does not mean that the tone and perhaps the very conception of story and character may not spring from the poet's experience. In poems already examined we have found much to support Coleridge's contrast of Milton's imagination with Shakespeare's, and this fact weights the scales in favour of a similar relation in *Samson*, where there are too many parallels with Milton's situation for these to be accidental or to have escaped his notice. The burden of proof rests not with those who would recognize the connection, but with those who would deny it.

The striking similarities of Samson's story to his own, Masson notes, gave Milton his opportunity.[11] Samson was a Nazarite dedicated to God from the womb: Milton from his early years was self-dedicated to God's service, determined to labour as ever in his great taskmaster's eye. With Samson God's service and his nation's were one: in Milton's view the peculiar situation of England in the Puritan Revolution wrought for him a similar result. Milton's Samson was endowed with special natural gifts and conscious of God's guiding and sustaining hand: and so was Milton. Yet, despite all this, each was a defeated champion, with all that he had laboured for lost, and himself rejected by his countrymen, apparently forsaken by God, in the power of his enemies, aging, ill, blind, and essentially alone. Up to a point, in order to capture Samson's emotions, the poet had only, it would seem, to look in his heart and write. But before that could happen he must have transformed Samson from the sanctified barbarian of the Book of Judges to something much more like himself; and this he clearly does. The Samson of Judges is innocent of self-knowledge, of religious experience, and of speculative intelligence: he never seeks, as does Milton's hero, to apportion responsibility, or to understand the workings of God's justice and his often mysterious providence, or to learn the limits which faith sets to reason. He would have been as incapable of declaring, 'That fault I take not on me,' as of acknowledging his sin and God's justice; as incapable of provoking and understanding the Chorus's outburst, 'God of our Fathers, what is man ... ,' as of the self-admonition, and its correction, 'Down Reason then, at least vain reasoning down.' The simplest explanation is that Milton wrote out of the fulness of his own experience and reflection when defeat had completed the parallel with his hero.[12]

The earliest moment at which this conviction obtained was when, with Milton fighting a desperate rearguard action in the *Ready and Easy Way*, the restored monarchy swept into power and, to escape its vengeance, the poet went into hiding, with one can only imagine what despair and bitterness at his heart. For there is despair in *Samson Agonistes*, and bitterness. The despair is exorcised by the poem; but the bitterness finds its expression in the catastrophe where Samson slays his thousands and with them himself. The event which is the sign and seal of Samson's restoration is an act of savage revenge. Nor is this a merely modern perception. Christian commentators had been embarrassed by it and had sought to justify Samson's action by insisting that the Philistines were God's enemies destined by him for destruction, that Samson acted by divine impulsion and so passed beyond the ordinary standards of ethics and politics, and that he acted not as a private person, but as a magistrate of the Hebrew people, who might, even without divine impulsion, strike at their *de facto* rulers. The first two points Milton accepts; the last he rejects in silence. Such bitterness and such vicarious vengeance are more understandable in the moment of utter defeat and in the humiliation of hiding than they would be at any later time, certainly than they would be when the hint, contained in the poem, that 'patience is more oft the exercise Of Saints' (1287–8), had taken firm root and been made part of the philosophy of *Paradise Regained*. The tone, the questionings, and the outcome of *Samson Agonistes* seem best suited to the months of hiding when friends like Marvell were labouring to effect his pardon, and opponents like Sir Roger L'Estrange were wanton in their triumph. Indeed if one were disposed to read *Samson* as allegory or veiled autobiography, Manoa and Harapha need not perhaps be far to seek.

If one is ever to understand the relation of *Samson Agonistes* to Milton's experience, one must remember that it is not a reflection of Milton's normal mood, which in his later years would seem to have been marked by tranquillity and even serenity, but of an altogether unusual state of depression and agitation which would be amply explained by his circumstances in 1660–1: his world in ruins around him, and himself blind, in hiding from his enemies, disillusioned, embittered, and alone. Of his experience as viewed in this mood *Samson* may well be our fullest and most authentic record. For who shall say what doubts and fears, and thereafter what visitings of grace, may not have had their part in his solitary retrospective musings? On any other hypothesis the parallels between Samson's experience and Milton's remain finally inexplicable because, while obvious, they are not central. They owe their cogency and power to Milton's conception of Samson's character and situation, to Samson as illustrating that series of states which were the preoccupation of Milton's later poetry: temptation, disobedience, repentance, obedience, restoration; but precisely at this point the parallel between Samson and Milton himself seems to fail. It fails because we cannot imagine it as obtaining, that is, as coming home to Milton himself, in his normal mood. But the mood of *Samson Agonistes* is far from Milton's normal mood.

The most determined readers of the tragedy as veiled autobiography (and I need scarcely add that I am not of their number) shy away from the possibility that for Samson's confession of error and sin there can be any basis in the experience of the poet. It may be that their instinctive response is right; or it may be merely that courage fails them, and with it such insight as they possess. Curiously, they feel no hesitation in associating Dalila with Mary Powell, and Samson's diatribe and the harsh doctrine of the Chorus with Milton's divorce pamphlets. They are apparently unconscious of the very real difficulties in the way of such a view (for Dalila is patently not a portrait of Mary Powell, and uxoriousness was not Milton's fault as a husband) ; and they are blind to the consequences which immediately follow for the relation of Samson to Milton. But indeed such heavy-handed equations fail to reach the problem, let alone to solve it. There may nevertheless be a relation between Samson's sense of error and sin and humiliation and Milton's experience in his marriage choices. If there is, it does not lie upon the surface; and its exposition will ask a few words of recapitulation.

There can be little doubt that Milton's unhappy first marriage, which embittered and gave a special application to his plea for free divorce, left a permanent scar. That he, the wise and dedicated spirit, prepared to chart England's course amid rocks and shoals, that John Milton should have suffered shipwreck in his domestic life and in a relation which common men came through with safety and credit! – (202–4)

> Tell me Friends,
> Am I not sung and proverbd for a Fool
> In every street ... ?

The brief, but ideally happy second marriage, whose only record is the sonnet 'Methought I saw my late espoused Saint,' did much to heal the wound, and the picture of the idyllic life in Eden, we have inferred, owes something to this second experience.[13] But it did not eradicate the effect of the first. In the mood of *Samson Agonistes*, a mood of depression and retrospective musing, it would seem that the brief and happy interlude is forgotten and the mind fastens with an intensification of bitterness on the old error and its attendant humiliation, just as Samson's lament for his blindness strikes a note of unrelieved anguish, with no hint of the hard-won acceptance and the compensations recorded in Milton's other poems. Milton's error, let us grant, seems to have little in common with the sin of Adam or of Samson, save as Milton may have come to regard the ill-judged marriage itself as a temporary conquest of reason by passion. Yet somehow error and humiliation have taken on the colouring of sin. And if this is so, the questions are how and why?

In any consideration of Milton's personality one must distinguish between Milton the natural man and what his religion made of him. Milton the natural man was marked by pride and even by egoism, and by what he himself once described as 'an honest haughtiness and self-esteem' (*Apology for Smectymnuus*, Col. 3 [i]: 305). The egocentric imagination which Coleridge detected is characteristic of the whole personality. But upon his proud, unyielding spirit, a profound, though limited, religious experience had worked. The result was at least a partial transformation. The proud spirit which would bow to nothing else would bow to the will of God. But there were other and subtler effects. Under the influence of his religion Milton's egoism was transformed into a sense of special dedication to God's service and of special, indeed unique, equipment for that service. No poet ever put forward more exalted claims to divine inspiration or intended them to be taken more literally. The assurance comes out most strongly in Milton the poet because poetry is central in his life; but it is part of the experience of Milton the man and extends to his view of his own function as prophet and leader.

In the hour of defeat, total and irrecoverable, Milton was able, quite justly, to place the responsibility for disaster upon the shoulders of the political leaders of the Puritan parties, who had heeded not at all his confessedly desperate counsels: 'That fault I take not on me'; and he himself retired to the citadel of his own inner life. But was he quite secure even there? That he later became so is certain: but not in 1660–1, under the first shock of defeat and in the mood of *Samson Agonistes*. Now, especially in such a mood, anything that could strike at Milton's sense of his own integrity, at his 'honest haughtiness and self-esteem,' might threaten the inner citadel. And precisely at this point, I would suggest, the half-obliterated memories of the first marriage, that record of error and of humiliation through error, reasserted themselves and menaced the whole structure by attacking its unrecognized base. But whatever could thus shake Milton's confidence in his dedication to God's service and his unique equipment therefor could hardly escape taking on some colouring of sin. The precise degree to which the idea took possession of Milton's mind we can never know, but merely that it was sufficient to ensure an extraordinary degree of insight into Samson's situation and of power in presenting it. But something like this is, I believe, the real though hidden connection of Samson's sin and Milton's error with its attendant humiliation, as the poet viewed it from the unaccustomed standpoint of a mood bordering upon despair.

But if despair is the beginning of *Samson Agonistes*, it is not the end. Here, as nowhere else in Milton's writings, we have a moving representation of a repentant sinner and the clear sense of a God (1172–3)

> Whose ear is ever open; and his eye
> Gracious to re-admit the suppliant ...

And the poem itself becomes an instrument of, and a contribution to, the poet's religious experience. The fact is, I believe, undeniable. Again the question is how? And the answer can best be given in words which are in part a recapitulation of results reached in our study of Milton's earlier poems.

In discussing the nature of poetry and its function, Milton adopts the view commonly held in the Renaissance and for long after, that the end of poetry is to edify by means of delight; but in expounding the theory he adds a significant phrase: poetry, he says, has power 'to allay the perturbations of the mind and set the affections in right tune' (*The Reason of Church Government*, Col. 3 [i]: 239). In other words, for Milton not tragedy alone, but all serious poetry effects its *katharsis*. Primarily, he is thinking of its result for the audience, but it seems to be not less true for the poet himself. And as we study Milton's poems, the process by which this result is achieved becomes fairly clear to us. In what may be called the typical Miltonic pattern, the poem appears to rise in some doubt or difficulty that besets him and in some emotional tension that requires to be resolved. In the poem these receive free, though sometimes veiled, expression, and this is the first step towards a resolution, but, second, there is marshalled to meet the situation Milton's profoundest convictions. Thus his thoughts and feelings are fully objectified. There is, however, a third condition that is necessary. The whole thing is expressed within the compass of an aesthetic pattern – or, in other words, the poet imposes upon his material significant form. With Milton the patterns chosen are emphatic and for the most part traditional, though he brilliantly adapts them to his needs.

Now aesthetic pattern or significant form carries its own emotional effect. For we may agree, I think, that there is such a thing as purely aesthetic emotion, though in poetry it can never perhaps be successfully isolated. But, to take an obvious example, it is the addition of aesthetic emotion, springing from pattern or significant form, that chiefly differentiates the effect of a tragedy from what we commonly, though inexactly, call tragedy in real life. In *Samson Agonistes* it is essental to the final resolution – to 'calm of mind all passion spent.' But the process which we have tried to analyse as it appears in Milton is not confined to *Samson Agonistes*. As we have seen, it appears at its simplest in the sonnet on his blindness, *When I consider how my light is spent*. The octave poses the problem: the sestet effects the resolution: 'They also serve who only stand and waite.' Here Milton resorts to no dramatization: he speaks in his own person, but within the compass of an aesthetic pattern, as he does in the earlier sonnet, *How soon hath Time*, and in the interjected passage on his blindness in Book 3 of *Paradise Lost*. In *Comus* and *Lycidas* he utilizes what may be roughly described as allegory, again within a traditional pattern. In parts of *Paradise Lost*, in *Paradise Regained*, and in *Samson Agonistes*, he reaches a method of dramatic projection, this time within a pattern that is not only traditional, but classical.

The effort to analyse a poem into its constituent elements inevitably, and properly, breaks down, though not perhaps before it has shed some rays of light on the poem or the poet. It is false to think of a poem as a mere record of experience on which an aesthetic pattern has been imposed. The poem is itself an experience, which is only realized in the act of expressing it. And from this truism, so often neglected, springs one final consideration of the highest importance.

In Milton, as in all genuinely religious poets, there is the closest inter-relation between aesthetic and religious experience, and the aesthetic may actually forward the religious. In his earlier poems, in the two sonnets, for example, mentioned above, and in *Lycidas*, we see Milton in different ways transcending his own egocentricity and bringing it under control. But from his earliest dedication of himself to God's service onward, we miss in Milton any sustained sense of his own fallibility, any sense whatever of his own un-worthiness and his utter dependence on God's mercy. By the help of *Samson Agonistes*, it would seem, that deficiency was at last made good.[14]

10

Last published poems, 2:
Paradise Regained

Though building upon a common ground of religious experience, and turning in part on the same pivotal ideas of temptation, obedience, and restoration, *Samson Agonistes* and *Paradise Regained,* the companion pieces of Milton's later life, differ markedly in tone and temper, and in the resolution which they achieve. The fact is fully explained by our hypothesis regarding the date of *Samson,* by the assumption, in other words, that the poems are separated by an interval of at least six years, and it seems to demand for its explanation some such hypothesis. The exact nature of the difference will become fully apparent as we proceed.

Paradise Regained, we have observed, is an appropriate, but not an indispensable, sequel to *Paradise Lost*. The Christian scheme of redemption is set forth in the earlier poem, and the victory over Satan, though not included in the action, is predicted and ensured: it is this which makes *Paradise Lost* a divine comedy.

But the principal emphasis in the two epics falls upon different aspects of the scheme of redemption: in *Paradise Lost,* upon the atonement, upon Christ's vicarious sacrifice; in *Paradise Regained,* upon his victory over Satan in the role of the second Adam who succesfully withstands temptation and by his firm obedience regains all, and more than all, lost by the disobedience of the first Adam. To avoid misapprehension it must be remembered that this second conception of Christ's mission is as much a part of orthodox Christian theology as the first and is recorded, though with subordination to the atonement, in the words of Michael to Adam: (*Paradise Lost* 12.393–410)

> hee, who comes thy Saviour, shall recure,
> Not by destroying *Satan*, but his works
> In thee and in thy Seed: nor can this be,
> But by fulfilling that which thou didst want,
> Obedience to the Law of God, impos'd
> On penaltie of death, and suffering death,
> The penaltie to thy transgression due ...
> So onely can high Justice be appaid.
> The Law of God exact he shall fulfill
> Both by obedience and by love, though love
> Alone fulfill the Law ... ,
> Proclaiming Life to all who shall believe
>   ... that his obedience
> Imputed becomes theirs by Faith, his merits
> To save them, not thir own ...

This is the doctrine of *Paradise Regained*.

To infer that by the time he wrote the second epic Milton had ceased to believe in the atonement is as much a *non sequitur* as it would be to infer that because *Samson Agonistes* does not invoke the dogma of personal immortality or regard Samson as a type of Christ, Milton has abandoned the whole Christian scheme. In *Paradise Regained,* as we shall see, Milton's general view of the nature and office of the Son is precisely what it is in *Paradise Lost.* On the other hand, it does not follow that the selection of subject and emphasis in *Paradise Regained* is arbitrary and without significance. The title taken alone would certainly suggest to nine readers in ten that Milton's subject was to be the atonement, and that he was about to execute, though in epic form, the *Christus Patiens* projected thirty years earlier. Instead, he centres upon the temptation in the wilderness, an episode in which, so far as we can discover, he felt no special interest until he made it the subject of his second epic. He chose it presumably because it invited, indeed necessitated, a heavy emphasis on the conception of the Redeemer as the second Adam.

It is easy to justify the choice on artistic grounds. The sequel to *Paradise Lost* must have not only theological or intellectual relations with that poem, but also aesthetic, and for every artist, and especially for Milton, the essential aesthetic relation is parallel with difference. Alone among the episodes of Christ's earthly ministry the temptation in the wilderness parallels, and was recognized as paralleling, the temptation in Eden. Nor must the second poem merely repeat and elaborate the doctrine of the first. In *Paradise Lost* the doctrine of the atonement was sufficiently set forth: the doctrine of Christ as the second Adam, the 'greater Man,' was recorded but not elaborated. It was a sound artistic instinct that led Milton to the central episode which he selected. That episode had been interpreted by commentators as the human Christ's first encounter with Satan and his preparation for the long struggle whose final victory was won in the apparent defeat of Calvary. Milton does not wholly abandon the idea of the temptation in the wilderness as Christ's preparation – indeed, as we shall see, he exploits it – but he regards it as more than preparation, more even than the first in a series of victories, rather as an event which epitomizes the whole meaning of Christ's ministry from baptism to crucifixion and holds in solution his complete victory over the powers of evil.[1]

Artistically, the choice was right. But, given Milton's view of poetry and of his office as a Christian poet, he would never have made it unless it had also had for him the sanction of truth, unless it had squared with his own deepest convictions. It seems probable that, in addition to the theological and the artistic, there was a third reason of a more personal kind. Its exposition must wait upon our analysis of the poem; but it may be again observed at this point that the close interrelation of experience, thought, and art in Milton and the high degree of integration achieved in his principal poems mean that in his choice of subject and form intellectual, artistic, and personal reasons converge, and to this generalization *Paradise Regained* is no exception. As it happens, the shift in emphasis from Christ the vicarious sacrifice to Christ the second Adam did not carry Milton beyond the pale of orthodoxy, though its doing so, we may be sure, would not alone have deterred him. Still within the compass of orthodoxy, it involved a second shift in emphasis, from Christ the Redeemer to Christ the Great Exemplar. For it is the special mark of the temptation in the wilderness that in one respect it sets the Saviour in the position of ordinary men, his followers. Elsewhere he is subjected, like them, to misinterpretation, injustice, insult, danger, and death: here he is subjected to temptation.

Of the nature and office of the Son the view which Milton takes is, as we have observed, unaltered in *Paradise Regained*: it is still Arian. Christ is 'This perfect Man, by merit call'd my Son' (1.165), and he is still the 'True Image of the Father' (4.596). There is neither advance on nor retreat from the doctrine of *Paradise Lost*; and even more emphatically than in that poem Milton's Arian view of the Son is shown to be for him wholly compatible with the impulse of worship. Indeed *Paradise Regained* may be read as the fulfilment of Milton's promise: (*Paradise Lost* 3.412–15)

Hail Son of God, Saviour of Men, thy Name
Shall be the copious matter of my Song

Henceforth, and never shall my Harp thy praise
Forget, nor from thy Fathers praise disjoine.

One might perhaps have expected Milton's Arianism to have aided in the resolution of a difficulty which must occur to every thoughtful reader of *Paradise Regained*. Adam could be tempted because, though his nature was as yet uncorrupted, he was simply able *not to sin*: otherwise, in Milton's own phrase, 'he ... had been a mere artificial Adam, such an Adam as he is in the motions.' But the second Adam, being God as well as perfect man, while he could share the feelings of humanity, evidently was not able to sin: how, then, can the temptation be real? If Milton had chosen to face this problem, he might have solved it by insisting that the Son was not God in the absolute sense, but the first born of every creature, and though raised, by merit more than birthright, to divine honours, that he was endowed with free will and, like the first Adam, able indeed not to sin, but not unable to sin. Actually, Milton, like Calvin[2] and the other commentators, does not face the problem. He is content to show that Christ in his human nature is able to repel all the assaults of the devil; so that the question of his ultimate vulnerability does not arise. That it does not is perhaps a dramatic weakness in the poem; and certainly it would have been interesting to know whether in Milton's opinion the Arian doctrine held a solution, but in the absence of evidence it is idle to speculate.

It is evident that in *Paradise Regained* the temptations of Satan move the Saviour no more than they do in the simple gospel story, but this need not be attributed to anything more than perfect fortitude and temperance. The attitude and experience of Milton's Christ in the presence of Satan's temptations remind us of Guyon's in his temptation by Mammon[3] in the second book of *The Faerie Queene*. According to Aristotle[4] the man perfect in temperance no longer experiences the solicitations of the passions, no longer meets temptation part way; and such is the case of Guyon and of Milton's Christ. To the temptations they respond not at all, wearing an armour from which these glance aside, though they experience the strain of the ordeal through which they pass.[5] By Spenser, in this book of his poem, as of course by Aristotle, the matter is treated on the level of natural ethics without any resort to divine grace.[6] Not so with Milton; but in effect he recognizes Christ to be in the state mistakenly assumed by Aristotle to be attainable by the natural man: the state in which perfect virtue, perfect impenetrability to temptation, is achievable. The result alike for Spenser and for Milton is that they are faced with the problem of presenting temptations which do not tempt. It is a redoubtable problem, in a literary view. Clearly to recognize it is essential to an intelligent and sympathetic reading of both poets. For their original readers the recognition was immediate and intuitive. Since some knowledge of the Christian tradition is today more widely diffused than is a knowledge of the classical, the conditions necessary for a proper understanding of *Paradise Regained* are no doubt more often fulfilled than for an intelligent reading of *The Faerie Queene*. Nevertheless, if the modern reader is to avoid disappointment, it is desirable to bring to his attention at the outset the limitations under which the human drama of Christ's temptation in the wilderness is inevitably presented, and which set a much more severe restraint upon it than any imposed on Milton's treatment of Satan, of Adam and Eve, or of Samson. If *Paradise Regained* seems less powerful than *Paradise Lost* and *Samson Agonistes*, the restraints entailed upon the poet by his subject are an important part of the cause.

II

Considered in itself the structural pattern of *Paradise Regained* presents points of special interest. The New Testament, it will be recalled, contains two detailed accounts of the temptation in the wilderness; and it is instructive to watch Milton making his selections from them. He recognizes the superior degree of concentration and finality in St Matthew's account, which places the temptations after the forty days of fasting in the desert, makes Satan's defeat and withdrawal permanent, and concludes with the ministering angels, a detail for which Milton has a special use. But in the yet more important matter of the order of the temptations he departs from the tradition at once of previous commentators and artists by following St Luke; and the reasons are significant.

In St Matthew the three temptations are for Christ 1/ to turn the stones of the desert to bread, 2 / to cast himself down from a pinnacle of the temple, 3 / to accept from Satan the kingdoms of the world. In St Luke the order of the latter two is reversed. It is evident that the last temptation in St Matthew's order, the temptation of the kingdoms, might have been made to furnish some sort of climax, but not as Milton proposed to treat it, that is, with an elaboration which had its own function, artistic and doctrinal, but which militated strongly against the effect of climax. The temptation of the temple, on the other hand, the last in St Luke's order, furnished in Milton's brief but impressive treatment exactly the climax required. In addition, however, to this matter of progression towards a climax, the balance of Milton's pattern demanded the choice he made. For his plan was to treat the temptation of bread and the temptation of the temple with something approaching the brevity of the scriptural accounts, but, as we have implied, to elaborate the temptation of the kingdoms by breaking it down into a series of incitements to the pursuit of worldly glory in its various forms – the glory of beauty, fame, wealth, power, and knowledge; and to have carried out this plan while adopting St Matthew's order would have thrown the whole poem off balance, or have made the other two temptations a mere prelude to the temptation of the kingdoms. There was, however, a third reason for adopting St Luke's order, and a compelling one. Beside its primary theme of Christ as the second Adam, *Paradise Regained* has a secondary theme, namely, the nature and office of the Son of God, significantly mentioned in the prelude. Throughout the poem this theme gets its recognition both in Satan's motives and in Christ's response, but in the final temptation the secondary theme comes forward and assumes the centre of the stage. This is the third and compelling reason for Milton's adoption of St Luke's order.

From what has been said so far of the structural pattern of *Paradise Regained*, it must be evident that it is marked by a very high degree of balance and symmetry. And this impression is strongly confirmed as we observe how the balance, so carefully maintained in the placing of the second and composite temptation of the kingdoms, extends to the internal structure, with the temptations to the active pursuit of glory framed by two which are contemplative rather than active in character, and when we further observe that the first temptation, to distrust, is balanced by the third, to presumption, the extreme of defect balanced by the extreme of excess.[7]

Though there is no evidence of Milton's special interest in the subject of the temptation in the wilderness before he wrote *Paradise Regained*, there is evidence of his early interest in the form which he chose for its elaboration. In the *Reason of Church Government* (1642) he speaks of 'that epic form of which the two poems of Homer, and those other two of Virgil and Tasso, are a diffuse, and the book of Job a brief model' (Col. 3: [ii]: 237); and nothing is more evident than that, almost thirty years later, he modelled his own brief epic, *Paradise Regained*, on Job. This book, unique in the canon of the Old Testament in so many ways, is seven times alluded to in the poem, and was frequently in Milton's thoughts in the years before it was written, as a large number of quotations, allusions, and echoes show. To us Job seems in no sense an epic, but a dramatized debate with the minimum of action and description, and in its total effects, as Moulton saw,[8] not unlike Sophocles; and this quality *Paradise Regained* clearly shares. Yet if the theme is not epic it is because it transcends the heroic. Milton echoes the claim put forward for the human action of *Paradise Lost*, but with a difference. If the story of the loss of Eden was 'not less, but more Heroic' than the wrath of Achilles, the story of its regaining is 'Above Heroic,' in its ordinary earthly meaning, altogether. Christ is, as Milton had sung forty years before, the 'most perfect *Heroe*' (*The Passion* 13), and more clearly than before this is now seen to involve that patience which is the exercise of saints, a willingness to forgo all action till God's good time and then to step forward and claim, not a throne, but the cross. The theme of *Paradise Regained* includes but also transcends that of Job. In Milton's last poem the conventions of epic are not quite abandoned, but are used sparingly and with little emphasis: there are few similes, which never, of course, found a place in epic debates, and of the conventions of epic action only the councils survive, and these are assigned to Satan who illustrates the futility of action. Besides the epic tradition, thus modified and subdued, there are few other literary influences on *Paradise Regained*: indeed only one of any importance, that of the Spenserians and notably of the second part of Giles Fletcher's *Christ's Victory and Triumph* which presents the temptation in the wilderness. Here the similarity is almost wholly in interpretation, and not in manner and effect, which are in fact very different; for Fletcher resorts to allegory and allows himself every licence of elaboration.

It is sometimes held that in *Paradise Regained* Milton not only adopts a style much simpler than that of *Paradise Lost*, but also adheres more closely to his biblical sources and eschews imaginative elaboration; but this thesis must not be accepted without examination. Any poet who will turn four verses of scripture into approximately 1025 pentameter lines must needs indulge in elaboration: and this is what Milton does in his treatment of the second temptation. But the elaboration is not of the imaginative order that one gets in the war in heaven, or the scenes in hell in *Paradise Lost*, but is more like that in the serpent's temptation of Eve: or, in other words, it is dedicated less to supplying epic action and effect than to drawing out the full implications of the scriptural narrative, and in that sense may be said to be closer to the biblical source.

With this much of introduction we may turn briefly to the content and pattern of the poem.

III

From the introductory lines onward everything in *Paradise Regained* is simpler and more compressed than in *Paradise Lost*. By a happy echo of Virgil the poet identifies himself, links the later poem with the earlier, and makes clear the parallel pattern and the doctrinal emphasis of the second epic: (1.1–7)

> I who e'rewhile the happy Garden sung,
> By one mans disobedience lost, now sing
> Recover'd Paradise to all mankind,

By one mans firm obedience fully tri'd
Through all temptation, and the Tempter foil'd
In all his wiles, defeated and repuls't,
And *Eden* rais'd in the waste Wilderness.

Then in the invocation to the Spirit who led Christ into the wilderness and brought him thence 'By proof the undoubted Son of God,' Milton introduces the secondary theme, as he does that of the creation in *Paradise Lost*, and introduces the claim which parallels one reserved in the earlier epic till the ninth book, that the subject is 'Above Heroic,' exhibiting perfect Christian heroism, which is in many ways opposed to merely classical, and making up in significance what it lacks in martial action. This is the implication of Milton's brief phrase 'Above Heroic.'

The story is taken up at the point where John is baptizing in Jordan. There is, properly speaking, no plunging *in medias res*, and no need for an elaborate narrative of antecedent action. We are introduced to the first council of demons, where Satan gives an account of Christ's baptism, testifies to his virtues, and raises the question which is to remain unanswered till the third temptation and to supply one motive for it and the other two temptations: (1.89–93)

His first-begot we know, and sore have felt,
When his fierce thunder drove us to the deep;
Who this is we must learn, for man he seems
... though in his face
The glimpses of his Fathers glory shine.[9]

There is some support for this Satanic motive in traditional commentary. Satan, it was argued, was in doubt as to Christ's identity and whether, as one contemporary phrased it, he was 'Son of God by nature' or merely perfect man and God's 'adopted Son by grace,'[10] though a second interpretation insisted that Satan well knew his adversary and persisted in his hopeless effort against him from impotent malice and sheer despair. Critics have usually assumed that Milton adopted the first alternative and with it the necessity of making Christ fence with Satan and deny him the proof which he sought. But this leaves much in the text unexplained – Christ's reply, for example, to the first temptation: (1.355–6)

Why dost thou then suggest to me distrust,
Knowing who I am, as I know who thou art?

It also does too little justice to the characterization; and it fails to fathom the nature of a Satanic doubt.

Though shorn of his grandeur, all of which he had in fact lost by the end of the earlier epic, the Satan of *Paradise Regained* is the same character as the Satan of *Paradise Lost*. He is the great romantic, the rebel not only against God, but against fact, who cannot bring himself to accept his place in the scale of being or to act upon what in his heart he knows to be the truth (that is the whole purport of the great soliloquy in Book 4 of *Paradise Lost*). And in *Paradise Regained* Satan's doubt respecting Christ is at once real and unreal. It is an assiduously fostered doubt because he will not let himself acknowledge the truth; and yet the doubt torments him. He would give anything to have it confirmed, or, failing that, to receive proof so categorical as to destroy it forever. As the poem proceeds, he returns to this doubt – Christ, indeed, is withstanding every temptation, but as perfect man, 'For Son of God to me is yet in doubt.' And, for the title, it (4.517–18)

> bears no single sence.
> The Son of God I also am, or was,
> And if I was, I am.

He clings to the doubt, but patently with diminishing conviction and mounting despair. And yet despair is, in a way, Satan's native element: (3.204–11)

> ... all hope is lost
> Of my reception into grace; what worse?
> For where no hope is left, is left no fear ...
> I would be at the worst; worst is my Port,
> My harbour and my ultimate repose,
> The end I would attain, my final good.

This is the very note of the great soliloquy, and Satan's assertion is not unjustified: (1.358–60)

> 'Tis true, I am that Spirit unfortunate,
> Who leagu'd with millions more in rash revolt
> Kept not my happy Station ...

One does well to remember this essential identity with the Satan of *Paradise Lost* when one seeks to appraise his motives.

Nor do I find any reliable evidence that the Christ of *Paradise Regained* tries to conceal his own identity. It is Satan who goes in for disguises, not Christ. There is a simpler and sounder explanation of Christ's words, namely, that from the experience in the wilderness he himself is gaining a progressively deeper insight into his own nature as well as into God's purpose, and a progressively strengthened conviction. This is a bold conception for the seventeenth century, and it is not surprising if Milton allows it to be borne in upon the reader rather than stating it in so many words; but woven into the texture of the poem there is a great deal to support such an interpretation.

As in *Paradise Lost* the council of demons is balanced by an announcement of the policy of heaven. Forgetful of his failure with Job, (1.148–9)

> Whose constant perseverance overcame
> Whate're his cruel malice could invent,

Satan boasts his power; but now God promises he shall encounter one 'far abler to resist All his solicitations,' 'This perfect Man, by merit call'd my Son,'[11] who finally shall win (1.154–60)

> by Conquest what the first man lost.
> By fallacy supriz'd. But first I mean
> To exercise him in the Wilderness,
> There he shall first lay down the rudiments
> Of his great warfare, e're I send him forth
> To conquer Sin and Death ...
> By Humiliation and strong Sufferance.

Thus the temptation in the wilderness is at once preparation for, and anticipatory fulfilment of, Christ's mission of redemption. And the angel choir answers with a chorus of praise to the Son, reminiscent of that which greeted his offer to redeem mankind, and to be balanced by the chorus with which *Paradise Regained* concludes.

There are, clearly, two terminal conceptions of Christ's nature and office: the Jewish conception of the Messiah, held, as we are shown, by his first followers, who are typical of their race and age, and the Christian (or, to speak more precisely, the Miltonic) conception on which the poem ends. When, after his baptism, he is led by the Spirit and his own deep thought into the wilderness, the Redeemer has already, through the teaching of his mother and his meditations on prophecy, got well beyond the simple messianic conception, though he still expects further light. The soliloquy in which he is introduced tells us this, and much beside.[12] Like the best dramatic soliloquies, it represents not words uttered, but the stream of thought passing through the mind; and, like the best dramatic exposition, it lays a foundation for all that is to follow. (1.196–269)

> O what a multitude of thoughts at once
> Awakn'd in me swarm, while I consider
> What from within I feel myself, and hear

What from without comes often to my ears,
Ill sorting with my present state compar'd.
When I was yet a child, no childish play
To me was pleasing, all my mind was set
Serious to learn and know, and thence to do
What might be publick good; myself I thought
Born to that end, born to promote all truth,
All righteous things: therefore above my years,
The Law of God I read ...
Made it my sole delight, and it grew ...
        yet this not all
To which my Spirit aspir'd, victorious deeds
Flam'd in my heart, heroic acts, one while
To rescue *Israel* from the *Roman* yoke,
Then to subdue and quell o're all the earth
Brute violence and proud Tyrannick pow'r
Till truth were freed, and equity restor'd:
Yet held it more humane, more heavenly first
By winning words to conquer willing hearts,
And make perswasion do the work of fear;
At least to try ...
These growing thoughts my Mother soon perceiving
       ... inly rejoic'd,
And said to me apart, 'high are thy thoughts
O Son, but nourish them and let them soar
To what highth sacred vertue and true worth
Can raise them, though above example high;
By matchless Deeds express thy matchless Sire ...'
This having heard, strait I again revolv'd
The Law and Prophets, searching what was writ
Concerning the Messiah, to our Scribes
Known partly, and soon found of whom they spake
I am; this chiefly, that my way must lie
Through many a hard assay even to the death,
E're I the promis'd Kingdom can attain,
Or works Redemption for mankind ...
Yet neither thus dishearten'd nor dismay'd,
The time prefixt I waited ...

And so on to John's baptism and the voice from Heaven. (1.290–3)

And now by some strong motion I am led
Into this Wilderness, to what intent

I learn not yet, perhaps I need not know;
For what concerns my knowledge God reveals.

These concluding words are surely a directive which tells how to read the experience on which the hero is about to enter: its purpose is revelation. The words also epitomize what is to be Christ's unshakable position throughout the ordeal: a position of absolute obedience and complete trust. And the two things taken together bring into relief an essential feature of the pattern of *Paradise Regained*, namely, the combination of two elements, the one static, the other progressive, and the dependence of pattern at this point wholly upon theme. But his does not exhaust the significance of the soliloquy. For it presently appears that Satan, like Christ's followers, assumes the common perception of the messianic mission, which Christ has already outgrown, but that, when he seeks to utilize it in the temptations, he is at least appealing to motives and emotions which Christ once entertained. This is typical of the close integration and artistic economy which mark the whole poem.

Immediately after the soliloquy comes the first temptation, and with it the primary theme of Christ as the second Adam gets under way. Scholarship has dwelt on the long tradition of commentary, patristic, scholastic, and Protestant, which lies behind Milton's treatment, but the attempt to show that he drew largely upon this tradition remains somewhat unconvincing. For the earlier commentators, not content as Milton generally is with the simple contrast between Christ's obedience and the disobedience of our first parents, sought to parallel the two temptations step by step and to plot them in an ascending scale of flesh, world, and devil, and this with a cheerful disregard of the order adopted, St Matthew's or St Luke's. 'Here,' said Calvin, in curt dismissal, 'the ancients amused themselves with ingenious trifles.' We may be sure that Milton, who likewise insisted on the words of scripture and their rational interpretation, would agree. Such parallels as he suggests are all with his own account of the earlier temptation in *Paradise Lost*, and these on occasion carry him outside the tradition altogether. For example, finding nothing to correspond to the predicament of his own Adam 'fondly overcome by female charm,' he has Belial propose, 'Set women in his eye and in his walk' (2.153), only to be rebuked by Satan for stupidity. But these are embellishments. The interpretation which Milton adopts as basic is the simplest current among Protestant theologians in his day, namely, that the first temptation is to distrust of God's providence, the second – of the kingdoms – to the glory of this world, the third to presumption.

Like Calvin,[13] Milton rejects the notion, superficial as well as ascetic, that Christ's first temptation is to satisfy his natural hunger. Christ's hunger is the occasion of the temptation: its essence, as Satan presents it and Christ rejects, is distrust: 'Why dost thou then suggest to me distrust?' (1.355). It is the temptation to take matters into his own hands, to save himself, not waiting upon God. This plain case conveys a valuable hint for the interpretation of the offer of the kingdoms. Like the apple in Eden the things offered are in themselves indifferent: they become evil in a religious sense only as they are preferred to obedience to God. For the rest, like all indifferent things, their use is governed by natural ethics and common prudence, and in this relation Christ comments upon them. In other ways the first temptation prepares for the second; for that too entails the taking of matters into his own hands, not to save himself, but to ensure the success of his messianic mission. And since this in turn involves a degree of presumption, it points on to the third temptation, which stands in patterned contrast to the first.

There is little elaboration. Skilfully Milton develops the Satanic 'If thou be the Son of God' so as to introduce from the outset the secondary theme of the poem, the nature of Christ, and its dramatic motivation in Satan's concern regarding this question. He also manages to suggest the significance of the coming of Christ and the Spirit, to glance back at the silencing of the pagan oracles and on to Christ's rejection of merely human love, and to allude to his own favourite doctrine of the inner mentor and oracle in the heart and mind of the believer: (1.460–4)

> God hath now sent his living Oracle
> Into the World, to teach his final will,
> And sends his Spirit of Truth henceforth to dwell
> In pious Hearts, an inward Oracle
> To all truth requisite for men to know.

For the rest, Satan appears in the guise of an aged dweller in the wilderness, the lineal descendant of Archimago through the Satan of Giles Fletcher, but Milton is careful to have his speech echo the Satan of *Paradise Lost* and at once bring home to us the parallel between Christ's temptation and Adam's, while at the same time he invites us to observe the deterioration of Satan in heroism and power. These things Milton achieves without sacrificing the effect of simplicity in the first temptation, on which depends the impression, noticed by Calvin, that here we are in the presence of such a temptation as may assail any believer. And for Milton the essential simplicity of the first temptation has a second function, this time in the aesthetic pattern of the poem: it contrasts sharply with his elaboration of the second temptation and is balanced by the simplicity and directness of the third.

The second temptation is clearly marked off from the first by the interval of a night, by one of the rare pieces of epic elaboration in the account

of the seeking for Jesus by those who believed in him at his baptism and
the perplexity of his mother, and finally by the second council of demons.
The purpose of what intervenes is not structural alone. Satan's rejection of
Belial's device, 'Set women in his eye,' is not wasted: Satan's device is as
futile as Belial's, but serves to activate his subsequent action. Christ's mind
is set wholly on the accomplishment of 'greatest things'; here, if anywhere,
the flaw in his armour must be found, and the satisfaction of natural hunger
may perhaps be used as a bridge to the subtler temptation: (2.225–33)

> Therefore with manlier objects we must try
> His constancy, with such as have more shew
> Of worth, of honour, glory, and popular praise;
> Rocks whereon greatest men have oftest wreck't;
> Or that which only seems to satisfie
> Lawful desires of Nature, not beyond;
> And now I know he hungers where no food
> Is to be found, in the wide Wilderness;
> The rest commit to me ...

And indeed the Saviour, now suffering the pangs of extreme hunger, has
dreamed of food all night. This dream parallels that of Eve before her temptation, but with a significant difference: it is inspired, not by Satan, but by
nature, and it betokens no predisposition to fall; for Christ has faced and
mastered his situation. I, he says, (2.257–9)

> from the sting of Famine fear no harm,
> Nor mind it, fed with better thoughts that feed
> Mee hungering more to do my Fathers will.

The dream is to be balanced by one, in the second night, which Satan is
permitted to inspire.

In Calvin's commentary the meaning of the second temptation (the
third in his order) is 'that Christ should seek in another manner than from
God the inheritance which he has promised to his children';[14] and this is,
clearly, part of the meaning in Milton's view, but not the whole. If the first
temptation is in no sense to a sin of the flesh, it cannot be deemed that the
second is to a sin of the world – or rather to a series of such sins, for Milton
breaks the temptation of the kingdoms down into parts, most of them presenting themselves as ways of claiming Christ's inheritance and even of fulfilling God's service, with no reference to the will of God, but all of them,
without exception, representing different examples of worldly or vain
glory.[15] Widely divergent as is *Paradise Regained* from *Christ's Victory*

and Triumph in method and effect, Fletcher likewise presents the temptation of the kingdoms as the temptations of vain glory (indeed, Panglory is
the temptress) and breaks the episode down into a series, very different from
Milton's indeed, for Fletcher joins the flesh to the world, but still a series,
crudely described in the marginal gloss as: 'pleasure in drinking'; 'in luxury'
(sensuality); 'avarice' (here the garden of Acrasia gives way to the Cave of
Mammon); and 'ambitious honour' (reminiscent of Spenser's Philotime).

The first episode in the series which makes up Milton's temptation of
the kingdoms is not entirely remote from Feltcher's beginning. It finds its
point of departure in Christ's natural hunger as had the first temptation. If
this is a defect, and perhaps it is, since it has led some critics to group the
banquet scene with the first temptation despite Milton's evident concern to
separate them, it has its uses, providing a natural transition from the first to
the second temptation, and showing Satan's persistence and his eagerness
to exploit to the full a fancied advantage. In harmony with the character
of the second temptation, Satan has changed his guise and appears 'As one
in City, or Court, or Palace bred' – for citizens, Milton would seem to have
discovered, may be no less worldly than courtiers. 'Tell me,' he says, (1.
320–3)

> if Food were now before thee set,
> Would'st thou not eat? Thereafter as I like
> The giver, answer'd Jesus.

It need not necessarily be assumed that Milton rejects as unlawful in themselves all or any of the things which Christ rejects. They are rejected because
they are untimely: because, in the circumstances, to accept them would entail disobedience to God, and finally (this is the point in the words just
quoted) because they are offered by Satan and with evil intent. As the apple
was in itself a thing indifferent and yet a test of man's obedience, so Satan's
offers are a test of Christ's obedience, of his utter submission to God's will.
The banquet appears with every accompaniment of luxury and indeed of
beauty. Building on the base of natural hunger, Satan piles up all the at-
tractions whereby art can minister to appetite, and the temptation becomes
in effect a temptation to the vain glory of art and beauty in the service of
luxury: (2.351–66)

> in order stood
> Tall stripling youths rich clad, of fairer hew
> Then *Ganymed* or *Hylas*, distant more
> Under the Trees now trip'd, now solemn stood,
> Nymphs of *Diana*'s train, and *Naiades*

> With fruits and flowers from *Amalthea*'s horn,
> And Ladies of th' *Hesperides*, that seem'd
> Fairer than feign'd of old, or fabl'd since
> Of Fairy Damsels met in Forest wide
> By Knights of *Logres* or of *Lyones*,
> *Lancelot* or *Pelleas*, or *Pellenore*,
> And all the while Harmonious Airs were heard
> Of chiming strings, or charming pipes and winds
> Of gentlest gale *Arabian* odors fann'd
> From their soft wings, and *Flora*'s earliest smells.
> Such was the Splendour ...

And Satan, whose habit, as Christ has observed, is 'By mixing somewhat true to vent more lyes,' now urges: (2.369–71)

> These are not Fruits forbidden, no interdict
> Defends the touching of these viands pure,
> Thir taste no knowledge works, at least of evil ...

Yet different as is the form from 'that crude Apple that diverted *Eve*,' this too is a test of obedience. And the vain glory of art and beauty Christ rejects, contrasting it with the heavenly glory which, if he chooses, he can summon to attend him: (2.383–91)

> I can at will, doubt not, ...
> Command a Table in the Wilderness,
> And call swift flights of Angels ministrant
> *Array'd in Glory* ...
> Thy Pompous Delicacies I contemn,
> And count thy specious gifts no gifts but guiles.

This first, as also the last episode in the series, stands somewhat apart from the rest, which turn on the assumption that Christ's 'heart is set on high designs. High actions' (2.410–11), and seek to play upon the will to power by offering either the attributes of power or the means to an immediate assumption of his messianic kingship and rule. The irony is that this is a conception of the messianic office which the Saviour, as we have seen, has already outgrown. The first thing offered is wealth. One fruit of riches, luxury, was implied in the temptation just rejected: now riches are offered as the means to kingship and power. 'They whom I favour,' boasts Satan, (2.430–4)

> thrive in wealth amain,
> While Virtue, Valour, Wisdom sit in want.
> To whom thus Jesus patiently reply'd:
> Yet Weath without these three is impotent,
> To gain dominion or to keep it again'd ...

And for dominion and kingship: (2.466–83)

> he who reigns within himself, and rules
> Passions, Desires, and Fears, is more a King;
> Which every wise and virtuous man attains:
> And who attains not, ill aspires to rule
> Cities of men, or headstrong Multitudes,
> Subject himself to Anarchy within,
> Or lawless passions in him which he serves.
> But to guide Nations in the way of truth
> By saving Doctrine, and from error lead
> To know, and knowing worship God aright,
> Is yet more Kingly ...
> Besides to give a Kingdom hath been thought
> Greater and nobler done, and to lay down
> Far more magnanimous than to assume.

Carefully read, Christ's role is far from passive. In principle, he rejects Satan's subsequent offers before they are made, and not simply as made with evil intent, and as entailing disobedience to God, though these would be all-sufficient reasons, but on their own intrinsic merits. For, though we have said that what Satan offers are things indifferent, this does not preclude a judgment upon them. They are judged by a scale of natural values; they are rejected because in the circumstances they would come between Christ and his mission and would entail disobedience to the will of God: because they cut across the scale of spiritual values. Lawful or unlawful in the order of nature, they would, in the circumstances, thwart the purpose of the order of grace.

   Satan next offers an attribute of power: the glory of fame. Christ rejects it, first upon its merits, then in relation to God's glory and his own mission: (3.47–107, italics mine)

> For what is glory but the blaze of fame,
> The peoples praise ... ?
> And what the people but a herd confus'd,
> A miscellaneous rabble, who extol

Things vulgar, and well weigh'd, scarce worth the praise ...
And what delight to be by such extoll'd,
To live upon thir tongues and be thir talk?
Of whom to be disprais'd were so small praise?
His lot who dares be singularly good ...
This is true glory and renown, when God
Looking on the Earth, with approbation marks
The just man, and divulges him through Heaven ...
He ask'd thee, hast thou seen my servant *Job*?
Famous he was in Heaven, on Earth less known;
Where glory is false glory, attributed
To things not glorious, men not worthy fame.
They err who count it glorious to subdue
By Conquest far and wide ...
But if there be in glory ought of good,
It may by means far different be attain'd ...
By deeds of peace, by wisdom eminent,
By patience, temperance ...
Shall I seek glory then, as vain men seek
Oft not deserv'd? *I seek not mine, but his*
Who sent me, and thereby witness whence I am.

'Well,' sneers Satan, in effect, 'if you are thus careless of glory, you are very unlike your Father'; whereto Christ replies by emphasizing once more the difference between creature and Creator, with the explanation, already discussed, that God created (3.123–6)

      chiefly not for glory as prime end,
But to shew forth his goodness, and impart
His good communicable to every soul
Freely ...

For this, as for every other mark of his absolute goodness, glory (3.141–4)

      to God alone of right belongs;
Yet so much bounty is in God, such grace,
That who advance his glory, not thir own,
Them he himself to glory will advance.

Repulsed and defeated, Satan replies, with assumed indifference, (3. 150–4)

> Of glory as thou wilt ... so deem ...
> But to a kingdom thou art born, ordain'd
> To sit upon thy father *David*'s throne;
> By Mothers side thy Father ...

It may be remarked in passing that the Satan of *Paradise Regained* is, significantly, but a shadow of his former self. Satan is designed to illustrate the deteriorating effect of evil, the impotence of malice, the bankruptcy, first, of heroism, and then its disappearance. All this imposes severe restraints upon the poet; yet Milton's characterization is not ineffective, and uses new devices. As very occasionally in *Paradise Lost*, now habitually Satan's defiance has given place to innuendo, to the tactic, in later phrase, of 'Sapping a solemn creed with solemn sneer.' This is by the way. Satan is defeated before he commences; for the temptation turns, as we have remarked, on the Hebraic conception of the Messiah as rescuer, conqueror, and king; and this concept Christ has already outgrown.

Then on to the offers of power, first power in its cruder military form, attained through alliance with Parthia, then the seeming climax, power in its plenitude set forth in the magnificent panorama of imperial Rome. I say, the seeming climax; for when Christ has rejected the grandeur that is Rome, Satan suddenly confronts him with the glory that was Greece: (4. 237–55)

> behold
> Where on the *Aegean* shore a City stands
> Built nobly, pure the air, and light the soil,
> *Athens* the eye of *Greece*, Mother of Arts
> And Eloquence ...
> See there the Olive Grove of *Academe*,
> *Plato*'s retirement, where the *Attic* Bird
> Trills her thick-warbl'd notes the summer long,
> There flowerie hill *Hymettus*, with the sound
> Of Bees industrious murmur oft invites
> To studious musing; there *Ilissus* rouls
> His whispering stream; within the walls then view
> The schools of ancient Sages; his who bred
> Great *Alexander* to subdue the world,
> *Lyceum* there, and painted *Stoa* next:
> There shalt thou hear and learn the secret power
> Of harmony ...

And so on, through the famous roll-call of the glories of Greek philosophy and poetry, with emphasis always on the knowledge and wisdom they enshrine, to the conclusion: (4.283–4)

> These rules will render thee a King compleat
> Within thyself, much more with Empire join'd.

Beside the obvious contrast of Athens, the symbol of knowledge, with Rome, the symbol of power, observe how the last in the series of temptations balances the first, the banquet scene. For both are in essence contemplative, yet one moves on the level of the sense, the other on the level of the intelligence; and if the banquet by contrast reminded the poet of Eve and the apple, Milton can now trust the reader to remember that the apple was in reality the fruit of the Tree of Knowledge. Yes, but can he trust the reader to cast his mind back over eight hundred lines to the banquet scene? Perhaps not; and so in the Roman panorama, which precedes the Athenian, he introduces in the words of Christ a palpable reminiscence, a reminder to the reader, of the earlier temptation. There is no more characteristic and revealing example of Milton's artistry than this.

To the consternation of many a reader, Christ's rejection of Athens is complete. 'Think not but that I know these things,' he says, 'or think I know them not': (4.288–312)

> he who receives
> Light from above, from the fountain of light,
> No other doctrine needs, though granted true;
> But these are false, or little else but dreams ...
> The first and wisest of them all profess'd
> To know this only, that he nothing knew [Socrates];
> The next [Plato] to fabling fell and smooth conceits,
> A third sort [the Sceptic] doubted all things ...
> Others in virtue plac'd felicity,
> But vertue join'd with riches and long life [Aristotle],
> In corporal pleasure he [the Epicurean], and careless ease,
> The Stoic last in Philosophic pride,
> By him call'd virtue; and his vertuous man,
> Wise, perfect in himself ...
> contemning all
> Wealth, pleasure, pain or torment, death and life ...
> Alas, what can they teach, and not mislead;
> Ignorant of themselves, of God much more,
> And how the world began, and how man fell
> Degraded by himself, on grace depending?

Nothing, in short, can they teach, (4.351–2)

> Unless where moral vertue is express't
> By light of Nature not in all quite lost.

Nor does Christ stop here: with equal decision he goes on to depress all Greek poetry and eloquence below those of the Old Testament.

No re-examination of the poem can refuse the challenge of these lines: they must be explained, and neither ignored nor explained away.

One must remember of course that all Satan's gifts and suggestions are offered with evil intent, to betray Christ, in one way or other, into disobedience to God. Even though what was offered were in itself a thing indifferent, like the apple in Eden, it would become evil in the circumstances as it came into competition with obedience to God; this fact alone would be sufficient to account for Christ's rejection of the proffered gift of knowledge, but not for the extremity or the terms of the rejection. Is Christ, then, rejecting all secular knowledge and art as in themselves worthless? Not necessarily, though it must be admitted that his tactic throughout the debate is to call in question the intrinsic worth of Satan's proffered gifts, and this indeed is an extreme example of his doing so. But there is an implied qualification: secular knowledge is of little worth when compared with divine revelation, and positively delusive when it trenches on questions that only revealed religion can answer.

In the earlier temptation of the banquet, which turns, as we saw, on the glory of beauty, an analogous question arises – Is Christ rejecting beauty as worthless or evil? – and it receives a partial and oblique answer. Immediately preceding the banquet scene is one of the very few descriptions of natural beauty which the poem contains. It commences with morning and the song of the lark; and then from an eminence Christ beheld (2.289–97)

> a pleasant Grove,
> With chaunt of tuneful Birds resounding loud;
> Thither he bent his way, determin'd there
> To rest at noon, and enter'd soon the shade
> High rooft and walks beneath, and alleys brown
> That open'd in the midst a woody Scene,
> Natures own work it seem'd (Nature taught Art)
> And to a Superstitious eye the haunt
> Of Wood-Gods and Wood-Nymphs; he view'd it round ...

The point is that Christ accepts this scene of natural beauty just before he rejects the splendours of the banquet speciously offered as homage from the powers of nature, but really of Satan's procuring and destined to vanish 'With sound of harpies' wings and talons heard.'[16] As in *Comus*, it is not beauty that is condemned, not natural beauty in its appointed place, but beauty in the service of evil, and, specifically, in competition with obedience to God. And actually there is some parallel for this in Christ's attitude to knowledge. For if he here rejects secular wisdom and natural ethics, he has often referred to them for a judgment on Satan's other offers. Nor should we forget the earlier citation of Socrates: made memorable next to Job, (3.91–8)

> By deeds of peace, by wisdom eminent,
> By patience, temperance, ...
> By what he taught and suffer'd for so doing,
> For truths sake suffering death unjust ...

The suggestion of a pagan approximation to Christian heroism can hardly be accidental.

Yet when all is said, a large residuum is left unexplained, which only history can explain. Christian humanism was a synthesis of the classical inheritance and the Christian, attempted under the aegis of Christianity. One need go no farther afield than Erasmus to get an idea of what this involved or to recognize an anticipation of Milton. Some things, says Erasmus in the *Enchiridion*, are in their nature good, others evil; many, however, 'are mediate, such as health, beauty, strength, eloquence, learning.'[17] Of these none should be sought on its own account but only 'as it conduces to the highest good' – only as 'it helps those who are going forward towards Christ,' and in this light 'it should be instantly accepted or rejected.' 'You love letters? Rightly, if for Christ's sake. But if you love them only that you may know, you have stopped where you ought to take a further step.' And again, in the *Education of a Christian Prince*: 'He whom you are reading is a pagan; you who are reading, are a Christian ... Measure everything by the Christian standard.'[18] Far more often than many writers on Christian humanism will allow, tensions between the two elements in the synthesis emerge, and the Christian supremacy issues in a partial repudiation of classical humanism. We see it in the later life and writings of Michelangelo; we see it in Spenser's *Fowre Hymnes*; and beyond all doubt we see it in *Paradise Regained*, where the phenomenon is intensified by Milton's Puritanism and by the drastic re-appraisal of values which appears to have followed the Restoration and the collapse of all his hopes.

Perhaps we shall not be far wrong if we infer that what Milton wishes to enjoin is that, as Erasmus says, things indifferent should not be pursued for their own sake but only as they conduce to the service of God, and, beyond this, that we should be *willing* to sacrifice them, and every other treasured possession, to that service. Plainly, the classics have not ceased to influence Milton's thought and art. The Christ of *Paradise Regained* is in effect a Christian version of Aristotle's temperate man, and of his magnanimous man as well. The mark of the temperate man is that he has reached a state of security where what is evil has no power to attract him: he cannot really be tempted in the full meaning of the word. And so it is with Christ. Satan proposes and Christ rejects: that is all. The fact is undeniable, and must be accepted by the reader though it severely restricts the possibility of interest in action and in character. The mark of the magnanimous man is that he knows himself to be equal to every situation, and is so; and here again the description is wholly applicable to the Christ of *Paradise Regained*. But how then does he differ from the temperate man and the magnanimous man of Aristotle; and how can he be said to represent a Christian version of the virtues? Obviously the difference lies in the religious motivation, in Christ's being not self-centred but God-centred, and in the resulting union of humility with magnanimity.

Now the pattern approaches its conclusion. The final temptation, the temptation of the temple, is, like the first temptation, briefly presented; and here, as we have said, the secondary theme comes forward and assumes the centre of the stage. Ostensibly a temptation to presumption, it is really Satan's last desperate effort to resolve, one way or other, the question that still plagues him, 'For Son of God to me is yet in doubt.' He has tempted Christ and found him (4.533-40)

> Proof against all temptation as a rock
> Of Adamant, and as a Center, firm
> To the utmost of meer man both wise and good,
> Not more; for Honours, Riches, Kingdoms, Glory
> Have been before contemn'd and may agen:
> Therefore to know what more thou art then man,
> Worth naming Son of God by voice from Heav'n,
> Another method now I must begin.

The method is to place Christ on the dizzy pinnacle of the temple: (4.551-62)

> There stand, if thou wilt stand; to stand upright
> Will ask thee skill; I to thy Fathers house
> Have brought thee, and highest plac't, highest is best,
> Now shew thy Progeny; if not to stand,
> Cast thy self down; safely if Son of God:

> For it is written, He will give command
> Concerning thee to his Angels, in thir hands
> They shall up lift thee, lest at any time
> Thou chance to dash thy foot against a stone.
> To whom thus Jesus: Also it is written,
> Tempt not the Lord thy God, he said and stood.
> But Satan smitten with amazement fell ...

It is easy to miss the full drama and the irony concentrated in these few lines. Satan's intention is that Christ shall fall and the result will answer his question. His injunction to stand is purely ironical: that it is possible, he never for a moment conceives. But if Satan can be ironical, so can Christ and the event. For the first and only time, he complies with Satan's suggestion; but it is not in surrender to Satan: it is obedience to God – like Samson's going to the festival of Dagon. This is Christ's supreme act of obedience and trust, and it is also the long-awaited demonstration of divinity. The poem's two themes are finally and securely united; and 'Tempt not the Lord thy God' carries a double meaning, for, in addition to its immediate application, it is Christ's first claim to participate in the Godhead. In an instant, and by the same event, Satan receives his answer and Christ achieves full knowledge of himself.

A poet less deeply grounded in classical form and effect might well have ended on this note of climax. Instead, Milton completes his pattern and proceeds to the quiet ending which that pattern and the parallel with *Paradise Lost* alike demand. The ministering angels balance the earlier banquet scene and to its contrast of Satanic beauty with natural add a third element, namely, heavenly beauty. The angels' song confirms Christ's divinity, newly apprehended but enjoyed from of old: (4.596–600)

> True Image of the Father whether thron'd
> In the bosom of bliss, and light of light
> Conceiving, or remote from Heaven, enshrin'd
> In fleshly Tabernacle, and human form,
> Wandring the Wilderness ...

always and everywhere, Christ is the true image of the Father. He defeated Satan and drove him from heaven; again he has defeated him, by vanquishing temptation, has 'aveng'd Supplanted *Adam*' and 'regain'd lost Paradise': (4.634–5)

> on thy glorious work
> Now enter, and begin to save mankind.

And, secure in the knowledge of his nature and his mission, the Redeemer 'Home to his Mothers house private return'd.'

Why to his *mother's* house? Because this also completes a pattern. The final accent, like the first, is on the humanity of Christ. But more than that: this is the third mention of Mary. She it was who had helped her son to his first conception of his nature and mission, and now, the revelation completed, he returns to her. But between these two events Mary herself has been introduced, realizing in her own person the essence of Christian heroism – the heroism exemplified by Christ: (2.91–4)

>   this is my favour'd lot,
>   My Exaltation to Afflictions high;
>   Afflicted I may be, it seems, and blest;
>   I will not argue that, nor will repine.

We are meant to remember these words also as we read the concluding line of the poem.

Notes

All citations of the English poetry and prose of Milton are from *The Works of John Milton,* ed. Frank Allen Patterson (New York, 1931–8), 18 vols. in 21. This Columbia edition is referred to throughout as 'Col.'

Editor's preface

1 A.S.P. Woodhouse also wrote the following essays and reviews concerning Milton and his critics: 'Milton, Puritanism and Liberty,' *University of Toronto Quarterly,* 4 (1934–5): 483–513; 'Milton and His Age,' *University of Toronto Quarterly,* 5 (1935–6): 130–9; review of A. Sewell, *A Study in Milton's 'Christian Doctrine,'* MLR, 34 (1939): 593–6; 'Background for Milton,' *University of Toronto Quarterly,* 10 (1940–1): 499–505; review of H.E. Fletcher, ed., *The Complete Poetical Works of John Milton,* JEGP, 41 (1942): 99–102; review of D.M. Wolfe, *Milton and the Puritan Revolution,* JEGP, 41 (1942): 102–5; review of M. Kelley, *This Great Argument, Philosophical Review,* 52 (1943): 206–8; 'Milton Today,' *University of Toronto Quarterly,* 13 (1943–4): 462–7; 'The Approach to Milton: A Note on Practical Criticism,' *Transactions of the Royal Society of Canada,* 3rd ser. 38 (1944): Section II, 201–13; 'Time and *Paradise Lost,' University of Toronto Quarterly,* 15 (1945–6): 200–5; review of J.S. Diekhoff, *Milton's 'Paradise Lost': A Commentary on the Argument, University of Toronto Quarterly,* 16 (1946–7): 433–5; review of B. Rajan, *'Paradise Lost' and the Seventeenth-Century Reader, University of Toronto Quarterly,* 18 (1948–9): 202–5; 'The Historical Criticism of Milton,' *PMLA,* 66 (1951): 1033–44, reprinted with minor revisions in *The Modern Critical Spectrum,* ed. Gerald J. and Nancy M. Goldberg (Englewood Cliffs, NJ, 1962), pp. 233–43; review of F.M. Krouse, *Milton's Samson and the Christian Tradition, MLN,* 66 (1951): 116–18; review of J.M. French, *The Life Records of John Milton,* Vol. 1, *University of*

Toronto Quarterly, 21 (1951–2): 193–6; *Milton the Poet*, Sedgewick Memorial Lecture at the University of British Columbia (Toronto and Vancouver, 1955); 'Some Reflections on How to Read Milton,' *Seventeenth Century News*, 16 (1958): 8–9; 'Milton,' in *The Poet and His Faith* (Chicago, 1965), 4: 90–122.

A bibliography of A.S.P. Woodhouse's publications, compiled by M.H.M. MacKinnon, and a review of his contribution as scholar, critic, and humanist, written by Douglas Bush, are to be found in *Essays in English Literature from the Renaissance to the Victorian Age: Presented to A.S.P. Woodhouse*, ed. Millar MacLure and F.W. Watt (Toronto, 1964).

Chapter 1   Prospect: the study of Milton

1 Further discussion of this theme by the author may be found in 'Nature and Grace in *The Faerie Queene*,' *ELH*, 16 (1949): 195–97; 'The Argument of Milton's *Comus*,' *University of Toronto Quarterly*, 11 (1941): 46–71; introduction, *Puritanism and Liberty*, ed. A.S.P. Woodhouse (London, 1951), 39–40. [ED.]
2 Coleridge, *Biographia Literaria*, ed. J. Shawcross (Oxford, 1907), 2: 20; *Table Talk* (Oxford, 1917), pp. 267–8.
3 Thomas B. Macaulay, '*Milton*,' in *Critical, Historical and Miscellaneous Essays* (New York, n.d.), pp. 156ff.
4 J.H. Hanford, *John Milton, Englishman* (New York, 1949), introduction.
5 E.H.W. Tillyard, *Milton* (London, 1930), pp. 8off.
6 Denis Saurat, *Milton, Man and Thinker* (London, 1944), p. 184.
7 'The Light Symbolism in "L'Allegro–Il Penseroso," ' in *The Well-Wrought Urn* (New York, 1947), pp. 47–61.
8 It now seems established that the Miltons lived in Hammersmith after leaving the city and did not move to Horton until 1635; see W.R. Parker, *Milton: A Biography* (Oxford, 1968), 2 vols. Here and throughout, Horton has been corrected to Hammersmith where necessary. [ED.]

Chapter 2   Milton's early development

1 *Ad Patrem*, translated by William Cowper (1808), in *Poetical Works of William Cowper*, ed. H.S. Milford (London, 1950), p. 606.
2 'Letter 100' in *Oliver Cromwell's Letters and Speeches*, ed. Thomas Carlyle (London, 1871), 3: 134.
3 Richard Ward, *Life of Henry More* [1710] (London, 1911), pp. 62–3.
4 William Haller, *The Rise of Puritanism* (New York, 1948).
5 J.H. Hanford, 'The Youth of Milton,' in *Studies in Shakespeare, Milton and Donne*, University of Michigan Publications in Language and Literature (New York, 1925) 1: 87–163; [reprinted in *John Milton: Poet and Humanist* (Cleveland, 1966), pp. 22ff. ED.].
6 EDITOR'S NOTE ON THE DATING OF THE MINOR POEMS   In the present chapter

Woodhouse sometimes writes as if there were little doubt concerning the dating
of all but a few of Milton's early poems. This is far from being the case. The
chronology of these early pieces has been the subject of continuous debate, and
had the author lived to complete his preface he would undoubtedly have
reviewed the entire question in an effort to comprehend the scholarship of
recent years. As it is, the justification of the chronology adopted here remains
unchanged from his 1943 article 'Notes on Milton's Early Development.' It
is worth reminding ourselves of some of the uncertainties: *Elegy* 7 has been
dated 1627, 1628, and 1630; *Arcades*, 1630, 1632, and 1634; Sonnet 7,
1631 and 1632; the set of three odes (*On Time, Upon the Circumcision, At a
Solemn Music*), 1630–1, 1631–2, 1637; *Ad Patrem*, 1631–2, 1634, 1637.
Even where there is a large measure of agreement (as with the dating of the
Italian sonnets and the companion pieces), it is frequently based almost entirely
on inference and internal evidence. The critic who wishes to make his way
through this sea of troubles must be armed with resolution, tact, and a clear
hypothesis. The value of the present chapter lies partly in the cogency with
which its hypothesis is explored. The argument turns on the belief that
Sonnet 7 (*How soon hath Time*) represents the culmination of a gradual process of self-realization through which Milton's religious sense of 'calling' is
transferred to poetry. After this point in his career, according to Woodhouse,
there is no hesitation or turning back. Subsequent investigators have questioned
this account, or assessed the chronology of the early poems in terms of other
conceptions of the poet's psychology. Ernest Sirluck and J.T. Shawcross, for
example, agree in locating a vocational crisis in the period circa 1637 (although
for somewhat different reasons), and this affects their sense of the chronology
of the poems (e.g., both place *Ad Patrem* about 1637). Although the argument
of the present chapter was first advanced in 1943, it is, I believe, still forceful
and illuminating. The uninitiated reader can take heart at the thought that
none of the dates assumed in the course of the chapter have been finally
disqualified. Some support, as well as criticism, of the chronology adopted by
Woodhouse can be found in the following: *The Poems of John Milton*, ed.
John Carey and Alastair Fowler (London, 1968); *John Milton: Complete
Poems and Major Prose*, ed. M.Y. Hughes (New York, 1959); H.A. Barnett,
'A Time of the Year for Milton's "Ad Patrem," ' *MLN*, 73 (1958): 82–3;
Douglas Bush, 'The Date of Milton's "Ad Patrem," ' *Modern Philology*, 61
(1964); 204–8; John Carey, 'The Date of Milton's Italian Poems,' *Review of
English Studies*, 14 (1963): 383–6; W.R. Parker, *Milton: A Biography*
(Oxford, 1968), 2 vols; J.T. Shawcross, 'The Date of Milton's "Ad Patrem," '
Notes and Queries, 6 (1959): 358–9; 'Speculations on the Dating of the
Trinity MS of Milton's Poems,' *Modern Language Notes*, 75 (1960): 11–17;
'Certain Relationships of the Manuscripts of *Comus*,' *Papers of the Biblio-
graphical Society of America*, 54 (1960): 38–56; 'Milton's Decision to Become
a Poet,' *Modern Languages Quarterly*, 24 (1963): 21–30; 'The Dating of
Certain Poems, Letters, and Prolusions Written by Milton,' *English Language
Notes*, 2 (1965), 261–6; Ernest Sirluck, 'Milton's Idle Right Hand,' in *Milton
Studies in Honour of Harris Francis Fletcher*, (Urbana, 1961), pp. 141–77.
Summary and interpretation of problems concerning the dating of the minor
poems will be found in *A Variorum Commentary on The Poems of John Milton*,
gen. ed. M.Y. Hughes (3 vols., London, 1972).

7 Familiar Letters, 3: July 2, 1628.

8 *De Liberorum Educatione,* in W.H. Woodward, *Vittorino da Feltre* (Cambridge, 1897), p. 151.

9 *Elegy* 3, adapted from the translation of W.V. Moody and E.K. Rand, in *Complete Poetical Works,* ed. H.F. Fletcher (Cambridge, Mass., 1941).

10 Translation by Dryden (1704), in *Poems of John Dryden,* ed. J. Kinsley (Oxford, 1958), 4: 1769–70.

11 Translation by Moody and Rand.

12 *Elegy* 1, adapted from the translation of Moody and Rand.

13 *Elegy* 5, adapted from the translation of Moody and Rand.

14 *Milton* (London, 1930), p. 333.

15 The *Vacation Exercise* deserves more attention than it can here receive. It suffers from requiring to be read in the context of *Prolusion* 6, Milton's rather distressing effort to live up to the requirements of the Father (or leader of the revels), whose office of introducing the Sons, the poem is forced to complete, to the destruction of its own unity. The amusing parody of Spenser and other Elizabethan poets on the English rivers is insufficient compensation.

16 Adapted from the translation of Moody and Rand.

17 On the controversy see E.L. Tuveson, *Millennium and Utopia* (Berkeley, 1949), pp. 22–74, and Victor Harris, *All Coherence Gone* (Evanston, 1949), pp. 1–161.

17 Thus dated by W.R. Parker, *TLS,* December 17, 1938, p. 802.

19 Edward Bagshawe, *Mr. Boltons Last and Learned Worke of the Four Last Things: Death, Judgement, Hell, and Heaven ... Together with the Life and Death of the Authour* (London, 1633), p. 65.

20 Richard Baxter, *Treatise of Conversion* (1657), p. 111, spelling modernized. On the Puritan literature of conversion see Haller, *Rise of Puritanism,* pp. 83–127.

21 Richard Baxter, *Reliquiae Baxterianae* (1696), pp. 6–7, spelling modernized.

22 William Whately, *The New Birth or a Treatise of Regeneration* (1635), p. 43, spelling modernized.

23 *Elegy* 6, adapted from the translation of Moody and Rand.

24 This view of the poem is worked out by Arthur Barker in 'The Pattern of Milton's *Nativity Ode,*' *University of Toronto Quarterly,* 10 (1941): 167–81.

25 *The True Intellectual System of the Universe* (1678), preface.

26 On the chronology of the poems I have considered the evidence presented by Hanford, Grierson, Tillyard, W.R. Parker, Smart, and M.Y. Hughes. To all of them I am indebted. Grierson and Parker are especially valuable for their treatment of the Cambridge MS; and Parker for his dating of *How soon hath Time,* and of the *Fair Infant* (see *TLS,* December 17, 1938). [Unfortunately Woodhouse did not live to benefit from Parker's *Milton, A Biography* (Oxford, 1968). ED.]

27 John Milton, *Sonnets,* ed. J.A. Smart (Glasgow, 1921), p. 33.

28 Cf. Tillyard, *Milton,* p. 372.

29 Cf. *Passion,* 24–6 ('Cremona's trump'), and 13–14 ('The Hero' is Vida's favourite term for Christ).

30 I.e., from the Holy Sepulchre.

31 Cf. *Elegy* 5, l. 25.

32 Milton, *Sonnets,* ed. Smart, pp. 133ff.

33 I quote from the Italian sonnets in William Cowper's fine and remarkably close verse rendering, *Poetical Works,* ed. H.S. Milford (London, 1950), p. 623

(Sonnet 5), p. 622 (Sonnet 3). Nothing here requires a caution save his addition of 'on foreign ground,' the result of the mistaken impression that the sonnets belong to the Italian journey.

34 Tillyard (p. 373) would go further and read it as an allusion to the failure of *The Passion*.

35 E.M.W. Tillyard, 'Milton: *L'Allegro* and *Il Penseroso*,' English Association, Pamphlet no. 82 (London, 1932), reprinted in *The Miltonic Setting* (Cambridge, 1938).

36 In a passage from *Prolusion* 1, quoted by Tillyard as replete with images used in *L'Allegro*, we come upon the *roses* and *dew* of *L'Allegro* 23, but coupled with the marigold, not the violet, and with the dew connoting not freshness or fertility, but weeping. In *Carmina Elegiaca*, however, we read:

> Iam rosa fragrantes spirat silvestris odores,
> > Iam redolent violæ luxuriatque seges.
> Ecce novo campos Zephyritis gramine vestit
> > Fertilis, et vitreo rore madescit humus.

Here are the ideas and images – *roses, violets, dew* as the symbol of *freshness* and perhaps *fertility* – which are adapted and recombined in the parentage of Mirth:

> *Zephir* with *Aurora* playing ...
> There on Beds of Violets blew
> And fresh-blown Roses washt in dew,
> Fill'd her with thee a daughter fair ...

37 A fuller study of the poems would demand notice of Laurence Babb's valuable paper on melancholy, 'Background of *Il Penseroso*' (*Studies in Philology*, 37 [1940]: 257–73).

38 Giovanni Pico della Mirandola, *On the Dignity of Man*, trans. C.G. Wallis (Annapolis, 1940), pp. 5–6.

39 It is in the light of this line that we must also read Il Penseroso's reverie about the conclusion of Chaucer's *Squire's Tale*. Spenser's completion of a part of the tale in *The Faerie Queene* (4.2.30 to 4.3.52) would teach Milton to think of it in terms of moral allegory (l. 112 echoes Spenser 4.3.52.4); and this in turn accounts for a piece of literature, on the face of it better suited to *L'Allegro*, being mentioned instead in *Il Penseroso*.

40 John Milton, *Poems*, ed. Sir Herbert J.C. Grierson (1933), 1: xxii. Cf. Tillyard, p. 384.

41 Grierson, it must be noticed, is inclined to place the companion pieces with *Comus*, or even after it: 'That *Comus* was written some time later than *Arcades* is suggested not only by its more mature and sensuous art, but by the more puritan tone of the former ... But it is with the maturer art of *Comus* that *L'Allegro* and *Il Penseroso* associate themselves. They might conceivably have been written later than *Comus*' (p. xix). As to *Comus* and *Arcades* one may readily agree, but it is a dark saying that the companion pieces are more 'mature' than *Arcades* and as 'sensuous' as *Comus*.

42 Against this evidence there is nothing to urge but two lines repeated from *Ad Patrem* in *Mansus* (noticed by Grierson and Tillyard); for the fiery spirit with his 'inenarrabile carmen' (37) is not more closely linked with *Lycidas* than with *Il Penseroso*.

43 NOTE ON THE DATE OF ARCADES AND OTHER POEMS IN THE CAMBRIDGE MS   In the absence of any known record of the date of *Arcades*' performance, we are

thrown back chiefly on the evidence of the Cambridge MS (on which see Grierson; Parker; and Hanford, *Milton Handbook* [New York, 1946], pp. 153–4). Its first items are: 1 / *Arcades* (copy representing an advanced stage of composition); 2 / *At a Solemn Music* (wholly composed in the MS); 3 / Letter to a Friend (first draft) containing *How soon hath Time* (fair copy); 4 / *On Time* (fair copy); 5 / *Upon the Circumcision* (fair copy). In *Poems* (1645) the order within one group is, *Time, Circumcision, Solemn Music*, which is perfectly compatible with the evidence of the MS and probably represents the order of composition. Now Parker has shown that *How soon hath Time* was almost certainly composed in December 1632, and that the terms in which the Letter to a Friend speaks of the sonnet argue an interval of no great length between them, say two or three months at most, which would place the Letter early in 1633. The MS indicates that before the Letter *Arcades* and *At a Solemn Music* were certainly written. We also know the season of two poems: *Arcades* bears every appearance of having been written for outdoor (i.e., summer) presentation; and the *Circumcision* clearly belongs to January 1, in some year. Further, as Parker suggests, the theme of *On Time* connects it with *How soon hath Time*. Taking these facts and inferences into account, we get an order and tentative dating wholly compatible with the MS and the order in *Poems* (1645): 1 / *Arcades* (for performance in some summer prior to the date of the Letter, i.e., in the summer of 1632 or an earlier year); 2 / *How soon hath Time* (December 1632, copied into MS in the Letter which was written after *Arcades* and *At a Solemn Music*, or, as appears below, early in 1633); 3 / *On Time* (written later in December 1632, copied into MS after Letter); 4 / *Upon the Circumcision* (January 1, 1633, copied into MS after Letter); 5 / *At a Solemn Music* (written in MS before Letter, and before copying, but after composition, of *How soon hath Time, Time,* and *Circumcision*; i.e., later in January, or early in February 1633); 6 / Letter to a Friend, soon after *Solemn Music*, say early February 1633).

It is true that so far as the order in the MS alone is concerned 3 / *Time* and 4 / *Circumcision* might have been composed as late as December 1633 and January 1, 1634, i.e., shortly before *Comus*. But this would be to ignore a / the probable connection of 3 / *Time* with 2 / *How soon hath Time*, whose date is fixed (December 1632); b / the likeness in religious subject, metre, style, and tone, which strongly indicates that 3 / *Time*, 4 / *Circumcision*, and 5 / *Solemn Music* belong, as they occur in *Poems* (1645), together; and c / the point argued above, that these poems in fact represent a new essaying of religious verse after the resolve taken in 2 / *How soon hath Time* (December 1632). There is, of course, no evidence in favour of a date for 3 / *Time* and 4 / *Circumcision* later than December 1632 and January 1, 1633.

It is likewise true that so far as the order in the MS is concerned *Arcades* could have been written for performance in any summer up to that of 1634 itself, time being allowed between the composition of 1 / *Arcades* and *Comus* for the writing of 5 / *Solemn Music* and 6 / Letter, and the subsequent copying into the MS of 3 / *Time* and 4 / *Circumcision*. But to place *Arcades* in 1634 is to create the impossible interval between 2 / *How soon hath Time* and 6 / Letter, of some 16 or 17 months. To place *Arcades* in 1633 reduces this interval to some 4 or 5 months, which is still long. Since *Solemn Music* comes after *Arcades*, either date separates it from *Time* and *Circumcision*. The sole reason advanced (e.g., by Masson and Hughes) for placing *Arcades* this late is what

Hughes calls 'its obvious points of kinship to *Comus*.' But actually the similarity extends little farther than the genre and what pertains directly thereto. Whenever they were written this much of kinship must have appeared. Nor can anything be argued from the choice of genre since there was no choice, the masque form being dictated by the occasion of each piece and the directions which Milton must have received. Given the similarity in genre, the impression made by the two poems is one not of kinship but of astonishing difference. In its pure aestheticism *Arcades* (as I have pointed out above) is sharply contrasted with *Comus* and finds its kindred among the poems which in all probability belong to the years 1631–2. An added reason for placing *Arcades* at least a year before *Comus* is that the success of the first poem would serve to explain why the much more important commission of the second was given to him.

Of years for *Arcades* earlier than 1632: 1631 is ruled out (see Masson, *The Life of John Milton* [London, 1859–94], 1: 597n.) by the execution of Lord Castlehaven, son-in-law to the Countess. The year 1630 is favoured (according to Hughes, who nevertheless rejects the date for 1633) by the Countess' seventieth birthday falling in that year. But at Milton's age in 1630–2, the difference of two years in maturing powers is important. Nothing that he had written in 1630, not even *Elegy* 5 and the *Nativity*, seems certainly to justify us in placing *Arcades* so early, a consideration which exempts us from examining yet earlier years. On the evidence of maturity it is desirable to place the masque at the latest possible date compatible with all the known facts and the reasonable inferences therefrom. And this I take to be the year 1632, on which all the probabilities appear to converge.

It is proper that I should state (as I am enabled to do by his kind permission) that Mr Roger Stanton has found in the Bridgewater accounts, at the Huntington Library evidence that the Earl of Bridgewater with his retinue visited his stepmother, the Countess Dowager of Derby, at Harefield, *en route* to Ludlow, in the summer of 1634. There is no record of a performance of *Arcades* on this occasion. Nor do I think that the case for 1632 is at the moment at all impaired. But the possibility that the masque may have been commissioned for the visit of 1634 leads me to ask what, if proof were forthcoming that it was, the effect would be upon the pattern of Milton's early development which I have presented above.

In that pattern the date and significance of *How soon hath Time* are crucial. The poem records an experience of which three things may be said: that it springs immediately from the self-examination attendant on Milton's retirement to Hammersmith; that it forms the decisive culmination of a series of experiences going back to the *Nativity*, and implements their results; that, in other words, it leaves its mark on all the rest of Milton's career, not on the poems immediately undertaken merely, but on his view of the poet's office and on almost all the rest of the poetry which he wrote to the end of his days. It is obvious that to interject *Arcades*, with its pure aestheticism, after *How soon hath Time*, would break the pattern to the extent of introducing an important exception. Would it invalidate the pattern as a whole? It would not: because it would leave untouched all the rest of the evidence on which the pattern depends. No one wishes to deny that at rare intervals after 1632 Milton wrote occasional verse which bears no relation to the decision reached in *How soon hath Time*, such as the epistle to Mansus, the ode to Rouse, and half a dozen of the sonnets. It would be necessary to add *Arcades*, which is also in one aspect an occasional poem, to this list. If evidence should be turned up that *Arcades* was written for the visit to Harefield in the summer of 1634 (that is, written after *Comus* was commissioned, planned, and probably executed), it would seem natural enough that Milton, having so heavily freighted the main poem with religio-ethical content, should feel neither obligation nor desire to repeat the experiment in the minor poem.

44 For the doctrine there advanced see below, chapter 3.

45 *Nativity* 125–32; *Ad Patrem* 33–4; *At a Solemn Music* 18–28; *Comus* 1020–1. Tillyard (p. 376) recognizes no distinction between these instances and the use of the image in *Arcades* (see below). In dealing with *At a Solemn Music* (pp. 377–8) he makes Milton *identify* the music of the spheres with the song of the angels in heaven, which only the hundred and forty and four thousand could learn (Rev. 14:1–4). But Milton is careful always to distinguish the music of the spheres from the angels' song. They are not identical, but complementary, and parallel on different levels. In the *Nativity* the spheres, with their 'nine-fold harmony,' are bidden to complement, to 'Make up full consort to th' Angelicke symphony'; in *Ad Patrem* the stars echo the songs of heaven; and in *At a Solemn Music* the song of those on earth, which is distinguished alike from the music of the spheres and the song of the angels, is bidden once more to 'answer' the latter. Only in eternity, when the world is destroyed, will the first and third songs be merged, and the second superseded, the triumph envisaged at the end of the poem. Thomas Heywood (*Hierarchy of the Blessed Angels* [1635], p. 582), telling how the various orders of God's angels 'all Resound his praise in accents musical,' adds, 'So do the heavens and planets, much below them.' He further (p. 272) carefully parallels, not identifies, the different parts of the natural world with the hierarchy of the celestial, dwelling on

> what reference the seraphim
> Hath [sic] with the primum mobile; then what kin
> The cherub from the starry heaven doth claim, [etc.]

It is this traditional association of the cherubim with the starry heaven that explains Milton's allusion (*Ad Patrem* 35–7) to the fiery spirit flying through the swift spheres and singing his *inenarrabile carmen*. The spirit is, I take it, not the Platonic soul of the world (as Tillyard supposes) or the interfused and sustaining spirit and mind of Virgil's *Aeneid* 6.724–7 (as Hughes suggests), but the cherub whose song harmonizes with the music of the spheres, and (because it is angelic) is by man 'unutterable.' The link is with the cherub of *Il Penseroso*. Like Heywood and Milton, Donne (*Upon the Translation of the Psalms* 23–9) maintains the distinction and parallel between the music of the spheres and the angelic song. Milton (*Paradise Lost* 5.618–27) describes the dance of the angels, with its accompanying harmony,

> which yonder starrie Spheare
> Of Planets and of fixt in all her Wheeles
> *Resembles nearest.*

Again the distinction and the parallel are maintained. The reason is this. The music of the spheres represents the highest degree of perfection (expressed as harmony) in the order of nature; the angelic song represents the highest perfection and harmony of the order of grace. Thus Virtue (*Comus* 1019–21)

> can teach ye how to clime
> Higher then the spheary chime.

But if 'the spheary chime' were identical with the 'unexpressive nuptial song,' there could be nothing higher. To confuse the two orders of nature and grace is to break up the pattern of Milton's thinking.

46 Milton is echoing Pindar, *Nemean Odes*, 4.43: 'But whatever merit King Fate has given me, I shall know that time in its course will accomplish what is destined' (Lewis Campbell, 'A Parallel in Milton and Pindar,' *Classical Review*, 8 (1894): 349. The fact intensifies the impression of fatalism which the lines convey to a modern reader. The impression requires to be corrected by recalling the Christian view of fate which subjects it to the will of God – the view which Milton later sums up with beautiful precision (*Paradise Lost* 7.172–3):
> Necessitie and Chance
> Approach not mee, and what I will is Fate.

47 Much turns on the precise meaning of the last two lines. In the Cambridge MS there is no punctuation. The punctuation in *Poems* (1645), which editors retain, is ambiguous:
> All is, if I have grace to use it so,
> As ever in my great task Masters eye.

At first glance the commas appear to be a pair setting off the words between them as a conditional clause. But it conditions nothing; and this reading reduces the lines to something between redundancy and nonsense, making them say: Everything is, if I have grace to recognize it, as it ever has been, in my great taskmaster's knowledge. But obviously it is so whether Milton recognizes it or not: God's knowledge does not depend upon man's attitude, as Milton, who was not in the habit of thinking loosely, very well knew. Further, if God's eye betokens only his cognition, why is he described as the poet's *task*master? The commas are not a pair. The function of the first could be discharged just as well, perhaps slightly better, in modern punctuation by the colon which I have substituted for it. The meaning is then clear, with no redundance: All [that matters] is: whether I have grace to use it so, as ever [conscious of being] in my great taskmaster's [enjoining] eye. One editor, J.S. Smart, evidently adopts some such reading of the lines, but indicates it by omitting the second comma instead of changing the first to a colon.

48 For a very suggestive (though not in every detail acceptable) analysis of *Lycidas* in this connection, see Tillyard, pp. 80–5.

49 For their probable dates see n. 43.

Chapter 3 *Comus, Lycidas, Epitaphium Damonis*

1 I have one substantial debt to record. It is to J.H. Hanford's 'The Youth of Milton' in *Studies in Shakespeare, Milton and Donne*, University of Michigan Publications in Language and Literature (New York, 1925), 1: 87–163, especially 139–43, 152. Since I shall have occasion to disagree with him at some points, I wish to express here not only my deep sense of obligation, but also my conviction that his is in general the wisest and most penetrating essay on Milton ever written. In dealing with Spenser I have been helped by the *The Works of Edmund Spenser: A variorum edition*, ed. Edwin Greenlaw (Baltimore, 1932–49), and by C.S. Lewis' brilliant *Allegory of Love* (Oxford, 1936). Douglas Bush has made some very valuable criticisms and suggestions.

2 Enid Welsford, *The Court Masque* (New York, 1927), pp. 320–1.

3 W.W. Greg, *Pastoral Poetry and Pastoral Drama* (London, 1906), pp. 399, 402.

4 Ben Jonson, *Masque of Queens* (1609), preface

5 See Gretchen L. Finney, 'Comus, Drama per Musica,' *Studies in Philology*, 37 (1940): 102–15.

6 'She Walks in Beauty,' from *Hebrew Melodies, Works of Byron* (Cambridge, 1933), p. 216.

7 The words, if compared with *Epitaphium Damonis* 150–2, strongly suggest that the allusion is to Charles Diodati.

8 *Faerie Queene* 2.12; see *Areopagitica*, Col. 4: 311.

9 *Faerie Queene* 3.6; cf. Lewis, *Allegory of Love*, pp. 324ff.

10 *Comus* 727–35. The last lines echo, and pervert, the imagery of the Attendant Spirit (21–3) when he describes
>   the Sea-girt Iles
>   That like to rich and various gemms inlay
>   The unadorned boosom of the Deep ...

11 For the charge of ingratitude, the Lady has already detected in the sound of Comus's revelry the noise of those who (175–6)
>   In wanton dance ... praise the bounteous *Pan*
>   And thank the gods amiss.

And she will soon retort the charge: Comus is one who 'Cramms and blasphemes his Feeder' (778).

12 See A.S.P. Woodhouse, 'Nature and Grace in the *Faerie Queene*,' *ELH*, 16 (1949): 194–228; [reprinted in *Elizabethan Poetry: Modern Essays in Criticism*, ed. Paul J. Alpers (Oxford, 1967), pp. 345–79. ED.]

13 In Spenser, of course, in its extended Aritotelian sense.

14 *An Hymne in Honour of Beautie* 132–3.

15 'Youth of Milton,' pp. 140–1.

16 See 'Nature and Grace in the *Faerie Queene*.'

17 Nor have the minor characters in which Spenser deals with other aspects of chastity more relation than Britomart to Milton's masque, with one possible exception, Belphoebe, Spenser's version of the classical Diana. To Britomart Hanford would trace 'the martial conception [that] underlies such passages as *Comus* 44off.' (*Youth of Milton*, p. 141). But the conception though militant, is not martial; and to me the lines with their allusions to Diana and Minerva recall the spirit of Spenser's portrait not of Britomart, but of Belphoebe. More plausible is Hanford's contention that the Lady's rescue, which can be completed only by the reversal of the enchanter's charm, owes something to the rescue of Amoret (*Faerie Queene* 3.12.36), though there is a possible common source in Ovid, *Metamorphoses* 14.301–2 (M.Y. Hughes, *John Milton: Complete Poems and Major Prose* [New York, 1957]). But least plausible of all is the assumption that Milton's emphasis on providential intervention to guard chastity requires a source and finds it in the rescue of Florimel by Proteus (*Faerie Queene* 3.8.29ff.). And anyway these would be mere surface borrowings: the characters and situations of Amoret and Florimel have nothing in common with the Lady's. In one instance Hanford exaggerates Milton's divergence from Spenser: it is the one certain and significant borrowing from Book 3, the allusion to the Garden of Adonis.

18 See, for example, Hughes's note on l. 822.

19 Nor, perhaps, does the debt to Spenser stop here. The power of grace to destroy

evil is part of its function in freeing the good. In slaying Maleger (2.11.45–46) by casting him into the standing lake, Prince Arthur invokes the power of grace, symbolized by water, to destroy evil, just as Sabrina sprinkles the precious drops, not only upon the Lady, freeing her by an infusion of grace, but upon Comus's throne, destroying its evil effect.

20 See 'Nature and Grace in the *Faerie Queene*,' p. 207.

21 Welsford, *Court Masque*, p. 321.

22 The allusion would serve to recall the reference to 'the wide Atlantic' in the original Prologue of the Attendant Spirit and to the 'Stygian pool,' with which was Comus's real affinity (cf. 131–2, where he invokes 'the dragon womb Of Stygian darkness').

23 This couplet is italicized because, for all its beauty and seeming innocence, it is untrue. The spheres with their 'ninefold harmony,' audible only to the pure in heart, have for Milton a special significance. The ordered motion and harmonious music of the spheres symbolize the highest degree of perfection in the natural order, and parallel the dance and song of the angels. The irony is evident.

24 The non-classical reader will not appreciate the full extent of licentiousness conveyed by the name, though he will recognize the association with evil implied by Hecate and the blotting out of light. See C.G. Osgood, *The Classical Mythology of Milton's English Poems* (New Haven, 1900), pp. 24–5.

25 This is meant to contrast with the 'calm and serene air' (4) in the abode of the Attendant Spirit. Midway between the two (to be purified by one or corrupted by the other) is the 'Smoke and stir of this dim spot Which men call earth' (5–6). The Cambridge MS first has 'And makes a blot of nature,' deleted in favour of above.

26 Another seemingly innocent couplet, which instantly reminds us indeed of a genuinely innocent one,

> Com, and trip it as ye go
> On the light fantastick toe,

a type of the 'unreproved pleasures free' of *L'Allegro* (33–34, 40). But, as Osgood makes clear, Comus is still alluding to the obscene rites of Cotytto.

27 Hanford, 'Youth of Milton, p. 152.

28 *Faerie Queene* 3.6.

29 One should record Hughes' note on *Assyrian Queen*, l. 1002, that 'according to Pausanias 1.14–6, 'the Assyrians were the first men to revere the Celestial Aphrodite.'' But surely the phrase *Assyrian Queen* is sufficiently accounted for by the myth of Venus and Adonis itself, which, as Milton well knew (cf. *Nativity*, 204) is of Eastern origin. Thammuz was adopted as Adonis. Astoreth or Astarte, the original of the Venus of this myth, was herself identical with the Assyrian goddess Istar. *Assyrian Queen* is thus one of Milton's learned devices of poetical ornament. Cf. A.W. Verity's note on *Comus* 1002, and *Paradise Lost* 1.438–41.

30 Brents Stirling in *Variorum Spenser*, 3: 347–52.

31 See Lewis, *Allegory of Love*, pp. 324ff., 361ff.

32 *Defensio Secunda* (1654), Col. 8: 248–50, as translated in John Milton, *Prose Works*, ed. J.A. St John (London, 1846), 1: 298.

33 *Lycidas* 176. E.M.W. Tillyard, in *Milton* (London, 1930), pp. 376ff., seems to hold that in *At a Solemn Music* Milton identifies the two, and to wish to read *Comus* in the light of this supposed identification. What the text says is that the two strains *answer* each other. Milton does not divorce the different orders of

existence, but neither does he confuse them. There is something *higher then the Spheary chime*. It is the unexpressive nuptial song.

34 Andrew Lang's translation of a Greek poem addressed to Bion, in *The Poetical Works of Andrew Lang* (London, 1923), 2: 217.

35 Trans. H. Rushton Fairclough in *Virgil* (London, 1916), 1: 73.

36 'Lament for Damon: the *Epitaphium Damonis of Milton,' University of Toronto Quarterly*, 16 (1947): 341.

37 Trans. W.V. Moody and E.K. Rand, in John Milton', *Complete Poetical Works*, ed. H.F. Fletcher (Cambridge, Mass., 1941), p. 539.

38 Letter 10, trans. David Masson, Col. 12: 49.

39 Trans. Moody and Rand, *Poetical Works*, pp. 539, 540.

40 The lines (155–9) do not state that the inability to proceed with his poetry, symbolized by the shattered pipes, is the result of the news of Damon's death. But I find my interpretation of them supported by M.Y. Hughes's note in *Paradise Regained, The Minor Poems and Samson Agonistes* (New York, 1937), p. 330: 'Milton's grief for Diodati, as the broken exclamations are intended to suggest, prevents him from prosecuting the poetical ambitions which we know, from *Mansus* 80–84, that he cherished in Italy.' The lines read:

> Ipse etiam – nam nescio quid mihi grande sonabat
> Fistula – ab undecimâ iam lux est altera nocte –
> Et tum forte novis admôram labra cicutis,
> Dissiluere tamen rupta compage, nec ultra
> Ferre graves potuere sonos ...

41 Trans. Moody and Rand, *Poetical Works*, p. 541.

42 *Ibid.*

43 William Cowper's verse translation (1808), in *Poetical Works of William Cowper*, ed. H.S. Milford (London, 1950), p. 618.

44 It will be unnecessary to burden the text with footnotes if one may discharge one's debts by mentioning now two pieces of pioneer work on *Lycidas*, from which all subsequent investigation must start: J.H. Hanford's in 'The Pastoral Elegy and Milton's *Lycidas*,' *PMLA*, 25 (1910): 403–44 [reprinted in *Milton's Lycidas*, ed. C.A. Patrides (New York, 1961), pp. 217–63 – ED.], and E.M.W. Tillyard's in his *Milton* (London 1930); and one may add a reference, perhaps, to A.E. Barker's suggestive rounding out of Tillyard's analysis, in 'The Pattern of Milton's Nativity Ode,' *University of Toronto Quarterly*, 10 (1941): 171–2.

Chapter 4 The reformer

1 For a fuller treatment of Puritanism, see the Introduction to *Puritanism and Liberty*, ed. A.S.P. Woodhouse (London, 1951). [ED.]

2 Colonel Thomas Rainborough made the remark during the Army debate held at Putney on October 29, 1657; see Woodhouse, ed., *Puritanism and Liberty*, p. 53.

3 *Ad Patrem*, William Cowper's translation (1808), in The *Poetical Works of William Cowper*, ed. H.S. Milford (London, 1950), p. 606.

4 Adapted from the translation in John Milton, *Prose Works*, ed. J.A. St John (London, 1846), 1: 257–8.

5 By Thomas Edwards (London, 1647).

6 John 1: 17, cited by Milton in *De Doctrina Christiana*, 1: 27 (Col. 16: 153).

7 Adapted from the translation in *Prose Works*, ed. St John, 1: 298.

8 See *Prolusion* 7.

9 The limits of Milton's Baconianism are clearly seen if we compare the tractate with William Petty's *Advice to Samuel Hartlib* (*Harl Misc.* 1810.6.141–58), also an educational utopia and one of wider range than Milton's, extending all the way from the primary school to the institute of research, and including a 'college of tradesmen' concerned with the useful crafts, a museum, a botanical garden, a zoo, an aquarium, an astronomical observatory, so that his school would be 'an epitome or abstract of the whole world' (though this, he admits, is utopian, and rather what should than what will). More practicable, he thinks, is the addition of an experimental hospital and place of medical research and training. In four respects, besides its range, this scheme differs from Milton's and in general declares its affinity with the aims of Bacon: 1 / At the lowest level it is to offer an elementary education to all, however poor. Their primary training is to be in observation, not in reading and writing: 'Few children,' he says, 'have need of reading before they know or can be acquainted with the things of which they read, or of writing before their thoughts are worth the recording.' (Here, indeed we see the so-called progressive educationist afar off.) Foreign languages may be yet further postponed. But all children are to be taught a trade. 2 / This emphasis on the practical, indeed the vocational, is characteristic of the whole scheme. 3 / In all the higher reaches there is an emphasis on research and invention, not merely the acquisition of knowledge, but the advancement of science. A principal task is to carry on Bacon's work by recording all useful experiments and inventions achieved in the past and to set down what still requires to be explored. 4 / Save for a rather perfunctory assertion at the end that the purpose is to promote 'piety, virtue, and learning in all things divine and human as they are subordinated to the glory of God,' there is little or no reference to religious and ethical training which is central in Milton's scheme.

10 Samuel Johnson, 'Milton,' in *Lives of the English Poets*, ed. G.B. Hill (Oxford, 1905), 1: 157.

11 See D. Neal, *History of the Puritans* (London, 1822), 2: 110–11, and W.H. Burgess, *John Robinson* (London, 1920), p. 239.

12 John Goodwin, *Imputatio Fidei* (1642), preface.

13 *An Apologetical Narration* (1664), p. 101.

14 Henry Robinson, *Liberty of Conscience* (1644), p. 50.

15 *The Ancient Bounds* (London, 1645), chap. 6, in Woodhouse, ed. *Puritanism and Liberty*, p. 259.

16 As translated in *Prose Works*, ed. St John, 1: 294.

17 See Maurice W. Kelley, *This Great Argument* (Princeton, 1941), chap. 2.

18 In his determinism and voluntarism, Hobbes presents a secular (and indeed anti-religious) parallel to extreme Calvinism, as was in effect recognized, if not by Milton, at least by the Cambridge Platonists and Shaftesbury.

19 See John S. Diekhoff, 'Eve, the Devil, and *Areopagitica*,' *MLQ*, 5 (1944): 429–34.

20 *Milton* (London, 1956), p. 282.

21 *The Marriage of Heaven and Hell*, in *The Complete Writings of William Blake*, ed. Geoffrey Keynes (Oxford, 1966), p. 150.

Chapter 5   The theologian, 1: Milton's Christian doctrine

1 Reference here and in subsequent citations is to book and chapter of *De Doctrina Christiana* and then to volume and page in the Columbia edition of Milton's works.
2 See Maurice W. Kelley, *This Great Argument* (Princeton, 1941).
3 *Gangraena* (London, 1646), Part i, No. 66, No. 7.

Chapter 6   The theologian, 2: the creation; the Son of God

1 I have reduced to a minimum the references to previous investigators. It is to be understood that I am familiar with, and have profited by reading, the well known works of Baldwin, Curry, Fletcher, Grierson, Greenlaw, Hanford, Hughes, Kelley, McColley, Saurat, Sewell, Williams, Williamson, though this is the only reference to most of them by name.
2 To call this power nature or fate, he argues, is to become involved in absurdity. For nature can mean only 'the essence of a thing, or that general law ... under which everything acts'; and to attribute the production of all things to nature is really to 'associate chance with nature as a joint divinity,' while 'fate can be nothing but a divine decree emanating from some almighty power' (*De Doctrina*, 1: 7 [Col. 15: 5] and 1: 2 [Col. 14: 27]). Cf. *Paradise Lost* 7.172–3: 'Necessity and Chance Approach not me, and what I will is Fate.'
3 James Ussher, *A Body of Divinity* (1649), pp. 93–4: 'For reason teacheth, that there must needs be a first cause of all things ... ; that all perfections which are in other things by participation, should bee in it essentially, and that the same must bee of infinite wisdome, in that all things are made and ordered unto so good purposes as they are: none of which things can agree to any but to God alone ... *Is not Creation then an article of faith above reason?* Yes; in regard of the time and manner of it: as likewise in respect of a full and saving assent unto it with comfort.'
4 *Exposition of the Creed* [first published in 1659] (1676), p. 56.
5 *Ethics* I, prop. 17, in Spinoza, *Chief Works*, trans. R.H.M. Elwes (London, 1884), 2: 59–62.
6 Ibid., prop. 29, 2: 68.
7 Ibid., prop. 32, 2: 70.
8 Ibid., prop. 33, 2: 70.
9 *Body of Divinity*, pp. 94–5.
10 The omission of reference to God's wisdom here is not significant in the light of the passage quoted above.
11 See pp. 154ff.
12 In Milton's usage *soul* is a synonym for living being.
13 *Timaeus* 29e.
14 On this difference, see A.O. Lovejoy, *The Great Chain of Being* (Cambridge, Mass., 1936), passim.
15 See pp. 216ff.
16 Edward Stillingfleet, *Origines Sacrae* [first published in 1663, 3.2.7], in *Works* (1709), 2: 276.
17 *Exposition of the Creed*, p. 65.

18 William Ames, *The Marrow of Sacred Divinity* (1642), p. 40.

19 *A Friendly Debate ... betwixt Mr Samuel Eaton and Mr John Knowles, concerning the Divinity of Jesus Christ* (1650), p. 35.

20 *Logic* 1.4 (Col. 11: 37): 'Instruments ... are reckoned among the helping causes ... Instruments, however, do not act of themselves, but are used or help. And a cause which has no helping cause except an instrument can properly be called a solitary cause, however wide the significance given to the word *instrument*.'

21 *De Genesi ad litteram libri duodecim* 1.15.29,30; *Confessions* 12.12.

22 *De Genesi ad litteram imperfectus liber* 3.10, 4.12.

23 *Commentary on the First Book of Moses*, trans. John King (1847), 1: 70.

24 *Exercitationes in Genesin* (1633), quoted by Arnold Williams, 'Renaissance Commentaries on Genesis and ... the Theology of *Paradise Lost*,' *PMLA*, 56 (1941): 157.

25 *Exposition of the Creed*, pp. 52–3. The supporting passages of scripture Pearson interprets in a sense opposed to Milton's, notably Heb. 11:3. For the argument from reason, he draws from the attribute of omnipotence the traditional inference of God's independence of any pre-existing matter. Stillingfleet (*Origines Sacrae* 3.2.8, p. 277) admits that *bara* does not commonly denote creation *ex nihilo*; but, finding that Moses had no other word better calculated to convey this meaning, he protests against what is to be Milton's inference, that Moses teaches creation from some pre-existent matter: 'All that can be rationally inferred is that from the mere force and importance of that word [*bara*] the contrary cannot be collected.'

26 *Ad Philosophiam Teutonicam Manuductio* (1648), p. 19. Hotham interprets Heb. 11:13 in the sense to be adopted by Milton.

27 *Origines Sacrae* 3.2.8, p. 277. While Milton is no Socinian, it seems probable that Racovian theology forms an essential part of his background.

28 See Johannes Volkelius, *De Vera Religione* (Racoviae, 1630), 2.4 (books separately paged, pp. 5–7); and Robert Fludd, *Mosaicall Philosophy* (1659), 1.2.2, pp. 44–5. The argument, common to Volkelius and Fludd, may be briefly summarized. Both resort to what is described as a scholastic distinction between two meanings of the term *nothing*: *nihilum negativum* (absolute nonentity) and *nihilum privatum*, which denotes the absence of forms, and hence of actuality, but equally entails the presence of potentiality, of something upon which forms can be imposed, a substance or substratum that is to underlie all actual beings. To *nothing* in this privative sense, that is to say, to the substratum, St Paul refers as 'the things which do not appear' (Heb. 11:3), and the Apocryphal writers when they speak of the world as created *ex rebus quae non erant* (2 Macc. 7:28) or *ex informi materia* (Wisd. 11:18). The apparent contradiction between the last two phrases is resolved by the scholastic distinction; for the *res quae non erant* of Maccabees are the same as the *materia informis* of Wisdom. Thus a comparison with other passages of scripture shows that it is in the sense of *nihilum privatum* merely that Moses can be said to teach creation *ex nihilo*; and the heaven and earth, the earth without form and void, the deep and the waters, to which he refers, are indeed the *materia informis*. Its creation *ex nihilo negativo* was for St Augustine and orthodoxy the first stage of the creative act. For Volkelius and Fludd, as for Milton, it was uncreated.

29 *Origines Sacrae* 3.2.10, p. 280.

30 See Jacques Farges, *Méthode d'Olympe, Du Libre Arbitre, Traduction* (Paris, 1929).
31 *De Genesi ad litteram imperfectus liber* 1.2.
32 See p. 156.
33 Rom. 11:36 is cited by St Augustine to refute creation from an independently pre-existent matter (*De Genesi ad litteram imperfectus liber* 4.13).
34 In summing up his position, Milton describes his method of reaching it in the phrase: '... it has (I conceive) been satisfactorily proved, under the guidance of scripture, that God did not produce everything out of nothing, but of himself ...' (*De Doctrina*, 1: 7 [Col. 15: 27]). Having discovered in the opening verses of Genesis, and in the passage of scripture commonly cited to elucidate them, no support for creation *ex nihilo*, he turned to reason, that is, to the logic of causation, and to what appeared to be the inescapable inferences from the divine attributes, reverting finally to scripture (Rom. 11:36) for a formulation which logic would sustain. This is the characteristic relation of scripture and reason in the *De Doctrina*.
35 Cf. *Logic* 1.3 (Col. 11: 31–3).
36 On Milton's interpretation of the attribute of infinity see p. 156.
37 Du Bartas, *Divine Weekes and Workes*, trans. Josuah Sylvester (1621), p. 2.
38 See the passage from *Mosaicall Philosophy*, pp. 44–5, quoted on pp. 153–4.
39 *Preparation for the Gospel* 4.1, trans. E.H. Gifford (Oxford, 1903). As a possible influence on Milton, and notably on his view of the Son, Eusebius has been strangely overlooked.
40 'Quel que soit le sens exact de la pensée de Platon sur le Devenir, peu importe pour l'histoire des idées dans les siècles postérieurs. Les commentateurs prendront ses affirmations à la lettre. Ce qu'ils retiendront surtout du *Timée*, ce sera le Chaos initial ramené a l'ordre par le Demiurge, le règne de la Nécessité opposé à celui d'une puissance intelligente, l'antagonisme entre le sensible et l'intelligible' (Farges, *Méthode d'Olympe, Du Libre Arbitre*, p. 15).
41 *Mosaicall Philosophy* 2.1.2, p. 139.
42 Ibid., 2.2, pp. 44–5. Among other passages of scripture Fludd utilizes Heb. 11:3, Wisd. 11:18, putting upon them the same sense as does Milton. The references introduced into the text here and elsewhere are given by Fludd in the margin.
43 *Ethics* 1, prop. 3.
44 *Short Treatise*, appendix 1, axiom 5, trans. A. Wolf (London, 1910), p. 153.
45 *Mosaicall Philosophy* 1.3.1, 2, pp. 42–3, 44.
46 Ibid., p. 44.
47 William Ames, *Marrow of Sacred Divinity* (1642), p. 14. Ussher explains that God is chiefly to be known 'by denials or removing of all imperfections whatsover: as of composition, by the titles of simple, spirituall, and incorporeall; of all circumscription of time by the title eternall; of all bounds of place, by that of infinite ...' (*Body of Divinity*, p. 32); for the rest he uses the world only adverbially, as in the sentence 'God is ... infinitely great and good' (ibid.). Ralph Cudworth, *True Intellectual System* (1678), 1.5.1, declares that God's 'infinity is really nothing else but perfection.'
48 *Confessions* 1.3.
49 *Divine Dialogues* (1668), pp. 104–6.
50 'Extension is an attribute of God' (*Ethics* 2, prop. 2). 'Every substance is necessarily infinite' (1, prop. 8). 'Besides God no substance can be granted' (1, prop. 14).

51 *Timaeus* 53b. That Milton was not unmindful of the *Timaeus* as he wrote is put beyond reasonable doubt by the reference, which immediately follows, to necessity and chance.

52 '... God (contrary unto Aristotle's assertion, with the opinion of divers Ethnick Philosophers) does not operate of necessity for the creation and continuation of his creatures; but of his proper will and benigne inclination' (*Mosaicall Philosophy* 1.4.7, p. 79; cf. p. 81).

53 Ibid. 2.1.2, p. 138.

54 Ibid. 1.3.4, pp. 48–9.

55 Ibid. 2.1.1, p. 131.

56 *Milton, Man and Thinker* (1925), p. 124.

57 *Origines Sacrae* 3.2.10, pp. 281–2. Milton does not, of course, place God in the matter, but thinks of the matter as comprehended in God.

58 *Timaeus* 48a, 52e–53b.

59 F.M. Cornford, *Plato's Cosmology* (London, 1937), p. 165.

60 See, for example, *Mosaicall Philosophy* 1.4.6, p. 77; and 2.1.3, pp. 138–9.

61 It must, for example, be plain to every reader of *Paradise Lost* that the description of the chaos there throws a very much heavier emphasis on its formlessness and disorder than does the account of the original matter in the *De Doctrina*, so that it is difficult to escape the inference, denied in the treatise, that this disorder is, or at all events has some affinity with, evil. Less obtrusive, but not less significant, is the assertion (7.237–9) that before it is fit for the imposition of forms matter must, by the action of the Spirit, be purged of its

> black, tartareous, cold, infernal dregs,
> Adverse to life.

It would appear that this is a relic of some anxious consideration of the problem of evil. In the dialogue of Methodius, *Concerning Free-Will*, a Valentinian explains that originally matter 'was without quality or form and, besides this, was borne about without order and was untouched by divine art'; that God did not leave it in this condition, however, 'but began to work upon it and wished to separate its best parts from its worst, and thus made all that was fitting for God to make out of it. But so much of it was like lees, so to speak, this being unfitted for being made into anything, he left as it was ... , and from this ... what is evil has now streamed down among men' (trans. in *The Ante-Nicene Fathers*, ed. Alexander Roberts and James Donaldson [Buffalo, 1880], 6: 358). This separation of the matter to be used in the creation from its lees or dregs is closer to the purgation glanced at by Milton than is the division of the waters ascribed by Fludd to the Spirit, whereby 'the purer, brighter and more worthy waters' that were to form the heavens were separated from 'the grosser, viler and darker sort of waters' that were to form the earth (*Mosaicall Philosophy* 1.3.3, p. 47), though it is possible that Fludd may help to explain some of the details of Milton's image by associating cold and darkness as synonyms for evil, and by speaking, in another context, of 'the dregs which issue out of the lower waters' (ibid., p. 76).

62 If our concern were with the problem of evil in general, the Christian solution of the problem at its various levels, and Milton's response thereto, we should have to observe: 1 / that the cosmological aspect of the problem is merely one among several; 2 / that Christianity has always laid more stress on its solution of the problem at other levels – on its solution, for example, in terms of God's providence, his power and will to subordinate evil to the purposes of the good, and out of evil itself to bring forth good, or again on its solution in terms of

man's free will, whereby good and evil are within his choice, and the responsibility lies with him, not with his Maker, to which must be added the whole machinery of the fall, with its loss of free will, and of grace, with the restoration of freedom; 3 / that these other solutions of the problem had been fairly fully formulated before St Augustine attacked it on the cosmological level, and an especially heavy emphasis had been thrown on man's free will; and, finally 4 / that Milton retains these other Christian solutions and lays a particular stress on free will.

63 The following brief summary is based on St Augustine's many pronouncements on the subject in the *Confessions* and in his writings against the Manichaeans.

64 Philippe de Mornay, *A Worke concerning the Truenesse of the Christian Religion* (1604), pp. 23–5.

65 Into Milton's attempted solution we cannot go here since it entails an effort to define more precisely his conception of the good and an examination of his view of creation in its later phases (or of what St Augustine would describe as the second logical stage in the creative act, and Milton as the whole of it).

66 We have seen above (p. 158) that *Paradise Lost* 7.169–72 does not, as Saurat claims (*Milton*, p. 124), contain Saurat's version of 'retraction,' but yields a meaning, supported by Fludd, utterly opposed to it. But the 'retraction' (which is not present) is essential to the whole scheme which Saurat thrusts upon Milton. By the 'retraction' God is enabled to cast 'outside of himself the evil parts of himself ... because (*Paradise Lost* 5.117–18)

> Evil into the mind of God or man
> May come and go ...

Terrible words, applied to God ...' (*Milton*, p. 133). It would be easy to show how improbable it is that these casual words, wrenched from their context in a speech of Adam's about dreams, should contain a central doctrine in Milton's scheme: easy, but superfluous. For the fact is obvious (though faintly obscured by Saurat's suppression of the capital letter in Man) that 'God or Man' means angel or man, and the lines do not refer to the deity at all: the quotation is simply irrelevant. Cf. *De Doctrina*, 1: 5 (Col. 14: 245).

67 Another proposition debated on the same day was that the world's creation may be known by the light of nature.

68 Two years later Hotham permitted its translation under the title *An Introduction to the Teutonick Philosophie. Being a Determination concerning the Original of the Soul ... By C. Hotham ... Englished by D.F.* (1650). Curiously, the Epistle of the Translator to the Author contains a highly laudatory reference to Milton, noted in W.R. Parker, *Milton's Contemporary Reputation*, (Columbus, 1940) p. 84, which suggests that he was on terms of personal friendship with one or both of them. But the interest of the analogue does not depend on such a tenuous connection.

69 *Introduction to the Teutonick Philosophie*, p. 38.

70 *Hudibras* 1.1, ed. A.R. Waller (Cambridge, 1905), pp. 17–18. Ralph professed to understand such writers as Floud and Jacob Behmen and to have seen *First Matter*

> Before one Rag of Form was on.
> The Chaos too he had descry'd
> And seen quite through, or else he ly'd.

71 H.J. McLachlan, *Socinianism in Seventeenth-Century England* (London, 1951), pp. 187–93.

72 *Friendly Debate*, p. 5.

73 Ussher, *Body of Divinity* (1649), p. 76.
74 See *The Racovian Catechism*, trans. Thomas Rees (London, 1810), pp. 65–6.
75 *De Trinitate*, cap. 31.
76 See J.F. Bethune-Baker, *Introduction to the Early History of Christian Doctrine* (London, 1920), p. 159.
77 *Friendly Debate* (1650), pp. 15, 17.
78 Ibid., pp. 20–1.
79 Ibid., p. 20.
80 Ibid., pp. 15, 20.

Chapter 7   *Paradise Lost*, 1: theme and pattern

1 'Girl's Song,' *Collected Poems* (London, 1926), p. 341. By permission of Mr M. Gibson and Macmillan London and Basingstoke.
2 Samuel Johnson, 'Milton,' in *Lives of the English Poets*, ed. G.B. Hill (Oxford 1905), 1: 171.
3 Alexander Pope, *Essay on Man* 1: 16.
4 *Faerie Queene* 1.10.53–4.
5 'Preface to Poems, 1656,' in *Abraham Cowley: The Essays and Other Prose Writings*, ed. Alfred B. Gough (Oxford, 1915), p. 16.
6 See Sir Walter Raleigh, *Milton* (London, 1900), p. 133; and G.R. Hamilton, *Hero or Fool: A Study of Milton's Satan* (London, 1944). [ED.]
7 J.T. Sheppard, *Pattern of the Iliad* (London, 1922).
8 See Helen Gardner, 'Milton's Satan and the Theme of Damnation in Elizabethan Tragedy,' *English Studies*, n.s. 1 (1948): 46–66. [ED.]
9 *Iliad* 18.490–535, trans. A.T. Murray (London, 1925), 325–9.

Chapter 8   *Paradise Lost*, 2: the elaboration of the pattern

1 Trans. H. Rushton Fairclough (London, 1916), 2: 527–9.
2 Ibid., 2: 537.
3 Samuel Johnson, 'Dryden,' in *Lives of the English Poets*, ed. G.B. Hill (Oxford, 1905), 1: 349.
4 'To Augustus,' *Imitations of Horace*, 102.
5 E.M.W. Tillyard, 'The Crisis in *Paradise Lost*,' in *Studies in Milton* (London, 1951), pp. 8–13.
6 *The City of God*, 14: 13, trans. Marcus Dods (Edinburgh, 1871), 2: 25–6.
7 Denis Saurat, *Milton: Man and Thinker* (London, 1944), p. 184.

Chapter 9   Last published poems, 1: *Samson Agonistes*

1 The foregoing facts are summarized from W.R. Parker, 'The Date of *Samson Agonistes*,' *Philological Quarterly*, 28 (1949): 145–7, where the authorities will be found. [Parker amplified and revised his argument in *Milton: A Biography* (Oxford, 1968). ED.]
2 David Masson, *Life of Milton* (London, 1880), 6: 662ff.

3 Parker, 'The Date of *Samson Agonistes*,' pp. 163–4.

4 See M.M. Ross, *Milton's Royalism* (Ithaca, N.Y., 1943), pp. 120ff.

5 *Samson Agonistes*, 1660–8; *De Civitate Dei* 1.21; cf. J.H. Hanford, *Milton Handbook* (New York, 1926), p. 289 and n.

6 Had he been content, like Vondel, to adhere more closely to the Book of Judges, and to the Hebrew tradition of Samson as a national hero, as exemplified in Josephus, the problem would have been simpler, but the result far less powerfully moving. 'Such,' writes Josephus 'was his [Samson's] end after governing Israel for twenty years. And it is but right to admire the man for his valour, his strength, and the grandeur of his end, and also for the wrath which he cherished to the last against his enemies. That he let himself be ensnared by a woman must be imputed to human nature, which succumbs to sins; but testimony is due to him for his surpassing excellence in all the rest. His kinsmen then took up his body and buried him at Sarasa, his native place, with his forefathers' (*Jewish Antiquities*, 5: 316–17; see Loeb edition [Heinemann, 1950], 5: 140–1). Here is a legend not altogether incomparable with those on which the Greek tragic poets worked, and a character with the requisite greatness and the requisite tragic flaw. Samson, it was early observed, is in some sort the Hebrew counterpart of the Greek Hercules. Such a legend Sophocles might at once have humanized and treated with a sense of cosmic background and the memorable decrees of destiny and Zeus. To the justice of these decrees the Greek poet is not indifferent; nor on the whole does he present his hero as coming within their danger save as sin or error brings him there. But the Greek conception of justice differs very markedly from the Hebrew view. (The curse which pursues a family in the Greek tragic cycles is not wholly remote from that retributive justice, as conceived by the Hebrews, which visits the sins of the fathers upon the children unto the third and fourth generation [Exod. 20: 5, 34: 7; Num. 14:18; Deut. 5:9]). The Greek conception of culpability, unlike the Christian, includes ignorance, as the case of Oedipus clearly shows, and does not of necessity presuppose any defection of the will. Nor do the Greek decrees of Destiny or of Zeus add up to anything like the Christian or even the much more severely limited Hebrew conception of eternal providence. Milton humanizes the figure of Samson and gives the story its setting in God's providential scheme; but both these things he does in the light of perfected Hebrew-Christian tradition and of Christian commentary on the legend of Samson. Inevitably this sets Samson at a distance from Greek tragedy and at a remove also from Hebrew legends. But Milton, whether or not he was conscious of any problem posed by the effort to interpret Hebrew legend in the fuller light of Christianity, was certainly well aware of that presented by the effort to embody Christian concepts in Greek forms, and in *Samson* took steps to meet the problem.

7 The critical works alluded to in the following discussion include: Sir Richard Jebb, '*Samson Agonistes* and Hellenic Drama,' *Proceedings of the British Academy* (1907–8); W.R. Parker, 'The Greek Spirit in Milton's *Samson Agonistes*,' *Essays and Studies of the English Association*, 20 (1935): 21–44; A.S.P. Woodhouse, '*Samson Agonistes* and Milton's Experience,' *Transactions of the Royal Society of Canada*, 3rd ser. 43 (1949); Section II, 157–75; D.C. Allen, *The Harmonious Vision* (Baltimore, 1953), chap. 4; H.D.F. Kitto, *Greek Tragedy* (London, 1954).

8 If Jebb is right in thinking that despair of happiness or of relief from suffering has its part to play to the very end in motivating Samson's ready acceptance of

death, there is support for this view in Christian commentary. 'This advantage,' says Joseph Hall, 'shall Samson make of their [the Philistines'] tyranny that now death is no punishment to him, that his soul shall fly forth in this bitterness without pain, and that his dying revenge shall be no less sweet to him than the liberty of his former life' (*Contemplations Upon the Principal Passages in the Holy Story*, in *Works* [London, 1837], 1: 252). But the deeper grounds of Samson's despair it was necessary first to expose and then to remove.

9 It is of the essence of Milton's interpretation of Samson's story that he adopts the idea of one group of commentators that Samson, though a 'saint,' had sinned, that his afflictions were a punishment for his sin, that he repented, and that his revenge upon his enemies was the seal of his repentance and of his full restoration to God's service. To derive from the narrative of Judges any indication of Samson's repentance taxed the ingenuity of commentators. Richard Rogers, in his *Commenary upon the whole Booke of Judges, preached in sundrie lectures* (London, 1615), pp. 769–70, frankly admits the difficulty, but argues his repentance from his election (for a Nazarite dedicated to God was of the elect), from his prayer (which shows faith, and faith is inseparable from repentance), and from his being listed among those who lived and died in faith (Heb. 11:2,32). Like Peter Martyr, in *The Commentary of Master Peter Martyr, upon the Booke of Judges* (London, 1564?), p. 235v, Rogers insists that it was not Samson's patience under affliction or any other virtue in him that deserved forgiveness and restoration, but God's free grace and mercy that bestowed them. But of Samson's sin Milton takes his own view: it is no simple matter of sensuality, of unchastity, as the commentators had assumed, but, like the sin of Adam, an act of disobedience which takes the form of uxoriousness: in its form an offence against nature (for Samson has set the woman above himself, her natural lord), in the event a betrayal of God's cause (for Samson has in effect set the woman above his obedience to God and his dedication to God's service). It is the sense of these things that is the deeper ground of Samson's despair.

10 Trans. E.F. Watling, in *Sophocles: The Theban Plays* (New York, 1947), p. 135.

11 Masson, *Life of Milton*, 6: 670ff.

12 In the *Doctrine and Disciple of Divorce* Milton had admitted that God 'in some ways of his providence is high and secret, past finding out' (Col. 3 [ii]: 445) ; but clearly the problem became acute with the Restoration. After his bold applications of the canons of logic in his writings on liberty, and in the *De Doctrina* on Christian dogma, the pronouncement on reason suggests a new development in Milton's thought.

13 I cannot follow Parker in redating this sonnet and making it refer to Mary Powell.

14 It is true that he has always recognized, as a theological proposition, original sin and the natural depravity of fallen man: 'For though it were granted us by divine indulgence to be exempt from all that can be harmful to us from without, yet the perverseness of our folly is so bent, that we should never lin [cease] hammering out of our own hearts, as it were out of flint, the seeds and sparkles of new misery to our selves ... And no marvel if out of our own hearts, for they are evil ...' (Col. 3 [ii]: 281). In the divorce pamphlets he likewise writes with a sense of his own error in his marriage choice and its attendant misery. These two facts are significant; but so is their isolation. For Milton does not bring the

two facts together; he is content to invoke human depravity only to explain the errors of others, who superstitiously oppose free divorce, not his own error. In retrospect, apparently, the two facts are brought into a new alignment.

Chapter 10   Last published poems, 2: *Paradise Regained*

1 In *The Meritorious Price of our Redemption, Justification, etc. Clearing it from Some Common Errors* (London, 1650), William Pynchon seeks to show that 'Christ did not bear our sins by God's imputation, and therefore he did not bear the curse of the Law for them ... Christ hath redeemed us from the curse of the Law (not by suffering the said curse for us, but) by a satisfactory price of Atonement; viz., by paying our performing unto his Father that invaluable precious thing of his Mediatoriall obedience, whereof his Mediatoriall Sacrifice of Atonement was the master-piece' (title page). 'And according to this tenor the Apostle Paul doth explain the matter. He teacheth us to place the obedience of the Mediator in a direct opposition to the first disobedience of Adam (Rom. 5.19)' (p. 84).
2 Calvin, in his *Commentary on a Harmony of the Evangelists,* trans. William Pringle (Edinburgh, 1845), 1: 212, raises the question how Christ, having our feelings as well as our flesh, could be tempted without, like us, suffering contamination from contact with evil; for 'Satan never attacks us without doing some injury, or at least without inflicting a slight wound.' His solution is that Christ was neither in our state (unable not to sin) nor in Adam's (able not to sin), but 'fortified by the Spirit with such power that the darts of Satan could not pierce him.' Though in *Paradise Regained* Christ is likewise fortified by the Spirit, the problem does not exist for Milton since the suggestion of evil, if unapproved and meeting no response from the will, carries no implication of sin (*Paradise Lost* 5: 117–19).
3 *Faerie Queene* 2.7 The impression made upon Milton by the episode is recorded in *Areopagitica* (Col. 4: 311).
4 *Nicomachean Ethics,* 3: 11.
5 The absence of response to temptation is as evident in Guyon as in Christ, but lest we should fail to observe it Spenser introduces his figure of the fiend who glides behind Guyon and who not merely at his first attempt to take the treasures, but at the first manifestations of desire to do so, would destroy him.
6 See A.S.P. Woodhouse, 'Nature and Grace in the *Faerie Queene,*' *ELH,* 16 (1949): 194–228.
7 Indeed, if one relied merely upon a structural analysis of the poem one might suspect that the symmetry was too emphatic and ran some danger of becoming mechanical in its effect. But this danger Milton countered by a simple device – simple once you have recognized it. I confess that I had read *Paradise Regained* a good many times before I did so – had read it and puzzled over the principle, if any, on which it was divided into four books. For the division appeared to be entirely arbitrary with nothing of the reason, approaching inevitability, that divides *Paradise Lost* in its revised form into twelve. Almost it looked as if the fourfold division had no other purpose than to measure off in sections of comparable length a poem short enough to be read at a sitting. The significant breaks are not at the endings of books but between the three tempta-

tions, and these are marked by the falling of night and dawning of a new day with the return of Satan in a fresh guise. Book 1 ends with the falling of night after the first temptation, but the description of night and the new dawn is postponed till we are halfway through the second book. The rest of this book, the whole of Book 3, and the first two-thirds of Book 4 go to the elaborated second temptation ere night again falls, and with the dawn Satan returns for his final effort. But this staggered effect (for the modern phrase exactly describes it) is clearly deliberate. It partially conceals, without breaking, the symmetry of the pattern and allows that symmetry to impress itself gradually upon the attentive reader. Moreover, the first two books with their frequent change of scene differ markedly from the latter two, where poet and reader never once quit the presence of Christ. These are points of pure technique: they belong to the pattern, not to the theme; but nothing could better demonstrate Milton's sensitivity and his conscious artistry in elaborating an aesthetic pattern. It is seldom profitable, however, to consider (as momentarily here) Milton's patterns without reference to the themes which they support and advance. And with theme and pattern must be reunited such other elements as criticism may temporarily disengage; action, character, setting, imagery, whatever they may be.

8 See Richard G. Moulton, *The Literary Study of the Bible* (London, 1898), pp. 25ff. [ED.]

9 This echo of *Paradise Lost* 3.384–6, and the many others, must not be missed if one is to get the full value of the poem:

> Begotten Son, Divine Similitude,
> In whose conspicuous countenance, without cloud
> Made visible, th' Almighty Father shines.

Immediately a second echo follows in Satan's boast how he 'when no other durst' successfully undertook the voyage of exploration and destruction to earth which now, under easier conditions, he will repeat.

10 Edward Leigh, *Annotations upon All the New Testament Philological and Theologicall* (London, 1650), p. 104, as quoted in E.M. Pope, *Paradise Regained: The Tradition and the Poem* (New York, 1962), p. 32.

11 Cf. *Paradise Lost* 3.309: 'By merit more than birthright Son of God.' There is no change in doctrine.

12 With the greatest economy and naturalness, his retrospective soliloquy sketches in the antecedent action: the memory of his early years, reminiscent (it would seem) of Milton's own, and influenced perhaps by the representation in St Paul's School of the boy Christ instructing the doctors in the temple, the story of his birth, the conviction that he was indeed the promised Messiah, God's owning of him in his baptism as the beginning of his public ministry, the need of further clarification, which indeed the temptation in the wilderness helps to supply. It is this last fact which justifies our assertion that, so far from abandoning the idea of this episode as preparation, Milton exploits it.

13 A perfectly adequate gloss upon the first temptation is furnished in Calvin's *Commentary:* 'it is absurd to suppose [with medieval commentators] that it arises from the intemperance of gluttony when a hungry person desires food to satisfy nature ... Satan made a direct attack on the faith of Christ, in the hope that after destroying his faith, he would drive Christ to [what were in the circumstances] unlawful and wicked methods of procuring food. And certainly he presses us very hard when he attempts to make us distrust God and consult our own advantage ... Now though he holds out the divine power of Christ to

turn the *stones* into *loaves*, yet the single object which he has in view is to persuade Christ to depart from the word of God and follow the dictates of infidelity ... Such was the kind of temptation which Satan employed, the same kind with which he assails us daily. The Son of God did not choose to undertake any contest of an unusual description, but to sustain assaults in common with us, that we might be furnished with the same armour and might entertain no doubt as to achieving the victory (1 : 213–14).

14 Calvin, *Commentary*, 1 : 220.

15 The second temptation as a series of incitements to worldly glory is discussed by A.A. Gilbert in 'The Temptation in *Paradise Regained*,' *JEGP*, 15 (1916): 599–611.

16 I am well aware that this interpretation is not without its difficulty, caused by the ambiguous line, 'Nature's own work it seemed – nature taught art.' Taken by itself, the implication seems to be that this is not natural beauty, as is the beauty of the morning, just described, but art imitating nature – and art imitating nature in order to deceive has (especially in Spenser) evil implications. On the other hand, it must be observed: 1 / that the lines immediately following indicate the circumstance in which the scene might prove deceptive and evil, namely, 'to a superstitious eye'; 2 / that not the scene of beauty, but only 'the banquet which Satan presents in this setting, vanishes 'with sound of harpies' wings'; and 3 / most important, that Christ, who is never deceived, accepts the scene as beauty, in other words, as a thing indifferent – good if put to use as he intends, evil if put to evil use as Satan intends.

17 *Enchiridion Militis Christiani*, 'General Rules for the Christian Life: the Fourth Rule,' Chap. 12.

18 *Education of a Christian Prince*, trans. Lester K. Born (New York, 1965), p. 199.

Index